Bring History Alive!

A Sourcebook for Teaching United States History

EDITED BY:

Kirk Ankeney
Richard Del Rio
Gary B. Nash
David Vigilante

National Center for History in the Schools
University of California, Los Angeles

Ordering Information

Bring History Alive: A Sourcebook for Teaching United States History
ISBN 0-9633218-5-4

Contact:

UCLA Book Zone
The UCLA Store
308 Westwood Plaza
Ackerman Union
Los Angeles, CA 90024-8311
Phone: (310) 206-0788
Fax: (310) 825-0382

INTRODUCTION

This book is a resource manual created by teachers and for teachers. It is not a curricular plan, not a textbook, and not a prescribed set of classroom exercises. It is presented for the consideration of those who wish to engage in an inquiry-based approach to historical knowledge and historical understanding. We hope that if your house catches on fire, this is the one book you'll reach for on your way out the door.

The book has a history of its own. *Bring History Alive!* is built around some 1,200 classroom activities. A large majority of these were first published as illustrative examples of how students could master the *National Standards for United States History*. The controversy over the *National Standards* is a story in itself, one that would take an entire chapter—perhaps even a book—to rehearse and analyze. It need only be said here that these examples of student achievement, not to be confused with the standards themselves, were omitted from the revised version of the United States History Standards, published in April 1996. Hundreds of teachers have strongly urged that these teaching activities be republished, with appropriate revisions and improvement.

How were the classroom activities written in the first instance? They are the work of a task force of teachers from various parts of the country, and evenly divided among elementary, middle, and high schools, who worked from 1992 to 1994 at UCLA as part of the National History Standards Project. These teachers were selected by the National Center for History in the Schools after soliciting nominations from nine principal organizations that participated in the Project: The American Historical Association, the Association for Supervision and Curriculum Development, the Council of Chief State School Officers, the Council for State Social Studies Specialists, the National Council for History Education, the National Council for the Social Studies, the Organization of American Historians, the Organization of History Teachers, and the World History Association Most of the examples written by these teachers had been tried out in their own classrooms.

In preparing this book for publication, its editors have combed the original examples of student achievement to ensure that each activity raises questions about important topics without dictating or inferring answers. The activities and questions are meant to be open-ended. They are invitations to explore historical issues, problems, ideas, values, behaviors, interests, motives, and personalities. Many thoughtful critiques of the hundreds of classroom activities are gratefully acknowledged, and the editors have carefully considered every criticism and suggestion. Many of the original examples have been discarded; others have been newly created; many have been rewritten.

Though numbering in the hundreds, the activities are explicitly not meant to add up to a curriculum. Nor are they intended to cover every important topic—or every personage—in United States history. Such a comprehensive book would be overwhelming. It is true that the examples have been created by a diverse group of accomplished teachers who have tried to spotlight what inexperienced or overburdened colleagues will find most helpful, and this means giving pride of place to the less familiar rather than to activities that have been conventionally addressed for years.

Every reader of this book should understand that the teaching examples are simply examples—ones chosen to enliven classrooms with material that is not customarily found in curricular materials. It goes without saying that teachers will choose as they will from these examples, redesign them to meet their students' needs, and, we hope, find in them particles of inspiration that will lead teachers to create many others of their own.

The teaching examples, organized by grade level and by era, are supplemented by essays of two kinds. In Part I, we have brought together a number of short essays by experienced teachers that explore ways of bringing history alive in the classroom and ways to discourage a passive reliance on textbooks and rote exercises. These essays may help teachers emulate what the most engaging history instructors have accomplished: leading and inspiring students to become active, inquisitive learners who sharpen their skills on the way to seeing the excitement and relevance of the past.

In Part II, essays have been selected to introduce each of the ten eras of United States history. None of these essays describes the era, defines the era, or addresses all the major events and issues of each era. Rather, each essay dwells on a particular theme or approach relevant to the era. Regard each essay as a pep pill, not a nostrum; simply a lively essay to get one started with students.

While this book is a stand-alone resource book, it has several links to the *National Standards for United States History*. First, the ten eras are borrowed from the *National Standards*, though as these standards point out, the periodization of history is always arbitrary and open to negotiation. Second, in Part I, Historical Thinking Skills are reprinted from the *National History Standards* because history thinking skills are the *sine qua non* of historical literacy. Third, Part III draws upon the resources provided in the National History Standards, although the resources recommended here are substantially enlarged.

The editors of this volume wish to thank the following members of the Advisory Board of the National Center for History in the Schools who reviewed the format, design, and philosophy of the book: Joyce Appleby, Robert Bain, Jerry H. Bentley, Daniel Berman, Douglas Greenberg, Melinda Hennessey, Linda Heywood, David Hollinger, Evelyn Hu-DeHart, Donna Rogers-Beard, Gloria Sesso, Donald Woodruff, and Judith P. Zinsser. We also gratefully acknowledge four exceptional teachers from different regions of the country who reviewed a draft of the book and made valuable suggestions: Ron Briley, Carl Schulkin, John Tyler, and Emily Warner.

Kirk Ankeney
Richard Del Rio
Gary B. Nash
David Vigilante
Los Angeles, California
October 1996

TABLE OF CONTENTS

PART I

Approaching United States History: Foundations of Good Teaching

Rationale: Why Study History*

The Case for History in Our Schools

Americans have long said that universal education is essential to securing the people's rights to life, liberty, and the pursuit of happiness. But those who run our schools have rarely agreed on what is most worth teaching to every learner in a modern democratic society. So difficult has this question appeared that we have repeatedly turned away from it, to busy ourselves instead with methods and logistics, as though these were more important and could be applied without regard to the subject matter we choose to teach, or our purposes in choosing it. The consequences are evident. All subjects and disciplines have suffered, at all levels of schooling from kindergarten through the graduate years.

By its nature, history has suffered more than most subjects from permissive or simply ill-founded curriculum making. History's enormous scope and detail require more choices than many people, educators and historians included, are able or willing to make. It is, and ought to be, complex and often controversial. In its style and methods, it is both an art and a science. As a school subject, it embraces both the humanities and the social studies, neither of which can prosper without history's context and perspectives. It is the most synthesizing of all the disciplines, not just another bundle of subject-matter, but a way of ordering and apprehending reality. To be well taught it calls for more than ordinary knowledge and pedagogical skill on the part of those who teach it. As historians and teachers of history, we must admit its difficulties

---

*Reprinted from *Lessons From History, Essential Understandings and Historical Perspectives Students Should Acquire*, edited by Charlotte Crabtree, Gary B. Nash, Paul Gagnon, Scott Waugh (Los Angeles, CA: The National Center for History in the Schools, 1992), pp. 1-10.

and labor to overcome them, for if the proper place of history in our schools is not accepted by the public and those who shape the schools, the larger campaign to improve the quality, and equality, of American education will surely fail.

Why Study History?

The purposes of historical study must reflect the three ultimate purposes of education in a free society: to prepare the individual for a career of work, to sustain life; for active citizenship, to safeguard liberty and justice; and for the private pursuit of happiness. The last of these purposes—personal fulfillment, whether it be defined in secular or spiritual terms—is of first importance, providing the reason we struggle to maintain life and liberty, its necessary conditions. Each of the three aims of education, of course, calls for traits of minds and character that are useful to the other two. Historical study contributes to all three, but in preparing the individual for citizenship and for personal fulfillment its offerings are unique, and together with those of literature and philosophy, are indispensable.

The argument for more history in the schools and for its centrality to the social studies has usually stressed its role in preparing informed, sophisticated citizens. Thomas Jefferson long ago prescribed history for all who would take part in self-government because it would "enable every man to judge for himself what will secure or endanger his freedom." History's main use, he believed, was to prepare people for things yet to come. By reflecting on the past, on other times, other people, other nations, they would be able "to judge of the future" and to make up their own minds on the "actions and designs of men."

In 1892, the Committee of Ten's subcommittee on History, Civil Government, and Political Economy (which included Woodrow Wilson) urged that four years of history be required for all secondary school students, whether or not they were destined for college, because history, more than any other subject, readied the student to exercise "a salutary influence upon the affairs of his country." It was, they said, vital to "the invaluable mental power which we call judgment." A succession of committees, from the American Historical Association's "Seven" in 1899 through its study panels in the 1930s, pressed similar arguments for history as the basis for civic education.

Nearing the end of the 20th century, in a populous and ethnically and racially diverse society caught up in an interdependent global society, we reaffirm the central importance of history in preparing students to exercise their rights and responsibilities in the democratic political process. As historians of human behavior, we know better than to claim too much. "Neither history nor any social studies course intended to teach citizenship can *make* good citizens," said the Council for Basic Education's Commission on the Teaching of History in 1982; but without knowing the past, citizens cannot know the choices before them. And historian William McNeill, in a report for the American Historical Association in 1985, similarly argued that "democratic citizenship and effective participation in the determination of public policy require citizens to share a collective memory, organized into historical knowledge and belief.

Lacking a collective memory of important things, people lapse into political amnesia, unable to see what newspapers are saying, to hear what is in (or left out of) a speech, or to talk to each other about public questions. A historical education should prepare us for times of trouble, when we are tempted to put aside inefficient democracy and to lash out, to exclude, or to oppress others. Why have past societies fallen or survived, turned ugly or retained their humanity? Citizens need to know and to be able to tell each other, before it grows too late, what struggles and sacrifices have had to be accepted, what comforts given up, to keep freedom and justice alive. Historical knowledge and historical perspective ward off panic, cynicism, self-pity, and resignation.

Students of history come to see, as James Howard and Thomas Mendenhall said in *Making History Come Alive*, that not every difficulty is a problem and not every problem is a crisis. To take but one example, democracy must cherish both liberty and equality. The two impulses repeatedly clash, yet each is necessary to the other. This "concept" may serve as a starting point, but only history can each us why it is so, by presenting the tough human experience that has convinced us of it. Students then grasp why conflict is to be expected—even welcomed— and is not some failure of a system that should run itself and leave them alone. They also understand how hard it has been to improve human life but how often it has nonetheless been done in the past. Historical study has a way (annoying to some) of rejecting both optimism and pessimism, of refusing us the comforts of either. In sum, it offers citizens the sense of reality and proportion that is the first mark of political wisdom.

It is hard to see how better to prepare students for life in the 21st century, about which there is so much talk these days in the social studies field. Unhappily, enthusiasts for "futures studies" are quick to reject history and the humanities in general as "past-oriented" and thereby useless in preparing citizens for what is to come. Apart from flying in the face of centuries of human experience, such notions ignore—as they would have our young people do— everything that can be learned from the lives of countless men and women whose historical and humanistic education prepared them for great work in the "futures" of their own eras. If they knew how to meet the unexpected, it was not out of formulas and "skills" but out of first knowing themselves and the human condition. History, philosophy, biography, literature, and the arts had liberated their imaginations, informed their judgments, and imbued them with a sense of human dignity. The social sciences standing alone help to describe today's and tomorrow's problems, but they alone cannot explain them; nor should they be expected to nourish those values and qualities of mind required to deal with them wisely. For these purposes the long-term explanatory perspectives that history provides and the habits of thought it uniquely develops are essential.

Along with educating citizens for public affairs—a role it shares with the social sciences— history has a deeper, even more fundamental responsibility: the cultivation of the individual private person, in whom self-knowledge and self-respect support a life of dignity and fulfillment. The public and private purposes of educational and historical study are, of course, inescapably interrelated. Only the self-respecting, fully-rounded person is likely to make a good citizen for a self-governing society, as ready to serve as to resist, depending upon the circumstances of the hour. Only a free society can provide a setting for personal dignity and fulfillment, what Jefferson called the pursuit of happiness.

The liberal education of the private person is preeminently the role of history and the humanities. The study of history reveals the long, hard path of human striving for dignity. It can be, as Jerry Martin puts it, "a source of *pietas*, the reverent acknowledgment of the sources of one's being." Historical memory is the key to self-identity, to seeing one's place in the stream of time, in the story of humankind. We are part of an ancient chain and the hand of the past is upon us—for good and ill—as our hands will rest on our descendants in the future. Such perspective is essential to one's morale, perhaps even to sanity, in a complex, troubled present. "It is true that history cannot satisfy our appetite when we are hungry, nor keep us warm when the cold wind blows," says the New York Chinatown History Project. "But it is also true that if younger generations do not understand the hardships and triumphs of their elders, then we will be a people without a past. As such, we will be like water without a source, a tree without roots."

The human mind seems to require a usable past. Unfurnished with historical knowledge that approximates reality, we are like to conjure up a past that is false or nostalgic, misleading in one form or other. Or we may subscribe to versions of the past peddled by partisan or special interests. Either way we are deluded, lose our way, perhaps even become dangerous to ourselves and our contemporaries, not to speak of posterity. We remain prisoners of our milieu, ignorant, in bliss or despair, of the possibility for personal liberation that history opens to us by revealing the immense range of approaches people have taken to political, economic, and social life, to personal integrity and salvation, to cultural creativity.

The dignity of free choice can proceed only out of knowing the alternatives possible in private and public life, the knowledge that only history, and the humanities taught in conjunction with history, can provide. Is such education "past-oriented" and obsolete? Exactly the contrary. The study of history opens to students the great case book of centuries of human experience. The quicker the pace of change, the higher the flood of "information," the more troubled and confused we become, the more relevant and essential history becomes in preparing people for private life and public auction.

As to the third purpose of education—preparation for work—historical studies are central for such careers as journalism, law, diplomacy, international business, government service, politics, the military, teaching, and management of many public and private enterprises. Knowledge of history informs many other academic disciplines and creative professions. Insofar as personal morale, integrity, and dignity are conducive to all kinds of good work, history's contributions are obvious, as is its development of analytical skills and modes of critical judgment. As more and more employers assert the importance of a liberal education to their workers' inventiveness, their aptitude for continued learning and changes of career, the uses of historical studies should be more commonly appreciated.

Given the importance of history for all three purposes of education, and its centrality to citizenship and personal life, it is clear that both the amount and the quality of history taught in American schools must be sufficient to the task. That they are clearly not sufficient has alarmed many observers in recent years. In 1975, a report by the executive secretary of the Organization of American Historians, Richard S. Kirkendall, found history enrollments shrinking and history being displaced by other social studies subjects. In 1982 the Council for Basic Education's Commission on the Teaching of History deplored both the quantity and the quality of history being taught in the schools. History, said the Commission's report, was "overshadowed and undervalued in the curriculum, often neglected by professional historians, and found boring by many students."

Data reported by the National Center for Education Statistics indicated that in 1981-82 only 60 percent of the nation's high schools were offering a comprehensive course in United States history, though courses in state history, special eras, or special topics were being offered in some of the schools not providing the basic United States history course. By 1989-90 this picture had improved, probably as a result of the curriculum reforms launched in 1983. A national survey conducted in 1989-90 by the National Center for History in the Schools found that 89.9 percent of the high schools were offering one or more General Enrollment classes in United States history, and an additional 5 percent not offering the General Enrollment course were offering one or more special enrollment classes such as Advanced Placement or Remedial.

Fully 5 percent of the high schools, however, were offering no United States history courses, and of the courses that were offered, only 81 percent provided a full year of instruction; the rest were offered for one semester or less. Only 70.2 percent of the high schools were offering a General Enrollment course in world history, with only 66 percent of these schools requiring the course for graduation. Only 3.7 percent were offering a course in Western Civilization, a significant decline from a decade earlier when 14 percent were offering such a course. Serious problems were observed in the middle school/junior high school offerings. Close to 40 percent were offering no courses in United States history and 87 percent reported offering no courses in world history. For a significant number of students, then, the only history they currently study is what is offered in a year or less of high school instruction.

The gap between what a modern democratic school system needs and what the curriculum in this country now provides is very great. Putting aside for a moment the paucity of history in the elementary and middle school curriculum of most schools, there is simply no way that the one and one-half years, or less, of history now taken by the average American high school student can possibly fulfill the purposes we have set forth above, or develop the essential knowledge and understandings we shall presently discuss. This view is shared by every major reform proposal of recent years. Theodore Sizer, in *Horace's Compromise* (1984), makes the joint study of history and ideas one of his four required areas of learning throughout the secondary years. *The Paideia Program* (1984) places narrative history and geography at the core of the social studies from the upper elementary years through high school. In the Carnegie report, *High School* (1983), Ernest Boyer recommended a year of United States History, a year of Western Civilization, and at least a term's study of a non-Western society. The Council for Basic Education's report of 1984 set an "irreducible minimum" of two years of American history, one of European and the historical study of at least one non-European society in depth. In 1987, the American Federation of teachers published *Education for Democracy: A Statement of Principles*, signed by 150 national leaders across the political spectrum, and calling for the reordering of the entire social studies curriculum around a continuing core of history and geography. Also in 1987 the National Endowment for the Humanities issued *American Memory*, Lynne V. Cheney's report on humanities in the schools, which urged that "both history and enduring works of literature" be a part of every school year for every student. Most recently, the Bradley Commission recommended that the social studies curriculum from kindergarten through grade six be history-centered and that no fewer than four years of history be required of all students sometime during the six-year span from 7th through 12th grade.

All of these reports set reasonable goals, and they also agree that a reformed social studies curriculum should be required of all students in common, regardless of their "track" or further vocational and educational plans. Only such a common core is democratic, because wherever the curriculum in history and ideas is truncated or optional, the students' right to know is violated and democracy is wanting. Something is wrong when the learning often considered necessary and appropriate for university-bound students is treated as unnecessary or irrelevant for the others. This first principle of democratic education, enunciated by the Committee of Ten a century ago, is an idea whose time has come again. In order that it not again be abandoned, diverse and imaginative teaching methods must be applied in developing the common core of what is most worth learning with all of our diverse learners. A common core and varied methods are the twin imperatives for democratic schooling. A curriculum that is trivial, optional, or differentiated according to track produces a class system of education, no matter how innovative the methods or how many students receive a diploma. But the most wondrous subject matter just as surely produces a class system of education if inflexible teaching methods and school structures impede its being conveyed to the great majority of young people.

Methods: Historical Thinking Skills*

The study of history, as noted earlier, rests on knowledge of facts, dates, names, places, events, and ideas. In addition, true historical understanding requires students to engage in historical thinking: to raise questions and to marshal solid evidence in support of their answers; to go beyond the facts presented in their textbooks and examine the historical record for themselves; to consult documents, journals, diaries, artifacts, historic sites, works of art, quantitative data, and other evidence from the past, and to do so imaginatively—taking into account the historical context in which these records were created and comparing the multiple points of view of those on the scene at the time.

Real historical understanding requires that students have opportunity to create historical narratives and arguments of their own. Such narratives and arguments may take many forms—essays, debates, and editorials, for instance. They can be initiated in a variety of ways. None, however, more powerfully initiates historical thinking than those issues, past and present, that challenge students to enter knowledgeably into the historical record and to bring sound historical perspectives to bear in the analysis of a problem.

Historical understanding also requires that students thoughtfully read the historical narratives created by others. Well-written historical narratives are interpretative, revealing and explaining connections, change, and consequences. They are also analytical, combining lively storytelling and biography with conceptual analysis drawn from all relevant disciplines. Such narratives promote essential skills in historical thinking.

Reading such narratives requires that students analyze the assumptions—stated and unstated—from which the narrative was constructed and assess the strength of the evidence presented. It requires that students consider the significance of what the author included as well as chose to omit—the absence, for example, of the voices and experiences of other men and women who were also an important part of the history of their time. Also, it requires that students examine the interpretative nature of history, comparing, for example, alternative historical narratives written by historians who have given different weight to the political, economic, social, and/or technological causes of events and who have developed competing interpretations of the significance of those events.

Students engaged in activities of the kinds just considered will draw upon skills in the following five interconnected dimensions of historical thinking:

1. Chronological Thinking
2. Historical Comprehension
3. Historical Analysis and Interpretation
4. Historical Research Capabilities
5. Historical Issues-Analysis and Decision-Making

These skills, while presented in five separate categories, are nonetheless **interactive and mutually supportive**. In conducting historical research or creating a historical argument of their

---

*Reprinted from National Standards for History, Basic Edition, National Center for History in the Schools, UCLA (Los Angeles, CA: The National Center for History in the Schools, 1996), pp. 59-70.

own, for example, students must be able to draw upon skills in all five categories. Beyond the skills of conducting their research, students must, for example, be able to comprehend historical documents and records, analyze their relevance, develop interpretations of the document(s) they select, and demonstrate a sound grasp of the historical chronology and context in which the issue, problem, or events they are addressing developed.

In short, these five sets of skills, developed in the following pages as the five Standards in Historical Thinking, are statements of the **outcomes** we desire students to achieve. They are not mutually exclusive when put into practice, nor do they prescribe a particular teaching sequence to be followed. Teachers will draw upon all these Thinking Standards, as appropriate, to develop their teaching plans and to guide students through challenging programs of study in history.

Finally, it is important to point out that these five sets of Standards in Historical Thinking are defined in the following pages largely independent of historical content in order to specify the quality of thinking desired for each. It is essential to understand, however, that these skills do not develop, nor can they be practiced, in a vacuum. Every one of these skills requires specific historical content in order to function.

STANDARD 1

Chronological Thinking

Chronological thinking is at the heart of historical reasoning. Without a strong sense of chronology—of when events occurred and in what temporal order—it is impossible for students to examine relationships among those events or to explain historical causality. Chronology provides the mental scaffolding for organizing historical thought.

In developing students' chronological thinking, instructional time should be given to the use of well-constructed **historical narratives:** literary narratives including biographies and historical literature, and well-written narrative histories that have the quality of "stories well told." Well-crafted narratives such as these have the power to grip and hold students' attention. Thus engaged, the reader is able to focus on what the narrator discloses: the temporal structure of events unfolding over time, the actions and intentions of those who were there, the temporal connections between antecedents and their consequences.

In the middle and high school years, students should be able to use their mathematical skills to measure time by years, decades, centuries, and millennia; to calculate time from the fixed points of the calendar system (BC or BCE and AD or CE); and to interpret the data presented in time lines.

Students should be able to analyze *patterns of historical duration*, demonstrated, for example, by the more than two hundred years the United States Constitution and the government it created has endured.

Students should also be able to analyze *patterns of historical succession* illustrated, for example, in the development, over time, of ever larger systems of interaction, beginning with trade among settlements of the Neolithic world; continuing through the growth of the great land empires of Rome, Han China, the Islamic world, and the Mongols; expanding in the early modern era when Europeans crossed the Atlantic and Pacific, and established the first world-wide networks of trade and communication; and culminating with the global systems of trade and communication of the modern world.

Standard 1: *The student thinks chronologically:*

Therefore, the student is able to:

A. **Distinguish between past, present, and future time.**

B. **Identify the temporal structure of a historical narrative or story:** its beginning, middle, and end (the latter defined as the outcome of a particular beginning).

C. **Establish temporal order in constructing historical narratives of their own:** working forward from some beginning through its development, to some end or outcome; working *backward* from some issue, problem, or event to explain its origins and its development over time.

D. **Measure and calculate calendar time** by days, weeks, months, years, decades, centuries, and millennia, from fixed points of the calendar system: BC (before Christ) and AD (*Anno Domini*, "in the year of our Lord") in the Gregorian calendar and the contemporary secular designation for these same dates, BCE (before the Common Era) and CE (in the Common Era); and compare with the fixed points of other calendar systems such as the Roman (753 BC, the founding of the city of Rome) and the Muslim (622 AD, the hegira).

E. **Interpret data presented in timelines and create timelines** by designating appropriate equidistant intervals of time and recording events according to the temporal order in which they occurred.

F. **Reconstruct patterns of historical succession and duration** in which historical developments have unfolded, and apply them to **explain historical continuity and change.**

G. **Compare alternative models for periodization** by identifying the organizing principles on which each is based.

STANDARD 2

Historical Comprehension

One of the defining features of historical narratives is their believable recounting of human events. Beyond that, historical narratives also have the power to disclose the intentions of the people involved, the difficulties they encountered, and the complex world in which such historical figures actually lived. To read historical stories, biographies, autobiographies, and narratives with comprehension, students must develop the ability to read imaginatively, to take into account what the narrative reveals of the humanity of the individuals involved—their motives and intentions, their values and ideas, their hopes, doubts, fears, strengths, and weaknesses. Comprehending historical narratives requires, also, that students develop historical perspectives, the ability to describe the past on its own terms, through the eyes and experiences of those who were there. By studying the literature, diaries, letters, debates, arts, and artifacts of past peoples, students should learn to avoid "present-mindedness" by not judging the past solely in terms of the norms and values of today but taking into account the historical context in which the events unfolded.

Acquiring these skills begins in the early years of childhood, through the use of superbly written biographies that capture children's imagination and provide them an important foundation for continuing historical study. As students move into middle grades and high school years, historical literature should continue to occupy an important place in the curriculum, capturing historical events with dramatic immediacy, engaging students' interests, and fostering deeper understanding of the times and cultural milieu in which events occurred.

Beyond these important outcomes, students should also develop the skills needed to comprehend—historical narratives that *explain* as well as recount the course of events and that *analyze* relationships among the various forces which were present at the time and influenced the ways events unfolded. These skills include: 1) identifying the central question the historical narrative seeks to answer; 2) defining the purpose, perspective, or point of view from which the narrative has been constructed; 3) reading the historical explanation or analysis with meaning; 4) recognizing the rhetorical cues that signal how the author has organized the text.

Comprehending historical narratives will also be facilitated if students are able to draw upon the data presented in historical maps; visual, mathematical, and quantitative data presented in a variety of graphic organizers; and a variety of visual sources such as historical photographs, political cartoons, paintings, and architecture in order to clarify, illustrate, or elaborate upon the information presented in the text.

Standard 2: *The student comprehends a variety of historical sources:*

Therefore, the student is able to:

A. **Identify the author or source of the historical document or narrative and assess its credibility.**

B. **Reconstruct the literal meaning of a historical passage** by identifying who was involved, what happened, where it happened, what events led to these developments, and what consequences or outcomes followed.

C. **Identify the central question(s)** the historical narrative addresses and the purpose, perspective, or point of view from which it has been constructed.

D. **Differentiate between historical facts and historical interpretations** but acknowledge that the two are related; that the facts the historian reports are selected and reflect therefore the historian's judgement of what is most significant about the past.

E. **Read historical narratives imaginatively,** taking into account what the narrative reveals of the humanity of the individuals involved—their probable values, outlook, motives, hopes, fears, strengths, and weaknesses.

F. **Appreciate historical perspectives**—the ability (a) to describe the past on its own terms, through the eyes and experiences of those who were there, as revealed through their literature, diaries, letters, debates, arts, artifacts, and the like; (b) the historical context in which the event unfolded—the values, outlook, options, and contingencies of that time and place; and (c) to avoid "present-mindedness," judging the past solely in terms of present-day norms and values.

G. **Draw upon data in historical maps** in order to obtain or clarify information on the geographic setting in which the historical event occurred, its relative and absolute location, the distances and directions involved, the natural and man-made features of the place, and critical relationships in the spatial distributions of those features and historical event occurring there.

H. **Utilize visual, mathematical, and quantitative data** presented in charts, tables, pie and bar graphs, flow charts, Venn diagrams, and other graphic organizers to clarify, illustrate, or elaborate upon information presented in the historical narrative.

I. **Draw upon visual, literary, and musical sources** including: a) photographs, paintings, cartoons, and architectural drawings; b) novels, poetry, and plays; and, c) folk, popular and classical music, to clarify, illustrate, or elaborate upon information presented in the historical narrative.

STANDARD 3

Historical Analysis and Interpretation

One of the most common problems in helping students to become thoughtful readers of historical narrative is the compulsion students feel to find the one right answer, the one essential fact, the one authoritative interpretation. "Am I on the right track?" "Is this what you want?" they ask. Or, worse yet, they rush to closure, reporting back as self-evident truths the facts or conclusions presented in the document or text.

These problems are deeply rooted in the conventional ways in which textbooks have presented history: a succession of facts marching straight to a settled outcome. To overcome these problems requires the use of more than a single source: of history books other than textbooks and of a rich variety of historical documents and artifacts that present alternative voices, accounts, and interpretations or perspectives on the past.

Students need to realize that historians may differ on the facts they incorporate in the development of their narratives, and disagree as well on how those facts are to be interpreted. Thus, "history" is usually taken to mean what happened in the past; but *written* history is a dialogue among historians not only about what happened but about why and how it happened, how it affected other happenings, and how much importance it ought to be assigned. The study of history is not only remembering answers. It requires following and evaluating arguments and arriving at usable, even if tentative, conclusions based on the available evidence.

To engage in these activities requires that students draw upon their skills of *historical comprehension* as well as go beyond those skills to conduct *thoughtful analyses* of the line of reasoning or argument in which the historian has engaged in creating the narrative. There is no sharp line separating the skills involved in comprehension and in analysis. For example, unless students are first able to comprehend what a document, historical narrative, or artifact divulges concerning the ideas, perspectives, or beliefs of a particular person, culture, or era, it is impossible for students to engage in the analytic skills of comparing the ideas, perspectives, or beliefs held by different individuals, cultures, or societies at a particular time, or of comparing instances of continuity and change in ideas, perspectives, and beliefs over time. Similarly, unless students comprehend the credibility of the historical documents, artifacts, or other records on which the historian bases his or her interpretation of the past, students will be unable to analyze whether a narrative is grounded on sound historical evidence and merits, therefore, their thoughtful attention. In this sense certain of the skills involved in comprehension not only overlap the skills involved in analysis, but are essential to conducting these more demanding analytic activities. Analysis, however, builds beyond the skills of comprehension, and carries the student more deeply into assessing the authority of historical records themselves, assessing the adequacy of the historical evidence on which the historian has drawn, and determining the soundness of the interpretations historians have created from the evidence. It goes without saying that, in acquiring these skills, students also develop the capability to differentiate between expressions of opinion, no matter how passionately delivered, and informed hypotheses soundly grounded in historical evidence.

Well-written historical narrative has the power to promote students' analysis of historical causality—of how change occurs in society, of how human intentions matter, and how ends are influenced by the means of carrying them out, in what has been called the tangle of process and outcomes. Few challenges can be more fascinating to students than unraveling the often dramatic complications of cause. And nothing is more dangerous than a simple, monocausal explanation of past experiences and present problems.

Finally, well-written historical narratives can also alert students to the traps of *lineality and inevitability*. Students must understand the relevance of the past to their own times, but they need also to avoid the trap of lineality, of drawing straight lines between past and present, as though earlier movements were being propelled teleologically toward some rendezvous with destiny in the late 20th century.

A related trap is that of thinking that events have unfolded inevitably—that the way things are is the way they had to be, and thus that humankind lacks free will and the capacity for making choice. Unless students can conceive that history could have turned out differently, they may unconsciously accept the notion that the future is also inevitable or predetermined, and that human agency and individual action count for nothing. No attitude is more likely to feed civic apathy, cynicism, and resignation—precisely what we hope the study of history will fend off. Whether in dealing with the main narrative or with a topic in depth, we must always try, in one historian's words, to "restore to the past the options it once had."

> ### Standard 3: The student engages in historical analysis and interpretation:

Therefore, the student is able to:

A. **Compare and contrast differing sets of ideas**, values, personalities, behaviors, and institutions by identifying likenesses and differences.

B. **Consider multiple perspectives** of various peoples in the past by demonstrating their differing motives, beliefs, interests, hopes, and fears.

C. **Analyze cause-and-effect relationships** bearing in mind **multiple causation** including (a) **the importance of the individual** in history; (b) **the influence of ideas,** human interests, and beliefs; and (c) **the role of chance,** the accidental and the irrational.

D. **Draw comparisons across eras and regions in order to define enduring issues** that transcend regional and temporal boundaries.

E. **Distinguish between unsupported expressions of opinion and informed hypotheses grounded in historical evidence.**

F. **Compare competing historical narratives.**

G. **Challenge arguments of historical inevitability** by formulating examples of historical contingency, of how different choices could have led to different consequences.

H. **Hold interpretations of history as tentative,** subject to changes as new information is uncovered, new voices heard, and new interpretations broached.

I. **Evaluate major debates among historians** concerning alternative interpretations of the past.

J. **Hypothesize the influence of the past,** including both the limitations and the opportunities made possible by past decisions.

STANDARD 4

Historical Research Capabilities

Perhaps no aspect of historical thinking is as exciting to students or as productive of their growth in historical thinking as "doing history." Such inquiries can arise at critical turning points in the historical narrative presented in the text. They might be generated by encounters with historical documents, eyewitness accounts, letters, diaries, artifacts, photos, a visit to a historic site, a record of oral history, or other evidence of the past. Worthy inquiries are especially likely to develop if the documents students encounter are rich with the voices of people caught up in the event and sufficiently diverse to bring alive to students the interests, beliefs, and concerns of people with differing backgrounds and opposing viewpoints on the event.

Historical inquiry proceeds with the formulation of a problem or set of questions worth pursuing. In the most direct approach, students might be encouraged to analyze a document, record, or site itself. Who produced it, when, how, and why? What is the evidence of its authenticity, authority, and credibility? What does it tell them of the point of view, background, and interests of its author or creator? What else must they discover in order to construct a useful story, explanation, or narrative of the event of which this document or artifact is a part? What interpretation can they derive from their data, and what argument can they support in the historical narrative they create from the data?

In this process students' contextual knowledge of the historical period in which the document or artifact was created becomes critically important. Only a few records of the event will be available to students. Filling in the gaps, evaluating the records they have available, and imaginatively constructing a sound historical argument or narrative requires a larger context of meaning.

For these purposes, students' ongoing narrative study of history provides important support, revealing the larger context. But just as the ongoing narrative study, supported by but not limited to the textbook, provides a meaningful context in which students' inquiries can develop, it is these inquiries themselves that imbue the era with deeper meaning. Hence the importance of providing students documents or other records beyond materials included in the textbook, that will allow students to challenge textbook interpretations, to raise new questions about the event, to investigate the perspectives of those whose voices do not appear in the textbook accounts, or to plumb an issue that the textbook largely or in part bypassed.

Under these conditions, students will view their inquiries as creative contributions. They will better understand that written history is a human construction, that certain judgments about the past are tentative and arguable, and that historians regard their work as critical inquiry, pursued as ongoing explorations and debates with other historians. By their active engagement in historical inquiry, students will learn for themselves why historians are continuously reinterpreting the past, and why new interpretations emerge not only from uncovering new evidence but from rethinking old evidence in the light of new ideas springing up in our own times. Students then can also see why the good historian, like the good teacher, is interested not in manipulation or indoctrination but in acting as the honest messenger from the past—not interested in possessing students' minds but in presenting them with the power to possess their own.

Standard 4: The student conducts historical research:

Therefore, the student is able to:

A. **Formulate historical questions** from encounters with historical documents, eyewitness accounts, letters, diaries, artifacts, photos, historical sites, art, architecture, and other records from the past.

B. **Obtain historical data from a variety of sources,** including: library and museum collections, historic sites, historical photos, journals, diaries, eyewitness accounts, newspapers, and the like; documentary films, oral testimony from living witnesses, censuses, tax records, city directories, statistical compilations, and economic indicators

C. **Interrogate historical data** by uncovering the social, political, and economic context in which it was created; testing the data source for its credibility, authority, authenticity, internal consistency and completeness; and detecting and evaluating bias, distortion, and propaganda by omission, suppression, or invention of facts.

D. **Identify the gaps in the available records and marshal contextual knowledge and perspectives of the time and place** in order to elaborate imaginatively upon the evidence, fill in the gaps deductively, and construct a sound historical interpretation.

E. **Employ quantitative analysis** in order to explore such topics as changes in family size and composition, migration patterns, wealth distribution, and changes in the economy.

F. **Support interpretations with historical evidence** in order to construct closely reasoned arguments rather than facile opinions.

Error of opinion may be tolerated where reason is left free to combat it.

— THOMAS JEFFERSON
FIRST INAUGURAL ADDRESS, MARCH 4, 1801

STANDARD 5

Historical Issues-Analysis and Decision-Making

Issue-centered analysis and decision-making activities place students squarely at the center of historical dilemmas and problems faced at critical moments in the past and the near-present. Entering into such moments, confronting the issues or problems of the time, analyzing the alternatives available to those on the scene, evaluating the consequences that might have followed those options for action that were not chosen, and comparing with the consequences of those that were adopted, are activities that foster students' deep, personal involvement in these events.

If well chosen, these activities also promote capacities vital to a democratic citizenry: the capacity to identify and define public policy issues and ethical dilemmas; analyze the range of interests and values held by the many persons caught up in the situation and affected by its outcome; locate and organize the data required to assess the consequences of alternative approaches to resolving the dilemma; assess the ethical implications as well as the comparative costs and benefits of each approach; and evaluate a particular course of action in light of all of the above and, in the case of historical issues-analysis, in light also of its long-term consequences revealed in the historical record.

Because important historical issues are frequently value-laden, they also open opportunities to consider the moral convictions contributing to social actions taken. For example, what moral and political dilemmas did Lincoln face when, in his Emancipation Proclamation, he decided to free only those slaves behind the Confederate lines? The point to be made is that teachers should not use critical events to hammer home a particular "moral lesson" or ethical teaching. Not only will many students reject that approach; it fails also to take into account the processes through which students acquire the complex skills of principled thinking and moral reasoning.

When students are invited to judge morally the conduct of historical actors, they should be encouraged to analyze the values that inform the judgment. In some instances, this will be an easy task. Students judging the Holocaust or slavery as evils will probably be able to articulate the foundation for their judgment. In other cases, a student's effort to reach a moral judgment may produce a healthy student exercise in analyzing values, and may, in some instances, lead him or her to recognize the historically conditioned nature of a particular moral value he or she may be invoking.

Particularly challenging are the many social issues throughout United States history on which multiple interests and different values have come to bear. Issues of civil rights or equal education opportunity, of the right to choice vs. the right to life, and of criminal justice have all brought such conflicts to the fore. When these conflicts have not been resolved within the social and political institutions of the nation, they have regularly found their way into the judicial system, often going to the Supreme Court for resolution.

As the history course approaches the present era, such inquiries assume special relevance, confronting students with issues that resonate in today's headlines and invite their participation in lively debates, simulations, and socratic seminars—settings in which they can confront alternative policy recommendations, judge their ethical implications, challenge one another's assessments, and acquire further skills in the public presentation and defense of positions. In these analyses, teachers have the special responsibility of helping students differentiate between (1) relevant historical antecedents and (2) those that are clearly inappropriate and irrelevant. Students need to learn how to use their knowledge of history (or the past) to bring sound historical analysis to the service of informed decision making.

Standard 5: The student engages in historical issues-analysis and decision-making:

Therefore, the student is able to:

A. **Identify issues and problems in the past** and analyze the interests, values, perspectives, and points of view of those involved in the situation.

B. **Marshal evidence of antecedent circumstances** and current factors contributing to contemporary problems and alternative courses of action.

C. **Identify relevant historical antecedents** and differentiate from those that are inappropriate and irrelevant to contemporary issues.

D. **Evaluate alternative courses of action,** keeping in mind the information available at the time, in terms of ethical considerations, the interests of those affected by the decision, and the long- and short-term consequences of each.

E. **Formulate a position or course of action on an issue** by identifying the nature of the problem, analyzing the underlying factors contributing to the problem, and choosing a plausible solution from a choice of carefully evaluated options.

F. **Evaluate the implementation of a decision** by analyzing the interests it served; estimating the position, power, and priority of each player involved; assessing the ethical dimensions of the decision; and evaluating its costs and benefits from a variety of perspectives.

Students at West Milford High School, West Milford, NJ. Photograph taken by John Jordan

Explorations

Adding Inquiry To The "Inquiry" Method*
by Clair W. Keller

Clair Keller outlines approaches to teaching based on open-ended questions which engage students in the study of history. The teacher's role is to encourage curiosity; to motivate students using a creative process of describing, explaining, and evaluating data. Based on observations as classroom teacher and supervisor of student teachers, Keller argues that what usually passes for class discussions are one-to-one exchanges rather than a mutual commitment of teacher and student to investigate and utilize data. In the following article Keller offers several practical approaches to the development of creative inquiry in the classroom.

The author holds a joint appointment as Associate Professor in History and Education at Iowa State University. He teaches Colonial History and Social Studies Methods classes as well as supervising student teachers. Previous to going to ISU, he taught for ten years in high schools near Seattle, Washington. His present research interest is an analysis of committee assignments as a key to political power in the Pennsylvania Assembly, 1703-1743.

The newest method promising instant success in teaching social studies, "packaged inquiry," does not seem to provide students with the open-end experiences the term "inquiry" implies. In fact, "Inquiry," as it is now being commercially packaged, actually prevents the student from practicing at least two essential and creative skills he must learn in order to be inquisitive and skeptical, a true inquirer. First, by providing questions similar to those at the "end of the chapter," the materials stifle the opportunity to ask questions; second, the materials limit the scope of investigation by selecting the data from which a student is to draw conclusions. There is increasing danger that, in the hands of many teachers, these new materials will become new textbooks rather than new methods of teaching.

It is possible for students and teachers through the use of open-end questions to become truly engaged in creative inquiry, by which we mean the process of explaining various relationships between social science phenomena by developing inquiry models to ask the questions needed to solve, clarify or explain a subject.

The method we advocate is based upon the following suppositions.

1. That the most important learning which takes place in a classroom is not what is taught but the way it is taught (a Marshall McLuhan derivative).
2. That the primary objective of social studies teaching should be to provide students with the skills needed to explore and explain relationships between various kinds of social science data.
3. That the above objectives can best be accomplished when students and teachers are mutually engaged in the process.

The ability to ask the right questions is at the center of inquiry and good teaching. Yet teachers either are not being taught to ask good questions or they are not using this training successfully, judging from the observations of this writer as both classroom teacher and supervisor of student teachers. Class discussions are usually a one-to-one exchange between teacher and student: one question asked, one question answered. More honest and less time consuming would be giving the questions to the students in written form—either with or without answers—rather than continuing the pointless charade of "guess what I'm thinking." Included in this charade are those questions requiring several parts for a full answer, for while they are

*Reprinted with permission from *The History Teacher*, Vol. IV, No. 1 (Nov. 1970), pp. 47-53.

more complex, they differ only in length. When teachers quit talking and begin listening to their students, they usually hear a recapitulation of the lecture or textbook. The argument so often offered to justify such a catechism is that students must know the "facts" before they can think. Even granting this dubious assumption, few teachers ever get beyond the first level. Most social studies teaching stops at the point where it should be beginning.

In contrast to the "guess what I'm thinking" approach to class discussions, teachers need to ask questions for which there are no pat answers. These questions generally fall into two categories: those which focus upon the subject matter of the discipline and those which focus upon the methodology of the discipline. Both are essential, but the latter are the most crucial and the most neglected. As far as the social sciences are concerned, a student's education will never become self-starting until he can skillfully propose questions leading to investigation and utilization of the data of the social sciences.

To teach students to ask such questions, the teacher's role must change so that he too is engaged in a creative process of describing, explaining and evaluating the various relationships between data in the social sciences. Such an approach calls for a new honesty in the classroom as class discussions shift from "question-and-answer" to a mutual commitment of finding out. Think of the excitement and revelation when students discover that the teacher also wants to learn, It could be contagious.

Most inquiry models follow the steps outlined by Massialas and Cox in *Inquiry in the Social Studies*, consisting of Orientation, Hypothesis Formation, Exploration, Evidencing and Generalizing. These steps are usable, but the Exploration and Evidencing parts should be expanded. Students need to speculate, not only in forming the original hypothesis, but in "Evidencing" as well, by answering the question: How can we know that my hypothesis is valid? Students speculate in model building, first, by determining what questions need to be answered to prove the hypothesis, and second, by deciding what evidence would be needed to substantiate these answers. It is here that the student and teacher become engaged in creative inquiry.

Inquiry itself presupposes curiosity. The first step—and the major role of the teacher—is to present an episode in the class which enables students to hypothesize about the subject under investigation. It is this class session which should make each student's reaction and line of inquiry unique, momentum coming from the dialogue of students and teacher. This can be done in numerous ways; a great deal depends upon the imagination and resources of the teacher in making students curious and motivating them—although the motivation can grow with the process itself. Visual presentations are often effective. Some current films are designed to raise questions or get students to hypothesize. Another approach is providing students with conflicting interpretations. An imaginative teacher can utilize the textbook as well, as has been illustrated by Massialas and Cox, encouraging students to speculate about the subject. For the purposes of demonstrating this approach to inquiry, the causes of the American Revolution will serve as the "medium" through which the "message" will be explained. These speculations might include some of the following statements about the causes of revolutions in general and about the American Revolution in particular:

Revolutions occur when people are poor or getting poorer.
Revolutions occur when people's rights are taken away by a despotic government.
People revolt because they want greater voice in their own affairs.
Revolutions occur because the masses are led by a few agitators.
The American Colonists declared independence in order to escape the mercantile system.

The American Colonists revolted because they wanted to have a greater control over their own lives.

The American Colonists wanted to main the control of their own affairs to which they had become accustomed prior to 1763.

For purposes of illustration, the class will test the last statement.

The teacher should turn to developing a model substantiating the claim that the "American Colonists" sought independence in order to maintain the control over their own affairs to which they had grown accustomed prior to 1763." The process involves several interacting episodes consisting of determining what kinds of data are needed for verification, if they exist, where they can be found, and whether they are reliable. Model building and data accumulation should go on simultaneously as questions are raised and data collected to answer them or supportive statements made in class.

Model building should begin with speculation about the requirements necessary for verification. Such speculation could consist of the following:

Colonists must have had control over their own affairs prior to 1763.
Colonists must have believed that this freedom existed.
This idea must have been sufficiently widespread to have a mass following.
The colonists must have believed that this freedom was disappearing.
Those who were responsible for independence must have believed that Great Britain was substantially reducing local control.

Each statement is then evidenced. First the class must determine what kind of evidence would substantiate the statement and then proceed to gather that which exists. If the data cannot be acquired, or if they do not exist, then students need to recognize the weakness of the supporting statement. For example, class discussion and investigation of the statement, "Colonists must have had control over their own affairs prior to 1763," might revolve around the following:

What affairs would be important for the colonists to control?
 Control over their livelihood.
 Control over the way they were governed.
How would you determine that colonists had control over their own livelihood?
 Must identify what colonists did to make a living and that they were unhampered in these pursuits.
 Show that the colonists were not prohibited from pursuing some economic endeavors that were important to their economic welfare.
How would you establish that the colonists had control over their own political affairs?
 Must identify what political institutions were important to the Colonists.
 Must show that these political institutions were controlled by the Colonists.
How would you determine what political institutions were important to the colonists?
 Those institutions which had the greatest effect upon their lives.
 Those institutions which, if not controlled, could significantly alter their lives.
What data would you accept to identify those political institutions which were important to the colonists.

Answers might include:

Statements by colonists to that effect.
Polls which asked the question, which of these institutions are you most concerned with?
Analysis of decisions made by institutions and the impact these decisions had on the lives of people.
Analysis which shows what institutions received greatest participation by colonists.
Which political institutions produced the greatest struggle for control among the colonists and between the colonists and Great Britain.

When specific data has been identified, students must locate and gather the data. Again the work could be divided among groups in the class and research begun as students search for the data. It is obvious that a reasonably good library or resource center would be required. If sufficient resources are not available, topics should be pursued which lend themselves to the materials readily obtainable.

Model building is complex and varies greatly in sophistication. The example illustrated above would certainly pose difficulty for the average high school class in American history. It is possible, however, to relate the questions mentioned above to more contemporary and perhaps more understandable issues without sacrificing the open-endedness of this approach. Such an investigation could begin by asking and pursuing the following:

What political institutions are most important today?
How could we find out?
Who would you ask?
Who should decide which institutions are most important?
What kind of data would you accept as verification that certain political institutions were most important?

A discussion of a possible analogy to the colonial period could then be developed.

How valid is an analogy between the present and the colonial evaluation?
How would you decide is such an analogy were valid?
What assumptions would have to be made if the analogy were valid?

Once a model has been constructed it provides a useful tool for analysis of various interpretations by comparing the arguments and data historians used with that developed in the class model. The emphasis which each interpretation places on parts of the model not only identifies the interpretation more clearly but helps to account for the differences.

This approach can easily be adapted to different forms of instruction. It lends itself to individual instruction for it enables a student to do two things: first, choose his own topic; second, develop his own model at his own level of sophistication. Group work may be more feasible, however, because a large amount of interaction between student and teacher and among students is desirable. Group work best provides for such interaction, as well as affording the opportunity for variety. Because data from all the social sciences are useful for evidencing, this method make possible a true inter-disciplinary approach.

The development of a new technique in the teaching of social studies does not mean that it should be employed exclusively. Social studies teaching should be eclectic. The procedure suggested in this article is flexible enough to allow teachers to use as little or as much as students can digest. It can be implemented as rapidly or as slowly as teachers desire. It can be the focal point for an entire course, a unit, ore merely a day's work. The procedure can be adopted by an entire school system which provides workshops and training for the teachers or by an individual teacher who, after reading this article, understands the technique. No new materials need be purchased, although a good selection of primary and secondary sources are necessary. Even here, it is possible to collect materials for a particular unit and follow this process without a large investment. What makes this proposal acceptable is that it focuses upon the art of teaching an not, as so many proposals of today, upon expensive gimmickry.

Edward Hicks (1780-1849), Peaceable Kingdom. *Courtesy of National Gallery of Art, Washington, D.C.*

Primary Sources in the Teaching of History*
Gerald Danzer and Mark Newman

What is more gratifying than the gleam of excitement reflected in the eyes of engaged students? Using primary sources in history instruction helps to generate that spark of enthusiasm which is one of the greatest rewards in the teaching profession. The authors, Gerald Danzer and Mark Newman, make a realistic appraisal of the benefits of incorporating a variety of primary source materials in history instruction at all grade levels without losing sight of the difficulties involved in constructing meaningful curricular programs.

Gerald Danzer, Professor of History, and Mark Newman, Media Consultant for Harper Collins Publishers, have collaborated on a number of projects promoting history education at the University of Illinois at Chicago.

"Tuning in," teachers tell us, is the great key to teaching history in the schools. But how can we get teenagers to "tune in" to the world around them? We live in a cultural environment shaped by the interplay of people, space, and time. Yet, many young people seem oblivious to it all. How can we transform the oblivious into the observant? One way is to supplement the basic textbook with primary source-based lessons.

Using primary sources in the classroom is not a new trend or fad; it is as old as the teaching of history in American schools. The earliest textbooks included documents along with narrative accounts. Noah Webster's celebrated 1787 reader contained the Declaration of Independence and other source materials. The popular *The Life of George Washington* by Mason Locke Weems devoted an entire chapter to reprinting Washington's Farewell Address.

Nearly a century later, Albert Bushnell Hart reported that the use of original materials was a frequent topic in discussions on methods of teaching history. In 1945, Robert E. Keohane sounded a familiar theme, declaring that the teaching of history in the secondary schools "would profit greatly from more extensive, intelligent, varied, and continuous use of primary sources." This discussion continues today in the pages of various educational journals.

But the promise of primary source lessons has seldom been realized. Students complain that source readings are too long, too difficult, or just plain boring. Some teachers are uneasy about using sources. They point to the area as a major deficiency in their professional education. Others become fearful when they realize that the use of sources encourages pupil participation, which often means that they must yield some of the initiative in the classroom. Moreover, educational literature frequently does not cover the various ways to employ historical sources in the high school. The typical methods textbook devotes only a few pages to the topic. Clearly a need currently exists for a brief discussion on the theory and practice of primary source materials in secondary school history classes.

Basic Questions: What and Why

What Are Primary Sources? Primary sources are difficult to define. Norman F. Cantor and Richard I. Schneider have defined a primary source as "a work that was written at a time that is contemporary or nearly contemporary with the period or subject being studied." Walter T. K. Nugent expanded the definition to include non-literary objects: "A 'primary source' is some direct record left behind from the period or by the people who are the subject of the historian's study. They are the actual records which have survived from the past." Henry Johnson long

*Reprinted from Tuning In: Primary Sources in the Teaching of History, Gerald A. Danzer and Mark Newman (World History Project, University of Chicago, 1991), pp. 5, 7-9, and 11. Reprinted with permission of the authors.

ago spelled out this expanded concept in greater detail: primary sources include all "the traces left by the human past—present ideals, present social customs and institutions, language, literature, material products of human industry, physical man himself, and the physical remains of men."

Some authorities have suggested using the term "original sources," but this has not really clarified the situation because, as Louis Gottschalk has noted, there are at least five different ways in which a document can be original. It might be original (1) in the sense that it contains fresh materials, or (2) because it is not translated, or (3) because it is in its earliest state, or (4) because the text has not been altered, or (5) because it contains the earliest available information.

Most teachers will need to spend time explaining the concept of primary sources to their students. Perhaps it is preferable to devote several short conversations to the problem of definition rather than one long one. Students will soon realize that the boundary line between primary and secondary sources often is arbitrary, sometimes shifts depending on how the source is used, and frequently is quite blurred or indistinct.

Why Are Primary Sources Valuable in the Classroom? Primary sources are the ore from which history is made. Without them there can be no history. It is reasonable, therefore, to expect that a course of history would devote some attention to these basic materials. Primary sources concretely present the uniqueness of each situation. An appreciation of this singularity, an awareness that each circumstance has special aspects, is one of the major contributions that the historical approach makes to human understanding. As students try to make sense out of individual events or documents, however, they must place them in a larger context. In doing so, they will be forced to develop generalizations to *invest* the facts with meaning and significance. This is the primary task of the student of history: to appreciate the peculiar situation of the individual event and at the same time to see its broader significance. To become "historical," the information gained from primary sources must be used to illustrate a general proposition, provide an example of a common phenomenon, or furnish a piece of a larger picture.

This dynamic between the specific and the general, between the unique location of individual events and their place in a larger schema, forms the essential structure of historical studies. Without specific remains there is no past; without concepts there is no meaning. Both are essential pillars supporting the temple of history. Tear one of them down and the edifice falls.

Perhaps much of the dissatisfaction with the quality of history teaching in the schools can be attributed to the lack of proportion in this basic structure. Have teachers spent too much time on generalizations and on the main outlines of the story so that students get a distorted view of what history is all about? This is precisely where the use of primary source materials enters the discussion. Their major pedagogical function is to provide roots for generalizations, to introduce that creative tension between the specific and the general which makes the historian's world go around.

Many statements about the value of using primary sources point to this vitalizing quality. Primary sources make history come alive providing the "warmth, color, and flavor of the time." Editors often introduce anthologies of source materials with the observation that "the freshness" of the documents will help readers "recapture the spirit of the times." By conveying some of the drama and variety of the past, teachers can use primary sources to compensate for the dryness of secondhand summaries often found in textbooks and lectures.

How Can Primary Sources Be Used To Best Advantage? The excitement generated by penetrating inside a historical event can often help students see the provocative character of many contemporary writings. What arguments do these documents advance either by direct advocacy or by their implicit assumptions? Who did these works provoke at the time? Who would they upset now? Is this true of visual materials and artifacts as well as texts? Following this line of questions, teachers can challenge a student's assumptions and explode the possibility of any simple, one-dimensional approach to the past.

At the same time, even simple documents have great emotive power. Voices from the past retain the ability to move people when viewed from a historical angle of vision. Transporting oneself back in time and across space will reveal the eloquence in the funeral oration of Pericles, the bite in the satires of Juvenal, the splendor of Byzantine mosaics, the soaring thrust of a Gothic cathedral, the power of a Bach fugue, the freshness of an impressionist painting, the silent indictment presented in a photograph of trench warfare, and the ringing confidence of John F. Kennedy's inaugural address. These qualities are not dimmed by the passage of time. As monuments of human achievement, they can stand on their own. But each one will increase in its power as it is placed in its context, viewed as an argument, and treated as a historical document.

In other words, to simply "read" a document is not enough; a student must use it as a historical source. He or she must analyze its content, assess its significance, and in the process become his or her own historian. Using source materials in this way will encourage critical reading and can also serve as an impetus to synthesize diverse materials. A familiarity with the methods of a historian is certainly an important contribution that history courses can make to general education. The idea that historical studies will equip the citizenry is as old as Jefferson: "History, by apprising them of the past, will enable them to judge of the future; it will avail them of the experience of other times and other nations; it will qualify them as judges of the actions and designs of men; it will enable them to know ambition under every disguise it may assume; and knowing it, it defeats its view."

Students always benefit when they utilize a wide range of study skills, enlarging their vocabularies and extending their ability to locate information in the process. A major goal of historical instruction is always to have the student leave a course possessing in some measure the skills of a historian: posing significant questions; locating sources; subjecting the data to critical analysis; synthesizing diverse materials; and expressing the results in readable, convincing prose. These skills, of course, can be acquired only by practice. Lectures, textbooks, videotapes, and so on, will not, by themselves, do the job. If teachers are serious about the development of these skills, they must be prepared to devote a substantial amount of class time to the task. The effort must be continuous, and it must permit work on an individual basis. The use of sources in teaching history thus demands much from the teacher, but it also carries the great reward of helping students become their own teachers. Surely one of the most compelling arguments for the documentary approach to the study of history is "the opportunity it affords to get the student well started on the way to his own self-education."

What Are Some Disadvantages of the Source Method? The use of primary sources in the teaching of history also has certain limitations. As noted above, the method is very time consuming. It is obviously impossible for any student to gain a general understanding of historical development through the use of sources alone. Life is too short and the documents are too numerous. The quantity of original materials that can be used in one school year is necessarily restricted. Moreover, the sources will be one-sided and prevent a full consideration of opposing views. Indeed, the value of any particular source in isolation will largely depend on the setting and background—the historical context—provided by secondary materials. Thus primary sources supplement but they cannot replace the textbook or the lecture. Long ago Albert

Bushnell Hart phrased the point in a most appropriate metaphor. "Sources," he said, "do not tell all their own story; they need to be arranged and set in order by the historian, who on the solid piers of their assurances spans his [or her] continuous bridge of narrative."

The World of Primary Sources

The world of primary sources is a varied as the real world it depicts. It is impossible to discuss all types of primary sources, and any categories we may establish are not hard and fast. A single source defies strict categorization. Yet some type of classification scheme is desirable when discussing primary sources and their value in the classroom. We have devised the system shown by the chart on p. 25. Note that it divides primary sources into five categories, with some convenient subcategories.

Print documents are written or published sources that encompass the wide range of written communication that has characterized human life since the beginning of civilization. This type of source includes formal government, personal, and institutional documents such as constitutions, wills, and membership registers of organizations, to name just a few examples. In addition, there are publications like newspapers and autobiographies.

The electronic media, to a large extent, are a development of the last two centuries. Included here are film, radio, television, and the personal home movies/videos that have become so pervasive. The media are visual and aural sources that span the spectrum of entertainment, information, news, sports, advertising, and documentary programming.

The arts include graphic and fine art forms. This category is difficult to define because while fine arts can be easily identified, the graphic arts almost defy classification. They include maps, illustrations, cartoons, posters, and illustrations of various sorts—such as the example from Diderot's *Encyclopedia*. Frequently there is little distinction between a graphic work and a fine art piece: the etchings of German artist Albrecht Durer or Japanese Hokusai prints, for example.

Folklore, folkways, and mythology present similar difficulties because this type of source extends beyond oral traditions of storytelling and song to traditional performance arts, folk crafts, foodways, rituals, family traditions, and even techniques of homebuilding and clothesmaking. The study of folklore and mythology examines what people do, how they do it, and why.

The physical environment and material culture produce two types of sources. The built environment includes architecture; all human-made physical structures; and any changes made to the natural environment by humans, such as landscaping and the making of fields or pastures. Using this type of source helps students understand just how people have interacted with their environment and how this has led to changes in ecology. The second type of source in this category is artifacts. This includes all objects made by humans. In this subcategory we can see a division between objects constructed for use and retention and those made for use and disposal. This latter kind of source is sometimes referred to as ephemera.

Primary sources help counteract the traditional complaints against the study of history: that it is boring and monotonous and that it is concerned solely with dates and names. The one key to successful teaching is variety in the use of materials and instructional techniques. By their very nature and because of their infinite assortment, primary sources dictate a variety of approaches. They have the power to bring history to life, to engage students creatively and analytically.

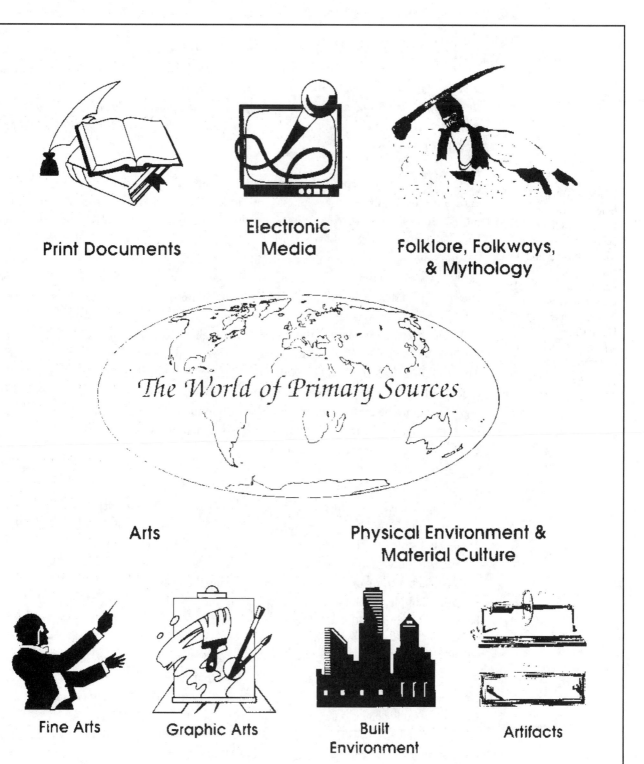

Print Documents

Electronic Media

Folklore, Folkways, & Mythology

The World of Primary Sources

Arts

Physical Environment & Material Culture

Fine Arts

Graphic Arts

Built Environment

Artifacts

Writing Essays that Make Historical Arguments*
by Ray W. Karras

Experienced history teachers often develop their best lessons through a long process of trial and error. Here, Ray Karras offers a ready-to-use formula for writing historical essays that is built on the timeless foundation of evidence and argument. The strategy is designed to avoid the twin pitfalls of student essays: the summary and the polemic. The author explicitly recognizes that what frequently motivates history students of all ages are the questions that prompt divergent responses.

Ray Karras has taught history at Lexington High School, Lexington, Massachusetts and is currently an educational consultant based in Nashua, New Hampshire, specializing in higher order thinking skills in history teaching.

For the valuable purpose of improving their students' critical thinking skills, history teachers are frequently urged to assign essay writing. There is, however, little critical thinking in most "reports" and other narratives which only summarize textbooks and other sources. Essays that testify to desirable citizenship attitudes or that promote particular political, social, or economic causes are often more polemical than thoughtful. Such writing too often and too easily fits Samuel Johnson's Dictionary definition of an essay: "A loose sally of the mind; an irregular indigested piece; not a regular and order composition. There must be a better way."

The essay that makes a historical argument may offer that better way, for it is hard to make an effective argument without expressing higher-order thinking skills. Yet even though teachers do sometimes ask students to argue in their essays, the results are often disappointing. The trouble is that simply telling students to argue seldom enables them to do so. For how, exactly are students to compose these arguments? How, exactly, are they to put them in writing? What is needed is an approach to historical argumentation that can be explicitly taught, performed, and evaluated. This paper suggests a method of essay instruction that can help teach history through argumentation.

History teachers might agree that an essay that argues should include the following. It should:

1. Ask a question of historical interpretation that invites controversy.

"Was the New Deal successful in handling the Great Depression between 1933 and 1940?" is such a question. However, "Discuss the main features of the New Deal" is not; discussion is not necessarily argument.

2. Claim a controversial hypothesis answering the question.

For example, "The New Deal was mainly successful in handling the Great Depression between 1933 and 1940," or "The New Deal was mainly unsuccessful..." are hypotheses that invite argument, since both cannot be simultaneously believed.

3. Claim controversial and logical reasons for believing the hypothesis.

For example, one logical reason for believing that the New Deal succeeded might be: "The New Deal successfully alleviated unemployment." Another reason might claim that "the New Deal successfully achieved its professed aim of preserving capitalism." These claims of reasons are conceptually narrower, and thus easier to defend than the overarching hypothesis they logically support. If we can be made to believe these reasons, we can, at least provisionally, be made to believe the hypothesis that the New Deal succeeded.

---

*Reprinted from *Magazine of History* (Summer, 1994), pp. 54-57, by permission of the Organization of American Historians.

4. **Apply specific and relevant factual evidence to support each reason and, if necessary, explain how this evidence supports the claimed reasons.**

For example, supporting the claim of New Deal success with unemployment are the facts that unemployment declined from about 24% of the total labor force in 1933 to 14% in 1937. By 1936 the WPA alone employed 3.4 million out of a total working labor force of 44.4 million. At this point we have a prima facie case for the claim that the New Deal eased unemployment through such agencies as the WPA.

5. **Make claims that oppose the supporting claims, give evidence for this opposition, and then rebut this opposing argument with new evidence in order to restore the arguer's original claim.**

Here is the heart of the argument, and it is where students need the most guidance and practice. Many students resist the notion that they should reveal claims and evidence that oppose their own claims and evidence. They have to be convinced that there is far more to argument than merely supporting their own side; they must also fairly present opposing arguments and defeat them.

Thus the opposing claim that the New Deal failed to ease unemployment might be supported by evidence that by 1938 recession again set in spite of the New Deal, with unemployment rising from 14% to 19% of the total labor force in one year. This counterargument—this package of claim and evidence—cannot be allowed to stand if the student is to sustain the unemployment success claim; it must be rebutted. This rebuttal might claim that the "Roosevelt recession" of 1938 shows that the New Deal actually succeeded because it was the weakening of its programs that brought back unemployment with a vengeance. For evidence, in the single year 1937 the Roosevelt Administration slashed government spending on the WPA and on other New Deal programs from $4.1 billion to a mere $800 million.

The very success of the New Deal between 1933 and 1937 made its leaders so understandably optimistic that they reduced New Deal activity, thus allowing the recession.

But how "understandably"? As the process of argument drives the arguer deeper into the historical subject, facts that at first may have seemed irrelevant can become very relevant indeed. In his 1936 presidential campaign FDR told Chicago businessmen, "Today those factories sing the song of industry; markets hum with bustling movement; banks are secure; ships and trains are running full." Yet only three months later in his Second Inaugural Address on 20 January 1937 FDR told the country, "I see one third of a nation ill-housed, ill-clad, ill-nourished"—and this was before the government spending cuts that were said to have brought about the 1937-1938 relapse. Could it be that New Deal publicity flew in the face of economic realities? Was hypocrisy at work here? A new argument might now address this interesting new question, one that arose only because the student set out to argue rather than simply to describe or "discuss" the New Deal.

Now the student's original hypothesis and its supporting reasons may need to be rejected, revised, or further strengthened. Perhaps the hypothesis will become "The New Deal mainly failed between 1933 and 1940;" and one reason for believing this might be that "New Dealers were hypocritical about economic realities." Though this claim is rather more sophisticated than the original claim about unemployment, it is probably not too sophisticated for young students who are, or who say they are, hypersensitive to hypocrisy—especially the hypocrisy of their elders.

All the evidence presented to this point is usually found in standard textbooks or in easily available reference works. The ambitious student may find an even more sophisticated claim about the main cause of the 1937-38 recession in, for example, Jordan A. Schwarz's *The New Dealers*. Schwarz argues that the timidity of investors caused a capital shortage which arose in the political climate of 1936-37, when many businessmen attacked the New Deal. The complexity of the capital shortage claim lies in requiring of students rather more economic knowledge than many of them are likely to possess. Ideally, an economic historian might weigh both claims by asking, "Which was more responsible for the 1937-38 recession: reduced government spending, or a shortage of private investment capital?"

But just because the capital shortage claim is more sophisticated than the government-spending claim does not make it necessarily a better argument. Effective argument can arise from cursory textbook evidence as well as from specialized sources. It is the process of argument itself—at any level of knowledge—that yields higher order thinking skill expression. The depth of the argument is limited only by the student's talent and by time and resources available for research.

The give-and-take of argument can serve a major purpose of studying history and of education itself. Through the structured expression of inferences, logic, and evaluation of evidence, students can learn that they can, and often must, change their opinions. Argument mounts a frontal attack on prejudice.

6. **Write inferential questions asking for new and unknown facts that, by inference, would help test the claim already made.**

Thus, to test the unemployment claim, the arguer might ask: "What percentage of the work force between 1933 and 1940 was employed by federal government agencies instead of by private business?" Those claiming New Deal success with unemployment would like to see—would infer—a low percentage in federal jobs. Those claiming New Deal failure with unemployment would like to see—would infer—a higher percentage of federal employment. For if the federal government addressed unemployment mainly by hiring workers into its own agencies it can hardly be said to have eased unemployment in the private sector, where most jobs would ultimately have to be found for recovery to occur. This inferential question assumes, of course, that the information it seeks was *not* included in available sources. If it were, the student should be expected to use it in the body of the argument.

Asking inferential questions also forces students to recognize that their available sources can never tell them all the facts they need to know to reach ironclad conclusions. There simply are no such conclusions about the New Deal or about any other historical question worth asking.

Almost by chance, argumentation often occur in everyday classroom work. Writing arguments in an orderly fashion is more challenging. Where to begin? What comes next? How to organize the work? Such problems can easily overwhelm the novice student. It is perhaps surprising, then, that a one-page instruction sheet can ease many of the difficulties facing the writer of an essay that argues.

How to Write Your Essay

1. In the first paragraph, write your historical question and claim your controversial hypothesis answering it. Say no more in this paragraph.
2. In the second paragraph, claim your first reason for believing your hypothesis in the first sentence. In the sentences that follow within this paragraph, write:
   a. facts that support this claim and explain how they do this.
   b. a claim that logically opposes the claim you have just made. Give and explain evidence for this opposing claim.
   c. a claim that rebuts your opposing claim. Write evidence for this rebuttal claim. Explain how this evidence does what you claim it does.
   d. an inferential question asking for new and unknown facts that will test the claims you made in this paragraph.
3. In the following paragraphs (except for the last one), do exactly what you did in the second paragraph for each additional reason you claim for your hypothesis.
4. In the final paragraph, simply restate your hypothesis. This is your "Q.E.D."

If you follow these instructions you will successfully show me what you think about the history you know.

This instruction sheet is designed for essay tests written during one class period, when there is usually time to develop only two main reasons. It can be adapted for longer research essays prepared outside the classroom by developing additional reasons and sub-reasons.

Instructions 2 and 3 in the sheet ask students to pack a great deal into the two central paragraphs. Though many teachers may want separate paragraphs for separate parts of the argument, it is crucial for the student to keep always in mind the claim made in each paragraph's first sentence; this must be defenced through all opposing and rebuttal claims and evidence. "Proper" paragraphing notwithstanding, paragraph indentations in mid-argument can sometimes let writers drift astray from their original intentions, especially in the stress of classroom essay testing.

Pacing classroom essay work. For students with little experience in writing arguments a good strategy is to build competence gradually. Suppose that during the academic year the teacher expects to assign five classroom essays, each on a different historical subject. The series might evolve in this way:

First essay. Ask students to offer a hypothesis and develop only one reason for believing it. Allow students to refer to their notes, textbooks, and to the "How to Write your Essay" sheet itself. Announce the essay question in advance: e.g., "HYPOTHESIS: The main cause of the American Revolution was economic conflict. Do you agree?" In preparation, let students compose their essays at home, but insist that they leave them at home; all actual writing must be done during the class period.

From this first experience students often learn that relying on notes and other "crutches" during class time encumbers more than helps them. This is a worthwhile lesson, for "open book" testing can tempt students to put off preparation instead of working out their arguments before they write. Pascal was surely right to advise that "the last thing one settles in writing a book is what one should put in first."

Second essay. Announce the essay question in advance, again require the development of only one reason, but rule out the use of notes, books and instruction sheet.

Third essay. Announce the essay question in advance, but require essays with two completely developed reasons for the hypothesis. Again, no notes, books or instruction sheet at hand.

Fourth essay. Remove all crutches. Ask students to complete two-reason essays without notes and without prior knowledge of the question, though students will, of course, know in advance the historical subject area on which they are to write. By this fourth essay, students should have gained some competence and confidence in developing arguments in writing and in everyday class work.

Fifth essay. Confirm the progress made. Once more, require full development, no outside materials at hand, and no prior question announcement.

A final examination essay might ask students for a grand sweep argument using evidence from various historical episodes they have studied. For example: HYPOTHESIS: Economic conflict more than racism best characterizes relations between Native Americans and white Americans. Do you agree? Argue for the period between 1789 and 1868 or between 1868 and the present.

HYPOTHESIS: Defending democratic ideals has been the main cause of the United States' foreign wars. Do you agree? Write your argument to cover any two U.S. wars with foreign countries.

Questions like these provide students with historical questions and suggest possible answering hypotheses. Also possible are open-ended assignments in which students develop their own questions and hypotheses. For example, a test item might say "Argue for a convincing hypothesis about the causes of the Civil War;" or "Argue for a convincing hypothesis about the history of affirmative action between 1965 and the present." All independently prepared research papers composed outside of class would be of this open-ended variety.

Evaluating Essays that Make Arguments. To make expectations clear, a check sheet like the following might be shared with students:

1. Did you follow *all* the instructions in "How to Write Your Essay"? For example, did you make the claims you intended to make? Remember the big difference between a claim and a factual statement; don't expect one to do the work of the other.
2. Did you give specific, adequate and accurate factual evidence to support your claims?
3. Did you make a logically convincing argument?
   To check, cover your hypothesis, revealing only your claims of reasons for believing it. From these reasons alone a reader should be able logically to infer your hypothesis.

Conclusion. There is good reason to believe that most students are well able to make arguments. They, in fact all of us, argue every day outside the classroom. To overhear students' conversations about ball games, their favorite music, about each other, and even about their teachers, is often to hear them express in irregular form all of the higher-order thinking skills of argumentation. Teaching history through argumentation gives structure to these skills so that students can use them in the classroom—which is where they belong.

Creative Book Reports*

By Kathryn Sexton

Recent research on learning styles has brought to the forefront of curriculum discussion what K-12 students have known intuitively for years. Variety is indeed the spice of life. The exemplary history teacher, as Kathryn Sexton does below, breathes new life into an old standard.

Kathryn Sexton served as librarian of Winston Churchill High School in San Antonio, Texas, from 1968 to 1989. Now retired, she continues to write for library, education, and history periodicals.

Teachers and students alike often find themselves caught in a vicious circle concerning that pedagogical veteran, the book report. "In the next six weeks read a historical novel about the American West. A book report of 250-300 words will be due at the end of the six week period." This is typical of how such an assignment is often presented. "Another book report," students groan. They do not realize, nor probably care that the teacher whose goal it is to foster reading also complains: "More reports to read and grade."

If teachers could get away from the traditional book report, perhaps reading student papers might become more enjoyable. Students can respond more creatively and more positively if they do not have to follow such traditional directions as: Give a summary of the plot. What did you learn about the historical period? Describe the setting or the characters. Students can answer these questions by looking them up in such publications as Cliff's Notes without ever looking at the assigned book!

I wish to share some techniques and approaches that will make the "read and report" assignment a more meaningful experience. First, students should be assisted in making their selections. The teacher and school librarian can draw up a list of the books to be found in the school library which cover the period or the type of book the students are supposed to read. Possible topics include: historical novels taking place in the ancient world, novels about the settling of the American West, biographies of famous nineteenth century figures, and books covering various aspects of life from the Renaissance to 1900. There are a myriad of topics depending on when in the curriculum you are calling for outside reading.

If the list is annotated, it is even more helpful for students. These lists are available from many sources such as text books, periodicals, and other libraries. Students can search out titles on their own by looking up the subject in a card catalog, computerized catalog, or in another format. The teacher, with or without the assistance of the librarian, can suggest subject headings the student might consult. Some examples include: Great Britain—History—Wars of the Roses, Middle Ages—Fiction, Arms and Armor—History, Costume-History, U.S.—History—Revolution, Rome—Social Life and Customs.

Once students have selected their books, give them suggestions about what to look for in their reading. Go over the following guidelines in class and list them on an assignment sheet. This will enrich their reading and help them to evaluate what they read.

1. What is the time period of the book?
2. Does the author interpret events or merely record them?
3. Is the book a social history showing how life was lived, or does it deal mainly with the politics and economics of the time?

---

*Reprinted from *Magazine of History*, Vol. 6, No. 1 (Summer 1991), pp. 5-7, by permission of the Organization of American Historians.

4. Does the author give an overall view of a historical period or rather concentrate on one aspect of that period?
5. Does the author write in a way that helped you understand the time period and why it was important in light of events which preceded or followed it?

If the assignment is to read a biography, the student should try to answer questions such as these:

1. What was the subject's motivation? What influence did it have?
2. What were the subject's weaknesses and strengths?
3. What were the subject's ideas of success? What did that person want to achieve? Did he reach his goals?
4. What was the period of time in which he lived? Did he influence events? Did events influence him?
5. Does the author make the subject come alive so that you understand him as a person as well as a historical figure?
6. Does the author merely report on events, or does he interpret the subject and the events?
7. What was the subject's chief contribution to history?

If students keep the following questions in mind as they read historical novels, it will give focus and direction to their readings.

1. Is history more important in this book than the plot?
2. Are the chief characters historical figures or the products of the author's imagination?
3. Does the historical period come alive for you?
4. Do you feel the author included too much detail or too little? Does the book move slowly? Do you like the way the book is written?
5. Is the plot simple or complicated one? Are there sub-plots?
6. Does the novel stress the historical events of the period, or does it give more emphasis to how people lived during that time?

There are many approaches to reporting on a history book which actually could be applied to history and biography (factual or fictional). The goals of the teacher are two-fold: to teach a perspective and evaluative approach to the reading of history, and to enhance and enrich the student's understanding of history. The following alternative choices to the traditional book report provide an opportunity for students to be creative and imaginative. Of course, there will be some who balk at any reporting, but using these alternatives should reduce the number of times librarians and teachers hear their students say, "I don't mind reading the book, but I hate to report on it."

Teachers can allow students to select one of the following assignments on the history book or the biography of a historical figure.

1. Write twenty trivia questions (with answers) based on the book you read.
2. Select the event you considered to be most important in the book and write it up as a newspaper article during that particular time period. (Keep in mind that good newspaper writing tells the who, what, when, why, and where of the event).
3. Design a poster which could be used in a bookstore to advertise the book.
4. Should the author of this book have taken Lord Acton's advice, "Advice to Persons About to Write History—Don't."
5. Should this book be required reading for every student who wants to be a history major in college? Why or why not?

6. Design a book jacket (unlike the one on the book) which you think would reflect the book's content and attract readers.

7. Is this book important enough to be included in a time capsule buried today to be dug up in a thousand years? Why or why not?

8. Does the book prove Thomas Carlyle's statement, "The history of the world is but the biography of great men?" How?

9. Compare the subject of the biography to a leader in the contemporary world.

10. If the class had been required to read this book, what objective test would you give them to evaluate their knowledge of the book's contents? Give five to ten questions with an answer key.

11. Locate a review or a critical article about the book. Explain why you agree or disagree with the article's author.

12. It has been said that "the past is never dead." Does this book prove this statement? Why or why not?

13. Could contemporary leaders learn from this book? What could they learn that you think would be helpful to them?

14. Do you think this book is a classic or will become one? In giving your answer include your definition of a classic, or quote someone else's definition with which you agree.

15. List the visual aids (maps, charts, etc.) that could have been included to help you better understand the book. Draw up an example of one of your suggestions.

If the student has chosen a book on a specialized subject, such as the history of costume or a book on castles, the teacher can suggest other projects and the students also will often suggest acceptable ideas. A model of a castle accompanied by a key to explain its various aspects might the appropriate for reporting in a book about castles. Costume history could be handled in many ways such as by drawing or sewing a dress. These are various creative ways in which to approach this subject.

Assignments for reporting on historical or period novels can also be different and more challenging than the traditional book report which stresses plot outlines and character descriptions. Of course there can be crossovers with the following list and the one suggested for non-fiction.

1. Somerset Maugham, the noted novelist, once wrote, "I would sooner read a timetable or a catalogue than nothing at all. They are much more entertaining than half the novels that are written." Would Maugham rather have read timetables than this book? Why?

2. Design a poster which a bookstore could use to publicize this book.

3. What would you write in a letter to the author? Topics could include your reactions to the book, or why you think the story should have been longer or shorter.

4. Someone once said that a classic is "a work of enduring excellence." Does this book meet that criterion? Give the reasons why you think it does or does not.

5. Do you think someone who does not like reading about history could still enjoy this book? Why or why not?

6. Discuss the title of the book. Does it have any particular significance? Does it indicate what the book is about? Do the words of the title appear anywhere in the text? Do you know if the title is a quotation? Did you find it in a book of quotations? Why do you think the title was chosen for the book? Did the title arouse your curiosity so that you wanted to read the book? Can you think of other titles that would have fit the book better? Whether you answer yes or no, give reasons for your answers.

7. Did the novel help you to understand the historical period in which it took place? What event or events were most interesting to you?

8. Design a book jacket which you think would attract more readers to the book than the one the publishers used on it.

9. Henry James once said, "The only reason for the existence of a novel is that it does attempt to represent life." Does this novel measure up to James' standard? Why or why not?

10. If the novel is not illustrated, do you think it should have been? What kind of illustrations do you think would have been appropriate? Paint or draw an example, such as a map that could have helped readers understand the book better.

11. If you were to interview the author, how do you think he would answer these questions?—Why did you write this book? What kinds of people do you think would like it? Do you think you will write a sequel? List any other questions—and the answers to use in the interview. (Reading a biographical article about the author would help when doing this assignment.)

12. Design an advertisement which a newspaper could use to promote this book.

Teachers are ever concerned that students won't read books assigned for outside reading unless they require a book report. Traditionally they ask students to give a somewhat detailed account of the book's contents. If the students select one of the alternative reports suggested in this article they will have to engage in critical thought and evaluation. Additionally, they will be forced to read the book if they are to complete the assignment successfully. For example, in order to write up a newspaper advertisement or create a poster, students must be able to summarize the book's contents, discern its strengths, and be perceptive in regard to the relationship between potential readers and the book. Such creative projects can become thinking experiences. There are challenges in these assignments, and as educators are well aware, if students are challenged in a significantly higher manner, the level of comprehension is higher as well.

Photograph by Bert Seal,
San Diego County
Office of Education

Toward Historical Comprehension: Essays and Examples of Classroom Activities

ERA 1

Three Worlds Meet (Beginnings to 1620)

The study of American history properly begins with the first peopling of the Americas more than 30,000 years ago. Students will learn about the spread of ancient human societies in the Americas, North and South, and their adaptations to diverse physical and natural environments. This prepares students to address the historical convergence of European, African, and Native American people starting in the late 15th century when the Columbian voyages began. In studying the beginnings of North American history it is important for students to understand that Indian societies, like peoples in other parts of the world, were experiencing change—political, economic, cultural—on the eve of the arrival of Europeans. The history of the Native Americans was complex, and it was continuing even as European settlers landed on South and North American shores.

European mariners were the agents of the encounters among these many peoples of the late 15th and early 16th centuries. To understand why the trans-oceanic voyages took place students must gain an appreciation of Europe's economic growth, the rise of bureaucratic states, the pace of technological innovation, intellectual and religious ferment, and the continuing crusading tradition in the late medieval period. Students' grasp of the encounters of diverse peoples in the Americas also requires attention to the history of West and Central Africa. This study will prepare students to investigate the conditions under which the Atlantic slave trade developed.

By studying the European colonization—and partial conquest—of the Americas to 1620, mostly played out in Central and South America, students will embark upon a continuing theme—the making of the many American people of the Western Hemisphere. As a people, we were composed from the beginning of diverse ethnic and linguistic strains. The nature of these manifold and uneven beginnings spawned issues and tensions that are still unresolved. How a composite American society was created out of such human diversity was a complicated process of cultural transformation that unfolded unevenly and unremittingly as the following eras will address.

By studying early European exploration, colonization, and conquest, students will learn about five long-range changes set in motion by the Columbian voyages. First, the voyages initiated a redistribution of the world's population. Several million voluntary European immigrants flocked to the Americas; at least 10-12 million involuntary enslaved Africans relocated on the west side of the Atlantic, overwhelmingly to South America and the Caribbean; and indigenous peoples experienced catastrophic losses. Second, the arrival of Europeans led to the rise of the first trans-oceanic empires in world history. Third, the Columbian voyages sparked a world-wide commercial expansion and an explosion of European capitalist enterprise. Fourth, the voyages led in time to the planting of English settlements where ideas of representative government and religious toleration would grow and, over several centuries, would inspire similar transformations in other parts of the world. Lastly, at a time when slavery and serfdom were waning in Western Europe, new plantation economies were emerging in the Americas employing forced labor on a large scale.

Theodore de Bry, Americae, 1602, *Courtesy of the Library of Congress*

Native-American Women in History*
by Nancy Shoemaker

Essay

Many aspects of early American history have come under scrutiny in recent decades, vastly increasing our knowledge of how European settler societies in the Americas emerged and how they were shaped through extensive contact with Native Americans and enslaved Africans. Among the many new topics being explored, women and the family are among the most important. Nancy Shoemaker's stimulating essay puts the spotlight on Native American women—a particularly difficult subject to explore because of the nature of the archival resources, which give slender evidence on Indian encounters with Europeans through Indian eyes. The new questions being explored by historians remind us how our picture of the emerging colonial societies is still very incomplete.

Nancy Shoemaker teaches history at the State University of New York at Plattsburgh and is the editor of *Negotiators of Change: Historical Perspectives on Native American Women.*

Ironically, Native-American women figure prominently in traditional narratives of American history, but until recently women's experiences and perspectives have been largely excluded from research in Native-American history. Ask any schoolchild to name famous Native Americans from before 1850, and most like you will hear of Pocahontas and Sacagawea. But pick up any book surveying American-Indian history, white-Indian relations in the United States, or the history of a particular tribe, and there will be little mention of either specific women or of women in general.

What exactly did Pocahontas and Sacagawea do to earn themselves a place in the pantheon of American-history heroines? Pocahontas was the daughter of the powerful Indian leader Powhatan, whose confederacy of different Indian nations in the Virginia region presented a significant challenge to the English colonists who settled at Jamestown in 1607. Pocahontas is remembered primarily for having saved Captain John Smith's life, an act which was probably part of a native captivity and adoption ritual but which endured in the narrative of American history because it implies that the conquered gladly assisted in their own conquest. Sacagawea became a historical figure for the same reason. As interpreter and guide to Meriwether Lewis and William Clark in their explorations of the Louisiana Purchase from 1804-1806, Sacagawea opened up the West to American settlement. At least that is how she has often been pictured in American popular culture, one arm extended, graciously directing Lewis and Clark to a landscape green with the promise of wealth. Although one Indian man, Squanto, was cast in that same role in the story of Pilgrim settlement of New England, Indian women seemed to fit this role much better, for the continents were themselves often depicted on maps and in promotional literature as gendered: the woman America, plump and naked except for a few leaves, embraced the iron-clad European conquistador, and the "New World" and "Old World" melded into one.

In the spirit of this uniting of two worlds and two peoples, Pocahontas's and Sacagawea's lives are often distorted to make a better story. Most people trying to recall who Pocahontas was, want to marry her off to John Smith. In reality, she married another English colonist, John Rolfe, who was instrumental in making tobacco the enormously profitable mainstay of the Chesapeake economy. Similarly, Sacagawea, in a movie from the 1950s starring Donna Reed,

---

*Reprinted from *Magazine of History*, Vol. 9, No. 4 (Summer 1995), pp. 10-14, by permission of the Organization of American Historians.

falls tragically in love with William Clark, but alas, must give him up because she is an Indian, and he is engaged to marry a white woman. Sacagawea's own story, as recounted in the journals of Lewis and Clark, seems much more tragic. A Shoshoni woman who as a girl had been captured by another Indian tribe, she was one of at least two wives of an abusive French fur trader named Charbonneau, the official guide hired by the exploring party. Popular renditions of these two women's lives get the details wrong, but the underlying reality may not have been all that different. Both Pocahontas and Sacagawea indeed married white men, and for that reason were well-placed to mediate the cultural and economic exchanges between Indians and Euro-Americans. Yet, as historian Clara Sue Kidwell has observed, it is difficult to discern Pocahontas's and Sacagawea's own motives, loyalties, and understandings of the historical events in which they participated.

It is equally difficult to know to what extent the histories of Pocahontas and Sacagawea can be generalized to shed light on Indian women's experiences in general. In other times and places, Indian women did become important go-betweens in the Indian and Euro-American cross cultural exchange. Sylvia Van Kirk's book, *Many Tender Ties*, a history of women in the beaver fur trade in Canada, showed how crucial Indian women were to the success of the fur trade in its early years. Women pressed furs, prepared foods such as pemmican (dried meat mixed with berries), and served as interpreters. And through their marital and sexual relationships with French and British fur traders, they linked their communities to Europeans in ways that both and complicated economic exchanges and political alliances. In later periods, Indian women continued to be important bicultural mediators, but may have felt increasingly divided by the competing interests of their own people and Euro-Americans. The Paiute woman, Sarah Winnemucca, for instance, served as a scout and interpreter for the United States, but later wrote her autobiography and made speaking tours to bring attention to the injustices that had been committed against her people.

Sarah Winnemucca cannot be considered any more representative than Pocahontas or Sacagawea, but currently much of what historians know about Indian women's lives in the past comes from the stories of individual women. Especially useful are autobiographies. Most of these autobiographies of Indian women were dual-authored, either with anthropologists or with a popular, mainstream writer. Whether the autobiography was part of an anthropologist's attempt to construct a life history that would also inform readers about culture, as in the case of Nancy Lurie's *Mountain Wolf Woman*, or a popular writer's nostalgic rendering of how Indian life used to be, as in Frank Linderman's *Pretty-Shield*, autobiographies can be useful documents for historians interested in understanding the changes in women's lives from their own perspective. Also, some autobiographies, *Pretty-Shield* and Gilbert Wilson's *Waheenee* for example, were originally published with a children's readership in mind, which means that they are very accessible to students.

The production of Indian women's autobiographies continues today. Wilma Mankiller, formerly principal chief of the Cherokee Nation, recently wrote an autobiography. And, Mary Crow Dog (now Mary Brave Bird) has published two accounts of her life. Her *Lakota Woman* provides a glimpse into women's participation in the restless political struggles of the 1960s and 1970s, focusing on the American Indian Movement and the 1973 militant takeover of the hamlet of Wounded Knee, South Dakota. Despite the tremendous importance of women's autobiographies, historians still face the difficulty of connecting individual experience to the broader issues of native women's changing roles and attitudes.

Other than autobiographies, most of the documents available to historians were written by white men: explorers, government agents, and missionaries. And although these Euro-American recorders of Indian cultures often included some commentary on Indian women, their observations were loaded with assumptions and expectations about what they thought Indians and women were supposed to be. Euro-American accounts of Indian cultures were especially critical of native women's work. Indian women either seemed to work too much or they did work which in Euro-American societies was defined as men's work. At the time of European contact, Indian women in tribes east of the Mississippi were largely responsible for the agricultural field-work. They grew the corn, squash, and beans. On the northwest coast, Indian women were active traders, much too shrewd and aggressive than their Euro-American trading partners wanted them to be. And throughout native America, women did much of the carrying. They brought wood and water into the village or camp, and in the case of Plains Indians women had charge of dismantling, packing, transporting, and re-erecting tipis. Euro-American men criticized Indian men for abusing "their women" by treating them like "squaw drudges" or "beasts of burden," a stereotype of Indian women much in contrast with the romanticized, "Indian princess" portrayals of Pocahontas and Sacagawea.

Euro-American descriptions of Indian politics imposed biases on the documentary record of a different nature. In the often detailed transcripts of Indian councils, why were women rarely mentioned? Is it because they were not there? Or, is it because Euro-American observers of the council did not notice they were there or did not think their presence was worth mentioning? In those cases where women did make their presence known in the political arena, Euro-Americans exaggerated women's political power and derided certain tribes, particularly the Iroquois, for being "petticoat governments" or "matriarchates," disorderly societies in which women ruled over men. While it is true that among the Iroquois clan mothers had the right to designate a chief's successor and remove or "dehorn" chiefs from office, Iroquois women did not rule over men.

Anthropologists and historians, who must rely greatly on a documentary record which for the most part excludes native women's voices, have been especially suspicious of how Euro-American descriptions of native societies portray them as having separate spheres: a public, male sphere of politics, diplomacy, war, and trade; and a private or domestic female sphere of childbearing, child rearing, food pressing, and household management. In reading the historical record, one would learn that women's labor usually took place within the proximity of the village or camp. While tending to their children, women worked in nearby cornfields or gathered nuts, berries, and other wild foods. They distributed food within the household, and were often said to own the houses. Men's work usually involved dealing with outsiders, and men were most often, but not always, the diplomats, traders, and warriors. Indian women do appear to have been most active in a private or domestic sphere, while men seemed to control the public sphere. But do the documents give this impression of gendered public and private space because Euro-American men imposed their own preferences about distinct male and female worlds on what they saw, heard, and noticed?

Much of the research in Indian women's history thus far has challenged the existence of public/male and private/female spheres in Indian societies by looking for Indian women in the public space and reconstructing a public role for them. Among different tribes in different time periods, there were some women chiefs, some women who spoke in council, some women who went to war, and some women who participated actively in trade with Euro-Americans. However, this literature produced by historians could just as easily be misrepresenting Indian women's experience in its eagerness to find Indian women in places which Euro-Americans defined as the locus of power. One could just as easily criticize the model of male/public and female/private by asking whether power resided only in the public sphere. Given the significance of the family, or clan, in native political systems, the private or domestic sphere may have been an important site for discussion and decision making about issues such as whether their people should go to war, move, or make alliances with other nations. In the Iroquois example, the political duties of clan mothers originated in the matrilineal clan structure of Iroquois politics, in which chiefs represented their clans in council. Although few tribes had such institutionalized political roles for women, women's significance within the family must have allocated them some influence on decisions affecting the larger community.

Instead of simply highlighting instances in which native women appeared in a public sphere, historians of Indian women's history and gender history are now bringing a more complex array of questions to their research. Much of this research has focused on the effects of Euro-American contact. Thus, historians researching United States Indian policy have shown how many government programs promoting Indian assimilation saw gender roles as crucially important to transforming Indian cultures. Indian women and men variously responded to these programs, sometimes with open resistance, sometimes by diverting the intent of the policies, and sometimes by selectively accepting certain aspects of the policies to fit more closely their traditional ideas about gender. The impact of missionization on Indian women is similarly being reconsidered. Historians used to believe that Indian women were more like than men to reject Christianity because missionaries also sought to restructure native families to fit a nuclear, patriarchal model. However, historians are now acknowledging the diversity of women's responses to Christian missions and acknowledge that many Indian women did choose to become Christian. Many even became leaders of women's church groups, and thus helped shape how Christianity became incorporated in native communities.

Few historians have conducted research upon Indian women's history in the twentieth century, even though the political and economic resurgence of native communities in recent decades raises interesting questions about women's participation in tribal government, the post-World War II migration to cities, and economic transitions from farming and ranching to wage labor. In the twentieth century, Indian women have been tribal chiefs, political activists, housewives, weavers, educators, provisioners of health care and social services on reservations and in urban communities, nuns, novelists, artists, and ranchers. Of course, they have also been mothers, daughters, wives, grandmothers, and aunts.

Scholars have long recognized the great diversity in the histories of American-Indian tribes and the impossibility of generalizing about Navajos and Cherokees, Menominees and Lakotas. Gender adds another dimension to this diversity. Within tribes, the experiences of men and women differed. Moreover, women within tribal groups may also have had different experiences based on their age, family background, religion, educational and work experiences, and choices they have made about where to live and what kind of life to pursue. While the growing interest in American-Indian women's history will make summarizing that history increasingly difficult, it will also bring us closer to understanding what Pocahontas and Sacagawea were really all about.

Sample Student Activities

I. *Comparative characteristics of societies in the Americas, Western Europe, and Western Africa that increasingly interacted after 1450.*

A. Patterns of change in indigenous societies in the Americas up to the Columbian voyages.

Grades 5-6

▶ Locate the Bering land bridge and the routes anthropologist believe were taken by Asian people migrating from Siberia and southward and eastward in the Americas during the periods when massive glaciers covered the northern latitudes. Use sources such as Helen Roney Sattler's *The Earliest Americans* to explore various theories regarding the earliest Americans.

▶ Describe how different Indian societies explain their own origins by drawing upon a variety of works such as *Myths and Legends of the Indian Southwest* by Bertha Dutton and Caroline Olin; *Myths and Legends of the Haida Indians of the Northwest* by Martine Reid; and *Grandfather's Origin Story: The Navajo Indian Beginning* by Richard Redhawk.

▶ Compare how location and physical geography affected food sources, shelter, and cultural patterns of Native American societies such as the Iroquois and Pueblo or Northwest and Southeast Indian societies. Draw evidence from *First Houses: Native American Homes and Sacred Structures* by Jean Guard Monroe and Ray Williamson to explore the differences in shelter and how different Indian societies adapted to the geography of the region in which they lived.

Grades 7-8

▶ Construct a map locating representative Native American peoples such as the Mississippian, Aztec, Mayan, Incan, Iroquois, Pueblo, and Inuit societies.

▶ Research the pre-Columbian development of agrarian societies among Native Americans. *How extensive were agrarian communities in the American Southwest? How prevalent were the "mound building" societies of the Mississippi valley? What can be deduced about these societies from their archaeological remains?*

▶ Write a historical narrative illustrating the cultural traditions, gender roles, and patterns of life of a specific Indian society.

Grades 9-12

▶ Make connections between the images in Native American origin stories and their beliefs about the peopling of the Americas. *What, for example, do Native American origin stories tell us about Native American values and beliefs? How are symbols in origin stories such as wood, rock, rivers, corn, and squash used to explain migration, settlement, and interactions with the environment? How do they help explain the Native American view of the earth?*

▶ Research the formation of the Iroquois Confederation explaining the ideals on which it was based and evaluating the League from the perspective of its Algonkian-speaking neighbors. *Who had been dispossessed by tribal warfare? How did other Native Americans of the Northeast respond to the Five Nations? What was the basis of the hostility among Native Americans before the arrival of European explorers? How did the French and Dutch rivalry over fur trade in the early 17th century exacerbate Huron-Iroquois hostilities?*

▶ Draw upon Native American and European artifacts, visual sources, oral traditions, journals and historical narratives to compare the different European perceptions of Native Americans. Compare, for example, John White's images of Native Americans with those of Theodore deBry in terms of perceptions of Native Americans. *How do their perceptions differ? What factors might account for the different representations of Native Americans in these images?*

B. Changes in Western European societies in the age of exploration.

Grades 5-6

▶ Describe an important European city in the fifteenth century such as Paris, London, Rome, or Seville. *How large was the city? What jobs did people who lived in large cities do for a living? How was life different in urban and rural areas in the fifteenth century? How different are our cities today?*

▶ Explain how a young person living in Europe in the fifteenth century received an education. *Were schools open to all people? How did young persons learn a trade?*

▶ Draw a language map of Europe during the last half of the fifteenth century. *What were the major languages spoken? How did educated people living in different countries communicate?*

▶ Write biographical sketches of King Ferdinand of Aragon and Queen Isabella of Castile. Explain how they united Spain and drove the Moors from Granada in 1492. *How did the expulsion of the Moors open the way for Spanish voyages of exploration?*

Grades 7-8

▶ Debate the issue: The Vikings rather than Christopher Columbus should be given credit as the first Europeans to discover America.

▶ Describe the advantages that written language has over oral language for the retention and expansion of knowledge. Analyze the effects that the spread of literacy and the increasing availability of texts have on society.

▶ Explain why it was Iberians and Italians, rather than other Europeans, that generated explorations during this period.

▶ Focusing on the lives of ordinary individuals, write a historical narrative illustrating the cultural traditions, gender roles, life cycle, and patterns of work for the people of a specific European state.

▶ Analyze the way in which the acquisition of knowledge was transformed using the techniques of scientific observation, experimentation, and exploration. Explain the contributions of such figures as Paracelsus, Gerardus Mercator, Nicolaus Copernicus, Tycho Brahe, William Gilbert, Georg Agricola, Galileo Galilei, and Francis Bacon.

▶ Assume the role of a merchant in the late fifteenth century and prepare a rationale for trading outside your native state. *What products would you select to trade? How would you finance your trading company? What role would you expect the state to play in trade and commerce?*

Grades 9-12

▶ Develop a historical argument of the cause-and-effect relationships that stimulated European overseas exploration, considering such factors as the Crusades and *Reconquista* of Islamic Spain, the rise of cities, the military revolution, the development of strong monarchies, the expansion of intercontinental commerce, and the expansion of scientific, geographic, and technological knowledge.

▶ Explain how the rebirth of interest in the arts, literature, and philosophy of antiquity during the Renaissance transformed the nature of inquiry. *Did this new mode of understanding affect encounters with unfamiliar societies?*

♦ Debate the claim that European exploration in the fifteenth and sixteenth centuries was fueled by devotion to "God, gold, and glory."

♦ Explain the basic view of leading religious reformers such as Luther and Calvin. *How did their beliefs challenge the practices and authority of the Roman Catholic Church? What were the consequences of the Protestant Reformation in Europe?*

♦ Explain how the rise of centralized states in western Europe such as those of Spain, Portugal, England, and France helped to promote the expansion of commerce and overseas expansion.

♦ Using historical evidence, draw a chart showing changes in men's and women's work options resulting from developments such as the increased division between capital and labor, and the increasing emphasis on wages as a defining characteristic of "work." *What effect did family roles, class, and geographic location have on men and women's work in this period? In what ways did their work situation remain unchanged?*

♦ List the factors which contributed to the growth of capitalism in Europe and explain how an emerging capitalistic economy transformed society.

C. Developments in Western African societies in the period of early contact with Europeans.

Grades 5-6

♦ Identify and locate the political kingdoms of Mali, Songhay, and Benin and major urban centers such as Timbuktu and Jenne. Explain how the physical geography of West Africa helped to make Timbuktu and Jenne major trading centers.

♦ Draw upon stories of Mansa Musa and his pilgrimage to Mecca in 1324 in order to analyze the sources of the wealth of Mali, the trans-Saharan trade, and the importance of Islam in Western Africa.

♦ Draw upon West African proverbs, folk tales and artifacts to illustrate and explain traditional family living and gender roles. *How were children taught about expected behavior in traditional West African communities? How did men and women divide family labor? How did West Africans use local materials to make masks, sculpture and artifacts reflecting their beliefs?*

Grades 7-8

♦ Draw upon the travel narrative of the Muslim scholar Ibu Ibn Battuta to describe the social customs, material conditions, and political organization of the Kingdom of Mali.

♦ Analyze representative examples of West African art such as terra cotta, wood, and bronze sculpture in order to illustrate West African social relationships and political structures.

♦ Analyze relationships between the geographic features, resources, and patterns of settlement of West Africa and the trade that developed between West Africa, North Africa, the Middle East, and Europe. *How did the trans-Saharan trade in gold affect West African states? Why was salt such an important import? Why were the slaves exported across the Sahara mostly women?*

Grades 9-12

♦ Develop a historical argument explaining the growing influence of Islam in West Africa. *Why were merchants and rulers in West Africa likely to adopt Islam? How were West African religious beliefs and practices affected by Islam?*

♦ Compare and contrast the impact of the Spanish on Mexico in the 16th century with the Portuguese impact on West Africa in the 15th and 16th centuries. *How did infectious and tropical diseases affect encounters between Iberians and peoples of Mexico and West Africa?*

▶ Draw upon historical narratives of Muslim scholars such as Leo Africanus and Ibn Battuta in order to describe the cultural, political and economic life of the African kingdoms of Mali and Songhay.

▶ Draw on E. W. Bovill's *The Golden Trade of the Moors* to explain why the trans-Saharan slave trade developed in medieval times. *Why was there a market for slaves from West Africa in North Africa and the Middle East? Under what circumstances were people likely to be enslaved in West Africa? Why did women compose a majority of slaves transported across the Sahara? What did Islamic teachings have to say about slavery and the treatment of slaves?*

D. Differences and similarities among Africans, Europeans, and Native Americans who converged in the western hemisphere after 1492.

Grades 5-6

▶ Describe how the daily life of Native Americans differed from region to region in the Americas. *Which Native Americans had large urban centers? Which lived in small rural communities? How did life differ among Native Americans at the time of the great convergence?*

▶ Compare the different ideas that Native Americans and Europeans held about how the land should be used.

▶ Write a short story which illustrates the differing attitudes of Europeans, Native Americans, and Africans towards one another in the Spanish colonies during the sixteenth century. *Were there similar or different attitudes in the French, Dutch, and English colonies in the late sixteenth and early seventeenth centuries?*

Grades 7-8

▶ Construct a chart or graphic organizer to show the different ideas and values of Native Americans, Europeans, and Africans in the Americas in the first half-century after the "great convergence." *How did the religious beliefs and practices differ? To what extent did attitudes toward gender roles differ? What differences existed in attitudes toward nature and the environment? How did differing attitudes and values affect relationships among diverse people?*

▶ Draw upon anthropological and historical data to develop a sound historical argument Native American societies at the times of the great convergence. *How did Europeans perceive Native American societies? What does historical evidence illustrate regarding social, economic and political development?*

Grades 9-12

▶ Marshal specific evidence from such Native American societies as the Hopi and Zuni cultures of the Southwest, the Algonkian and Iroquoian cultures of the Northeast Woodlands, and the earlier Moundbuilder and Mississippian cultures of the Ohio and Mississippi valleys to develop a historical argument on such questions as: *Were Native American societies such as the Hopi and Zuni different in their agricultural practices, gender roles, and social development from 15th-century peasant communities in Europe? To what extent did the striking differences among Native American societies reflect different phases of the agricultural revolution in the Americas? To what extent did they reflect different geographic environments and resources available to these societies?*

▶ Trace the evolution of systems of labor in 16th-century Spanish America and compare them to those of the French and English. *How did these European labor systems differ from those of Native American societies?*

II. *Early European exploration and colonization; the resulting cultural and ecological interactions.*

A. **The stages of European oceanic and overland exploration, amid international rivalries, from the 9th to 17th centuries.**

Grades 5-6

▸ Use literature, investigate stories of the early exploration of the Americas before Columbus. Discuss how myths and legends may have played a role in voyages of exploration using such sources as *Brendan the Navigator: A History Mystery about the Discovery of America* by Jean Fritz.

▸ Sketch a Viking ship and locate on a map major Norse settlements. Trace Viking ships' travel routes to western Europe, Russia, and the North Atlantic. *Where did the Vikings come from? Why did peoples of England fear them so much? How do we know that the Vikings had a settlement in Newfoundland, Canada? What happened to it?*

▸ Study pictures of Mediterranean galleys, Viking longships, and fifteenth-century caravels, and explain what features of caravels made them more suitable than the first two for the long-distance maritime voyages of the European age of exploration.

▸ For major early voyages of exploration, locate the Mediterranean and Atlantic seaports from which they sailed and map the routes each followed.

▸ Create a timeline of European exploration showing names, dates, countries of origin and destinations. Write short biographical profiles of European explorers such as Vasco de Balboa, Ferdinand Magellan, Hernando de Soto, Francisco Coronado, John Cabot, Francis Drake, Jacques Cartier, or Giovanni da Verrazano.

▸ Compare the perils and problems encountered on the high seas with the fears and superstitions of the time. Create "diaries" or role-play answers to such questions as: *What did sailors expect to find when they reached the "Indies"? How did explorers think and feel as they moved across the uncharted seas? What was daily life like aboard ship?*

▸ Investigate Columbus's first voyage by using illustrations, maps, charts, and *The Log of Christopher Columbus; First Voyage to America: In the Year 1492, as Copied Out in Brief by Bartholomew Las Casas.*

Grades 7-8

▸ Analyze how shipbuilding, navigational techniques, and knowledge of wind and currents contributed to Iberian exploration in the Atlantic. *How did the design of the caravel help to revolutionize sailing on the high seas? How did the North Atlantic "wind wheel" figure in Columbus's voyages to the Western hemisphere and back?*

▸ Draw upon evidence from Columbus's journal and other historical sources to appraise his voyages of exploration. *How, for example, did Columbus's description of the peaceful and pleasant nature of the Carib Indians compare with his treatment of them?*

▸ Analyze the immediate and long-term significance of the Columbian Exchange by developing historical arguments on such questions as: *How did the exchange of food such as maize affect population growth in Europe? What effect did it have on Native Americans and Africans in the Americas? How did the spread of diseases affect societies?*

▸ Explain how religious influences affected colonization in the Americas. *What inferences may be drawn from the establishment of the Spanish St. Augustine south of the French Protestant colonies of Fort Caroline and Charlesfort? Why did the English government promote the activities of "sea dogs" such as Hawkins and Drake?*

▶ Compare the motives for Spanish exploration to those of the English, French, and Dutch. *What were the expressed goals of the major European nations involved in exploration? How similar were their motives?*

Grades 9-12

▶ Contrast the perceptions of Columbus—the man and his exploits—in 1892 and 1992. *What accounts for the changing interpretations of Columbus and his exploits?*

▶ Analyze how religious antagonisms unleashed by the Reformation stimulated overseas expansion.

▶ Assess the long-range social and ecological impact of the Columbian Exchange in the Americas. *What was the significance of the great population change, including the forced relocation to the Americas of Africans, the migration of Europeans, and the decimation of Native American populations through disease?*

▶ Analyze the wording of early colonial patents and charters to determine motives for exploration and early colonization of North America. *What did Elizabeth's charter to Walter Raleigh (1584) and James I's charter of Virginia (1606) indicate regarding motives for exploration and settlement? To what extent did English motives differ from those of the Spanish, the French, or the Dutch?*

B. The Spanish and Portuguese conquest of the Americas.

Grades 5-6

▶ Explain Spanish motivations for settlement of the Americas.

▶ Trace and map Spanish exploration in the Americas for the century following Columbus's explorations.

▶ Examine the exploration and conquest of Spanish America using adventure stories such as *The King's Fifth* by Scott O'Dell, *Ferdinand Magellan* by Jim Hargrove, *De Soto, Finder of the Mississippi* by Ronald Syme, and *Walk the World's Rim* by Betty Baker.

Grades 7-8

▶ Construct a chart showing the various motives which prompted Spanish and Portuguese settlement in the Americas. *How similar were the motives of these two nation states in establishing colonies? Why did individuals from Spain and Portugal come to the Americas? To what extent did they represent a cross-section of Iberian society? How did their social and economic status in Spain and Portugal influence their decision to migrate?*

▶ Draw upon historical narratives and visual data to chronicle the Spanish conquest of the Aztec and Incan empires. *How were the Spanish able to conquer Indian empires with limited men and resources? Why was it possible for the Spanish conquistadores to recruit Indian allies to assist in their conquest of the Aztecs? What impact did internal rivalries have on the resistance of the Incas to the Spanish conquest?*

▶ Draw upon historical documents such as Hernando Cortés's letters on first viewing Tenochtitlan (Mexico City) to develop historical analyses of such questions as: *How did explorers react to the societies they encountered in the Americas? What kind of architecture, skills, labor systems, and agriculture did they find in these places? How did they compare with those of western Europe?*

▶ Use maps to show the trade routes of the silver mined in the Americas and show the crucial roles played by Potosi, Mexico City, Acapulco, Macao, Manila, Cadíz, and Amsterdam for this trade.

Grades 9-12

▶ Draw upon historical records to contrast and explain the Aztec view of the Spanish and the Spanish view of the Aztecs at the time of contact. *What role did religious beliefs play in the perceptions each held of the other?*

▶ Draw evidence from historical monographs to explain how Hernando Cortés and Francisco Pizarro were able to conquer the Aztecs and Incas. *How did the factors of disease, political and ethnic rivalry, succession problems, military strategy, religion, and trickery contribute to the success of these two expeditions?*

▶ Assess the Spanish justification for their treatment of Native Americans by developing historical arguments on such questions as: *What was the background and significance of the requierimiento? How did Juan Ginés Sepúlveda justify the Spanish treatment of Native Americans—morally, legally, and religiously? How did Bartolomé de Las Casas try to refute Sepúlveda's argument? Which argument is more persuasive and why?*

▶ Explain the *encomienda* system and describe the evolution of labor systems within the Spanish empire in the Americas.

▶ Explain the origin and expansion of the African slave trade in the Americas. *Why did African chattel slavery gradually replace Indian labor in the Spanish colonies? How did slavery as practiced in African societies contrast with chattel slavery as it developed in the Americas? What were the consequences for Africans and the Americas of the forced relocation and enslavement of Africans in the Spanish and Portuguese colonies?*

▶ Explain the consequences that the sustained influx of silver had on the economies of Europe and China. Compare and contrast the effects of an abundance of silver on different occupational groups and on material conditions in Western Europe.

Photograph by Bert Seal,
San Diego County
Office of Education

ERA 2

Colonization and Settlement (1585-1763)

The study of the colonial era in American history is essential because the foundations for many of the most critical developments in our subsequent national history were established in those years. The long duration of the nation's colonial period—nearly two centuries—requires that teachers establish clear themes. A continental and Caribbean approach best serves a full understanding of this era because North America and the closely linked West Indies were an international theatre of colonial development.

One theme involves the intermingling of Native Americans, Europeans, and Africans. Students first need to understand what induced hundreds of thousands of free and indentured immigrants to leave their homelands in many parts of Europe. Why did they risk the hardships of resettlement overseas, and how well did they succeed? Students must also address two of the most tragic aspects of American history: first, the violent conflicts between Europeans and indigenous peoples, the devastating spread of European diseases among Native Americans, and the gradual dispossession of Indian land; second, the traffic in the African slave trade and the development of a slave labor system in many of the colonies. While coming to grips with these tragic events, students should also recognize that Africans and Native Americans were not simply victims but were intricately involved in the creation of colonial society and a new, hybrid American culture.

A second theme is the development of political and religious institutions and values. The roots of representative government are best studied regionally, so that students can appreciate how European colonizers in New England, the mid-Atlantic, and the South differed in the ways they groped their way toward mature political institutions. In studying the role of religion—especially noteworthy are the foundations of religious freedom, denominationalism, and the many-faceted impact of the Great Awakening—a comparative geographic approach can also be fruitful. Comparison with the role of religion in Dutch, French, and Spanish colonies can be valuable as well.

A third theme is the economic development of the colonies through agriculture and commerce. A comparative approach to French, Spanish, Dutch, and English colonies, and a regional approach to the English mainland and West Indian colonies, as part of a developing Atlantic economy, will also be instructive. As in studying politics and religion, students should ponder how economic institutions developed—in ways that were typically European or were distinctively American—and how geographical variations—climate, soil conditions, and other natural resources—helped shape regional economic development.

Coerced religion on good days produces hypocrites, on bad days rivers of blood.

— ROGER WILLIAMS, C1635

Essay

American History, With and Without Religion: "... the whole truth ... so help me God"*
by Edwin S. Gaustad

Edwin Gaustad, one of the most accomplished historians of early American religion, reminds us that if we avoid the topic of religious history, we will never understand the intensely religious world of the seventeenth and eighteenth centuries. Nor will we understand American history fully in the nineteenth and twentieth centuries, though American society is far more secular than in the past. Gaustad's essay intends to remedy "the lowly and outcast state of religion in the school curriculum and in the treatment of American history." He points out the cost of such neglect. Teachers will see that their colleagues who constructed this book have harkened to Gaustad's plea to restore the role of religion to the history curriculum, while holding fast to the rule that as history teachers we do not mean to practice religion but study religion in the classrooms.

Edwin S. Gaustad, professor of history emeritus at the University of California, Riverside, is an authority on the history of religion. He is the editor of *Documentary History of Religion in America* and has written a number of works including *The Great Awakening* and *Liberty of Conscience: Roger Williams in America.*

Even in the final decade of the twentieth century, God receives some public notice in the United States: in oaths of office, in political campaigns, and in the courts' swearing in of a witness. Most of this falls in the category of the ritual use of language, so familiar and so routine that no one takes the mention of God very seriously. But in the educational profession, one purports to take seriously the issue of truth, wherever and whenever possible—even the whole truth. Though that may remain something of an ideal never fully attainable, few would argue that our collective reach should always be stretched out in that direction. In American history we are constantly being stretched regarding our particular share of the truth to make the story that we tell more faithful to the past that we share. We have been encouraged and instructed to come closer to the "whole truth" with respect to the role of women, the contributions of the minorities, the pall of poverty and racism, the failures as well as the triumphs. An American history survey text of the 1990s bears little resemblance to one of the 1950s—except in the area of religion. There the "whole truth" has continued to prove elusive or possibly even scary. Let us first consider some of the reasons for this anomaly, then some of the costs of a continued neglect of this rich and vibrant dimension of the human experience.

Both the judicial and the pedagogical establishments have made bold statements in favor of academic attention to religion at every level of the school curriculum. But bold announcements have been generally followed by timid actions on the part of publishers, principals, parents, and teachers. Often no action at all has been deemed not only the easier course, but the safer one as well. Religion remains a classroom pariah, a fact not to be explained simply in terms of an overcrowded curriculum or an underdeveloped school year.

Three factors help to account for the lowly and outcast state of religion in the school curriculum and in the treatment of American history. The first is confusion, sometimes honest and sincere, other times craftily preserved and promoted. That confusion has to do with the legality of teaching about religion as contrasted with the legality of practicing religion in the public schools. In the early 1960s the United States Supreme Court, amid clamorous public outcry and uproar, declared that prayers and Bible readings—as ritual acts of worship—were

*Reprinted from *Magazine of History*, Vol. 6, No. 3 (Winter 1992), pp. 15-18, with permission of the Organization of American Historians.

unconstitutional since, in violation of the First Amendment, they amounted to a state-endorsed establishment of religion. What the Court declared invalid was the *practice* of religion, not the *study* of religion. But knowing that this distinction might be too subtle for some, Justice Tom Clark (author of the majority opinion in *Abington v. Schempp*, 1963), took pains to point out explicitly that the Court in no way ruled out the appropriate, indeed the essential, attention to "the history of religion and its relationship to the advancement of civilization." Nearly thirty years old now, that opinion has been met by as much silence over what it encouraged as by uproar over what it prohibited. In 1987 the Court tried again to stir the cold ashes in curricular ground. On the one hand it outlawed the teaching of the biblical account of creation as contemporary science, but on the other hand (in a concurring opinion) called for a far greater and more appreciative understanding of the nation's religious heritage. In that same year, the Association for Supervision and Curriculum Development declared that "decisive action is needed to end the current curricular silence on religion." With no agenda in mind except that common one of pursuing the whole truth, the ASCD followed that clear statement with a series of equally clear recommendations designed to help local school districts, text book committees, state departments of education, and community leaders dispel this lingering darkness (see *Religion in the Curriculum: A Report from the ASCD Panel on Religion in the Curriculum*, 1987).

So if confusion persists on questions of legality, it is hard to see how such confusion can be doggedly maintained. A second factor in what is not really a conspiracy of silence, only a fortuitous combination of circumstances, is embarrassment. To be sure, it is difficult to imagine Americans in the 1990s being embarrassed about anything: from sex to corruptions of language and power. But embarrassment about religion remains, both with respect to one's own and that of another. If one is asked about his or her religion, the reply often takes the form of "I happen to be a . . . ," as in the sentence, "I happen to be left-handed." One's religion is a gift or a curse of birth; not much can be done about it except to indicate, apologetically, its strange or vestigial presence. With respect to someone else's religion, it is these days somehow more permissible to ask: "What is your sign?" than "What is your church?" Such embarrassment or restraint is perhaps more welcome than the strident question heard in other quarters, "Are you saved?", but in any case the teaching about religion calls for no confession of faith on the part of the pedagogue nor on the part of the pupil. American history is more than the expression of personal preferences, more than the raw exposure of potential sensitivities, be they political, racial, economic, or religious. If one wishes to be embarrassed, it should be over the willingness to settle—so obviously, so stubbornly—for less than the whole truth.

A third and final factor is the saddest of all: ignorance. It afflicts those teaching as well as those taught, to say nothing of those setting school policy or responding to parental complaints and those making the complaints. Happily, those most willing (sometimes even eager) to confess their ignorance in this area are the teachers. Ill-fed by a teacher education program that carefully avoided all discussion of religion and undernourished further by textbooks and readings that give the subject widest berth, many teachers welcome the opportunity to attend summer institutes or read handbooks that offer guidance and tell where even more can be found. (Of the latter, one of the best is Charles C. Haynes' *Religion in American History: What to Teach and How*, Association for Supervision and Curriculum Development, 1990.) But even when the problems of teacher ignorance have been resolved or at least ameliorated, surrounding pockets of ignorance remain: parents, community leaders, publishers, legislators, school boards or administrators, clergy, politicians, and any malcontent seeking a platform or a cause.

The enemy of ignorance, of course, is education, and that remains our principal business. The whole truth is not gained without cost.

The point of the remainder of this article, however, is to suggest that abandoning the pursuit of the whole truth has its awesome costs too. Narrowing our concern to the exclusion of religion from all learning about American history, what does such exclusion cost? We consider first the factual content that is lost, and second the meaning that is missed. With respect to the chronicle of the past, religion is a datum and point of reference as omnipresent and inescapable as the rivers and the mountains, the laws and the courts, the trade routes and the labor unions, the political parties and the national presidents. Should one attempt to tell the story of modern India or modern Ireland without reference to religion? Similarly, should one attempt to tell the story of modern America by leaving religion out of that picture entirely? In both cases, the questions are assumed to be rhetorical, but if not immediately perceived to be such, a swift chronological review may help to make the case.

In the sixteenth century, Spanish missionaries moved up from Mexico City to evangelize Native Americans in the American Southwest. One such missionary in the Caribbean attempted to persuade the Pope to restrain or modify—if he could—the brutality of the Spanish conquest. Place names, if not bestowed by the missionaries themselves in accordance with the ecclesiastical calendar, reveal that early religious presence from San Antonio to Santa Barbara. In the seventeenth century, French missionaries moved down from Quebec and Ontario into the very center of the American continent, leaving their cultural and religious mark on the land from St. Paul to St. Louis to St. Francisville. Meanwhile, the Dutch built their churches in Manhattan and Albany, the Swedes theirs along the Delaware, and the English theirs from Charlestown, South Carolina to York, Maine. Even the most superficial view of the landscape in the seventeenth century, from place names to buildings, make religion an unavoidable part of the record.

Religion's role in shaping American history, however, also went beyond the development of place names and other such superficialities. Soon after colonialization, both Massachusetts and Virginia passed laws in which religion provided both structure and content. England's persecution of religious minorities led directly to the founding of Massachusetts, as well as Maryland and Pennsylvania. Rhode Island's early history cannot be understood apart from the denominational development of Baptists and Quakers; even so remote an event as France's revocation of the Edict of Nantes in 1685 has direct implications for the colonial history of South Carolina and New York. In this same century, both the religion of displaced Native Americans and that of enslaved African-Americans engaged with the dominant force of Christianity, either by way of resistance or uneasy alliance.

At the turn of the century religious philanthropy in England led to the creation of the Society for Promoting Christian Knowledge as well as the even more influential Society for the Propagation of the Gospel. Both Anglican entities exercised considerable power down to the time of the Revolution. Such philanthropy also contributed directly to the founding of Georgia in 1732. By that time all thirteen colonies were soon engulfed by a powerful wave of revivalism, the most significant popular movement prior to the American Revolution. In that Revolution itself, religion acted as both causal factor (the widespread fear of an American episcopate) and interpretive theme (the millennial expectations). In the new state constitutions of the period, elected officials were obliged to take oaths testifying as much to their religious orthodoxy as to their political loyalty. In the United States Constitution of 1787, on the other hand, religion was conspicuous by its absence, a fact that requires understanding in terms both of the prevailing religious pluralism and the pervading Enlightenment allegiance to Reason and Nature. With the adoption of the First Amendment in 1791, of course, religious liberty at the federal level was granted a special status that would shape and re-shape the nation's ecclesiastical forces in dramatic fashion.

As the new nation began to give substance to the theories regarding executive, legislative, and judicial balance, voluntary forces throughout the country took on the tasks of reforming morals, founding colleges, printing Bibles, establishing model or utopian societies, and saving the West from barbarism and infidelity. Religiously motivated and affiliated individuals took the lead in this entire enterprise, as they did in the creation of new denominations such as the Disciples of Christ and Seventh-day Adventists. By the 1840s no issue demanded the attention of all citizens as did slavery, with the churches likewise being deeply involved. Unhappily, the moral voice of religion was muted and much of its moral authority lost as denominations split apart (Methodists, Baptists, Presbyterians) years before the nation itself plunged into Civil War.

After that tragic conflict, religion demonstrated its relevance and force in the new challenges of urbanization, industrialization, and mass immigration. By mid-century, Roman Catholicism had become the largest religious institution in America, a position of prominence not yielded thereafter. Judaism, of modest numbers and largely of Germanic origin before the Civil War, grew sharply from the East European influx for two generations after that war. In a pre-welfare state, some churches provided immigrants with food, clothing, shelter, and instruction, while other churches called for an end to unrestricted immigration or took the lead in the creation of nativist organizations. Newer entities like the Salvation Army and the YMCA and YWCA saw their special responsibility as ministering to the uprooted and homeless, the destitute and dispirited.

In the twentieth century, religious forces found themselves divided once more, not by disagreements over slavery, but by different understandings of the relevance of modern scholarship (historical, literary, archaeological) to the sacred scriptures. Much contemporary American history cannot be fully comprehended without some appreciation of "Modernism," "Fundamentalism," and the intermediary positions in between those poles. The impact of the founding of Israel (1948) upon the American Jewish community as well as the impact of Vatican II (1962-65) upon the American Catholic community demand special attention. Presidential elections such as those of Ronald Reagan in 1980 and the primary campaigns of Pat Robertson and Jesse Jackson in 1988 brought wide public notice to religion's power both to persuade and to produce votes.

So it is evident that religion in America did not end with the collapse of the Puritan experiment nor with the ratification of the First Amendment. Its forces—Protestant, Catholic, Jewish, now Buddhist, Muslim, New Age and more—continue to grow, continue to shape the culture in varying ways. To tell the story of the American past without giving full and steady attention to religion is to miss the whole truth by an inexcusably wide margin.

It is also, however, to miss much of the meaning in that story. We have named some of the monuments and movements, the denominations and the developments, but what do they (as well as many unnamed above) really mean? Does religion assist us in understanding the meaning of the age of discovery and exploration? As the colonies, one by one, came into being, how does religion help us to see what meaning the colonists themselves gave to their actions? Convenantal relationships, so central to Puritan theology, also remained central in the constitutional debates. Is religion relevant to the meaning of democracy and, perhaps, to its maintenance? If so, in what ways? Alexis de Tocqueville thought he saw a relationship between

America's religion and the nation's dedication to the idea of equality. Horace Bushnell thought the meaning of the Civil War could only be perceived in religious terms: that apart from the shedding of blood, there was no remission of sins. In their allegiance to Manifest Destiny, did Americans see themselves as a Chosen People, guided by a Divine Hand? In their quest for freedom, did slaves find meaning as well as hope in the deliverance of the Israelites from their Egyptian bondage?

G. K. Chesterton once remarked that the United States was a nation with the soul of a church. If so, we come much closer to the whole truth of the American past as we examine that past through the filter of religious motivations and aspirations, religious convictions and conflicts. As witnesses before the bar of history, our pledge is to the truth, the whole truth, and nothing but the truth. Anything less perverts the system of justice just as it perverts all our efforts in self-understanding.

Benjamin West (1738–1820), Penn's Treaty with the Indians. *Courtesy the Pennsylvania Academy of the Arts*

Sample Student Activities

I. **Why the Americas attracted Europeans, why they brought enslaved Africans to their colonies, and how Europeans struggled for control of North America and the Caribbean.**

A. **How diverse immigrants affected the formation of European colonies.**

Grades 5-6

- Construct a timeline of Spanish, Dutch, French, and English explorations in North America and map the route taken by each.

- Draw upon biographies, stories, and historical studies to develop a historical narrative about one of these explorers. *Who sent this expedition? Did the explorer plan to spread his religion? Did those on his expedition plan to find wealth and return home? What were the occupations, social background, and religion of the people on this expedition? What did this expedition achieve?*

- Draw upon stories, biographies, ships' passenger lists, and documentary records to analyze and compare the first settlers who established Jamestown, Plymouth, and Philadelphia. *What were their backgrounds, reasons for coming, occupational skills, leadership qualities, and ability to work together?*

- Contrast and compare an early English settlement with a Spanish settlement (e.g., St. Augustine or Santa Fe) and a French settlement (e.g., Quebec or New Orleans). *How did the people who came to these settlements differ from those in the English colonies?*

- Investigate why Europeans were willing to become indentured servants. *What was the typical term of an indentured servant? What could the indentured servant expect to get after the term of service? How did indentured servitude differ from slavery?*

- Use books such as Scott O'Dell's *My Name Is Not Angelica* and Paula Fox's *Slave Dancer* to describe the experience of enslaved Africans.

- Listen to a reading of the capture scene at the beginning of *Roots* and describe the visual imagery and express personal reactions to the episode.

Grades 7-8

- Trace English attempts to establish colonies in the Americas before the founding of Jamestown in 1607.

- Draw upon the accounts of such writers as William Bradford *(Of Plymouth Plantation)*, John Winthrop ("A Model of Christian Charity"), and John Smith *(The General History of Virginia)* to compare English motives for colonization and determine if their goals were achieved. Compare or contrast these goals to those of the Spanish, French, and Dutch.

- Compare the growth of the European colonies in the two centuries following their founding. *What new groups arrived either voluntarily or involuntarily? How did the colonies change as their population grew?*

- Explain the reasons why the English colonists began to abandon indentures as a labor force and turn toward slavery. *How cost effective was indentured servitude during the latter part of the seventeenth century? How did the English success in wars with the Dutch affect the slave trade and stimulate the growth of slavery in English colonial America?*

♦ Research statistical studies related to the numbers of slaves involved in the Atlantic slave trade. Construct a bar graph showing the different statistics.

Grades 9-12

♦ Analyze the influence of the enclosure movement, the growth of the urban poor, and the reign of Elizabeth I on early English attempts to colonize the Americas.

♦ Explain how accounts of Spanish wealth from the Americas, the popularization of *La Layenda Negra* (the Black Legend) the Protestant Reformation, and religious persecutions stimulated English, French, and Dutch colonization.

♦ Analyze the changing patterns of European immigration and settlement in the Americas in the 17th and 18th centuries by developing a historical narrative on such questions as: *How did the motives of 17th-century Puritans and Quakers differ from those of 18th-century immigrants such as Germans and Scots-Irish? Why did the colonies of New York and Pennsylvania attract the greatest diversity of immigrants?*

♦ Draw upon historical documents relating to the slave trade and the system of chattel slavery that evolved over the 17th and 18th centuries in order to develop a historical argument on such questions as: *Were there significant differences between slavery in the Spanish Caribbean and New Spain, the French Caribbean and Louisiana, the Dutch West Indies, and the English Caribbean and Chesapeake? Why did Brazil and the West Indies have more enslaved Africans than North America? Which colonies experienced the greatest increase and which experienced the most notable decrease in slave imports between the 17th and 18th centuries, and why?*

B. The European struggle for control of North America.

Grades 5-6

♦ Compare Puritan and Algonkian views of the land. *How did Puritan beliefs in private property and their claims to New England lands that were not "settled" or "improved" differ from Algonkian beliefs in ownership, property rights, and ways to use the land?*

♦ Compare William Penn's interactions with the Lenni Lenape and Susquehannocks with those of the colonial settlers and the Powhatans in Virginia (1622) and the Pequots in Massachusetts (1637). *Was conflict unavoidable in European relationships with Native Americans? What helped prevent such wars? What contributed to them?*

♦ Compare how Native Americans and European societies in North America were influenced by one another. *In what ways did the early settlers in Massachusetts and Virginia depend on the skills and assistance of Native Americans in order to survive? In what ways did trade benefit Native Americans and Europeans? How did association with Europeans change traditional ways of Native American life? In what ways were these changes beneficial? In what ways were they harmful?*

♦ Examine the interaction of American Indians and early European settlers through biographies and historical fiction using evidence from such books as *The Double Life of Pocahontas* by Jean Fritz; *The Serpent Never Sleeps: A Novel of Jamestown and Pocahontas* by Scott O'Dell and John Billington; *Friend of Squanto* by Clyde Robert Bulla; *Sign of the Beaver* by Elizabeth Speare; and *Squanto* by Fennie Ziner.

Grades 7-8

‣ Analyze examples of English colonists who opposed prevailing policies toward Native Americans and demonstrated that alternatives to hostility existed. *How did such individuals as Roger Williams, William Penn, and John Eliot differ in their actions toward Native Americans from most of their countrymen and with what results? What explains the generally friendly relations in Rhode Island and Pennsylvania?*

‣ Develop a historical argument explaining why French relations with the Hurons, Ottawas, and Algonkians were largely void of conflict. *In what ways did the relatively small numbers of French settlers, their dependence on the Indians for trade in furs, and the large presence of French Jesuit priests contribute to peaceable relations?*

‣ Develop a historical narrative, news report to a Boston, London, or Paris newspaper, or a "You Are There" dramatic interview to recreate the events culminating in the English victory over the French in the Seven Years War.

Grades 9-12

‣ Draw upon a variety of historical narratives, travel accounts, and visual sources to compare the diversity of Native American interactions with Spanish, English, French, and Dutch settlers. *How did the experiences of Native American societies in the interior differ from those who lived in coastal regions? How did they benefit from trade? How did trade alter their way of life and disrupt their societies? How did Native American societies such as the Pueblos, Catawbas, Iroquois, and Lenni Lenape respond to Europeans?*

‣ Analyze Pontiac's speech to the French on the reasons for making war in 1763, and compare his reasons with those of Opechacanough in 1622 and Metacomet (King Philip) in 1676. Explain the background and consequences of the Pueblo revolts of 1680 and 1696. Analyze the reasons for and results of the mission system in the Southwest and California.

‣ Analyze how the European wars for control of North America between 1675 and 1763 pitted the English, French, and Spanish against one another and allowed the Iroquois League, the Creek, and the Cherokee nations to strengthen their own position by playing one European nation off against another.

‣ Compare these wars with the events and consequences of the Seven Years War. *What was the significance of the Peace of Paris in ending European rivalry for control of North America? What options were left to Native Americans who had sided with the French?*

II.   *How political, religious, and social institutions emerged in the English colonies.*

A.   The roots of representative government and how political rights were defined.

Grades 5-6

‣ Draw upon stories of the arrival of the Pilgrims at in 1620 and explain the importance of the Mayflower Compact which they signed before leaving the ship. *How did the Mayflower Compact promote the self-government in colonial New England?*

‣ Explore how different colonies defined the right to vote or hold office. *Why were people required to own property in order to vote?*

‣ Describe the structure of roles and relationships within the Puritan family. Contrast Puritan family organization with the way families are structured today.

Grades 7-8

▸ Analyze how the Magna Carta, English common law, and the English Bill of Rights (1689) contributed to the concept of "the rights of Englishmen."

▸ Evaluate to what degree colonial society was democratic in practice. *How were political rights affected by gender, property ownership, religion, and legal status? What were the religious requirements for voting? Why did they exist?*

▸ Analyze what the following quotation from an 18th-century New Yorker tells us about changing values and the growth of prosperity in colonial America. *"The only principle of life propagated among the young people is to get money, and men are only esteemed according to what they are worth, that is, the money they are possessed of."*

▸ Assess whether Benjamin Franklin's thirteen virtues in his formula for moral perfection outlined in his *Autobiography* represented a change in values from the ideals of Puritan New England. Assess his proverbs relating to the acquisition of wealth, such as: *"Sloth makes all things difficult but industry all easy;" "It is hard for an empty sack to stand upright;" "Time lost is never found again."*

▸ Research the causes of 17th- and 18th-century colonial rebellions and assess the extent to which the insurgents resembled the patriots of the American Revolution. *How did the leadership of these revolutions differ from the leadership in the American Revolution of 1776?*

▸ Explain how political, geographic, social, and economic tensions led to Bacon's Rebellion and the Paxton Boys Massacre. *To what extent were these rebellions justifiable attempts of the people to change their government's policies? To what extent were they lawless attempts to overthrow legitimate governments?*

▸ Contrast the way in which property requirements restricted enfranchisement in England where land was scarce and expensive with similar requirements in colonial America where land was abundant and cheap. *What effect did broad suffrage in the colonies have on notions of citizenship?*

Grades 9-12

▸ Draw upon such documents as the Mayflower Compact (1620), the Fundamental Orders of Connecticut (1639), the Massachusetts Body of Laws and Liberty (1641), the New Jersey Laws, Concessions, and Agreements (1677), and the Pennsylvania Frame of Government (1701) to explain the growth of early representative government and institutions in the colonies. *How did geography and demography affect the different forms of government in colonial America? How did Pennsylvania's fluid social organization and Virginia's more rigid social hierarchy affect representative government in the two colonies?*

▸ Analyze how institutions such as the Virginia House of Burgesses, the county court system, parish vestries, congregational organization of churches, the Massachusetts General Court, and the New England town meeting contributed to the growth of representative government in the colonies. *How did such institutions promote the practice of "actual" as opposed to "virtual" representation? How democratic were such institutions in practice? Who could vote? Why did Jefferson call the New England town meeting "the wisest invention ever devised by the wit of man for the perfect exercise of self-government"?*

▸ Develop a historical argument on the question whether the political settlements of the Glorious Revolution expanded "the rights of Englishmen" in the colonies, or led to the establishment of more centralized administration and imperial control.

▸ Using selections from primary sources such as John Winthrop's *History of New England* and Thomas Jefferson's "Letters to His Daughters," explain why women were not allowed to vote.

▶ Analyze how the Puritan beliefs in a covenanted community, support of communal ideals, faith in a personal relation with God, and a commitment to a life of labor bred an individualism in marked contrast to the acquisitive and individualistic values associated with the early Chesapeake colonies. *To what extent did values in New England and Chesapeake colonies shape different societies?*

▶ Analyze how Puritan leaders in the 17th century might have appraised the spirit of individualism professed in Benjamin Franklin's *Autobiography* and *Poor Richard's Almanack*.

▶ Develop a historical argument about whether such factors as the abundance of land, devotion to private property, and the growth of individualism and a competitive entrepreneurial spirit in 18th-century colonial America challenged European ideas of hierarchy and deference and contributed to the idea of participatory democracy.

▶ Analyze the factors behind Bacon's Rebellion to illustrate the conflicts between the underrepresented backwoodsmen and the privileged tidewater planters. Compare with the ethnic and class tensions behind Leisler's Rebellion in colonial New York and with later conflicts of the Carolina Regulators and Pennsylvania Paxton Boys, involving similar grievances and tensions. *To what extent are the causes of Bacon's Rebellion, Leisler's Rebellion, and the revolts of the Carolina Regulators and Pennsylvania Paxton Boys similar? How are they different? Did Bacon's Rebellion lead to greater or less democracy in Virginia?*

▶ Analyze how the conflict between the lower houses of colonial legislatures and the governors over such items as "control of the purse" contributed to the development of representative government. *How did these conflicts affect their view of sovereignty and what was the significance of these developments?*

B. Religious diversity in the colonies and how ideas about religious freedom evolved.

Grades 5-6

▶ Explain why the Puritans came to North. *What restrictions had been placed on Puritans in England?*

▶ Create historical narratives, reenactments, or illustrations of children's roles in Puritan families drawing evidence from stories such as Elizabeth Speare's *The Witch of Blackbird Pond*, historical documents such as Eleazar Moody's *The School of Good Manners* (1772), pictures of hornbooks, replicas of *The New England Primer* (1727), family portraits, and other historical records. Compare these roles with their own lives in contemporary American society. *What religious beliefs and values were families trying to instill in their children? Why were children taught to read at an early age and apprenticed at age 13 to friends or relatives? How did the skills and values taught to boys and girls reflect the gender roles they were expected to assume as adults?*

▶ Examine opposition of dissenters to King James I as reflected in historical fiction such as *The House of Stink Alley* by F. N. Monjo.

▶ Describe the Bible commonwealth that the Puritans hoped to create. Explain the way in which individual goals were expected to be achieved within a mutually dependent community with shared values derived from their religious convictions.

Grades 7-8

▶ Draw upon historical records in order to analyze and debate the confrontation between Thomas Leverett and Anne Hutchinson at her trial and the justice of her banishment from the Massachusetts Bay Colony. *Did Anne Hutchinson violate Puritan mores? Was she justified in pursuing her acts of civil disobedience? Were the colonial officials justified in banishing her for her beliefs and actions?*

◗ Compare the treatment of dissenters in various colonies such as Puritan Massachusetts, Anglican Virginia, and Quaker Pennsylvania. *To what extent did Puritans immigrate in search of religious freedom and then deny it to others? What did Roger Williams mean by separation of church and state? Do we have the same meaning of separation of church and state today?*

◗ Draw evidence from biographies of Roger Williams, Anne Hutchinson, William Penn, and Cecilius Calvert on religious dissenters in the English colonies.

◗ Analyze how the tenets of faith expressed in John Winthrop's "A Model of Christian Charity" shaped the social, political, and religious life of the Puritan colony.

Grades 9-12

◗ Explain the major tenets of Puritanism such as predestination, the covenant of works, the covenant of grace, and the doctrine of sanctification; and demonstrate how these beliefs shaped the Puritan colony.

◗ Draw upon such sources as John Winthrop's "A Model of Christian Charity," John Milton's *Paradise Lost,* Increase Mather's "Predestination and Human Exertion" Michael Wigglesworth's "The Day of Doom," and the poetry of Anne Bradstreet and Edward Taylor in order to analyze the major tenets of Puritanism.

◗ Contrast Puritan New England's stress on religious conformity with the legislated religious tolerance of William Penn's Pennsylvania. Explain the ways in which the New England example influenced eighteenth-century political thought on republicanism as well as the way in which Penn's innovation became preserved in the first amendment of the United States Constitution.

◗ Draw upon such records as the *Trial of Anne Hutchinson at Newton* and the banishment of Roger Williams from Massachusetts in order to develop a historical argument or debate on such questions as: *How did Roger Williams and Anne Hutchinson justify their actions? Why did Puritans object to their ideas and behavior? Did Hutchinson threaten gender and hierarchy roles? How was the treatment of the two dissenters different? Was their treatment justified?*

◗ Analyze the reasons for the gradual decline of Puritanism in the later part of the 17th century, and explain its enduring legacy in the national character.

◗ Analyze how the presence of diverse religious groups in the English colonies such as Quakers, Catholics, Jews, Huguenots, and German Pietists contributed to the evolution of religious freedom. *Why did Roger Williams support the separation of church and state? What were the reasons for passage of the Maryland Act of Toleration in 1649? Why did the Pennsylvania Frame of Government (1701) guarantee religious freedom?*

◗ Explore the Great Awakening as the first American mass movement. Draw upon such sources as Jonathan Edwards's sermon, "Sinners in the Hands of an Angry God" and on historical accounts of the Great Awakening in order to create a historical argument agreeing or disagreeing with the statement: *The Great Awakening was a major influence in changing traditional relationships between rulers and the ruled and in the development of American "republicanism" and the nation's "civil religion."*

C. Social and cultural change in British America.

Grades 5-6

▶ Compare family life in Puritan society with that of other colonial North American families drawing evidence from such books as *Everyday Life in Colonial America*, popular stories, and historical records. Use a role-play activity or skit to show differences and similarities of a Puritan household to that of a Pennsylvania Quaker farm family; a farmer's family living in the Virginia piedmont; a craftsman's family from Williamsburg or Philadelphia; a New York merchant's family; a slave's family on a southern plantation; a family in French Quebec or New Orleans; or a family in Spanish Santa Fe or St. Augustine.

▶ Explain how differences in family housing, work, and the roles of men, women, and children reflected differences in family status and wealth; geographic region and resources; prior conditions of indentured servitude or slavery; ethnic traditions; and, religious beliefs.

Grades 7-8

▶ Analyze family portraits by such colonial artists as Charles Willson Peale, John Wollaston, Ralph Earl, and John Singleton Copley to determine what the pictures reveal about the relationships of parents and children, and how family and gender roles are reflected in the paintings.

▶ Examine the social order in Puritan New England and compare it with that of the middle and southern colonies. *How did family relationships differ? What were the established patterns of behavior of men, women, and children in different regions of English colonial America?*

▶ Explain the ways in which the Puritan family was a "little commonwealth" and the ways in which Puritan communities and political organization mirrored family structure.

Grades 9-12

▶ Draw evidence from a variety of secondary sources to investigate different patterns of family life in colonial North America. Compare the different ideals of family life among such diverse groups as the New England Puritans, the Virginia aristocracy, the frontier farmers, the Quakers, the Iroquois, the French in Quebec, the Indians of the Southwest, and the Spanish in Santa Fe. *How would you account for the similarities and the differences? To what extent are the families patriarchal? How were young children treated? Were boys treated differently from girls? What was it like to be a teenager in these different societies? What role did economic interests play in the development of family life and its relationship to the community? To what extent did family roles, values, and structure change during the colonial period?*

▶ Draw upon primary documents, secondary sources, and literary selections to analyze how men's and women's roles and status differed in Colonial America. *How, for example, did the following lines in Anne Bradstreet's poem, "The Prologue," illustrate the role of women in colonial Massachusetts?*

> *I am obnoxious to each carping tongue*
> *Who says my hand a needle better fits*

Why were women much more likely than men to be accused of witchcraft during the 17th century?

▶ Compare the property rights of single and married women in the English Atlantic seaboard colonies and the Spanish borderlands in the colonial period. *How did the community view single women and grant them property rights? Why did English common law deny married women [femme covert] property rights? How did property settlements on a first marriage differ from those settlements when a widow remarried?*

> ### III. *How the values and institutions of European economic life took root in the colonies, and how slavery reshaped European and African life in the Americas.*

A. Colonial economic life and labor systems in the Americas.

Grades 5-6

▶ Develop a historical map of the colonies by researching and locating the crops, animal products, minerals, and other natural resources found in New England, the Middle Atlantic, and southern colonies.

▶ Develop a map of economic relationships between the colonies, the Caribbean Islands, and the home country by locating major ports and shipping lanes between them. *What were the major ports in Europe and in the Americas that were involved in trade? What were the major items of trade?*

▶ Role play an international meeting of Spanish, British, French, and Dutch government leaders discussing colonial trade. *Why did countries attempt to prohibit their colonies from trading with other countries? How would governments attempt to prohibit smuggling? How would they deal with piracy? Would they be able to agree on a common trading policy?*

Grades 7-8

▶ Construct a list of goods traded between a European country and its colonies and explain the skills required of a merchant involved in the trans-Atlantic trade. Considering that merchants were said to have the boldness of gamblers and the caution and meticulous attention-to-detail of bookkeepers, write diary entries conveying their experiences in international trade. Describe the voyage, the buying and selling at different ports, life in the ports, and the hazards and rewards of trade.

▶ Analyze the advantages and disadvantages of mercantilism for both the mother country and its colonies.

▶ Compare the regions that produced sugar, rice, tobacco, timber, coffee, grains, fish, and minerals, and consider their value to the mother country.

Grades 9-12

▶ Drawing upon a variety of data relating to overseas trade between European countries and their American colonies, including statutory measures like the Navigation Acts, reports of colonial merchants and government officials, and graphical sources illustrating economic developments, analyze the advantages and disadvantages of mercantilism for both the mother country and its colonies. *How did the accumulation of gold and silver in its American colonies affect the Spanish economy? How did it promote further colonization? How was mining organized?*

▶ Compare the regions producing sugar, rice, tobacco, timber, coffee, grains, fish, and minerals, and evaluate their importance in terms of overseas colonization. *Which areas of the Americas became the most valuable colonies? Which areas exhibited the greatest imperial conflict? Why? How did climate and soil conditions affect the development of "money crops" in various regions? How did the economic development of French, English, and Spanish colonies differ?*

▶ Analyze the evolution of the Atlantic economy and describe the developing trade patterns. *To what extent was there a "triangular trade" and how significant was it?*

▶ Investigate ways in which the Spanish Council of Trade controlled commerce. *Why did Spain originally restrict trade to the Spanish ports of Cadíz and Seville? How did Spain attempt to restrict the entry of illegal commodities in their colonies? Did other European nations take similar actions in attempting to control trade with their colonies?*

B. Economic life and the development of labor systems in the English colonies.

Grades 5-6

▶ Draw upon historical stories and other descriptions of colonial economic life in various regions, and compare the similarities and differences in the work people did, the crops they grew, and the environmental conditions that supported their activities.

▶ Compare and contrast family farming in New England with plantation life in the Chesapeake and with small yeoman farming in the southern piedmont.

▶ Develop a product map showing the New England merchants' trading triangle and the goods and people regularly transported between the English colonies, West Indies, Africa, and Great Britain.

▶ Describe life in colonial America using stories such as *If You Lived in Colonial Times* by Ann McGovern, *How the Colonists Lived* by David McKay, and *Colonial Living* by Edwin Tunis.

▶ Examine labor patterns that emerged in the colonies. Drawing upon stories and diaries, describe the differences between free labor, indentured servitude, and slavery. Chart the rights, obligations, and opportunities for people under each form of labor. *Why did colonists bring more people to work the land? What was the hope of indentured people when they contracted to come to the colonies? What did chattel slavery mean for the Africans who were forced to come to work in the colonies?*

▶ Assume the role of a western Pennsylvania wheat farmer traveling to Philadelphia to sell grain, and describe the city and its waterfront. *What did farmers hope to purchase from the sale of their wheat?*

Grades 7-8

▶ Analyze how climate, land fertility, water resources, and access to markets affected economic growth in different regions.

▶ Explain the reasons for the passage of the early Navigation Acts and their relation to mercantilism.

▶ Investigate the hardships of indentured servitude by drawing evidence from historical fiction such as *Calico Bush* by Rachel Field and *Master Entrick* by Michael Mott.

▶ Explain why indentured servitude was more prevalent in the mid-Atlantic, Chesapeake, and southern colonies. Describe the typical terms of a contract for an indentured servant. *What is the reason for the headright system and why does it decline?*

▶ Examine laws enacted in Virginia and Maryland that helped institutionalize slavery. *What rights were taken away from enslaved Africans? What restrictions were placed on white-black relations? How was slavery made perpetual and hereditary?*

▶ Assume the identity of different individuals such as a London merchant, an English artisan, a West Indian sugar planter, a New England shipbuilder, a Cape Cod fisherman, a Chesapeake tobacco planter, and a Pennsylvania wheat farmer, and role-play a discussion on the merits of mercantilism. *What people benefit from the British mercantile system? What were the advantages and disadvantages of mercantilism for the mother country? For the colonies?*

▶ Analyze how climate, land fertility, and access to markets affected economic growth in the English West Indies and in the English North American colonies. *Which of the English colonies were most valuable to the mother country? Why? What factors accounted for the higher death rate among white settlers in the West Indian, Chesapeake, and southern colonies compared to the New England and Middle colonies in the colonial period? What were some of the major consequences of such developments?*

▶ Analyze the reasons for passage of the Navigation Acts and explain how they reflected traditional mercantile values. *To what extent did the Navigation Acts promote and retard economic growth in the colonies? To what extent were they obeyed?*

▶ Draw upon historical evidence to trace the gradual emergence of chattel slavery in Virginia and Maryland in the 17th century and compare historical interpretations concerning its origin and development.

▶ Differentiate between free labor and chattel slavery, and explain why neither provided a viable and effective alternative for labor in the Chesapeake colonies in the period before 1675. *How did the headright system and indentured servitude provide a better alternative for labor in the first half of the 17th century? Why did the increased life expectancy of indentured servants contribute to the transition to chattel slavery after 1660? How did laws enacted in the Chesapeake colonies institutionalizing slavery differ from laws regulating indentured servitude?*

▶ Examine artists' portrayal of individuals and family life in the mid-eighteenth century and explain how these works reflect an imitation of English culture. *How were the homes and furnishings of the upwardly mobile colonists a reflection of the lifestyles of the English gentry?*

▶ Explain how material success of many English colonists helped to promote a consumer society.

C. African life under slavery.

▶ Examine the slave trade drawing evidence from sources such as *A Slaver's Log Book: Twenty Years' Residence in Africa* by Theophile Conneau and *The Slave Ship* by Emma Sterne to examine stories of the slave trade.

▶ Trace the movement of enslaved Africans to different parts of the Caribbean and North America. *What was meant by the "middle passage"?*

▶ Describe chattel slavery using stories and narratives such as *Africa Remembered: Narratives by West Africans from the Era of the Slave Trade* edited by Philip Curtin, and slave narratives in *America's Children: Voices from the Past* edited by Matthew Downey.

▶ Describe the influence of African heritage on slave life in the colonies by drawing upon art, music, literature, and stories such as the Brer Rabbit folktales. *How did enslaved Africans draw upon their heritage in art, music, childrearing activities, and values to draw strength to cope with slavery and develop a strong culture in an unfamiliar land?*

▶ Describe the variety of measures used to resist slavery and discuss their effectiveness. *How did forms of resistance vary depending on the region and the slave's gender or age?*

▶ Investigate slave rebellions in colonial America such as New York, 1712 and 1740, and the Stono Rebellion in South Carolina in 1739. *What caused these rebellions? What were the results of these rebellions?*

▶ Describe the "middle passage" by drawing evidence from primary sources such as *The Interesting Narrative of the Life of Olaudah Equiano or Gustavus Vasa, Written by Himself.*

▶ Explain how slavery differed in colonial America from that practiced in West Africa and other parts of the world in the sixteenth and seventeenth centuries.

Grades 9-12

▶ Drawing upon the account of Olaudah Equiano, evaluate conditions faced by enslaved Africans and how survivors coped with the brutality of bondage.

▶ Explain the political, social, and economic circumstances under which African merchants, political elites, and other groups participated in the capture of slaves and their sale to European slave traders. *How did the African concept of slavery differ from that adopted by European settlers in the Americas?*

▶ Construct a comparative chart illustrating the ways in which ancient, medieval, and early modern societies instituted social bondage and slavery prior to the Atlantic slave trade. Compare and contrast ways in which bondage was practiced in the Islamic lands, Christian Europe, and West Africa. *How did the Atlantic slave trade differ from previous historical examples of slavery?*

▶ Investigate religious practices, dances, songs, holistic medicine, work chants, cuisine, and marriage and burial ceremonies to determine the degree to which African Americans retained and transmitted their cultural heritage.

▶ Compare slavery and slave resistance in different parts of the Americas. *How did slavery differ in Spanish America and British America? How did it differ in urban and plantation areas? Why were there more slave revolts in the Caribbean and South America than in North America?*

Students examining history projects at Lakeview Junior High School, Santa Monica, CA

ERA 3

Revolution and the New Nation (1754-1820s)

The American Revolution is of signal importance in the study of American history. First, it severed the colonial relationship with England and legally created the United States. Second, the revolutionary generation formulated the political philosophy and laid the institutional foundations for the system of government under which we live. Third, the revolution was inspired by ideas concerning natural rights and political authority that were transatlantic in reach, and its successful completion affected people and governments over a large part of the globe for many generations. Lastly, it called into question long-established social and political relationships—between master and slave, man and woman, upper class and lower class, office-holder and constituent, and even parent and child—and thus established an agenda for reform that would preoccupy Americans down to the present day.

In thinking about the causes and course of the Revolution, it is important to study the fundamental principles of the Declaration of Independence; the causes for the outbreak of the war; the main stages of the Revolutionary War and the reasons for the American victory; and the role of wartime leaders, from all strata of society, both on the battlefield and on the homefront.

In assessing the outcomes of the American Revolution, students need to confront the central issue of how revolutionary the Revolution actually was. In order to reach judgements about this, they necessarily will have to see the Revolution through different sets of eyes—enslaved and free African Americans, Native Americans, white men and women of different social classes, religions, ideological dispositions, regions, and occupations. Students should also be able to see pre- and post-revolutionary American society in relation to reigning political institutions and practices in the rest of the world.

Students can appreciate how agendas for redefining American society in the postwar era differed by exploring how the Constitution was created and how it was ratified after a dramatic ideological debate in virtually every locale in 1787-88. The Constitution of 1787 and the Bill of Rights should be broached as the culmination of the most creative era of constitutionalism in American history. In addition, students should ponder why the Constitutional Convention sidetracked the movement to abolish slavery that had taken rise in the revolutionary era. Nor should they think that ratification of the Constitution ended debate on governmental power, or how to create "a more perfect union." Economic, regional, social, ideological, religious, and political tensions would spawn continuing debates over the meaning of the Constitution for generations.

In studying the post-Revolutionary generation, students can understand how the embryo of the American two-party system took shape, how political turmoil arose as Americans debated the French Revolution, and how the Supreme Court rose to a place of prominence. Politics, political leadership, and political institutions have always bulked large in the study of this era, but students will also need to understand other less noticed topics: the beginnings of a national economy, the exuberant push westward, the military campaigns against Native American nations; the emergence of free black communities; and the democratization of religion.

The time to guard against corruption and tyranny is before they have gotten hold of us. It is better to keep the wolf out of the fold than to trust to drawing his teeth and talons after he shall have entered.

— THOMAS JEFFERSON, *NOTES ON THE STATE OF VIRGINIA* (1782)

Essay

Inspired Expedient
How James Madison balanced principle and politics in securing the adoption of the Bill of Rights*
by Jack N. Rakove

Jack Rakove's fresh essay on James Madison and the Bill of Rights provides a good example of how new scholarship continues to change our views of the past. In today's culture wars, "historical revisionism" is held in contempt in some quarters. Rakove's essay shows that the unending asking of new questions and the quest for new answers and interpretations is at the very heart of "doing" history. His elegant weighing of principle and politics in Madison's thinking about the Bill of Rights shows how our reverence for the Bill of Rights need not preclude a carefully exploration of Madison's motives and the changing view of the Bill.

Jack Rakove is Professor of History at Stanford University and is the author of *The Beginnings of National Politics: An Interpretive History of the Continental Congress, James Madison and the Creation of the American Republic* and *Original Meanings: Politics and Ideas in the Making of the Constitution.* He has also written numerous articles for historical journals and popular magazines.

Had James Madison been asked to rank his contributions to the American republic in order of importance, he would probably have given his role in the adoption of the Bill of Rights only passing mention. Although he guided the proposed amendments through the First Congress in 1789, Madison regarded bills of rights as "parchment barriers" of little practical use. He confided to a friend that his colleagues felt Congress had more important matters to decide and considered his labors "a nauseous project." Madison wrote often on constitutional matters during his long retirement after 1817, but he virtually ignored the amendments of 1789. His view of the Bill of Rights probably anticipated the judgment of many modern historians, who treat its adoption in 1791 more as a political expedient in the struggle over ratifying the Constitution than as a great milestone in the march of liberty.

From this vantage point, this early reaction to the Bill of Rights as irrelevant seems both puzzling and ironic, especially because interpretations of its provisions now stand at the heart of modern constitutional debate. This debate has increasingly centered on the original meaning of the Bill of Rights and its descendant, the 14th Amendment. No such inquiry can ignore James Madison. He was, after all, the principal author of the amendments of 1789 and the driving political force behind their passage through Congress. Indeed, had it not been for his persistence, there might never have been a Bill of Rights.

Yet important as it is to understand why Madison took the lead in framing the amendments of 1789, it is equally important to understand why he continued to question their value. The fact is he was convinced that the greatest dangers to the rights of citizens lay in the power of popular majorities within the states, and he doubted whether a federal bill of rights would do any good unless it somehow curbed the legislative authority of the state governments.

Madison came to his libertarian convictions early. The earnest young man who returned to Virginia in 1772 from collegiate studies at Princeton was already committed to the cause of religious freedom—the issue that at first engaged him more deeply even than the colonists' quarrel with Britain. Fittingly, his first notable public deed, as a delegate to his state's Provincial Convention, was to secure an amendment to the Virginia Declaration of Rights of 1776, broadening tolerance of religious dissenters to a wider affirmation that "all men are equally entitled to the free exercise of religion, according to the dictates of conscience." When he

---

*Reprinted from *Constitution*, Vol. 3, No. 1 (Winter 1991), pp. 25-30. Reprinted with permission of the author.

entered the Virginia Assembly in 1784, after long service in the Continental Congress, he led the fight against a proposed bill to levy a general assessment to support all ministers of Christianity, and then went on to secure passage of the celebrated Virginia Act for Establishing Religious Freedom that his friend Thomas Jefferson had drafted some years earlier.

Madison expressed his ideas on religious liberty most fully in his *Memorial and Remonstrance* against Religious Assessments, which he published anonymously in 1785 to rally public opinion against the assessment bill. He opened his *Memorial* by affirming the natural and unalienable right of every man to judge how "to render to the Creator such homage and such only as he believes to be acceptable to him," entirely free from the influence or control of "Civil Society."

Many of the political arguments that Madison marshaled against the assessment echoed the language of the revolutionary quarrel with Britain. Like Parliament, the Assembly seemed bent on usurping authority it could not legitimately claim; and if this "first experiment on our liberties" went uncontested, Virginians could expect future Assemblies to "sweep away all our fundamental rights" and reduce the people to the condition of "slaves"—the favored term that 18th-century Britons and Americans used to describe a people governed without their consent.

Yet if this rhetoric was familiar, the object against which it was directed was not. Americans had opposed Parliament because they believed that the security of their rights depended on being governed by legislatures they had elected. Where, however, was one to turn when the threat to popular rights came from the elected representatives themselves?

In 1785 Madison answered this question in two ways. The first and more conventional solution was to mobilize the people to defend their endangered rights—as he sought to do by publishing the *Memorial*. A second and potentially superior answer involved figuring out how to limit legislative authority by formal or constitutional means. That was where the Act for Establishing Religious Freedom marked a radical advance in American thinking. By treating the entire realm of religion as a matter of private belief, Madison and Jefferson identified the one area of governance in which private rights could be enhanced by forbidding legislatures from passing any laws about it at all.

In 1785 Madison believed that that a declaration of rights in the state constitution would also serve this end. Soon after he wrote his *Memorial* he received a letter from a college friend, soliciting his ideas about the kind of constitution that the Kentucky territory might adopt when it separated from Virginia. Madison's response is revealing. In his view, the great defects of the existing state constitutions lay in the composition of the legislative branch. Though he worried that legislative power was inherently difficult to define, he still thought it was "very practicable...to enumerate the essential exceptions. The Constitution may expressly restrain them [the legislators] from medling with religion—from abolishing Juries from taking away the Habeas corpus—from forcing a citizen to give evidence against himself, from controuling the press, from enacting retrospective [i.e., ex post facto] laws at least in criminal cases, from abridging the right of suffrage, from seizing private property for public use without paying its full Valu from licensing the importation of Slaves, from infringing the Confederation &c &c." [spelling not modernized]

Here, with remarkable ease, Madison had dashed off an impressive catalogue of basic rights—a list that anticipates some of the crucial elements of the federal Bill of Rights of 1789. But most significantly, it expressed Madison's conviction that of the three branches of government it was the legislature that most needed restraining.

In the period leading up to the Federal Convention in May 1787, Madison became increasingly critical of the ill-drawn and unjust laws that too many state legislatures were adopting and increasingly anxious to find constitutional means to control legislative power itself. He further came to fear that legislative misrule had deeper roots than the vices and ambitions of lawmakers. The real source of injustice lay not in government but in the passions and interests of society, or, more specifically, of whatever groups managed to make government the instrument of their own designs.

These concerns carried Madison well away from the orthodox understanding of rights that had prevailed circa 1776. The essential problem then had seemed to be to protect the ruled from their rulers. But in a republican regime, Madison now concluded, the problem was less to protect the ruled from arbitrary acts of their rulers than to protect one segment of the people from another.

Reviewing "the vices of the Political system of the United States" prior to the Federal Convention, Madison concluded that the "multiplicity," "mutability" and "injustice" of the laws that individual states had adopted since independence had called "into question the fundamental principle of republican Government, that the majority who rule in such Governments, are the safest Guardians both of public Good and of private rights."

In reaching these conclusions, Madison drew not only upon his own legislative experiences in Virginia but also on his observation of politics in other states. Especially disturbing were the measures that the states were adopting to deal with the economic and financial aftermath of the Revolution. Paper money and laws deferring payment of private debts alarmed him terribly, while the specter of Shays's Rebellion in Massachusetts left him wondering whether a time might come when a majority of Americans would support "agrarian" laws that would redistribute property. The writers of the state constitutions of 1776 had erred in assuming that by protecting "the rights of persons" they would also protect "the rights of property." Madison now understood "that in all populous countries, the smaller part only can be interested in preserving the rights of property."

As Madison completed his preparations for the Federal Convention, this deeper analysis of existing dangers to liberty left him even more skeptical about the utility of bills of rights. The difficulty was not that such bills were bad in themselves but rather that they would not reach the cases that most needed protection. Madison not only feared that populist majorities within the states would be able to enact legislation inimical to fundamental rights of property, but also that the nature of legislative power would make it nearly impossible to impose formal constitutional limits on the exercise of that power. This was especially true in the case of economic legislation, where the interests to be regulated were so complex, and the ends and means of legislation so intertwined, that no simple formula could defeat the ingenuity of lawmakers bent on mischief and spurred by the demands of their constituents.

Madison's careful analysis of the problem led to two proposals that he pressed at the convention. The first was to give the new Congress an unlimited veto over all state laws. This would enable the national government to act as a "disinterested and dispassionate umpire in disputes between different passions and interests" within the states (as well as allowing it to protect other federal powers against obstruction from the states). The second proposal called for the creation of a joint executive-judicial council of revision that would assess the merits of state laws under review and also enjoy a limited veto over national legislation. The benefits to be gained, Madison felt, far outweighed the damage that such a council would do to the strict theory of the separation of powers.

These two proposals, rather than a national bill of rights, were the measures that Madison thought would best safeguard liberty in America. But neither survived the scrutiny of the convention. With their rejection, Madison confided in a letter to Jefferson that he feared the Constitution "will neither effectually answer its national object nor prevent the local mischiefs which every where excite disgusts against the state governments." Even if restrictions that the Constitution placed on the states by prohibiting paper currency and laws impairing contracts proved "effectual as far as they go," he wrote in another letter, dated October 24, 1787, "they are short of the mark. Injustice can be effected by such an infinitude of legislative expedients, that where the disposition exists it can only be controuled by some provision which reaches all cases whatsoever."

This letter initiated the most engaging exchange in the near half century of correspondence between the two eminent Virginians. Over the next year and a half, amid delays imposed by the rush of events on both sides of the Atlantic—Jefferson was then serving as minister to France—the two men discussed the need for a bill of rights. And though Madison moved closer to the position with which his friend was quickly and publicly associated—"that a bill of rights is what the people are entitled to against every government on earth"—his basic doubts about the utility of bills of rights remained unaltered.

Like other Federalists, Madison had initially suspected that the call for a bill of rights masked a design to amend the proposed Constitution in radical and harmful ways. Once the document was ratified, however, he reconsidered the issue. By the early fall of 1788, he conceded that some declaration of rights could be safely added to the Constitution. Shortly thereafter, in the midst of a tough race against his friend James Monroe for election to the First Congress, he issued public letters affirming his support for a bill of rights.

Yet even as he moved toward this popular position, Madison believed that the principal value of a bill of rights would be to reassure moderate Antifederalists that the Constitution was not the dangerous blueprint for tyranny they imagined it to be. As he explained in a letter to Jefferson (dated October 17, 1788): "My own opinion has always been in favor of a bill of rights, provided it be so framed as not to imply powers not meant to be included in the enumeration." (For example, an amendment affirming rights of conscience could be falsely interpreted to imply that Congress was empowered to regulate religious matters.) "At the same time I have never thought the omission a material defect, nor been anxious to supply it even by *subsequent* amendment, for any other reason than that it is anxiously desired by others."

Madison then listed the reasons why he had never "viewed it in an important light." Like other Federalists, he held that the way in which the Constitution delegated particular powers implied that fundamental rights and civil liberties were still inherently "reserved." The independent existence of the states and their "jealousy" of the national government would provide further security against the abuse of federal power. Moreover, Madison repeated his often stated fear "that a positive declaration of some of the most essential rights [especially in the realm of religion] could not be obtained in the requisite latitude."

Finally and most crucially, there was his critique of republican politics—the danger of oppression of the minority by the majority. From his vantage point in monarchical France, Jefferson could still believe that rights had to be protected against government, but Madison had new "facts" to assimilate. In a monarchy, he observed, a bill of rights could usefully serve to rally the latent but ultimately "superior force of the community" against "abuses of power" by "the sovereign." But in a republic, where "the political and physical power" alike rested "in a majority of the people," no bill of rights could dissuade an impassioned or self-interested majority from pursuing its ends. What value, then, could a bill of rights have in a republic? Madison offered two answers. One use was educational: "The political truths declared in that solemn manner acquire by degrees the character of fundamental maxims of free Government, and as they become incorporated with the national sentiment, counteract the impulses of interest and passion." Second, Madison conceded that, at some future point, "the danger of oppression" might lie more in "usurped acts of the Government" than "the interested majorities of the people." In that case, a bill of rights would work much as it might in a monarchy, rallying the people to a standard of opposition. But in his view this remained an improbable scenario.

When Jefferson finally received this letter—a full four months later!—he was quick to respond that Madison had omitted one argument for a bill of rights "which has great weight with me, the legal check which it puts into the hands of the judiciary." Madison dutifully incorporated this crucial and prescient point in his June 8, 1789, speech presenting his plan of amendments to the House of Representatives, suggesting that "independent tribunals of justice will consider themselves in a peculiar manner the guardians of those rights...expressly stipulated for in the constitution by the declaration of rights."

In other respects, however, Madison hoped to use the debate over amendments to present his subsisting ideas about rights to both his fellow congressmen and the public who followed their deliberations in the press. Madison did not dissemble when the time came to defend the list of essential rights he had culled from the scores of amendments proposed by the state ratification conventions. Rather than endorse the Antifederalist claim that a constitution lacking a bill of rights was defective, he adroitly explained why standard Federalist arguments against amendments were both "plausible" but not "conclusive." The most pressing reason for amendments, he admitted, was to reconcile to the Constitution all those "respectable" citizens whose "jealousy...for their liberty...though mistaken in its object, is laudable in its motive."

Far from seeking to assuage public opinion at any cost, Madison then restated his essential positions about legislators and majorities. And again he sought to place restrictions on the legislative power of the states by proposing an amendment declaring that "No state shall violate the equal rights of conscience, or the freedom of the press, or the trial by jury in criminal cases." Though more limited than the veto he had initially proposed on all state laws, this measure marked one final effort to salvage part of his original recommendations to the convention. In subsequent debate, he boldly described this proposal as "the most valuable amendment on the whole list." Would the people not be equally grateful if "these essential rights" were secured against the state as well as the national governments?

This logic prevailed in the House but not the Senate, which was, in a sense, the constitutional guardian of states' rights. But in nearly every other respect, Congress approved his amendments much as Madison proposed them. For Madison, this must have been a source of some satisfaction, especially because in drafting his amendments he had taken pains to employ language of "requisite latitude" to express rights broadly. This was particularly the case in the Fourth Amendment's protection against unreasonable searches and seizures, the Fifth Amendment's prohibition on self-incrimination and the Sixth Amendment's promise of a right to counsel. By the legal standards of the day, these were expansive positions.

So, too, in the conference committee that resolved differences between the House and Senate versions of the Bill of Rights, Madison was almost certainly responsible for the final wording of the establishment clause of the First Amendment. Where the Senate had barred Congress only from "establishing articles of faith or a mode of worship," the committee agreed that "Congress shall make no law respecting an establishment of religion." If this phrasing was more ambiguous, it was also, for that reason, potentially more restrictive of the legislative power of Congress.

Another important concern of Madison's was addressed in the Ninth Amendment. The framer took seriously the objection of many Federalists to the very idea of a bill of rights. Any attempt, these men felt, to place a constitutional seal of approval on particular rights would imply that all rights not specifically mentioned would thereby be deemed less essential. Accordingly, for Madison the language of the Ninth Amendment expressed a vital principle when it declared: "The enumeration, in the Constitution, of certain rights, shall not be construed to deny or disparage others retained by the people."

What satisfaction Madison got from his parliamentary labors on behalf of the Bill of Rights was probably more that of an obligation discharged than of a goal fulfilled. Whatever benefits the adoption of the amendments would produce, Madison still believed, would take some time to unfold. A revealing passage in his notes for his essay "Public Opinion" (1791) suggests that he still thought that the primary value of bills of rights was educational. "In proportion as Government is influenced by opinion, must it be so by whatever influences opinion," he observed. "This decides the question concerning a bill of rights, which acquires efficacy as time sanctifies and incorporates it with the public sentiment."

Within a few years, Madison discovered that the pace of political and constitutional development in America was more rapid than he had anticipated. Disputes over the financial program of Alexander Hamilton and foreign policy led to the formation of two national political parties. In 1798, the ruling Federalists moved against Madison's Democratic-Republicans with the Sedition Act of 1798, in apparent defiance of the First Amendment clause prohibiting Congress from "abridging the freedom of speech, or of the press." Though Federalist judges refused to act as the independent, rights-protecting tribunals Jefferson had envisioned, Madison now saw more clearly just how effectively a bill of rights could be used to rally public opinion against "usurped acts of the Government."

More than the part of the Bill of Rights, however, the Democratic-Republicans became known as the party of states' rights. After the turn of the 19th century, the Bill of Rights itself had only symbolic value; its influence was felt mostly as a model for bills of rights for the new states joining the union. In 1833—when the 82-year-old Madison was troubled by the perverted uses to which the South Carolina nullificationists put his Virginia Resolutions of 1798—the Supreme Court definitively ruled (in *Barron* v. *Baltimore*) that the federal Bill of Rights did not apply to the states.

Another generation passed, and the evil of nullification evolved into the heresy of secession. When the civil war James Madison had lived to dread came and went, both the Constitution and American ideas of rights were transformed. Among the amendments adopted during Reconstruction, the 13th freeing the slaves was the most dramatic and revolutionary. But it was the 14th that laid the basis for many of the momentous constitutional developments and disputes of our own time—and in a way that more closely reflects the convictions of James Madison than any other single clause of the Constitution. We cannot safely claim that he would have approved all the subsequent extensions, but whatever its ambiguities, and the twists and turns in its interpretation, the 14th Amendment at last allowed the national government to act as Madison had originally thought it should: as a "disinterested and dispassionate umpire" capable of intervening to protect minority and individual rights against the democratic but potentially tyrannical impulses of popular majorities within the states.

Sample Student Activities

> I.   *The causes of the American Revolution, the ideas and interests involved in forging the revolutionary movement, and the reasons for the American victory.*

A.   The causes of the American Revolution.

Grades 5-6

▶ Identify such major consequences of the Seven Years War as the English victory, the removal of the French as a contending power in North America, and the reduced need of the colonists for protection by the mother country.

▶ Select in chronological order and explain the major events leading to the outbreak of conflict at Lexington and Concord.

▶ Construct biographical sketches of such persons as George Washington, Patrick Henry, James Otis, Samuel Adams, Thomas Paine, John Hancock, and Paul Revere to explain the importance of individual action in the defense of the rights of American colonists.

▶ Create historical arguments or narratives explaining at least one reason why the English Parliament felt it was justified in taxing the colonies to help pay for a war fought in their defense and at least one reason why the colonists, claiming their rights as Englishmen, challenged the legitimacy of the new taxes as "taxation without representation."

Grades 7-8

▶ Assemble the evidence about the consequences of the Seven Years War and listen to the voices of such resistance leaders as John Adams, Thomas Jefferson, John Dickinson, Thomas Paine, Patrick Henry, and Samuel Adams, and construct a sound historical argument on such questions as: *Was it reasonable for the English to tax the colonists to help pay for a war fought in their defense? Were the American colonists justified in their resistance to England's new imperial policies?*

▶ Explain the divisions in the colonies over these issues by comparing the interests and positions of Loyalists and Patriots from different economic groups such as northern merchants, southern rice and tobacco planters, yeoman farmers, and urban artisans.

▶ Marshal historical evidence including events leading up to "the shot heard 'round the world" and develop a historical argument on such questions as the following: *Was the outbreak of conflict at Lexington and Concord unavoidable? Could any action at that point have prevented war with England?*

Grades 9-12

▶ Drawing upon the arguments advanced by opponents and defenders of England's new imperial policy in order to construct a sound historical argument or narrative on such questions as: *Were the arguments against Parliamentary taxation a legitimate and constitutional defense of the historic and traditional rights of Englishmen under common law, or were they merely a defense for tax evasion? Was the British decision to station troops in the colonies at the end of the Seven Years War designed to defend the colonies or did it reflect a conscious decision to keep contentious and expansionist colonists under control?*

◆ Draw upon evidence of the mounting crisis as well as the efforts in Parliament and in the colonies to prevent a rupture with the mother country in order to construct a sound historical narrative or argument on such questions as: *Was the break with England avoidable? Could decisions on either side, other than those which were taken, have changed the circumstances leading to the escalation of the crisis and the outbreak war?*

◆ Drawing upon ideas of religious groups such as Virginia Baptists, mid-Atlantic Presbyterians, and millennialists, assess how religion became a factor in the American Revolution.

◆ Construct a historical narrative analyzing the factors which explain why a person chose to be a Loyalist or a Patriot. *Why did approximately one-third of the colonists want to remain neutral? Did economic and social differences play a role in how people chose sides? Explain.*

◆ Marshal evidence to explain how a Loyalist and a Patriot would view each of the following: The Tea Act of 1773, the Boston Tea Party, the "Intolerable" Acts, the cause of the skirmish at Lexington Green. *How might a Loyalist have interpreted the natural rights theory of the Declaration of Independence? How might a Loyalist have answered the charges in the Declaration of Independence?*

B. The principles articulated in the Declaration of Independence.

Grades 5-6

◆ Define the terms in the Declaration of Independence, including "all men," "created equal," "endowed by their Creator," "unalienable rights," "life, liberty, and the pursuit of happiness," "just powers," and "consent of the governed."

◆ Explain why Thomas Jefferson wrote the Declaration of Independence, what its signers risked in putting their names to the document, and what its consequences were for the newly declared nation.

◆ Explain the ideas expressed in the Declaration of Independence by drawing evidence from books such as *Fourth of July Story* by Alice Dalgliesh, and *Give Us Liberty: The Story of the Declaration of Independence* by Helen Peterson.

Grades 7-8

◆ Explain the major principles set forth in the Declaration of Independence including the basic rights of all people; the source of those rights; the purpose of government; the source of its just powers in the consent of the governed; and the right of the people to alter or abolish a government "destructive of those ends."

◆ Explain the historical antecedents of the Declaration of Independence in key ideas of Enlightenment thought; in traditions of English common law, the English Bill of Rights, and the Glorious Revolution; and in the traditions of natural law and the Judeo-Christian heritage which hold all persons to be of equal worth before God and before the state.

◆ Identify and analyze the fundamental contradictions between the institution of chattel slavery and the ideals expressed in the Declaration of Independence by formulating sound arguments in response to such questions as: *What rights, claimed by the Declaration of Independence to be the inalienable rights of all men, were denied to those held in slavery? Could such contradictions be justified?*

◆ Draw evidence from biographies of prominent individuals who were in the forefront of the struggle for independence such as George Washington, Benjamin Franklin, Thomas Jefferson, and Thomas Paine, as well as lesser known figures such as Mercy Otis Warren, James Lafayette, and Ebenezer MacIntosh, to examine their contributions to American independence.

▶ Examine Abraham Lincoln's Independence Hall speech, February 22, 1861, in which he remarked: "...[the] Declaration [gave] liberty not alone to the people of this country, but hope to the world for all future time. It was that which gave promise that in due time the weight should be lifted from the shoulders of all men, and that *all* should have an equal chance. This is the sentiment embodied in the Declaration of Independence." *How would Lincoln respond to the statement that the Declaration of Independence grew in importance to become the embodiment of American democracy?*

Grades 9-12

▶ Compare the ideas of the Declaration of Independence with those of John Locke in *Two Treatises of Government. How are they different? Similar? Why does Jefferson use the phrase "the pursuit of happiness" instead of "property"? What did Jefferson mean by "the pursuit of happiness"?*

▶ Draw upon the principles in the Declaration of Independence to construct a sound historical argument regarding whether or not it justified American independence.

▶ Compare and evaluate the arguments in letters, speeches, and other documents from advocates and opponents of slavery from different regions of the country, reflecting their perspectives on the ideals of the Declaration of Independence. *How did pro-slavery Americans justify their defense of slavery with their espousal of inalienable rights to freedom? How did the ideals of the revolutionary era inspire African Americans?*

▶ Compare the Declaration of Independence with the French Declaration of the Rights of Man and Citizen, and evaluate their influence on government and revolutionary movements around the world during the 19th and 20th centuries. *How did the natural rights philosophy of the Enlightenment influence the American and French declarations? How have these ideas, which inspired the American and French revolutions, influenced 19th-century revolutions in Latin America and Europe, and 20th-century revolutions such as those of Mexico, Russia, and China? How successful have these governments been in carrying out the ideals that inspired their revolutions?*

▶ Research how individuals in different periods of American history have interpreted the ideas set forth in the Declaration of Independence.

C. The factors affecting the course of the war and contributing to the American victory.

Grades 5-6

▶ Reconstruct the chronology of the course of the war as it moved from the North in 1775-78 to the South in 1778-81, climaxing at Yorktown.

▶ Identify and compare the leadership roles of at least two major political, military, and diplomatic leaders such as George Washington, Benjamin Franklin, Thomas Jefferson, John Adams, Samuel Adams, John Hancock, and Richard Henry Lee.

▶ Explain how the war affected the lives of people by drawing evidence from books such as *Jump Ship to Freedom, My Brother Sam is Dead* and *War Comes to Willy Freeman* by James Collier and Christopher Collier and *Johnny Tremain* by Esther Forbes.

▶ Research places in your state and local community which are named for Revolutionary War leaders. *What were the significant contributions of these individuals? What lessons can be learned from their lives?*

▶ Assess the importance of Benjamin Franklin's negotiations with the French government and of French aid to the Americans by constructing historical arguments on such questions as: *Could the underfinanced and undermanned Americans have defeated the most powerful military force in the Western world without French aid? What might have happened if the French army and navy had not been available to assist Washington at Yorktown?*

♦ Specify the terms of the Treaty of Paris and locate on a map the territorial changes agreed upon in the treaty.

Grades 7-8

♦ Analyze the major campaigns in the Revolutionary War and assess the leadership of both American and British military leaders.

♦ Analyze the varied responses of Native American nations to the American Revolution using the Iroquois and Cherokee as case studies. Construct a historical narrative examining the dilemma of establishing alliances or remaining neutral. *Why did both the British and Americans seek alliances with Indian nations? What were Mohawk chief Joseph Brant's reasons for supporting Britain after the Oswego Council (1777)? What impact did the war have on the Iroquois confederation? On the Cherokee?*

♦ Examine the Revolutionary War from the African American perspective and construct persuasive arguments or broadsides to enlist support for either the British or the patriot cause. *What was the impact of Lord Dunmore's proclamation? Why did free blacks and slaves join the patriots during the war? On what grounds did they base their appeals for freedom during and immediately after the conflict?*

♦ Draw upon diaries, letters, and historical stories to construct a narrative concerning how the daily lives of men, women, and children were affected by such wartime developments as the participation of men and women in the front lines; the need for women and children to assume men's roles in managing farms and urban businesses; the physical devastation caused by the fighting; the occupation and plunder of the cities by the British troops; and the economic hardship and privation caused by the war.

♦ Compare and contrast the interests, goals, and actions of France, Holland, and Spain in responding to American requests for assistance in their war with England.

♦ Develop a historical argument assessing the contributions to the American victory of such Europeans as the Marquis de Lafayette, Pierre de Beaumarchais, Baron Friedrich Wilhelm von Steuben, Baron Johann de Kalb, Thaddeus Kosciusko, Count Casimir Pulaski.

♦ Assess the position of the Native Americans at the close of the war. *What were their prospects, given the terms of the Treaty of Paris, which granted to the Americans sole rights to negotiate with them? How did land hunger, which had contributed to the tensions between the colonists and England over the Proclamation of 1763, express itself after the war?*

♦ Construct a dialogue between an Indian leader and George Washington at the end of the war regarding how a long-standing conflict between their peoples might be resolved.

Grades 9-12

♦ Construct an argument assessing the comparative advantages and disadvantages of such efforts to finance the Revolutionary War as taxing Americans, borrowing from foreign nations, confiscating goods and requiring services needed by the military, printing unbacked paper money, and repudiating debts.

♦ Construct a sound historical argument concerning the significance of the leadership traits and contribution of at least one of the major political, military, and diplomatic leaders of the war and hypothesize how the war might have been affected had this individual not been on the scene.

♦ Explain why the Battle of Saratoga has been considered the turning point of the Revolutionary War. *How did Benjamin Franklin use the battle to gain French aid? How important was French aid during the war?*

▶ Construct a position paper or historical narrative analyzing to what extent the American Revolution was a civil war as well as a war for national independence. *How does the battle at King's Mountain illustrate the civil war aspect of the Revolution?*

▶ Draw evidence from a variety of sources to explain how guerrilla warfare as well as conventional warfare was an aspect of the American Revolution. *Which was more important to the American victory?*

▶ Explain the factors that helped to produce the Treaty of Paris. *Was the treaty a military or a diplomatic victory? Why?*

▶ Explain how American diplomatic initiatives and the contributions of European military leaders affected the character and outcome of the American Revolution. Construct a historical argument agreeing or disagreeing with the statement: "The American Revolution succeeded because of a very small cadre of patriots, the intervention of foreign governments like France and Spain, and supreme good luck."

▶ Examine how the self-interests of France and Spain differed from the national interests of the United States. *What did France expect in return for its military and financial assistance to the United States during the Revolutionary war? What did Spain hope to get as a result of its war against Britain?*

▶ Compare how the terms of the Treaty of Paris and the national boundaries it specified affected economic, and strategic interests of the United States, Native American nations, Spain, England, and France. *What was the economic impact of the loss of trade with the British West Indies following the American Revolution? What boundaries remained in dispute after the Treaty of Paris? To what extent did the Treaty of Paris address issues of importance to the Indians? What was the impact of the Treaty of Fort Stanwix (1784) with the Iroquois and the Treaty of Hopewell with the Cherokee following the Revolution? What benefits could Indian allies of the United States expect to gain from their support?*

▶ Describe the boundary dispute between the United States and Spain resulting from the Treaty of Paris of 1783. Explain why the Jay-Gardoqui Treaty of 1786 resulted in regional economic conflict in the new nation.

> **II.** *The impact of the American Revolution on politics, economy, and society.*

A. Understanding of government-making at both national and state levels.

Grades 5-6

▶ Construct an explanation of how the 13 colonies settled the question of governing themselves after declaring their independence from England.

▶ Compare and explain the powers apportioned to the states and to the Continental Congress under the Articles of Confederation.

▶ Map the cession of western lands by various states to the national government.

Grades 7-8

▶ Develop a historical argument assessing the long-term importance of the Northwest Ordinance of 1787 in providing for the development of new states, restrictions on slavery, provisions for public education, and "the utmost good faith" clause for dealing with the Native Americans in the Northwest Territory.

▶ Analyze the issue of the western lands dispute by constructing sound historical arguments or narratives on such questions as: *Were states whose original charters had not granted them western lands justified in demanding that all western lands be ceded to the central government before they would sign the Articles of Confederation? Was the sale of these western lands important for a central government?*

▶ Assess the comparative accomplishments and failures of the national government under the Articles of Confederation. Debate the proposition: *"The Articles of Confederation was an effective government."*

Grades 9-12

▶ Draw upon specific provisions in any two state constitutions in order to demonstrate various applications of 18th-century republicanism such as virtue in government, balancing the interests of different social groups, service to the common good, representation, separation of powers, judicial independence, and the legitimacy of slavery. Analyze factors contributing to the differences in the selected state constitutions.

▶ Weigh historical evidence and construct a sound argument, debate, or narrative which evaluates the accomplishments and failures of the Continental Congress and Articles of Confederation. *How effective was the Continental Congress in waging war with Britain and negotiating diplomatic alliances with European powers? How difficult was it to reach an agreement on conflicting state claims to western lands? How successfully did the Continental Congress deal with Indian-white relations?*

▶ Formulate historical questions assessing the importance of the Northwest Ordinance based on a careful study of the document. *To what extent were the first two articles of the Northwest Ordinance a precursor to the Bill of Rights? How revolutionary was the antislavery clause of the Northwest Ordinance? Under the Ordinance, what was the status of free blacks in the territory? What was the "utmost good faith clause"? To what extent was it enforced? How did the Land Ordinance of 1785 and the Northwest Ordinance of 1787 promote public education? How did these ordinances lead to the opening of the West? What was their impact on Native Americans in the Old Northwest"?*

B.   Economic issues arising out of the Revolution.

Grades 5-6

▶ Assume the role of a Revolutionary War soldier who had not been paid for his services and write an appeal for back pay. Explain the reasons you need money and how inflation has affected your ability to borrow money to pay your debts including the taxes you owe.

▶ Explain the meaning of the phrase "not worth a continental." *What made continental currency virtually worthless?*

▶ Explain the issues which caused Massachusetts farmers to rebel in 1786. *What did the farmers who took part in Shays's Rebellion want? How did bankers and merchants to whom farmers owed debts react to the rebellion? How was the rebellion put down? What lessons can be learned from Shays's Rebellion?*

▶ Examine a map of the United States showing the overlapping state claims to western lands at the time of the Revolutionary War. Assuming roles representing the interests of the seven states which claimed land in the West and the six without claims, debate a fair settlement of the issue.

Grades 7-8

▶ Assuming the roles of representatives from Maryland and Virginia at the Continental Congress, debate the issues over western lands. *Why did Maryland refuse to ratify the Article of Confederation until the land issue was settled? Why did states which claimed large tracts of lands west of the Appalachians agree to turn over their claims to the national government?*

▶ Examine the effects of increasing the supply of paper money to finance the Revolutionary War. *What efforts were made to finance debt repayment after the war? To whom was the debt owed? What impact did the debt have on foreign relations? on domestic affairs?*

▶ Explain ways in which people were hurt by runaway inflation immediately after the American Revolution. *To what extent could the Continental Congress take steps to address the problem? How did different states deal with the problem? Why did merchants and tax collectors in some states refuse to accept inflationary currency?*

▶ Identify the issues involved in Shays's Rebellion. Debate the question: *Were the ordinary farmers who followed Daniel Shays justified in invoking revolutionary rights of petition and taking extralegal action to obtain redress of their grievances?*

▶ Research measures which were undertaken to rebuild the American economy after the Revolutionary War.

Grades 9-12

▶ Explain the measures taken by individual states and the Continental Congress to deal with the war debt. *What taxes were levied to help pay the debt? How did different states deal with debt payments? How did opportunists benefit from the inflationary spiral after the war? What effect did inflation and the lack of confidence in state currency have on economic transactions?*

▶ Research the size and scope of the U.S. debt at the close of the Revolutionary War and present alternative plans to retire the debt. Analyze the practicality and consequences of each proposal in the context of the post-Revolutionary era. *How practical would it have been to refuse payment of the debt? What were the sources of state and national revenue? What taxes could be imposed to retire the debt? What effect would these taxes have on different economic and social groups?*

▶ Examine how the resumption of trade with England after the Revolution and the extension of credit by English banks affected the American economy. *What was the initial effect of economic recession in England? How did the "debt chain" set off a spiraling crisis of credit in the United States? Which group in society was most severely affected by the credit crisis?*

▶ Explain the conditions in Massachusetts which prompted Shays's Rebellion and investigate how debtors in other states reacted to similar circumstances. *To what extent was Shays's Rebellion an isolated incident or a national phenomenon?*

▶ Evaluate the effectiveness of the Articles of Confederation and individual states in addressing inflation, trade, banking, and taxation.

▶ Evaluate the arguments made by creditors and debtors in attempting to prompt state governments to act on their behalf. *What actions did states take regarding private debt payments? How did legislative action of "creditor" states differ from those of "debtor" states?*

C. The Revolution's effects on different social groups.

Grades 5-6

▶ Compare the effects of the American victory on at least two of the following groups: small farmers; wealthy merchants; women who had contributed to the war effort; newly freed African Americans who had fought on the American or the English side; Native Americans who had fought on the American or the English side.

▶ Construct biographical sketches of women such as Abigail Adams and Mercy Otis Warren who made important contributions to American society during the Revolution.

Grades 7-8

▶ Interpret documentary evidence from diaries, letters, and journals to construct sound historical arguments, debates, or narratives on such issues as the following: *Were women justified in seeking new roles and rights in American society? To what extent were they influenced by such revolutionary ideals as liberty, equality and the right to representation? To what extent were they constrained by the social conventions of the 18th century?*

▶ Draw upon evidence from biographies and other historical sources to construct sound historical assessments of the contributions of such former slaves as Prince Hall, Paul Cuffe, Richard Allen, and Absalom Jones who worked to improve the lives of newly freed African Americans

▶ Construct historical arguments in the form of balance sheets, debates, or narratives which marshal historical evidence on such questions as: *To what extent were the revolutionary goals of those who supported the Revolution achieved? What were the goals of those who remained loyal to the English (Loyalists, Native Americans, and many African Americans), and what were the consequences for them of the American victory?*

▶ Examine the views of young people regarding life during the revolutionary era through a variety of historical fiction and primary source collections such as *Becoming American: Young People in the American Revolution*, edited by Paul Zall.

▶ Assume the role of a Virginia slave or indentured servant, and respond to Lord Dunmore's Declaration of Martial Law in Virginia (November 7, 1775). *What was the effect of Lord Dunmore's proclamation? How effective was Virginia's passage of the Manumission Act of 1782 in gaining the support of slaves in the struggle against the British? Why did some slaves and indentured servants join the Loyalists while others supported the Patriots?*

Grades 9-12

▶ Develop a sound historical argument concerning the degree to which the interests of such groups as enslaved and free African Americans and Native Americans were advanced or retarded by the American victory. *How did farmers, merchants, and artisans fare as a result of the American Revolution?*

▶ Draw upon biographies and other historical data to evaluate the importance of African American leaders in the early republic. *What institutions developed in the free black communities of the North to help overcome the obstacles of racial discrimination? How did individuals in the South resist slavery? What was the role of African American churches in building strong communities among free blacks in the North?*

▶ Draw upon arguments such as those offered by Abigail Adams's letters to John Adams (1776), Mary Wollstonecraft's *Vindication of the Rights of Women* (1792) and Judith Sargent Murray in "The Gleaner" (1798) to analyze how women's quest for new roles and rights for their gender continued to evolve, the extent to which they were successful in gaining new educational and political rights in the years following 1776 and the degree to which they were able to enter the public realm.

> **III.** *The institutions and practices of government created during the revolution and how they were revised between 1787 and 1815 to create the foundation of the American political system based on the U.S. Constitution and Bill of Rights.*

A. The issues involved in the creation and ratification of the United States Constitution and the new government it established.

Grades 5-6

- Draw upon a variety of historical sources such as biographies and narratives of the Constitutional Convention to construct a description of delegates such as George Washington, James Madison, Alexander Hamilton, James Wilson, and George Mason. Explain why they were assembled in Philadelphia and assess the importance of their work.

- Role-play a session at the Philadelphia Convention in which representatives of large and small states debated the Virginia and New Jersey plans. Draw evidence from sources such as *If You Were There When They Signed the Constitution* by Elizabeth Levy. *Why did the large states support the Virginia Plan? What was the Connecticut Compromise?*

- Compare the interests of those delegates who opposed and those who defended slavery, and explain the consequences of the compromises over slavery.

- Apply their understanding of the Constitutional separation of powers and system of checks and balances by constructing a flowchart, diagram, or narrative demonstrating the checks each branch of government can exert on the other two.

- Examine the importance of Shays's Rebellion in the decision to call for a convention to amend the Articles of Confederation. Draw evidence from a variety of sources including historical fiction such as *The Winter Hero* by Christopher Collier and James Collier.

- Describe the effects of the United States concept of democracy and individual rights on other nations. *How has the U.S. Constitution and Bill of Rights influenced other national constitutions?*

- Explain what it means to define our society as an "unfinished experiment in democracy" and the features in the Constitution that facilitate this ongoing process of creation. Analyze how Article Five of the Constitution makes changes in our government possible and discuss why relatively few changes have been made to the Constitution.

Grades 7-8

- Explain how fears over Shays's Rebellion contributed to the national call for a constitutional convention.

- Draw upon their understandings of the great debates and the compromises achieved by the delegates in order to construct a sound historical argument or narrative on questions such as the following: *Within the context of the late 18th century, were the compromises reached by the delegates reasonable? Were these compromises necessary in order to obtain approval of the Constitution?*

- Analyze the way in which power and responsibility are distributed, shared, and limited in the government established by the Constitution. Explain the ways in which it places limits on the governed as well as on those who govern. Consider the ways in which the Constitution is forever unfinished as a consequence of Article Five.

▶ Investigate the roles and influence of leading proponents and opponents of the Constitution at the Philadelphia Convention, including such persons as James Madison, Alexander Hamilton, William Paterson, James Wilson, George Mason, Edmond Randolph, and Charles Cotesworth Pinckney.

Grades 9-12

▶ Develop a sound historical narrative explaining the source and nature of the basic principles behind the separation of powers and the system of checks and balances established by the Constitution.

▶ Develop a sound historical argument on such questions as: *To what extent were the compromises reached in the Constitutional Convention the result of 18th-century republican ideals held by the delegates and to what extent were they the result of deep-rooted economic and political interests of the regions they represented?*

▶ Compare and analyze the major arguments for and against the Constitution of 1787 in leading Federalist and Anti-Federalist writings and major ratification debates.

▶ Analyze the differences between leading Federalists and Anti-Federalists in terms of their background, service during the Revolution, and political experience, and develop a historical argument concerning how these influences shaped their positions on such issues as individual rights, republican government, federalism, separation of powers, and popular sovereignty.

▶ Analyze a recent presidential election to demonstrate what elements of Anti-Federalist thought surfaced in party platforms, state initiatives, and candidate speeches.

▶ Examine the influence of the U.S. Constitution on the structure of democratic governments in other parts of the world. *What are the essential aspects of the U.S. Constitution that have been adopted by other governments?*

B. The guarantees of the Bill of Rights and its continuing significance.

Grades 5-6

▶ Develop sound arguments explaining and illustrating the importance of at least three guarantees in the Bill of Rights.

▶ Using art reproductions, photographs, or cartoons illustrate the relevance of the Bill of Rights in today's society.

▶ Research the roles of prominent Virginians such as George Mason and James Madison in the development of the Bill of Rights.

Grades 7-8

▶ Specify and explain the importance of the basic guarantees incorporated in the Bill of Rights. *Which do you feel is the most important guarantee? Why?*

▶ Compare the Virginia Declaration of Rights (1776) with that of other states such as Pennsylvania (1776) or Massachusetts (1780). *How do state declarations of rights compare to the U.S. Bill of Rights adopted in 1791? What accounts for these similarities and differences?*

▶ Draw evidence from primary and secondary sources to explain why the Anti-Federalists argued for the incorporation of a Bill of Rights in the Constitution. *What did they mean by a Bill of Rights? Were the Anti-Federalist suggestions incorporated into the Bill of Rights?*

▶ Construct classroom learning stations or collages incorporating illustrations and short quotations to examine the historical context and contemporary application of the Bill of Rights. Draw evidence from sources such as the Center for Civic Education's *We the People* and *With Liberty and Justice for All.*

Grades 9-12

▶ Draw evidence from "Federalist 84," James Madison's letter to Thomas Jefferson (October, 1788), Jefferson's response, and selections from the Anti-Federalist Papers to explain the arguments presented in the debate over whether there was a need for a Bill of Rights. *Was a Bill of Rights necessary? Why or why not?*

▶ Draw upon historical data and the Bill of Rights to construct a sound historical argument on such questions as: *Were the Alien and Sedition acts of 1798 and the arrest and imprisonment of critics of the Adams administration such as Benjamin Franklin Bache and Matthew Lyon violations of the First Amendment or were they justified by the crises confronting the new nation? Might these events have taken a different turn if the 1803 principle of judicial review had been developed at that time?*

▶ Using historical data and the First Amendment to the Bill of Rights, analyze the reasons why the Alien and Sedition Acts were passed and appraise their significance. *To what extent were the Alien and Sedition Acts a violation of the Bill of Rights? How did the Federalist party justify the need for the acts? Why did they feel it did not violate the Bill of Rights? How did they affect the growth of the Democratic-Republican Party? Were the Virginia and Kentucky Resolutions opposed to the restriction of rights under the Alien and Sedition Acts or were they concerned about the nature of federalism?*

C. The development of the Supreme Court's power and its significance from 1789 to 1820.

Grades 5-6

▶ Investigate the career of John Marshall and explain his importance as Chief Justice of the United States Supreme Court. *How difficult was it to be a "circuit rider" in the early 19th century?*

▶ Write a skit about the "Midnight Judges" and explain why president-elect Jefferson was upset with these last-minute appointments by President Adams.

▶ Explain what is meant by judicial review.

Grades 7-8

▶ Identify the powers and responsibilities of the Supreme Court set forth in Article III of the Constitution and in the Judiciary Act of 1789 which confers the power of judicial review of acts of state governments.

▶ Discuss why *Marbury* v. *Madison* is considered a landmark decision of the Supreme Court.

▶ Compare the power and significance of the Supreme Court in 1800 and 1820. *How did Chief Justice Marshall contribute to the growth of the Court's importance in relationship to the other two branches of the federal government?*

Grades 9-12

▶ Review *Marbury* v. *Madison* (1803) and at least one other major case such as *Fletcher* v. *Peck* (1810), *Dartmouth College* v. *Woodward* (1819) or *Gibbons* v. *Ogden* (1824) in order to construct a sound historical argument concerning how Chief Justice Marshall's decisions established important legal precedents and strengthened the role of the Supreme Court as an equal branch of government.

▶ Draw evidence from Marshall's decision in *McCulloch* v. *Maryland* to construct an argument or historical narrative appraising the position of the national government vis-à-vis state governments. *To what extent does McCulloch v. Maryland strengthen the powers of the national government? How does the decision impact the interpretation of the Constitution?*

▶ Consider the impact of the Marshall Court's decisions about contract and property rights on the growth of interstate trade and the development of national economy. *Which groups would tend to favor strengthening judicial protection of economic bargains?*

D. The development of the first American party system.

Grades 5-6

▶ Construct a project in the form of a classroom newspaper, skit, or role-play activity which examines the positions of George Washington, Alexander Hamilton, and Thomas Jefferson on a major issue confronting the new nation.

▶ Draw upon historical evidence and fictional accounts of the Whiskey Rebellion such as *Beyond the Allegheny* by Betty Koch to describe the issues which impacted the lives of farmers in western Pennsylvania.

Grades 7-8

▶ Identify the central economic issues of the 1790s on which people with varying economic interests and regional ties held different views and construct an argument regarding how these differences contributed to the development of the Federalists and the Democratic-Republicans.

▶ Prepare a list of probing questions to determine the policies advocated by leaders of the Federalist and Democratic-Republican parties, and through a "meeting of the minds" or "point counter-point" format debate the effectiveness of their positions on prominent issues.

▶ Analyze the social and economic bases of the two emerging political parties.

▶ Evaluate the role of ordinary people in the Whiskey Rebellion and in demonstrations against Jay's Treaty. *What were the causes of the Whiskey Rebellion? How were the demonstrations against the whiskey tax similar to those of the revolutionary period against British taxation? What were the differences? Why did western farmers object to the Jay Treaty?*

▶ Discuss the bitterly fought presidential election of 1800, including President John Adams's appointment of "midnight judges." *What were the issues in the election of 1800? During the campaign why was Jefferson accused of advocating anarchy and destroying Christian principles? Was Adams's appointment of Federalist judges in the last days of his administration appropriate?*

▶ Assuming the role of a Federalist or Democratic-Republican, write a position paper explaining your political party's views on Revolutionary France in 1789. Explain any changes in your viewpoint as the Revolution entered into the "Reign of Terror."

Grades 9-12

▶ Draw upon historical data disclosing the viewpoints of different constituencies in the North, South, and West concerning Hamilton's plans for promoting the economic development of the new nation. Construct a historical argument or debate in defense or opposition to Hamilton's plans from the viewpoint of several of these regional constituencies.

▶ Draw upon historical documents such as Jefferson's critique of Hamilton's economic program, Patrick Henry's "Resolution on the Assumption of State Debts," and the Hamilton-Jefferson disagreement on the constitutionality of the Bank of the United States. *What was the nature of the objections to Hamilton's financial plan? On what grounds did Hamilton use the "necessary and proper" clause of Article I, Section 8 of the Constitution to argue for the establishment of a national bank? How did Jefferson use the same clause to argue that a federally funded bank was unconstitutional? Who would benefit from the Bank of the United States? Who would benefit from funding the debt at par value?*

▶ Explain how differences concerning support for the French Revolution, foreign policy issues (such as the Gênet affair, the Jay and Pinckney treaties, the XYZ Affair, the undeclared war with France), and immigration contributed to the emergence of an organized opposition party led by Jefferson and Madison.

◆ Examine the social and economic make-up of the membership of the Federalist and Democratic-Republican parties in the 1790s. *To what extent does the social and economic status of the leadership of each of the two parties reflect their membership? Who would be most likely to support the Federalists? The Democratic-Republicans?*

◆ Analyze the factors which led to the Whiskey Rebellion and evaluate the following quotations from two political antagonists.

> *"An insurrection was announced and proclaimed and armed against, but could never be found."*
>   Thomas Jefferson

> Suppressing the rebellion *"will do us a great deal of good and add to the solidity of everything in this country."*
>   Alexander Hamilton

Was the government overreacting to the "Whiskey Rebels" or was the rebellion a threat to the security of the nation? Why or why not? Was the Whiskey Rebellion a confrontation between "haves" and "have-nots"? Compare the grievances of the "Whiskey Rebels" to those of the Regulators, Paxton Boys, and Shaysites.

Woodcut illustration of "A New Touch on the Times. Well adapted to the Distressing Situation of Every Seaport Town. By a Daughter of Liberty, Living in Marblehead" (1779). Courtesy The New York Historical Society.

ERA 4

Expansion and Reform (1801-1861)

The new American republic prior to the Civil War experienced dramatic territorial expansion, immigration, economic growth, and industrialization. The increasing complexity of American society, the growth of regionalism, and the cross-currents of change that are often bewildering require the development of several major themes to enable students to sort their way through the six decades that brought the United States to the eve of the Civil War.

One theme is the vast territorial expansion between 1800 and 1861, as restless Americans pushed westward across the Appalachians, then across the Mississippi, and finally on to the Pacific Ocean. Students should study how Americans, animated by land hunger, the ideology of "Manifest Destiny," and the optimism that anything was possible with imagination, hard work, and the maximum freedom of the individual, flocked to the western frontier. While studying how the frontier experience indelibly stamped the American character, students should explore its ambivalent aspects: the removal of many Indian nations in the Southeast and old Northwest, acquisition of a large part of Mexico through the Mexican-American War, and abrasive encounters with Native Americans, Mexicans, Chinese immigrants, and others in the West.

A second theme confronts the economic development of the expanding American republic—a complex and fascinating process that on the one hand created the sinews of national identity but on the other hand fueled growing regional tensions. In the North, the first stage of industrialization brings students face to face with the role of technology in historical change and how economic development has had profound environmental effects. In studying the rise of immigrant-filled cities, the "transportation revolution" involving railroads, canals, and trans-regional roads, the creation of a national market system, and the proliferation of family farming in newly opened territories, students will appreciate how Tocqueville might have reached the conclusion that the Americans seemed at one time "animated by the most selfish cupidity; at another by the most lively patriotism." In studying the expanding South, students must understand the enormous growth of slavery as an exploitive and morally corrupt economic and social system; but they should also comprehend how millions of African Americans struggled to shape their own lives as much as possible through family, religion, and resistance to slavery.

A third theme interwoven with the two themes above, can be organized around the extension, restriction, and reorganization of political democracy after 1800. The rise of the second party system and modern interest-group politics mark the advent of modern politics in the United States. However, students will see that the evolution of political democracy was not a smooth, one-way street as free African Americans were disenfranchised in much of the North and woman's suffrage was blocked even while white male suffrage spread throughout the states and into the newly developed territories.

Connected to all of the above is the theme of reform, for the rapid transformation and expansion of the American economy brought forth one of the greatest bursts of reformism in American history. Emerson captured the vibrancy of this era in asking, "What is man born for but to be a reformer." Students will find that the attempts to complete unfinished agendas of the revolutionary period and to fashion new reforms necessitated by the rise of factory labor and rapid urbanization partook of the era's democratic spirit and religious faith and yet also reflected the compulsion of well-positioned Americans to restore order to a turbulent society.

Essay

Women and the New Western History*
by Susan Armitage

The "New Western History," mostly the work of this generation of historians, has challenged many hoary myths about the western experience. We need not be alarmed that some of this scholarship has produced controversy. Students can benefit from understanding that new research—in any field—is likely to ruffle the feathers of those who cling to older versions of their discipline. In this essay, Susan Armitage shows that by studying relatively unexplored groups in the West (women in this case) we almost necessarily arrive at new understandings of "how the West was won." Rather than conceiving as the western frontier as a barrier dividing white Americans pushing west from Native Americans, the new western historians show that the frontier was a broad intercultural zone where people from various cultural backgrounds mixed and mingled, traded and fought, borrowed culturally from each other, forged new identities, and struggled for power. Armitage asks us to open our eyes to see how deeply and irrevocably women were involved in this complex meeting of different peoples.

Susan Armitage is Professor of History and Director of American Studies at Washington State University. She is the coeditor of *The Women's West* and *So Much to be Done.*

During the past five years, the "New Western History" has greatly changed the way historians view the West. One of its most surprising insights has been that the West, far from being an empty land awaiting the rapid settlement of white pioneers, has always been the most diverse and multiracial "meeting ground of peoples" in American history. The diversity of peoples in the West encompasses Native Americans and the Spanish Mexicans who pioneered New Spain's northern frontier; Hawaiians and Canadian Métis in the fur trade; European-American, Asian, Mexican and European ethnic migrants and immigrants in the nineteenth and twentieth centuries; and African Americans who were some of the earliest and the most recent migrants. The West, it appears, offers a historical model of multicultural race relations that is much more complex than the customary biracial model derived from the history of the American South. The conflict, collusion, and mingling of peoples in the American West cannot be told without women as an integral part of the story. Indeed, gender issues are fundamental to the notion of meetings between different peoples.

We need to begin by thinking clearly about the range of meanings encompassed in the phrase "meeting ground of peoples." Meetings can be peaceful or violent, and they can result in destruction, amalgamation, or any number of mixed outcomes between these extremes. Because of the way most western history has been written, we think first of violent conflict—Indian wars, in particular—and of the rapid European-American conquest of the western part of the continent in the mid to late nineteenth century. But, this nineteenth-century focus leads to a simple and truncated view of western history. A longer, more gendered perspective yields a much more complicated and fascinating story of real people of one cultural group, encumbered with their own ideas about race and gender, meeting strangers with different cultural ideas. Let's look first at the impact of some meetings on the first western women: Native American women.

Trade and Conquest. There are numerous unknown historical aspects of Native American cultures in the very long period before European contact. We do know, however, that there

---

*Reprinted from *Magazine of History*, Vol. 9, No. 1 (Fall 1994), pp. 22-26, with permission from the Organization of American Historians.

were many different groups, and we can assume that some of the relationships between them were peaceful and some hostile. Trade represented one means by which women from different groups acted peaceably, bringing diverse cultures together. Women produced many of the goods traded between different Native American groups; such goods included tanned hides, sewn and decorated clothing, and food crops. As producers they usually controlled the terms of the trade itself. Women as well as men participated in the large yearly intertribal trade rendezvous at sites like the Dalles on the Columbia River and the Mandan villages on the upper Missouri. As historians fully realize the size and complexity of these peaceful precontact trade relationships, we will better appreciate the activities of Native American women as traders.

It was, however, rare for a Native American tribe to live continuously at peace with all of its neighbors. The possibility of capture put women at extreme risk in hostile situations. War parties prized women and young children; invaders usually killed adult males whom they considered too dangerous and troublesome. Captive women had several benefits, especially as workers and as childbearers. They added to both the productive and reproductive capacity of their captors. Captivity, rather than death, was the most common fate of women when Native American societies warred with each other. As one can see from these two examples, women were valued for their sexuality as well as for their abilities to produce and trade.

In contrast, European contact brought with it an almost exclusive emphasis solely on the sexuality of native women. For example, Spanish men mixed freely with Indian women, thus creating the Mexican people in the early sixteenth century. Similarly, in the Canadian West, unions between Indian women and European fur trappers of the Hudson's Bay and Northwest Companies created the Métis (literally "mixed" in French). And in the nineteenth-century United States West, the mixed-race offspring of American trappers and traders and their Indian wives were more numerous than most European-American settlers, conditioned to think in rigid black and white terms, recognized. Nevertheless, the rapid European-American settlement of the American West forestalled the growth of the mixed race or mestizo population that would undoubtedly have occurred otherwise.

Women's sexuality played an important role in European conquest in other ways as well. It is well documented that Spanish-Mexican soldiers in Spanish California and New Mexico used rape as a weapon of conquest. Intermarriage, too, served as a tool of conquest. European-American traders, eager to advance economically, often married the daughters of the Spanish-Mexican elite in California, New Mexico, and Texas before 1848. Women of Northwest Indian coastal groups traded furs with American and British ships, and soon found themselves trading sex as well as sea otter pelts. Europeans, unaccustomed to women in trading roles, uniformly labelled the women's sexual activity as prostitution. Captivity practiced by Europeans as well as Native Americans and ransom of both Indian and Spanish-Mexican women were two important elements in the relationship between native groups and Spanish-Mexican settlements in colonial New Mexico. The most famous captive came from the Northern Plains. Sacajawea, a Shoshone girl captured by the Hidatsa and later traded to the French-Canadian Charbonneau accompanied the Lewis and Clark expedition of 1804.

As these examples show, the first and most common result of the "meetings" of Europeans and indigenous peoples in the American West was sexual contact between interloping males and native women. These sexual contacts may have been as forcible as rape or as mutual and formal as an elaborate church wedding. In either case, the result was the engendering of new, mixed-race offspring.

Communities. Although the history of the West is often tied up with military ventures, neither the concept of "victory" nor "defeat" on the field of battle adequately describes the complex relationships between cultural groups. We must look beyond the battle itself to its aftermath. In the West the creation and segregation of distinct racial groups followed the Mexican-American War of 1846 to 1848, the Indian wars of the 1870s, and the Chinese Exclusion Act of 1882. Native Americans were herded together (sometimes with former enemies) onto reservations. Mexican Americans of different ancestry were, with the exception of a small number of elites, treated as a monolithic, subordinate group throughout the region that was now called the American Southwest. Asians were restricted or excluded from emigrating to the United States on the basis of race. Finally, European Americans were divided by ethnicity but united in their confident racial superiority over the subordinated groups. Women of all races and ethnicities played central roles in the creation and continuation of the different cultural groups. Learning ways in which women culturally survived and adapted offers us a way to think specifically and deeply about the continuous process of change that everyone—"winners" and "losers" alike—experienced in the settlement of the West.

Events surrounding the Chinese Exclusion Act of 1882 provide the clearest examples of the differences women made. Large numbers of Chinese men first came to the United States in the 1860s to build the Central Pacific railroad. (The first transcontinental rail link was completed in 1869.) When many Chinese subsequently moved into agriculture, they met a wall of prejudice that culminated in the Chinese Exclusion Act of 1882 which admitted only diplomats and members of their immediate families, students and teachers, and merchants. Laborers already in the United States, many of whom had wives in China, were unable to bring their spouses to the United States. Thus, federal legislation skewed the normal press of settlement and the Chinese in America were subsequently characterized and reviled for the very "bachelor society" that United States laws had created. In addition, western states passed antimiscengenation laws outlawing intermarriage between Chinese (later Filipino and Japanese) men and European-American women. These immigration and marriage laws remained in force until after World War II, thereby preventing the vast majority of Asian immigrants from building communities with the promise of continuity through the generations.

The community-building activities of European-American women have not yet been fully documented. This is partly because the boisterous boosterism of male business interests in western towns drowned out the evidence of smaller-scale and more informal efforts by women. Historians are just now beginning to recognize the extent of women's activities as they study the vast network of women's clubs that stretched across the West in the nineteenth century.

A more basic reason for the dearth of research on women's community building in the West is that many studies of European-American pioneer women still suffer from the what might be called the "snapshot fallacy." Because of historians' fascination with the initial experiences of settlement, and because of the nature of existing sources, many have often forgotten to ask what happened after the first encounter with the West. Those first reactions have left some vivid vignettes like this one from Kansas:

> When our covered wagon drew up beside the door of the one-roomed sod
> house that father had provided, he helped mother down and I remember how
> her face looked as she gazed about that barren farm, then threw her arms
> about his neck and gave way to the only fit of weeping I ever remember seeing her indulge in.

Women's dismayed reactions to the initial hardships of settlement loom larger than they would have if they had been seen from the longer perspective of an entire lifetime. Although it certainly is important to explore the specific difficulties pioneer women faced, one should also realize that if the analyses stop there, we merely perpetuate the stereotype of European-American women as reluctant pioneers, unable to adapt to the rough-and-ready masculine West.

Some of the fullest accounts of female community-building have resulted from studying women of color. In Colorado during the early part of the twentieth century, women maintained Dearfield, a Black homesteading community while their men raised cash through wage work. As one woman recalled, "the Negro women, of course, were the backbone of the church, the backbone of the family, they were the backbone of the social life, everything." Similarly, the success of Hispañas in maintaining their communities in northern New Mexico while the men were away doing distant wage work clearly indicates that the definition of "community" needs to be wider and less place-specific. A new definition that encompasses long-distance relationships will cause some rethinking of classic western figures like the "single" men who participated in the West's many gold rushes. European-American women's letters and diaries reveal that many of these men were supported, financially as well as emotionally, by the wives they left behind. Women not only kept farms and businesses going while the men were away, but they also did their best to stay in communication by mail and in some cases even sent money to help unsuccessful goldseekers.

By far the most common intercultural experience of women of color was that of defending their families and communities from the interference of European Americans bent on "civilizing" them. The cultural damage done by missionary efforts to Native Americans—boarding schools, for example—has been well documented, and there are a few biographies of women such as the Paiute woman, Sarah Winnemucca, who attempted to act as cultural brokers between their people and European-American officials. However, we have only recently realized the rich cultural and historical insights available at the "cultural crossroads" where women of different races and classes meet. The bonds of gender, which strongly attracted many European-American women to interracial reform and humanitarian efforts in the West, were offset by racial, class, and cultural differences between women of which the reformers were often unaware. A number of women's historians are now studying the complex process in which *both* sides of the exchange adapted to, resisted, and changed each other. The richness of the first few historical studies of western women in these "relations of rescue" attests to the promise of work still to come.

Migration and Work. Studying successive waves of migration to the West and the ways in which immigrant families adapted to the people already there provides yet another way by which we can think of the West as a "meeting ground of peoples."

For too long, western historians were preoccupied with "pioneers," by which they meant only the first European American to settle in a particular town or region. This made it very hard to get western history out of the nineteenth century. One happy result of the New Western History is a new appreciation of the continuities between nineteenth- and twentieth-century western history, especially the similarity between the experience of twentieth-century immigrants to that of the fabled nineteenth-century pioneers. In the broadest sense, issues of adaptation are similar over time; what changes is the extent and effectiveness of opposition from earlier peoples, whether it be Red Cloud and the Sioux who closed the Bozeman Trail to goldseekers in 1866, or the Anti-Asiatic Association that opposed Japanese land-ownership on the west coast in the 1920s. Indeed, one author gave her recent study of an agricultural community founded by Japanese immigrants the title, *Farming the Home Place*, a phrase clearly meant to underline the basic continuities of immigration and settlement.

The linked concepts of work and family are essential for historians who wish to compare the successive waves of immigration to the West. Asian-American and Chicañoa/o historians have taken the lead in western labor studies. They have expanded the regional boundaries of traditional western history by linking the work patterns of (mostly male) racial and ethnic immigrants to international labor movements. Studies of the wage work of Asian and Chicaña women have, in their turn, provided the field of women's labor movements with valuable comparisons with the industrial work of Italian, Jewish, Slavic, and other immigrant women in the East. Comparative study of the work available to immigrant women provides a new source of insight into the ways in which different regions of the United States have structured racial and class differences.

In a different way, recognition of the limited range of wage work available to European-American women in the West well into the twentieth century has led to other comparisons which at first seemed startling. Horace Greeley doubtless did not realize how gender-specific he was when he urged opportunity-seekers to "Go West, young man." Because of the economic underdevelopment of the West, the place of economic opportunity for the single woman was not the West but the eastern city. This observation has led to the realization that popularly-held myths about the West as the site of freedom and opportunity were deeply gendered. It also raised the question of the nature of opportunity for western women.

One clear answer to this question was that opportunity for women in the West was often not so much individual as familial. Native Americans, long-settled and recent Mexicanas, and immigrant families of all races and time periods have all worked for and with their families over the span of western history. As we have seen, the most common unit of economic survival and adaptation was not the solitary man but, rather, the family. One must agree with Kathleen Neils Conzen's forthright summation that "a family story lies at the heart of American western history." Women are central to the study of family adaptation to the land and to other peoples. In all societies, women's work has included a commitment to the future: to nurture the next generation and transmit the central messages of the culture to them. This was as true in the American West as elsewhere, but the task was complicated by the fluid patterns of conquest, migration, and intermingling of peoples that continue to make the West a "meeting ground of peoples." Exploring and explaining women's activities in the multicultural arenas described in this essay—and rewriting western history to reflect those findings—will keep western history new for many years to come.

Sample Student Activities

I. *United States territorial expansion between 1801 and 1861, and how it affected relations with external powers and Native Americans.*

A. The international background and consequences of the Louisiana Purchase, War of 1812, and the Monroe Doctrine.

Grades 5-6

▶ Identify the boundaries of United States and French territorial claims in the Western Hemisphere in 1801 and compare with the boundaries of the U.S. following the Louisiana Purchase. *Why did Napoleon agree to sell the Louisiana territory to the United States?*

▶ Examine the achievements of the Meriwether Lewis and William Clark expedition using sources such as *Bold Journey: West with Lewis and Clark* by Charles Bohner, *Streams to the River, Rivers to the Sea* by Scott O'Dell and *Sacagawea: Indian Interpreter to Lewis and Clark* by Marion Marsh Brown.

▶ Draw upon journals, maps, stories, and other historical records to assess the influence of such explorers and mountain men as Zebulon Pike, John C. Frémont, Jedediah Smith, James Beckwourth, and Kit Carson. *Would the development of the United States have been different if these men had not blazed the trails and provided the information used by the thousands of settlers who moved west?*

▶ Draw upon maps of the Western Hemisphere showing territories held by Spain, France, Britain, and Russia in 1800 and locate the nations that declared their independence by 1823. *How did President Monroe propose to deal with attempts by Europe to reestablish their control in the hemisphere?*

▶ Explain why the War of 1812 is often called the Second War for Independence. *Who were the leading American heroes of the war? How important was General Andrew Jackson's victory at the Battle of New Orleans?*

▶ Assume the role of a young adult during the War of 1812, and through a diary or journal write firsthand accounts of memorable events during the conflict. *How would a British soldier, Shawnee, or Creek report on these same events?*

▶ Assume the role of Francis Scott Key and describe the British attack on Fort McHenry on the night of September 13, 1814. *What do the words of Key's poem tell about his feelings about the United States?*

Grades 7-8

▶ Develop a historical argument whether or not the War of 1812 helped to unite the new nation. *Why did New Englanders oppose the war? Why did the War Hawks want to move against Native Americans in the Northwest Territory? Was the war a "Second War for Independence," a war of expansion, or a war for maritime rights?*

▶ Construct a historical argument assessing the case for and against the acquisition of Louisiana. *What effect did war in Europe and black rebellion in Haiti have on France's decision to sell Louisiana? Why did Jefferson believe that the Louisiana Purchase provided the opportunity for an "Empire of Liberty"? Why did Senator Samuel White (Delaware) refer to the Louisiana Purchase as "the greatest curse that could befall us"? What were the advantages and disadvantages of doubling the territorial holdings of the United States?*

▶ Draw upon evidence from the diaries of Lewis and Clark to construct a historical narrative assessing the importance of the newly acquired Louisiana Territory and analyze the effects of the expedition. *Why is it considered one of the most successful scientific expeditions in United States history? How did it contribute to friendly relations with Native Americans in the region? What were its long-term effects?*

▶ Construct a historical argument on the impact of territorial expansion from the perspective of different Native American societies. *How did the acquisition of the Louisiana Territory affect Native Americans in the region?*

▶ Explain the diplomatic problems facing the U.S. as a result of the renewal of English-French hostilities, including their seizure of American ships, English impressment of American sailors into the English navy, and economic losses in trade.

▶ Analyze the causes of the War of 1812 by drawing upon evidence from a variety of primary sources, including excerpts from Henry Clay's speeches, President James Madison's declaration of war, and Congressional debates. *Was the war a "Second War for Independence," a war of expansion, or a war for maritime rights?*

▶ Explain the interests and actions of Native Americans in different regions of the country during the war of 1812. Use Tecumseh's speeches in recruiting Indian allies between 1809 and 1811 to explain the Native American perspective on the encroachment of white settlers on tribal lands. *Why did Tecumseh join with the British during the War of 1812? What did he hope to achieve by an English victory?*

▶ Place the Monroe Doctrine in its historical context and explain its major provisions and significance. *Why did President James Monroe issue a statement regarding Latin American independence? Was the Monroe Doctrine a departure from earlier foreign policy? What was its historical significance? What is its impact today?*

Grades 9-12

▶ Assemble evidence on such matters as the black rebellion in Haiti, French losses in the Santo Domingo campaign, pending hostilities with Great Britain, and American opponents to French designs on New Orleans in order to create a position paper or argument such as French Minister Talleyrand might have developed in 1803 to advise Napoleon to sell all of Louisiana to the United States.

▶ Assemble the evidence and develop a historical narrative on such questions as: *How did President Jefferson, a strict constructionist, devotee of limited government, and frugality in terms of government spending, justify the purchase of Louisiana? On what grounds did many New England Federalists justify their opposition to the purchase? What were the consequences of the Louisiana Purchase in terms of economic development, slavery, and politics?*

▶ Analyze the responses of Presidents Jefferson and Madison to impressment and the harassment of U.S. shipping prior to the outbreak of the War of 1812. *How effective were the Embargo Act, Macon's Bill No. 2, and the Nonintercourse Act? What was the domestic political and economic impact of the Embargo Act? Why was it repealed?*

▶ Create a historical argument that explains the opposing positions of Congressmen from Pennsylvania, the South, and the West in supporting the war resolution of June 3, 1812. *Why did representatives from New England and the mid-Atlantic states vote against it even though President Madison's war message focused on the maritime issues most directly affecting their interests?*

▶ Research the various interests of Native Americans during the war of 1812 and explain why some nations supported the British while others joined with the United States. *What impact did the opening of the Old Northwest territory have on Native America? How did the support of some Indian nations for the British feed war fever? Why did the Cherokee remain neutral? Why did the Cherokee join General Jackson against the Red Stick Creeks at Horseshoe Bend? Why did Jackson recruit the Choctaw to assist in the defense of New Orleans? What were the consequences of the war on Indian nations in the Northwest and South?*

▶ Draw data from the Hartford Convention resolutions to explain New England's resentment of the war. *If the war of 1812 was fought to guarantee rights on the "high seas," as Madison maintained, why did New England oppose the war? Were the proposed constitutional amendments reasonable? How do the sectional interests expressed at the Hartford Convention compare with those of the Kentucky and Virginia Resolutions of 1798? Why was the Hartford Convention considered the death-knell of the Federalist party?*

▶ Analyze the reasons why individuals in different regions of the country supported the War of 1812 and viewed it as a "Second War of Independence." *What were the grievances that led the United States to go to war? Why did residents of the Northwest and the South support the war effort?*

▶ Draw on historical sources, maps, and documents in order to analyze the three major provisions of the Monroe Doctrine and their significance. *To what extent was the major purpose of the Monroe Doctrine to protect the newly won independence of Latin American states? Why did the U.S. and other countries ignore the provisions of the Monroe Doctrine for so long?*

B. Federal and state Indian policy and the strategies for survival forged by Native Americans.

Grades 5-6

▶ On a map, identify (1) the original lands in the Old Northwest Territory occupied by the Shawnee, Miami, and Pottawatomie, and (2) the Seminole, Creek, Cherokee, Chickasaw, and Choctaw nations of the Southeast.

▶ Draw upon stories and historical accounts of such leaders as Tecumseh, the Prophet, and Black Hawk in order to develop a historical narrative, news report, or story of the Native American efforts to hold on to their lands and return to the ways of their ancestors.

▶ Examine personal stories of the Trail of Tears using such sources as *Only the Names Remain: The Cherokee and the Trail of Tears* by Alex Bealer, and *Yunini's Story of the Trail of Tears* by Ada Loomis Barry.

Grades 7-8

▶ Draw upon evidence from biographies and other historical sources to appraise the survival strategies employed by Native Americans such as John Ross, Sequoyah, Tenskwatwa (the Shawnee prophet), Tecumseh, Osceola, and Black Hawk.

▶ Draw upon the Cherokee Nation and Worcester cases before the U.S. Supreme Court in order to compare state and federal policy towards Native Americans. *What were Georgia's apparent motives in passing laws governing the Cherokees? How did Georgia respond to the Marshall Court's decisions in the two cases? What factors contributed to President Jackson's opposition to the Court's decisions?*

▶ Examine ways in which the Cherokee adopted the values and lifestyles of the southern gentry.

▶ Use a physical map of the United States to compare the topography and climate of Cherokee and Choctaw lands in the southeastern United States with resettlement areas in western Arkansas and eastern Oklahoma. *How did the geography of the two regions differ? How would the region's topography, climate, and resources affect Cherokee and Choctaw societies?*

▶ Draw evidence from historical fiction such as *In the Shadow of the Wind* by Luke Wallin, *Sequoyah and the Cherokee Alphabet* by Robert Cwiklik, and *No Resting Place* by William Humphrey to examine accounts of the removal of the Creek and Cherokee to Oklahoma in the 1830s.

▶ Examine Robert Lindneux's 1942 painting, *"The Trail of Tears." Is Lindneux's painting an accurate or a romanticized account of "The Trail of Tears"?*

Grades 9-12

▶ Analyze the U.S. government's changing policies toward Native Americans from an assimilationist strategy in the early 19th century to removal and isolation after 1825. *Were the policies of Indian removal announced by President Monroe in his last annual message (December 1824) and implemented by President Jackson the result of Jeffersonian paternalism toward Native Americans or a decided reorientation of U.S. policy? Did Northerners, Southerners, and Westerners agree in regard to policy toward Native Americans or were there clear-cut sectional and/or political differences? How, for example, did northern Whigs respond to removal, and why?*

▶ Compare and evaluate the arguments in favor of removal advanced by President Jackson in his second annual message and the arguments against removal advanced by Native American leaders such as Chief John Ross in his 1836 message to Congress. *Why did Jackson refuse to enforce the Supreme Court's decision in the Worcester case on the state of Georgia?*

▶ Using selections from primary and secondary sources, including articles from the *Cherokee Phoenix*, describe Cherokee values, their integration of European culture, and their resistance to removal. *How do stories regarding the sacrifices on the "Trail of Tears" help one understand Cherokee adaptation and resistance? How did the Cherokee define law, property rights, heroism, and freedom?*

▶ Examine the Black Hawk War and federal and state removal policies in the Old Northwest. Compare the removal of Indians of the Old Northwest to that of the Cherokees and Choctaws of the Southeast.

C. The ideology of Manifest Destiny, the nation's expansion to the Northwest, and the Mexican-American War.

Grades 5-6

▶ Draw upon biographies of such individuals as Stephen F. Austin, Davey Crockett, Jim Bowie, William Travis, and Sam Houston to explain the resistance to Mexican authority in Texas. Write accounts of the defense of the Alamo from the perspectives of one of its defenders and a Mexican soldier.

▶ Draw evidence from historical novels such as *The Far Battleground* by F. M. Parker and *The Dunderhead War* by Betty Baker to investigate personal stories of the Mexican-American War. Analyze the events that led to war with Mexico. *What could President Polk and the Mexican government have done to prevent war?*

▶ Analyze why the people known as "expansionists" believed that it was the nation's destiny to stretch "from sea to shining sea." *How might life be different in Mexico and in the U.S. today if these lands had not become part of the United States?*

Grades 7-8

▶ Draw upon documents such as John O'Sullivan's editorial (1845), Major Auguste Davezac's speech of 1846, and lithograph of Currier & Ives, "Westward the Course of Empire," and John Gast's later painting "America's Progress" to construct a historical narrative explaining the ethos of Manifest Destiny and its appeal to 19th-century American industrial workers and small farmers.

▶ Interpret documentary evidence from maps, political speeches, diaries, and letters to construct sound historical arguments, debates, or narratives on such questions relating to the Mexican-American War as: *What role did the annexation of Texas and the American desire for California play in leading to the outbreak of war between Mexico and the United States? Was the war justified? On what grounds did such critics as Abraham Lincoln, Frederick Douglass, and Henry David Thoreau oppose the war? On what grounds did supporters of President Polk's policies justify going to war? To what extent did the terms of the Treaty of Guadalupe Hidalgo reflect the spirit of Manifest Destiny?*

▶ Identify the issues surrounding the controversy over Oregon and evaluate Polk's campaign slogan "54° 40' or fight." *How practical was Polk's call for annexation of the entire Oregon Territory? Would it have been realistic for the United States to conduct a war over disputed territories with Mexico and Great Britain simultaneously? To what extent was the negotiated treaty of 1846 a satisfactory solution to interested parties in the United States and Great Britain?*

Grades 9-12

▶ Examine the seeds of Manifest Destiny in John Winthrop's vision of a "City Upon a Hill" and the subsequent belief in the divine mission of the United States to build a model Christian community. Develop a historical narrative explaining various reasons for the 19th-century belief in Manifest Destiny.

▶ Contrast Mexican and American perspectives on the War for Texas Independence. Assess how the establishment of the Lone Star Republic affected social relationships in Texas.

▶ Draw upon evidence such as President James K. Polk's diplomatic correspondence with Mexican officials and American officials such as Thomas Larkin, John C. Frémont, and James Slidell, Polk's War Message and the timing of its delivery, Senator Thomas Corwin's speech against the war in the Senate on February 11, 1847, and the ensuing debate in Congress in order to develop a historical regarding the justification of war with Mexico.

▶ Analyze the terms of the Treaty of Guadalupe Hidalgo and assess its impact on Mexico and on the U.S. *How did Mexican perspectives on the war differ from the perspective of those in the U.S. who supported the war and its outcomes? Why did the U.S. Senate reject the land grant provisions in Article 10? How did the treaty affect relations with Native Americans in the Mexican cession? What have been its lasting consequences for the U.S? For Mexico?*

II. *How the industrial revolution, increasing immigration, the rapid expansion of slavery, and the westward movement changed the lives of Americans and led toward regional tensions.*

A. How the factory system and the transportation and market revolutions shaped regional patterns of economic development.

Grades 5-6

▶ Draw upon stories, paintings, folk songs, and picture books such as *The Erie Canal* by Peter Spier to compare transport by wagon, flatboat, and clipper ship before the invention of the steam locomotive with rail and steamboat travel afterwards.

⬧ Use historical accounts and biographies of such individuals as John Deere (steel-bladed plow), Cyrus McCormick (mechanical harvester), Samuel B. F. Morse (telegraph), and Samuel Slater (cotton mill) in order to create a time line or historical narrative identifying and explaining the importance of such inventions as the spinning jenny, the steam locomotive, the steamboat, and the telegraph. Illustrate the timeline with pictures of the inventors and their inventions.

⬧ Examine historical maps locating the Erie Canal, the other canals developed after 1825, and the railroads built by 1860. *How were the lives of people changed as travel became faster and the cost of shipping goods cheaper?*

⬧ Draw upon historical paintings, stories, and other records to compare the lives of farm children and urban children. *How were their lives different? Why were there no laws to prevent child labor and to guarantee all children an education? Why was Horace Mann's crusade for free public education for all children important at this time?*

⬧ Use sources such as *Mill* by David Macaulay and *A Gathering of Days: A New England Girl's Journal, 1830-1832* by Joan Blost to examine life in New England milltowns in the early 1800s.

Grades 7-8

⬧ Draw from primary and secondary sources, such as diaries, interviews, art reproductions, and biographies to compare the effect of technological developments on business owners, farmers, and workers in different regions.

⬧ Draw upon data from maps and historical research to develop a historical argument or debate on whether the federal government should invest in internal improvements. *What was the nature of the controversy surrounding internal improvements? Are there parallels in the controversies over "public" investment in the national infrastructure today?*

⬧ Construct a narrative which marshals historical evidence on such questions as: *Should the federal government impose protective tariffs? Do tariffs promote or hinder commercial development? To what extent did economic issues intensify political and sectional differences in the antebellum era?*

⬧ Draw evidence from diaries, letters, paintings and lithographs, literature such as Charles Dickens's *American Notes*, and personal stories revealed in *The Mill Girls: Lucy Larcom, Harriet Hanson Robinson and Sarah G. Bagley* by Bernice Selden and fictional accounts such as *A Spirit to Ride the Whirlwind* by Athena Lord to explore child labor in the New England mills.

⬧ Construct historical arguments in the form of "balance sheets," debates, or narratives which marshal historical evidence on the advantages and disadvantages of the factory system from the opposing viewpoints of owners and laborers. *To what extent did the factory system create wealth and improve the lives of Americans? Did it stimulate the rise of the labor movement? In what has been called the "age of the common man," was social mobility improving and to what extent were class distinctions narrowing?*

Grades 9-12

⬧ Compare and analyze the advantages and disadvantages of a protective tariff, a national bank, internal improvements at federal expense, and a cheap price for the sale of western lands to residents of the North, South, and West. *How did such issues affect regional interests and the growth and development of political parties during the period?*

⬧ Use Andrew Jackson's veto of the bank recharter bill on July 10, 1832, and the opposition to it in order to construct a sound historical argument or debate on whether or not the veto served the national interest.

▶ Construct an argument explaining how one of the following Supreme Court cases promoted the market revolution: *Fletcher v. Peck* (1810), *McCulloch v. Maryland* (1819), *Dartmouth College v. Woodward* (1819), *Gibbons v. Ogden* (1824), *Charles River Bridge v. Warren Bridge* (1837).

▶ Draw upon a variety of historical and statistical data to analyze the causes and results of the onset of depression in 1819, 1837, and 1857.

▶ Using paintings from the Hudson River school and writings by Henry Thoreau and Ralph Waldo Emerson, analyze their reaction to the impact of industrialization on the environment. *How did Asher Brown Durand and artists of the Hudson River school view nature and the American land? How did Henry David Thoreau's* Walden *express skepticism over the disruption of nature by the machine?*

▶ Analyze the growth and spread of the factory system in New England and compare the early "piece work" and "putting out" systems with the factory system of production. *Did the transformation from household to factory labor erode the earlier artisan tradition? To what extent did it impose a new industrial discipline on the workforce? Did it affect the lives of men, women, and children? How did workers respond to the changes? How did the development of interchangeable parts by such inventors as Eli Whitney and Samuel Colt and the machine tool industry contribute to American economic growth in the antebellum era?*

▶ Construct a historical narrative using selections from a variety of primary and secondary sources to analyze reasons for the strikes at Lowell in 1834 and 1836. *How did women use community bonds to mobilize protest in times of crisis? Did the Lowell example influence others? How did immigration affect labor organization in the New England mills?*

▶ Compare the pattern of economic development in the different regions and explain why the North became increasingly associated with industry and finance, the South with plantations and subsistence farms, and the Northwest with family farms, meatpacking and food processing, and the manufacture of agricultural machinery. *What impact did the transportation revolution have on the pattern of economic development in each region?*

▶ Analyze labor conflict during the antebellum period such as the Lowell Strike of 1834, the textile strikes in Rockdale, Pennsylvania, in 1836 and 1842, and the Lynn, Massachusetts, shoemakers' strike in 1860. *How did the perspectives of industrial workers and employers differ? What were the goals of the unions, and how did such groups as owners and managers, state and federal governments, and political parties respond to the workers' demands? How did ethnic, religious, and racial tensions divide the working classes, and what effect, if any, did such conflicts have on the emergence of a unified labor movement?*

B. The first era of American urbanization.

Grades 5-6

▶ Analyze historical maps in order to compare the location and size of cities before and after the development of the canals and railroads. *Why did the growth of transportation after 1820 spur the development of cities? Why were so many immigrants coming to America and settling in the cities?*

▶ Draw upon diaries, stories, pictures, newspaper advertisements, historic sites, and records to compare city life between 1840 and 1850 with city life today. *Would life in a city of that time have been more or less satisfying than life in a city today?*

Grades 7-8

▶ Identify the major cities of the United States in 1800 and compare their size with large urban centers in 1860. Construct a sound historical narrative explaining the forces that caused urbanization. *What accounted for increased emigration from Europe and for the growth of free black communities in the North? To what extent were cities able to meet the demands and problems caused by rapid growth? What issues facing today's cities are similar to those of the mid-19th century?*

▶ Draw upon historical evidence from biographies and other historical sources to construct sound historical assessments of the contributions of individuals such as Benjamin Banneker, Prince Hall, Richard Allen, and Absalom Jones to free black communities. *What explains the growing white hostility they faced in the cites, particularly among new immigrants? How did the African American communities respond?*

Grades 9-12

▶ Draw on a variety of historical sources such as city directories, maps, old city plans, photographs, and newspapers in order to analyze the factors that led to the rapid growth of northern, southern, and western cities such as Boston, New York, Philadelphia, Baltimore, Charleston, New Orleans, Chicago, Cincinnati, Salt Lake City, and San Francisco, or smaller cities such as Paterson (N.J.), Rochester (N.Y.), Lexington (Ky.), and Fall River and Lowell (Mass.).

▶ Draw on several examples of urban conflict in the period 1830-1861 in order to analyze the factors contributing to tensions in cities during the period. *What was the social composition of the city's population in terms of ethnicity, religion, class, and race? Were there discernible differences in terms of where people lived and worked in the city? What were some of the major problems facing the city in the period? Were cities less violent places to live in the mid-19th century than they are today?*

▶ Draw on such sources as the *Dictionary of African American Biography* to explain how former slaves like Richard Allen, Peter Williams, Prince Hall, and Absalom Jones gained their freedom, became instrumental leaders of the burgeoning African American communities in northern cities, and advanced the interests and rights of African Americans.

▶ Explain the appeal of novels, the popularity of the theater for all classes, the minstrel shows, and P.T. Barnum's "American Museum." *Why were sentimental novels so popular among to women? How was Shakespeare transformed by the popular theater? How was P.T. Barnum's "American Museum" different from other museums? Why did it attract large crowds?*

C. How antebellum immigration changed American society.

Grades 5-6

▶ Draw upon data from historical narratives and fictional accounts of the experiences of immigrants and explain the factors which led them to emigrate. *Why was there an increase in immigration in the antebellum period? Why were so many people willing to risk their lives and worldly possessions to seek a new life in America? From which European countries did most people emigrate? What accounted for Asian emigration?*

▶ Construct a case study of an immigrant family of the 1840s. Write journal entries from the perspective of a 10- or 11-year-old member of the family explaining his or her views of life in the United States. *How different was life in America to what was experienced in Europe or Asia? What problems did immigrants face and what opportunities were afforded them in the 1840s?*

▶ On a map of the United States identify areas in which immigrants settled. *How was the geography of the region different or similar from that of their homeland?*

Grades 7-8

◗ Examine graphs and charts to explain trends in immigration between 1820 and 1860. *How did the number of Scandinavians, Germans, and Irish immigrant change over time? What accounts for the ebb and tide of immigration to America?*

◗ Compare and contrast the experiences of Irish and German immigrants with those of Chinese immigrants in the antebellum period. *Why did many German immigrants settle in the Midwest, Irish in urban areas of the Northeast, and Chinese in the West? What jobs were open to new immigrants? How did their experiences differ?*

◗ Draw upon data from a variety of sources including eyewitness accounts, political cartoons, and historical fiction to assess the relationship of industrial development in the United States to increased immigration.

◗ Research the lives of prominent immigrants such as Mathew Carey, Levi Strauss, or Carl and Margareta Meyer Schurz and explain how they contributed to American society. *What opportunities did immigrants seek? How did they help build the American nation?*

◗ Explain the reasons for widespread Chinese immigration in the antebellum period.

◗ Assume the role of an American industrialist and construct an illustrated flyer to attract immigrants. *What assurances would you give prospective immigrants of improving their standard of living?*

◗ Research the rise of the Know-Nothing Party. *What accounts for the appeal of the Know-Nothings?*

Grades 9-12

◗ Explain how immigration changed between the 1820s and 1850s. *What nationalities composed the largest group of immigrants in each decade? What economic factors led to an increase in immigration by the 1850s?*

◗ Assess the impact of the European revolutions of 1848 on immigration.

◗ Research the conditions on board ocean liners that carried emigrants to North America. *Why did a U.S. commissioner for immigration remark in the 1840s that "If crosses and tombs could be erected on water, the route of the emigrant vessels from Europe to America would long since have assumed the appearance of a crowded cemetery"? Was this an accurate portrayal of the six-week ocean crossing? If so, why would emigrants be willing to risk dangers to seek a new life in North America? Were conditions similar in the ocean voyages from China?*

◗ Explain the factors which contributed to the rise of nativism in the antebellum era and analyze the impact of public speeches and writings of prominent figures such as Theodore Parker, Lyman Beecher, and Samuel F. B. Morse on anti-Catholic and anti-Irish feeling. *What cultural issues of the 1840s and 1850s intensified support for nativism? What factors account for the anti-Catholic riots in northern urban centers in the 1840s?*

◗ Explain the position of political parties on immigration during the antebellum period. *To what extent did the Democratic party appeal to immigrants? Why did Northern Whigs blame their defeat in the 1852 election on immigrants?*

◗ Research ways in which immigrants transplanted their culture in America. *What institutions helped to preserve their cultural heritage?*

D. **The rapid growth of slavery "the peculiar institution" after 1800 and the varied experiences of African Americans under slavery.**

Grades 5-6

▶ Draw upon historical accounts, diaries, narratives by freed slaves, stories, and other records to compare life among the poor yeomen farm families of the South with life on the southern plantations. *How did life differ for poor white and free black farm families of the South, the families of plantation owners, and the enslaved men, women, and children who labored in the great houses, in skilled crafts, and in the fields?*

▶ Draw upon stories such as *The People Could Fly* and Virginia Hamilton's "Carrying the Running Aways," biographies of Harriet Tubman, and the *Autobiography of Frederick Douglass* to develop a historical narration, dramatic reading, or mural depicting the experiences of those who resisted slavery by escaping, the courage of those who helped them, and the terrible costs of being caught.

▶ Draw from children's literature such as the novel *Nightjohn* by Gary Paulsen to examine the human impact of slavery.

▶ Use children's stories such as *Brady* by Jean Fritz, *Drinking Gourd* by Jeanette Winter, *Runaway to Freedom* by Barbara Smucker, and *Get on Board: The Story of the Underground Railroad* by Jim Haskins to examine personal experiences of men and women involved in the Underground Railroad.

Grades 7-8

▶ Analyze quantitative data to explain the impact of the invention of the cotton gin on the maintenance and spread of slavery.

▶ Construct a historical narrative, graph, or illustrative chart which explains roles and responsibilities of different classes and genders in the plantation system. *How did the plantation system affect family life of slaveholders and of the enslaved? To what extent was the plantation a "self-contained" world?*

▶ Draw upon sources such as slave songs, black spirituals, folklore, and narratives and testimony of freed slaves in order to describe the ways in which enslaved Africans survived an oppressive regime, forged their own culture, and resisted slavery.

▶ Draw from a variety of historical sources such as slave narratives, diaries, autobiographies, court records, handbills and reward posters, folk tales, and political tracts such as David Walker's *Appeal* and Henry Garnet's *Address to the Slaves of the United States of America* to evaluate the effectiveness of various methods of passive and active resistance to slavery. *What factors contributed to the failure of slave conspiracies and revolts such as those of Gabriel (Virginia, 1800), Denmark Vesey (Southern Carolina, 1822), and Nat Turner (Virginia, 1831)? Was passive resistance to slavery a more effective response?*

▶ Draw upon historical accounts of the Denmark Vesey conspiracy in order to construct a historical narrative examining the influence of the Republic of Haiti on slavery in the United States. *What was the attitude of southern political leaders towards an independent Haiti? What influence did the Republic of Haiti have on African Americans?*

▶ Use personal accounts of the exploits of individuals such as Frederick Douglass, Henry "Box" Brown, and Harriet Tubman in escaping slavery.

Grades 9-12

▶ Draw upon economic data and historical maps in order to document the expansion of the cotton kingdom between 1801 and 1861, and explain the impact of such factors as the invention of the cotton gin and the opening of new lands in the South and the West.

▶ Develop a historical argument on such questions as: *What was the extent of slave ownership in the South? Why did many non-slaveholding whites support slavery? How did slavery affect the South's economy? How did slavery affect the development of a middle class in the South?*

▶ Draw on a variety of historical and literary sources such as autobiographies, diaries, newspapers, and other periodicals to analyze the plantation system and the consequences for southern society of a hierarchical system based on paternalism and slave labor.

▶ Analyze the major causes and consequences of the rebellions led by Gabriel (Virginia, 1800), Denmark Vesey (South Carolina, 1822), and Nat Turner (Virginia, 1831). *What did these events signify about the view of slavery held by those who were enslaved? How did the Haitian Revolution affect slave resistance in the South? Why did Nat Turner's rebellion create such widespread consternation throughout the South in particular? What kinds of restrictions on slaves and free blacks were instituted by most southern states in the aftermath of Turner's insurrection?*

▶ Research the role of families, community, and religion in efforts to cope with life under slavery.

E. The settlement of the West.

Grades 5-6

▶ Locate and compare the overland trails west to Santa Fe, Oregon, Salt Lake, and California; the trail north from Mexico; and the water routes around the Horn and by way of Panama to California. Draw upon pioneer journals, letters and diaries, newspaper advertisements, paintings and literature to develop a diary, reenact events, or illustrate episodes on the trails.

▶ Analyze why various groups undertook hazardous journeys to the West on the basis of books for young adults such as *Westering* by Alice Putnam, *Beyond the Divide* by Kathryn Lasky, *On to Oregon!* by Honore Morrow, and *Walking up a Rainbow* by Theodore Taylor. *What were the hazards they endured? What goals did they hope to achieve? How accurate are these fictionalized accounts of the journey west?*

▶ Identify Joseph Smith and Brigham Young and explain why the Mormons headed west.

▶ Analyze the movement of settlers from the perspective of Native Americans on the plains and in California from the perspective of Mexicans already living in these territories. *How did the relations between Native Americans and settlers change as more and more newcomers arrived? What was the cost to Mexican rancheros of California and New Mexico?*

▶ Locate on a map the California gold fields and indicate the routes migrants took to reach the region. *How did the physical geography of the United States help or hinder travel to California? What route did most migrants take to reach California? What impact did the discovery of gold have on the settlement of the American West?*

Grades 7-8

▶ Draw evidence from contemporary periodicals, diaries, journals, folklore, music, and art to compare the dream of a western utopia with the realities of everyday life on the frontier. *How did the image of the West depicted in popular folklore differ from everyday life on the frontier?*

▶ Draw upon evidence from a variety of sources including biographies and historical novels to explain the interaction of different cultural groups in the West. *To what extent were the motives for settlement in the West similar among different groups of people? What factors brought people together in a cooperative spirit? What factors caused disagreements and open conflicts?*

▶ Use a variety of primary and secondary sources including diaries, journals, biographies, and the art of C.C.A. Christensen, to construct a historical narrative explaining the founding of the Church of Latter Day Saints, the struggles that led Mormons to establish communities in Utah, and their contributions to settlement of the West. *How did Mormons differ from other Christian churches in their religious beliefs and practices? How were the Mormons able to turn the desert region of the Salt Lake basin into thriving farms?*

▶ Use novels such as *West Against the Wind* by Liza Ketchum Murrow to trace the personal story of a family moving west.

▶ Construct a journal from the perspective of a migrant seeking a fortune in California. *How easy was it to build a fortune during the gold rush? What hardships did the "forty-niners" face? How did the discovery of gold affect the development of towns, the price of goods, and the general standard of living in California? What impact did it have on the economy of the nation? On immigration?*

Grades 9-12

▶ Assemble the evidence and prepare a narrative analyzing one example of cultural interaction between different peoples and societies in the West. *What arguments did white settlers in the West advance to expropriate Native American lands? What factors contributed to the disunity of the Plains Indians? What obstacles did they pose to white expansion? What conflicts arose between Hispanic and Anglo settlers in the Southwest and California and between Anglo and Chinese settlers in California?*

▶ Analyze the impact of the Second Great Awakening and religious revivals of the early 19th century on Joseph Smith and his followers in the "burned over district" of western New York. *How did Mormons' beliefs differ from the major Protestant denominations? Why were the Mormons persecuted and forced to migrate westward? How did the Mormon political organization, settlement pattern around the Great Salt Lake, and relations with Native Americans differ from others in the West?*

▶ Examine the West as the "Crucible for Democracy" and analyze the debate among historians over the Frederick Jackson Turner thesis on "The Significance of the Frontier in American History." *Was political democracy characteristic of the West?*

▶ Using diaries and letters of women in the West, describe the roles they played, the hardships they faced, and the importance of family ties in the development of the West. *How were gender roles defined in the West? Did gender roles differ among different cultural groups?*

III. The extension, restriction, and reorganization of political democracy after 1800.

A. The changing character of American political life in "the age of the common man."

Grades 5-6

▶ Draw evidence from journals, diaries, and caricatures of President Jackson's inauguration to explain why his administration is said to have supported the interests of the "common man." *What do stories of the inaugural parties and open house at the White House tell about Jackson and the people who supported him? What was the "spoils system"? Was Jackson interested in providing the "common man" the opportunities to serve in government?*

● Examine different interpretations of Andrew Jackson using historical accounts of his presidency and drawing evidence from political cartoons such as "King Andrew the First, Born to Rule." *How did political cartoonists portray Jackson? Do historical accounts of his presidency support these views?*

Grades 7-8

● Construct a historical narrative that examines the changes in electoral qualifications of adult white males. *What accounts for changes in state policies regarding voter qualifications? What impact did these changes have on local, state, and national elections? To what extent did the style of political campaigns change with the increase of voter participation and the rise of regional interest groups? Why were women excluded from electoral reforms?*

● Draw upon the arguments used to support universal white male suffrage to illustrate the paradox in continued disenfranchisement of free African American males. *What arguments were made to justify white male suffrage? Why were these same arguments not applied to free African Americans in most northern states?*

● Draw from primary and secondary sources including letters, speeches, and biographies, to construct a historical narrative or oral presentation evaluating the influence of the West and western politicians in supporting equality of opportunity.

● Explain the controversy over the "Tariff of Abominations" and debate the proposition that a state has the right to nullify laws passed by Congress. *What roles did President Jackson and former Vice President Calhoun play in the tariff controversy?*

● Trace the controversy over the Bank of the United States from the Hamilton-Jefferson controversy during the Washington administration through the establishment of the Second Bank of the United States after the War of 1812. Explain Jackson's position on rechartering the bank. *Which regions of the United States were more like to support the bank?*

● Analyze how Jackson's actions in the bank war and the nullification controversy affected voters supporting the Democratic party and contributed to the rise of the Whig party.

Grades 9-12

● Interpret data presented in political maps of the United States and voting data for the 1800, 1832, and 1852 elections in order to support a sound historical argument on such questions as: *Which states and sections experienced the most significant growth in population and electoral votes in the period 1800-1832 and 1832-1852? Why? What factors account for the changing percentage of total white male population voting in the presidential elections of 1800, 1832, and 1852?*

● Analyze how George Caleb Bingham's paintings *Verdict of the People* and *County Election Number Two* reflect the changing character of American politics between the first and second party systems.

● Analyze how the selection of candidates by the political parties and the style of political campaigns changed in the 1830s and 1840s. *How did such changes influence regional interest group politics and affect the turnout of voters?*

● Interpret documentary evidence such as party platforms, political speeches, broadsides, and cartoons between 1820 and 1852 to illustrate how major political parties, such as the National Republicans, Democrats, Whigs, and "Know-Nothings," stood on paramount issues of the day.

▶ Construct a historical argument evaluating opposing views on Jackson's position on the bank recharter and nullification issues. *What were the political motives behind proponents and opponents of the U.S. Bank recharter? Was Jackson's position on the Bank a reflection of the will of the "common man"? Was Jackson or Calhoun more in line with the principles of Jefferson and Madison during the nullification crisis? What might have happened if South Carolina had succeeded in nullifying the tariff?*

B. How the debates over slavery influenced politics and sectionalism.

Grades 5-6

▶ On a map of the United States, draw the Missouri Compromise line and locate Maine. Compare the land areas open to slavery to those in which slavery was prohibited. Write a speech in defense of the compromise from the northern or southern point of view.

▶ List the issues which divided the North and South before the Civil War. *What compromises would you propose to settle the differences?*

Grades 7-8

▶ Construct a historical argument or conduct a debate supporting or opposing the Missouri Compromise of 1820. *Why was there such bitter argument over the admission of Missouri to the Union? Why did the Missouri Compromise fail to resolve the debate over slavery? Was the compromise over the admission of Missouri an appropriate response? How would you have proposed to solve the problem?*

▶ Devise simulated political platforms reflecting the position of Whigs and Democrats on important issues in 1832. *What party positions had special appeal to different sections of the country? What platform issues would have special appeal to different regions?*

▶ Assemble evidence from various sources to construct a historical narrative or position paper on the impact of the debate over slavery from the late 1830s to the Compromise of 1850. *Why did certain states oppose the Wilmot Proviso? Should slavery or involuntary servitude have been permitted in territory acquired after the war with Mexico? Did Congress have the constitutional right to interfere with slavery in states where it was established? Did Congress have the right to prohibit slavery in the territories? To what extent did questions such as these inflame sectional interests?*

Grades 9-12

▶ Analyze the issues created by the Missouri controversy which Thomas Jefferson characterized as "a firebell in the night," sounding for him the death knell of the Union. *How did the free white male population of the South compare to that of the North in the 1790s and 1840s? What factors caused the demographic change? What political dividend did the South have as a result of the three-fifths compromise at the Constitutional convention? How did southern spokesmen attempt to compensate for the minority status of the South's political position in the House of Representatives vis-à-vis the North in the period 1819 to 1845? How did Calhoun's argument in favor of a "concurrent majority" attempt to deal with this imbalance?*

What was the constitutional and legal argument asserting that Congress had the right to exclude slavery in a territory? What was the constitutional and legal argument asserting that Congress did not have the right to exclude slavery in a territory? How was the Missouri controversy finally resolved and with what results?

◆ Draw on a variety of historical sources and documents in order to analyze the reasons why the Mexican War strained national cohesiveness and fostered intraparty squabbles and sectional conflict. *Which policy, "free soil" as outlined in the Wilmot Proviso or Lewis Cass's espousal of "popular sovereignty," best served the interests of the United States? How did the outcome of the Mexican War exacerbate sectional tensions? How did "Conscience Whigs" differ from "Cotton Whigs"? What was the basis for the Free Soil party? What did all of this indicate about the impact of the Mexican War on politics?*

◆ Draw on historical data to contrast the positions of northern antislavery advocates and southern proslavery spokesmen on the issues of race, chattel slavery, wage slavery, the nature of the Union, and states' rights. Then develop a sound historical argument explaining how such differences undermined national political parties in the antebellum period, and with what consequences for national unity.

◆ Draw upon evidence for the major sectional issues, debates, and compromises over slavery between 1819 and 1857 in order to construct a historical argument or debate the question: *Was the rupture of the Union and eventual civil war probable or could it have been avoided?*

IV. *The sources and character of cultural, religious, and social reform movements in the antebellum period.*

A. The abolitionist movement.

Grades 5-6

◆ Develop biographical sketches of black and white abolitionists such as Frederick Douglass, Ellen Watkins, William Lloyd Garrison, Charles Finney, Angelina and Sarah Grimké, and Arthur and Lewis Tappan. *How did they differ in attempting to achieve their goals? How successful were they in bringing about the abolition of slavery? Why are they remembered today?*

◆ Compare the arguments of those who opposed and those who defended slavery.

◆ Draw upon literature and slave narratives, such as "Carrying the Running Aways" by Virginia Hamilton, in order to analyze the great risks and heroism of those who fled to freedom in the North and of those who helped them escape by means of the Underground Railroad.

Grades 7-8

◆ Draw upon primary and secondary sources to compare arguments used to defend slavery in the 18th and 19th centuries. *How did the arguments change over time? What accounts for this change?*

◆ Interpret documentary evidence from abolitionist literature, slave narratives, and biographical studies to construct a historical narrative, debate, or persuasive argument which illustrates and compares different viewpoints in the abolitionist movement. *Were the fundamental beliefs of abolitionists consistent with the Constitution? Did abolitionists advocate the fundamental equality of African Americans? To what extent did abolitionists agree on strategies to end slavery? What were the issues that divided the abolitionists? Why did William Lloyd Garrison and Frederick Douglass reject the goals of the American Colonization Society? How did Quaker abolitionists such as Benjamin Lundy respond to David Walker's Appeal?*

♦ Write biographical sketches of leading women abolitionists of the nineteenth century such as Sarah and Angelina Grimké, Abbe Kelley, Harriet Tubman, and Sojourner Truth. *What role did women play in the abolitionist movement? Did they have an equal voice to men in the movement? How effective were they in promoting an immediate end to slavery?*

♦ Explain the issues that divided the abolitionists. *Why were Black abolitionist societies founded? What was the position of most leading Black abolitionists on the American Colonization Society schemes?*

Grades 9-12

♦ Draw on the arguments of southern spokesmen such as John C. Calhoun, Thomas R. Dew, George Fitzhugh, and James H. Hammond, in order to prepare a legal brief defending chattel slavery from the perspectives of the 19th-century southern slaveholder. *What arguments did southern spokesmen advance to defend the institution of slavery as a positive good? Why did Fitzhugh believe chattel slavery to be superior to the "wage slavery" of the North?*

♦ Draw upon historical evidence of the growing hostility toward free blacks in the antebellum North in order to develop a historical argument explaining the following statement by Alexis de Tocqueville: "The Negro is free, but he can share neither the rights, nor the pleasures, nor the labor, nor the afflictions, nor the tomb of him whose equal he has been declared to be; and he cannot meet him upon fair terms in life or in death." Consider such evidence as the laws enacted by several northern states barring the immigration of free blacks, the urban anti-black riots in northern cities such as Philadelphia and Cincinnati, and Pennsylvania's 1838 state constitution denying the vote to African Americans. *To what extent were legal restrictions on free African Americans in the North and South a violation of the Constitution?*

♦ Analyze the ways in which leaders such as Paul Cuffe, Frederick Douglass, Henry Highland Garnet, Harriet Tubman, William Still, Sojourner Truth, and David Walker fought for the rights of their fellow African Americans.

♦ Draw on such sources as *Notable American Women, The Dictionary of American Biography*, and *The Dictionary of African-American Biography* in order to contrast the positions of African American abolitionists and white abolitionists on the issue of the African American's place in American society. *How did the strategies of abolitionist leaders differ? What were the major differences between "immediatists" and "gradualists"? To what extent did black and white abolitionists cooperate, and what was their view of each other? What forces and arguments did the abolitionists confront in the North and the South?*

♦ Explain the arguments over slavery and abolition from different perspectives. *To what extent did leaders of established and evangelical churches speak out on these issues?*

B. How Americans strived to reform society and create a distinct culture.

Grades 5-6

♦ Draw upon stories and historical accounts in order to describe and explain the great religious revival that swept across the nation in the early 19th century. *What was it like to attend one of the great camp meetings that drew thousands of people to hear such famous preachers as Charles Finney and Peter Cartwright? What was their message? Why did they believe that if each individual took responsibility for living a good life, all of society could be better?*

♦ Explain how Noah Webster helped promote American culture. *Who were other leaders in establishing a distinct American identity?*

♦ Read passages from McGuffy's *Eclectic Reader. How were values taught in schools during the nineteenth century. What were the subjects included in the Reader?*

Grades 7-8

▶ Assess the importance of the revivalist spirit of the Second Great Awakening and explain its impact on American society by constructing a historical narrative or argument on such questions as: *How did the Second Great Awakening advance social reform? What was the significance of Charles Finney's statement: "Away with the idea that Christians can remain neutral and keep still, and yet enjoy the . . . blessings of God"?*

▶ Drawing from current social issues and contemporary reform movements, assess the relevance of the Second Great Awakening in contemporary society.

▶ Construct an evaluative chart listing major utopian communities of the era and their objectives, and appraising the degree of success in attaining their goals. *What does the popularity of utopian communities tell you about early 19th-century society?*

▶ Analyze primary sources such as the Massachusetts school law of 1832 to explain the relationships between religion and the development of public schools.

Grades 9-12

▶ Draw on historical sources to analyze the impact of the Second Great Awakening on the following reform movements: public education, temperance, women's suffrage, and abolitionism. *What were the major goals and ideology of Great Awakening leaders such as Charles Finney and what was his impact on ordinary people? How did the belief in individual responsibility for salvation and millennialism influence the reform movements? What was the role of moral suasion, social control, and compromise in the particular reform movement?*

▶ Draw on examples of the work of Transcendentalists such as Ralph Waldo Emerson, Henry David Thoreau, Theodore Parker, Bronson Alcott, and Margaret Fuller in order to examine their views concerning individualism, society, the nature of good and evil, authority, tradition, and reform; and compare their ideas with those of evangelical Protestants such as Charles Finney and Lyman Beecher. *What were the similarities and differences in their respective views on the role of the individual and the nature of reform? How were the views of Nathaniel Hawthorne and Herman Melville different from those of the Transcendentalists?*

▶ Compile a 20th-century version of *The Dial* that applies the philosophy of Transcendentalism to contemporary issues.

▶ Draw on a variety of historical sources to describe the origin, beliefs, approximate size, and significance of one of the following utopian communities: the Shakers; the Oneida community; New Harmony; and Charles Fourier's utopian socialist communities. *How was the community similar or different from the Transcendentalists in terms of the rights of the individual, the relationship between the individual and the community, and the nature of society?*

▶ Examine the literary and artistic movements of the period and explain how they promoted a distinct American identity. *How did authors such as James Fenimore Cooper reflect American life and society? How did painters of the Hudson River school promote a distinctive American art?*

▶ List specific examples to support or refute Tocqueville's observation that religion and the democratic spirit were deeply united in the American character. *What were the religious roots of antebellum reform? How did the Second Great Awakening influence reform movements?*

C. Changing gender roles and the ideas and activities of women reformers.

Grades 5-6

▶ Draw upon biographies to create a historical narrative, mural, or diary depicting the struggles and contributions of one of the women who was prominent in the reform movements of the antebellum era.

♦ Create a speech, newspaper editorial, "letter to the editor" for a classroom newspaper, or a role play reenacting the struggle for one of the reforms women sought at that time: the vote for women, temperance, free public education, and the abolition of slavery.

♦ Draw upon children's stories such as *Bloomers!* by Rhoda Blumberg to investigate how fashion became involved in the movement for women's rights.

Grades 7-8

♦ Draw upon evidence from biographies, speeches, journals, and caricatures to evaluate the leadership role women played in major reform movements of the period. *Who were the women who helped various reform movements and utopian communities during this era? How did the public at large view women who held leadership roles? What is meant by the "cult of domesticity"? Did it prevent women from taking a more active role in society?*

♦ Drawing from historical evidence, evaluate the Seneca Falls "Declaration of Sentiments" as a response to the inequities of the period. *How effective was the use of the language in the Declaration of Independence in expressing the sentiments of women? How successful were women in gaining a redress of these grievances? If Elizabeth Cady Stanton were alive today, would she construct a new "Declaration of Sentiments"? If so, what might she list as major grievances?*

♦ Utilize books for young adults such as *Mother, Aunt Susan, and Me* by William Jacobs to examine the efforts to gain equal rights for women.

Grades 9-12

♦ Draw on biographical, historical, and literary sources to examine the pivotal contribution of women in the reform movements of the antebellum period: *What were the contributions of Catharine Beecher, Emma Willard, and Mary Lyon in education? Of Dorothea Dix, Fanny Wright, Margaret Fuller, and Amelia Bloomer in social welfare? Of Angelina and Sarah Grimké, Sojourner Truth, Harriet Beecher Stowe, Harriet Tubman, and Prudence Crandall in abolitionism?*

♦ Utilizing such sources as diaries, letters, newspaper accounts, and reminiscences, compare gender roles in different geographical regions and across class, ethnic, racial, and religious lines in the antebellum period. *How did gender roles change in the antebellum period, and how did such changes affect different classes of men and women? Under what circumstances was the notion of "separate spheres" challenged?*

♦ Compare the Seneca Falls "Declaration of Sentiments" (1848) with the Declaration of Independence, noting the similarities and differences in language and style. *Why did Elizabeth Cady Stanton model the "Declaration of Sentiments" after the Declaration of Independence? What specific political, social, economic, and legal grievances are outlined in the document? What objectives for women were included in the twelve resolutions at the end of the Declaration of Sentiments?*

♦ Analyze the connection between the evangelical movement and the idea of southern womanhood. *To what extent did southern women endorse the "Declaration of Sentiments"?*

♦ Compare the women's struggle of the early 19th century with women's status today. *To what extent have the goals and objectives presented in the "Declaration of Sentiments" been achieved? In what respects was the antebellum women's movement similar to and different from 20th-century feminism?*

ERA 5

Civil War and Reconstruction (1850-1877)

The Civil War was perhaps the most momentous event in American history. The survival of the United States as one nation was at risk and on the outcome of the war depended the nation's ability to bring to reality the ideals of liberty, equality, justice, and human dignity.

The war put constitutional government to its severest test as a long festering debate over the power of the federal government versus state rights reached a climax. Its enormously bloody outcome preserved the Union while releasing not only four million African Americans but the entire nation from the oppressive weight of slavery.

The war can be studied in several ways: as the final, violent phase in a conflict of two regional subcultures; as the breakdown of a democratic political system; as the climax of several decades of social reform; and as a pivotal chapter in American racial history. In studying the Civil War, students have many opportunities to study heroism and cowardice, triumph and tragedy, and hardship, pain, grief, and death wrought by conflict. Another important topic is how the war necessarily obliged both northern and southern women to adapt to new and unsettling situations.

As important as the war itself, once the Union prevailed, was the tangled problem of Reconstruction. Through examining the 13th, 14th, and 15th amendments—fundamental revisions of the Constitution—students can see how African Americans hoped for full equality as did many white lawmakers. They can assess the various plans for Reconstruction that were contested passionately. The retreat from Radical Reconstruction—the first attempt at establishing a biracial democracy—should be of concern to all students who need to understand how shared values of the North and South sharply limited support for social and racial democratization. The enduring republican belief in the need to respect local control made direction by central government power unpopular. Northerners, like southerners, did not support schemes to redistribute wealth under Reconstruction because of the need to protect private property. Northerners, like southerners, believed in the social inferiority of blacks.

Students should learn how southern white resistance and the withdrawal of federal supervision resulted in the "redemption" of the South through the disfranchisement of African Americans, the end of their involvement in Reconstruction state legislatures, greater racial separation, the rise of white intimidation and violence, and the creation of black rural peonage.

Balancing the success and failures of Reconstruction should test the abilities of all students. Too much stress on the unfinished agenda of the period can obscure the great changes actually wrought. Moreover, it needs to be remembered how most white Americans were diverted from completing Reconstruction toward new goals brought about by social change. A new generation sought new fields of endeavor afforded by industrialization. They were not imbued by the reformist idealism of their predecessors. Indeed, they were receptive to new doctrines of racial and social inequality. The legacies of the era of war and reconstruction needs to be considered with reference to the North and West as well as the South.

To us [Mexico] was an empire and of incalculable value; but it might have been obtained by other means. The Southern rebellion was largely the outgrowth of the Mexican war. Nations, like individuals, are punished for their transgressions. We got our punishment in the most sanguinary and expensive war of modern times.

— ULYSSES S. GRANT (1892)

Essay

The Continuing Evolution of Reconstruction History*
by Eric Foner

In the short essay that follows, Eric Foner summarizes the historiographical evolution of Reconstruction history. Readers will come to understand how inherently racist depictions of the period, perhaps best exemplified by the classic movie "Gone With the Wind," have sprung from seeds planted by generations of historians who failed to see and hear the roles played by African Americans in the aftermath of the Civil War. Foner suggests that immense social, political, and economic changes began with the signing of the Emancipation Proclamation in 1863 and that the latest turn of the interpretive wheel shows that Reconstruction marked the beginning of a revolution in American society.

Eric Foner is Professor of History at Columbia University. He has written extensively on Reconstruction and his latest book, *Reconstruction: America's Unfinished Revolution, 1863-1877* received many awards, among them the 1988 Los Angeles Times Book Prize and the 1989 OAH Avery O. Craven Award.

In the past thirty years, no period of American history has seen a broadly accepted point of view so completely overturned as Reconstruction—the dramatic and controversial era that followed the Civil War. Since the early 1960s, a profound alteration of the place of blacks within American society, newly uncovered evidence, and changing definitions of history itself, have combined to transform our understanding of race relations, politics, and economic change during Reconstruction.

Anyone who attended high school before 1960 learned that Reconstruction was an era of unrelieved sordidness in American political and social life. Drawing on scholarly studies that originated in the work of William Dunning, John W. Burgess, and their students soon after the turn of the century, the "traditional" interpretation argued that when the Civil War ended, the white South accepted the reality of military defeat, stood ready to do justice to the emancipated slaves, and desired above all a quick reintegration into the fabric of national life. Before his death, Abraham Lincoln had embarked on a course of sectional reconciliation, and during Presidential Reconstruction (1865-1867) his successor, Andrew Johnson, attempted to carry out Lincoln's magnanimous policies. Johnson's efforts were opposed and eventually thwarted by the Radical Republicans in Congress. Motivated by an irrational hatred of Southern "rebels" and the desire to consolidate their party's national ascendancy, the Radicals in 1867 swept aside the Southern governments Johnson had established and fastened black suffrage upon the defeated South. There followed the period of Congressional or Radical Reconstruction (1867-77), an era of corruption presided over by unscrupulous "carpetbaggers" from the North, unprincipled Southern white "scalawags," and ignorant blacks, unprepared for freedom and incapable of properly exercising the political right Northerners had thrust upon them. After much needless suffering, the South's white community banded together to overthrow these governments and restore "home rule" (a euphemism for white supremacy). All told, Reconstruction was the darkest page in the American saga.

During the 1920s and 1930s new studies of Johnson's career and new investigations of the economic wellsprings of Republican policy reinforced the prevailing disdain for Reconstruction. Johnson's new biographers portrayed him as a courageous defender of constitutional liberty; his actions stood above reproach. Simultaneously, historians of the Progressive School, who viewed political ideologies as little more than masks for crass economic ends, further

*Reprinted from *Magazine of History,* Vol 4, No. 1 (Winter 1989), pp. 11-13, with permission from the Organization of American Historians.

undermined the Radicals' reputation by portraying them as agents of Northern capitalism, who cynically used the issue of black rights to fasten economic subordination upon the defeated South.

From the first appearance of the Dunning school, dissenting voices had been raised, initially by a handful of survivors of the Reconstruction era and the small fraternity of black historians. In 1935, the black activist and scholar, W. E. B. Du Bois, published *Black Reconstruction in America*, a monumental study that portrayed Reconstruction as an idealistic effort to construct a democratic, interracial political order from the ashes of slavery, as well as a phase in a prolonged struggle between capital and labor for control of the South's economic resources. His book closed with an indictment of a profession whose writings had ignored the testimony of the principle actor in the drama of Reconstruction—the emancipated slave—and sacrificed scholarly objectivity on the altar of racial bias. "One fact and one alone," Du Boise wrote, "explains the attitude of most recent writers toward Reconstruction; they cannot conceive of Negroes as men." *Black Reconstruction* anticipated the findings of modern scholarship, but at the time of its publication, it failed to influence prevailing views among academic historians, or the account of the era in school texts.

Despite its remarkable longevity and powerful hold on the imagination, the demise of the traditional interpretations was inevitable. Its fundamental underpinning was the conviction, to quote one member of the Dunning School, of "negro incapacity." Once objective scholarship and modern experience rendered its racist assumptions untenable, familiar evidence read very differently, new questions suddenly came into prominence, and the entire edifice had to fall.

It required, however, not simply the evolution of scholarship but a profound change in the nation's politics and racial attitudes to deal the final blow to the Dunning School. If the traditional interpretation reflected, and helped to legitimize, the racial order of a society in which blacks were disenfranchised and subjected to discrimination in every aspect of their lives, Reconstruction revisionism bore the mark of the modern civil rights movement. In the 1960s the revisionist wave broke over the field, destroying, in rapid succession, every assumption of the traditional viewpoint. First, scholars presented a drastically revised account of national politics. New works portrayed Andrew Johnson as a stubborn, racist politician incapable of responding to the unprecedented situation that confronted him as president, and acquitted the Radicals—reborn as idealistic reformers genuinely committed to black rights—of vindictive motives and the charge of being the stalking-horses of Northern capitalism. Moreover, Reconstruction legislation was shown to be not simply the product of a Radical cabal, but a program that enjoyed broad support both in Congress and the North at large.

Even more startling was the revised portrait of Republican rule in the South. So ingrained was the old racist version of Reconstruction that it took an entire decade of scholarship to prove the essentially negative contentions that "Negro rule" was a myth and that Reconstruction represented more than "the blackout of honest government." The establishment of public school systems, the granting of equal citizenship to blacks, and the effort to revitalize the devastated Southern economy refuted the traditional description of the period as a "tragic era" of rampant misgovernment. Revisionists pointed out as well that corruption in the Reconstruction South paled before that of the Tweed Ring, Credit Mobilier scandal, and Whiskey Rings in the post-Civil War North. By the end of the 1960s, Reconstruction was seen as a time of extraordinary social and political progress for blacks. If the era as "tragic," it was because change did not go far enough, especially in the area of Southern land reform.

Even when Revisionism was at its height, however, its more optimistic findings were challenged, as influential historians portrayed changes in the post-Civil War years as fundamentally "superficial." Persistent racism, these post-revisionist scholars argued, had negated efforts to extend justice to blacks, and the failure to distribute land prevented the freedmen from achieving true autonomy and made their civil and political rights all but meaningless. In the 1970s and 1980s, a new generation of scholars, black and white, extended this skeptical view to virtually every aspect of the period. Recent studies of Reconstruction politics and ideology have stressed the "conservatism" of Republican policymakers, even at the height of Radical influence, and the continued hold of racism and federalism despite the extension of citizenship rights to blacks and the advanced scope of national authority. Studies of federal policy in the South portrayed the army and Freedmen's Bureau as working hand in glove with former slave-owners to thwart the freedmen's aspirations and force them to return to plantation labor. At the same time, investigations of Southern social history emphasized the survival of the old planter class and the continuities between the old South and the new. The post-revisionist interpretation represented a striking departure from nearly all previous accounts of the period, for whatever their differences, traditional and revisionist historians at least agreed that Reconstruction was a time of radical change. Summing up a decade of writing, C. Vann Woodward observed in 1979 that historians now understood "how essentially non-revolutionary and conservative Reconstruction really was."

In emphasizing that Reconstruction was part of the ongoing evolution of Southern society rather than a passing phenomenon, the post-revisionists made a salutary contribution to the study of the period. The description of the reconstruction as "conservative," however, did not seem altogether persuasive when one reflected that it took the nation fully a century to implement its most basic demands, while others are yet to be fulfilled. Nor did the theme of continuity yield a fully convincing portrait of an era that contemporaries all agreed was both turbulent and wrenching in its social and political change. Over a half-century ago, Charles and Mary Beard coined the term "The Second American Revolution" to describe a transfer in power, wrought by the Civil War, from the South's "planting aristocracy" to Northern capitalists and free farmers." And in the latest shift in interpretive premises, attention to changes in the relative power of social classes has again become a central concern of historical writing. Unlike the Beards, however, who all but ignored the black experience, modern scholars tend to view emancipation itself as among the most revolutionary aspects of the period.

The most recent effort to provide a coherent account of the Reconstruction era is my own *Reconstruction: America's Unfinished Revolution*, published in 1988 (abridged version, *A Short History of Reconstruction*). Drawing upon the voluminous secondary literature that has appeared in the last thirty years, the book seems to provide a coherent, comprehensive modern account of the period. Necessarily, it touches on a multitude of issues, but certain broad themes unified the narrative. The first is the centrality of the black experience. Rather than the passive victims of the actions of others or simply a "problem" confronting white society, blacks were active agents in the making of Reconstruction, whose quest for individual and community autonomy did much to establish Reconstruction's political and economic agenda. Black participation in Southern public life after 1867 was the most radical development of the Reconstruction years. Other themes include transition from slave to free labor and the evolution of racial attitudes and patterns of race relations.

The book also seeks to place the Southern story within a national context, especially by stressing the emergence during the Civil War and Reconstruction of a national state possessing vastly expanded authority and a new set of purposes, including an unprecedented commitment to the ideal of a national citizenship whose equal rights belonged to all Americans regardless of race. Originating in wartime exigencies, the activist state came to embody the reforming impulse deeply rooted in postwar politics. And Reconstruction produced enduring changes in the laws and Constitution that fundamentally altered federal-state relations and redefined the meaning of American citizenship. Yet because it threatened traditions of local autonomy, produced political corruption, and was so closely associated with the new rights of blacks, the rise of the state inspired powerful opposition, which, in turn, weakened support for Reconstruction. Finally, the study examines how changes in the North's economy and class structure affected Reconstruction, and especially the retreat from the commitment to equality that accelerated during the 1870s.

My account of Reconstruction begins not in 1865, but with the Emancipation Proclamation in 1863, to emphasize that Reconstruction was not merely a specific time period, but the beginning of an extended historical process: the adjustment of American society to the end of slavery. The destruction of the central institution of antebellum Southern life permanently transformed the war's character, and produced far-reaching conflicts and debates over the role former slaves and their descendants would play in American life and the meaning of the freedom they had acquired. These were the questions on which Reconstruction persistently turned.

They were also questions that confronted every society that abolished slavery in the Western hemisphere, from Cuba and Jamaica to Brazil. Indeed, it may well be that the future of Reconstruction studies lies in comparative analysis of the differences and similarities between various aftermaths of slavery. I made a brief beginning in this direction in my *Nothing But Freedom*, published in 1983. But comparative study of the economic, political, and social consequences of emancipation remains in its infancy. As was true for the study of slavery, a comparative approach to emancipation can broaden our perspective, introduce new questions and concepts, and illuminate what was and was not unique in the American experience of Reconstruction.

David Gilmore Blythe (1815–1865), "Abraham Lincoln Writing the Emancipation Proclamation." Courtesy the Carnegie Museum of Art

Sample Student Activities

I.   *The Causes of the Civil War.*

A.   **How the North and South differed and how politics and ideologies led to the Civil War.**

Grades 5-6

▶ Locate northern and southern states on a map, describe their geographic features and resources, and compare northern industries and agricultural products with those in the South.

▶ Draw upon letters, stories, and pictures to describe views held by people in the largely rural South with its agricultural economy and slavery and the industrial North, with its industry and small family farms.

▶ Explain the growing influence of abolitionists drawing upon accounts such as Gwen Everett's *John Brown, One Man Against Slavery,* Ann Turner's *Nettie's Trip to the South,* and the writings of Frederick Douglass, Harriet Beecher Stowe, and William Lloyd Garrison. Develop a skit to portray family life and children's roles under slavery.

▶ Create a timeline from the Missouri Compromise of 1820 to the election of Abraham Lincoln in 1860 and identify the issues which divided North and South. Explain how these differences contributed to the causes of the war.

Grades 7-8

▶ Construct a balance sheet listing the social and economic differences between the North and the South on the eve of the Civil War. *How did the free labor system of the North differ from that of the South? To what extent did the different social and economic convictions contribute to tension between the North and the South?*

▶ Construct a timeline listing the events from the Compromise of 1850 through John Brown's raid on Harper's Ferry, and write a persuasive speech, create simulated newspaper editorials, or a position paper for a debate which clarifies sectional issues surrounding these events.

▶ Interpret documentary evidence from a variety of sources to construct an argument on such questions as: *To what extent was slavery the primary cause of the Civil War? What other issues led to the conflict?*

▶ Appraise the effectiveness of President James Buchanan's leadership during the secession crisis and compare it with that of President Abraham Lincoln between his inauguration and the attack on Sumter. Use a Venn diagram or some other graphic organizer to indicate differences.

Grades 9-12

▶ Examine the political and sectional conflicts over slavery and compare how the Missouri Compromise, Wilmot Proviso, Kansas-Nebraska Act, and the Dred Scott case polarized the North and South. *How did the advocates of each position justify their point of view? What were the advantages and disadvantages of each position? Why? Was secession inevitable following passage of the Kansas-Nebraska Act?*

▶ Analyze the Supreme Court's decision in *Dred Scott v. Sandford* (1857). Compare the main points of the Court's decision presented by Chief Justice Taney with Justice Benjamin Curtis's dissent. *How do the issues and the arguments of this case reflect the controversy over slavery that led to the Civil War?*

▶ Read excerpts from the Lincoln-Douglas debates of 1858 to identify political issues which divided the Republican and Democratic parties. Analyze the arguments presented in the debates and explain how the two senatorial candidates differed. *To what extent did the debates set an agenda for political discussion throughout the nation? How did the debates help make Lincoln a national political figure?*

▶ Analyze the party platforms in the election of 1860 and the reasons why people voted as they did. *Was the Republican party platform and Lincoln's election a real threat to southern states' rights?*

▶ Contrast the leadership of President Buchanan and President Lincoln during the secession crisis. *Might Buchanan have avoided a more serious crisis had he adopted sterner measures following South Carolina's decision to secede? Is it justifiable to call Lincoln "the railsplitter who split the nation"? Should he have supported the Crittenden Compromise? Should he have attempted to supply Fort Sumter? How did Lincoln's First Inaugural Address reflect both a "carrot and stick approach" to southerners?*

▶ Analyze the southern justification for secession as expressed in such ordinances as the Mississippi Resolutions on Secession (November 30, 1860) and the South Carolina Declaration of Causes of Secession (December 24, 1860). *How did southerners use the Declaration of Independence to support their position? What areas of the South remained bastions of Unionism throughout the war?*

▶ Construct an argument or debate using historical evidence to support or reject the following proposition: *The Civil War was an unavoidable result of sectional differences.*

> **II.** **The course and character of the Civil War and its effects on the American people.**

A. How the resources of the Union and Confederacy affected the course of the war.

Grades 5-6

▶ Explain how the military leaders and resources of the Union and the Confederacy such as Robert E. Lee, Thomas "Stonewall" Jackson, Ulysses S. Grant, and William Tecumseh Sherman affected the course and outcome of the Civil War.

▶ Compare population, armies, and resources of the Confederacy with those of the Union at the beginning of the war.

▶ Draw upon historical accounts, diaries, literature, and songs to describe attitudes toward the war by both Union and Confederate soldiers and civilians at different stages of the conflict between 1861 and 1865.

▶ Explain why the Civil War is called the "first modern war." Illustrate innovations such as: communication by telegraph, extended railroad lines, observation balloons, ironclad ships, submarines, repeating and breechloading arms. *Did the new technology give the soldiers a better chance in battle? Did technological innovations make war more devastating?*

▶ Explain the reasons why President Lincoln issued his wartime Emancipation Proclamation. Read accounts to determine how different people in the North and South responded to the Proclamation.

‣ Locate and label major areas of combat on a historical map. Explore first-hand account of a major battle using letters, diaries, photographs, and art reproductions. Plan a hypothetical "class trip" and map a selected battle or campaign. Explain how the physical geography of the area played a part in the battle.

Grades 7-8

‣ Draw upon statistical information from charts and graphs, topographic maps, and other historical sources to construct arguments that compare the economic, technological, and human resources of the Union with those of the Confederacy.

‣ Draw upon Stephen Crane's *Red Badge of Courage* and Michael Shaara's *The Killer Angels*, paintings, photographs, art prints, biographies, and historical narratives in order to evaluate the importance of military technology and to appraise its effect on combatants.

‣ Construct a historical narrative explaining how major battles and military leaders, such as Robert E. Lee, Thomas "Stonewall" Jackson, James Longstreet, George McClellan, William Tecumseh Sherman, and Ulysses S. Grant contributed to the outcome of the war.

‣ Analyze the Emancipation Proclamation and assess its impact on the outcome of the Civil War. *What were President Lincoln's reasons for issuing the Emancipation Proclamation? Did the Emancipation Proclamation affect the foreign recognition of the Confederacy? How did abolitionists respond to the Emancipation Proclamation? What was the Confederate reaction?*

‣ Compile a list of innovations in military technology and explain the impact each had on humans, property, and the final outcome of the war. Describe how each side made use of new technology.

Grades 9-12

‣ Draw on a variety of biographical and historical accounts in order to contrast the wartime leadership of Jefferson Davis and Abraham Lincoln and prepare a sound historical narrative explaining the importance of presidential leadership in the outcome of the war. *How did their leadership styles contrast? Did Davis's military experience make a difference in his leadership? How did Lincoln's sense of humor and pragmatism affect his leadership? Which of the two men best exemplified better presidential leadership?*

‣ Analyze the reasons for the impact of the Emancipation Proclamation in transforming the goals of the Civil War. *How did the Emancipation Proclamation transform the goals of the Civil War? How does A.E. Lamb's painting,* The Emancipation Proclamation *portray the theme of the proclamation?*

‣ Explain the meaning of the Gettysburg Address and analyze its significance as one of the most effective political speeches in our nation's history. *What did Lincoln say the Declaration of Independence meant? Did Lincoln change the meaning of the Declaration or explain its true vision? How did Lincoln relate the Constitution to the Declaration?*

‣ Explain how the "hammering campaigns" of Generals Ulysses S. Grant and William Tecumseh Sherman affected the outcome of the war. *Did the South's emphasis on the eastern theater doom the Confederacy? What was the impact of the Civil War on the trans-Mississippi West?*

‣ Debate the statement: *Military leadership and manpower were secondary to technology in winning the Civil War.*

‣ Draw upon historical sources in order to assess the varied Native American responses to the Civil War. *How were Native Americans in the West affected by the Civil War? What were the internal conflicts among the "Five Civilized Tribes" regarding their support for the Union or Confederacy? What were the long-term consequences for them once the North emerged victorious?*

B. The social experience of the war on the battlefield and homefront.

Grades 5-6

▶ Explain how the Civil War changed the lives of American women, men, and children by comparing personal accounts, letters, and photographs. Use resources such as Virginia Hamilton's *The People Could Fly*, Patricia Lee Gauch's *Thunder at Gettysburg, A Child's Account of the Battle of Gettysburg*, and F. N. Monjo's *The Vicksburg Veteran*.

▶ Explain how the war affected the lives of women by drawing evidence from diaries, letters, and stories about the lives of Clara Barton, Harriet Tubman, and Rose Greenhow. *What responsibilities did women take on at home during the war? What role did women play on the battlefield?*

▶ Explain the motives of fighting men in the Civil War by examining documentary and literary accounts such as Milton Meltzer's *The Black Americans: A History in Their Own Words* and novels by Peter Burchard such as *Jed, The Deserter, North by Night*, and *Bimby*. *What reasons might have been given by Confederate or Union soldiers for fighting in the Civil War? What were the motives of African American soldiers? Why were African American soldiers in special danger during the war?*

Grades 7-8

▶ Use historical fiction such as *The Slopes of War* by N.A. Perez, *Thunder on the Tennessee* by Clifton Wisler, *Rifles for Watie* by Harold Keith, and *The 290* by Scott O'Dell to compare the experiences of Union and Confederate soldiers. *How were the motives which compelled Union and Confederate soldiers similar or different? To what extent did these motives change as the war progressed?*

▶ Examine the battlefield experiences of Union and Confederate soldiers using biographies, diaries, and visual depictions of battles such as the Kurz and Allison prints of the "Battle of Antietam" and the "Siege of Vicksburg."

▶ Appraise the contributions of African American soldiers during the war by drawing upon excerpts from the movie *Glory* and books such as *Between Two Fires: Black Soldiers in the Civil War* and *Which Way Freedom* by Joyce Hansen.

▶ Draw upon historical evidence to construct a narrative illustrating different perspectives on conscription during the Civil War and Union provisions for avoidance of service. *What alternatives to the draft, if any, were opened to conscientious objectors such as Quakers or members of the Shaker communities? To what extent have policies toward conscientious objectors changed during other wars of the 19th and 20th centuries?*

▶ Drawing upon a variety of sources including letters, biographies, and visuals, construct a skit or oral presentation which accurately evaluates the role and contribution of women on both sides of the conflict.

▶ Explain the effects of divided loyalties during the Civil War using historical fiction such as *Hew Against the Grain* by Betty Sue Cummings and *Across Five Aprils* by Irene Hunt.

Grades 9-12

▶ Drawing on a variety of historical sources, develop a historical narrative analyzing the treatment of African American soldiers in the Union army and by the Confederacy during the Civil War. *How was the concept of liberty viewed by African Americans? How did Confederate leaders determine to deal with African American soldiers? What happened to African American Union soldiers at Fort Pillow? What reasons account for the decision to differentiate between soldiers' pay for white troops and African American soldiers in the Union Army before June 1864?*

▶ Analyze the causes and consequences of the New York City draft riots in July 1863 and the irony of African Americans fighting for liberty and democracy at Fort Wagner a few days after the outbreak of violence against blacks in New York City. *How did city officials respond to the riots? How did the federal government respond? What do the riots reveal about support for the Union's war objectives in 1863?*

▶ Interpret documentary evidence from a variety of sources reflecting differing perspectives to construct a historical argument or debate on such questions as: *What circumstances would justify a restriction of civil liberties? How might President Lincoln's suspension of the writ of habeas corpus during the war be justified?*

▶ Using diaries and letters, explain the roles of women on the home front and battle front during the Civil War. *What new occupations were open to women during the war? To what extent did the war change gender roles and traditional attitudes toward women in the work force? How did the actions of Clara Barton, Belle Boyd, Rose Greenhow, and Harriet Tubman affect the war?*

▶ Using diaries, paintings, photographs, statistics, and newspaper articles, explain the human costs of the war. *How did photographs of death and destruction affect people of the North? Of the South? What do the paintings of Winslow Homer say about courage and leadership during the Civil War?*

III. *How various reconstruction plans succeeded or failed.*

A. **The political controversy over Reconstruction.**

Grades 5-6

▶ Use resources such as photographs, narratives, and literature such as Zachary Kent's *The Surrender at Appomattox Court House* to describe the end of the Civil War, the demobilization of the armies, and popular expectations for peace.

▶ Compare the leadership abilities of Presidents Abraham Lincoln and Andrew Johnson. *How did the two men differ? What was the effect of Lincoln's assassination on the nation? Why was President Johnson impeached?*

▶ List the basic provisions of the 13th, 14th, and 15th amendments. *How were the lives of African American freedmen changed by these amendments? Did they obtain the rights and freedoms promised to them? How did the Ku Klux Klan attempt to block these rights?*

Grades 7-8

▶ Identify and analyze the fundamental differences in the Reconstruction plans advocated by President Lincoln, Congressional leaders, and President Johnson as a background to creating the students' own position paper or editorial, advising and justifying their recommendation for a Reconstruction policy.

▶ Construct a historical narrative explaining how President Johnson's resistance to Congressional authority led to his impeachment. *How did Congress respond to President Johnson's attempts to control Reconstruction policy? To what extent did Johnson's personality play a role in the conflict with Radical Republicans? What was the Tenure of Office Act and how did it play a role in the impeachment of Andrew Johnson?*

▶ Explain the basic principles incorporated in the Reconstruction amendments and examine different perspectives on the effectiveness of these constitutional amendments. *What was the intent of these amendments? How did African American freedmen experience change following these amendments? How did southern "Redeemers" restrict the civil rights of African Americans?*

▶ Construct a historical argument, debate, or narrative which appraises the Compromise of 1877 from the perspectives of African Americans, southern political leaders, and northern Republicans. *Was the compromise an effective way to end the political stalemate over the election of 1876? To what extent did the Compromise of 1877 abandon reconstruction goals? What were the long-range consequences of the Compromise of 1877?*

Grades 9-12

▶ Compare the Lincoln, Johnson, and Radical Republican plans for Reconstruction. *How did each plan view secession, amnesty and pardon, and procedure for readmission to the Union? How did the issue of Federalism influence the debate over Reconstruction policy? How did President Andrew Johnson's personality and character affect relationships with congressional leaders, particularly Radical Republicans, in the period 1865-1868? Were the Radical Republicans motivated by genuine humanitarian concerns or crass political ones for maintaining control over the government?*

▶ Evaluate the reasons Republicans gave for impeaching the president. *Was Johnson's impeachment justified under the Constitution? Had the Senate convicted the president, what impact would his removal from office have on the nation?*

▶ Construct a historical narrative analyzing the meaning and intent of the 14th and 15th amendments. *How is citizenship being defined? Why were the clauses of "equal protection of the laws" and "due process" included? Were the 14th and 15th amendments necessary? Explain. Why is the word "male" used for the first time in the Constitution in the 15th Amendment? Why were women excluded in the amendment?*

▶ Analyze how violence helped to produce the Compromise of 1877 and the consequences of the compromise on the South. *Did northern Republicans and congressional leaders abandon African Americans in the 1870s? Would you agree or disagree that the Compromise of 1877 made the end of the Civil War a draw rather than a victory for the North?*

▶ Analyze the origins of the Ku Klux Klan. *How did southerners justify the origin of the Ku Klux Klan? Was the Ku Klux Klan a form of "guerrilla" warfare?*

B. How Reconstruction programs transformed social relations in the South.

Grades 5-6

▶ Interpret diaries, letters, journals, biographies, and cartoons such as those of Thomas Nast to describe how the Union victory and emancipation changed life in the South during Reconstruction. *What did defeated Confederate soldiers find when they returned home? What were the needs of nearly four million African American freed men and women?*

▶ Examine ways in which former slaves organized into communities to improve their position in American society. *Why were former slaves eager to build schools and get an education? How important were the black churches in working to improve the condition of African Americans in the South? How did they work together to obtain land? Why did some move to the North and West after the Civil War?*

▶ Explain the goals of the Freedmen's Bureau and give examples of how people from the North traveled south to help with Reconstruction? *What was the most important need the Freedmen's Bureau faced?*

Grades 7-8

▶ Compare the economic base of the South before and after the Civil War.

▶ Interpret documentary evidence from diaries, letters, journals, and biographies in order to construct a historical narrative, examining the problems facing different groups of people in the South at the close of the war.

▶ Draw from a variety of historical sources, including diaries and journals of administrators and participants, to evaluate the successes and failures of the Freedmen's Bureau. *What were the goals of the Freedmen's Bureau? To what extent were the services of the Freedmen's Bureau offered to southern poor whites? How did the Freedmen's Bureau propose to deal with abandoned land in the South? To what extent was the policy effective? What political, economic, and social factors hindered the success of the Freedmen's Bureau?*

▶ Formulate examples of historical contingency by explaining how different choices regarding land redistribution during Reconstruction could have led to different consequences. *Why were former slaves calling for "forty acres and a mule"? Would widespread land ownership among freedmen have made Reconstruction more successful?*

Grades 9-12

▶ Analyze how traditional beliefs and values inhibited the role and success of the Freedmen's Bureau. *How did the belief in limited government, the sanctity of private property and self-help affect the Bureau's success? To what extent was the Freedmen's Bureau successful in securing employment, education, and support services for African Americans and white refugees? In what ways did the Freedmen's Bureau contribute to the economic and social transformation of the South during Reconstruction? In what ways did the Bureau contribute to racial stereotyping and paternalism? How did the labor contracts negotiated by the Freedmen's Bureau affect African Americans?*

▶ Analyze the struggle between former masters aiming to recreate a disciplined labor force and former slaves seeking to create the greatest degree of economic autonomy, and explain how such conflicts affected economics, politics, and race relations in the postwar South. *How did the southern Black Codes limit the freed slaves' newfound freedom? What effect did passage of such laws in the South have on northern Republicans?*

▶ Examine how black churches and schools formed the basis for self-help within the African American community. *To what extent were African American goals of education, economic development, and establishing and reaffirming community achieved? What examples illustrate the desire of African Americans to establish independence and gain control over their own lives and destinies? How effective were Black churches in dealing with social, economic, and political issues of importance to the African American community?*

▶ Research efforts of African Americans to achieve economic independence during Reconstruction by examining letters, government documents reflecting the appeals and demands of freedmen for land ownership. *What did a South Carolina freedman mean when he said "If I can't own de land, I'll hire or lease land, but I won't contract"? How did the insistence on land ownership provide a major impetus for change from contract labor to tenancy and sharecropping?*

C. The successes and failures of Reconstruction in the South, North, and West.

Grades 5-6

▶ Make a chart comparing northern and southern economic conditions and family life before and after the Civil War. *How did conditions in each area change over the war years?*

▶ Examine the lives of African Americans such as Charlotte Forten, Robert Elliot, Hiram Revels, and Blanche Bruce, who served as teachers and political leaders during Reconstruction. *What significant contributions did African Americans make to further the aims of Reconstruction?*

▶ Construct a response in the form of an editorial, speech, or role-play activity to the passage of the 15th amendment from the perspective of Susan B. Anthony and Elizabeth Cady Stanton. *Why did Anthony and Stanton, who had supported the abolition of slavery, voice opposition to the 15th amendment?*

◗ Investigate personal accounts of life during Reconstruction using historical fiction such as *Two Tickets to Freedom* by Florence Freedman and *Words by Heart* by Ouida Sebestyen.

Grades 7-8

◗ Draw upon evidence from biographies and other historical sources, including legislation passed in southern states during Reconstruction to assess the contributions of African Americans who served in state and national offices, such as Hiram Revels, Blanche Bruce, and B. S. Pinchback.

◗ Draw upon different historical interpretations of Reconstruct-ion and documentary evidence to construct a sound historical argument agreeing or disagreeing with the statement: *"Reconstruction failed because of a lack of commitment to carry out its basic goals and objectives."*

◗ Examine personal challenges to Freedmen during Reconstruction using historical fiction such as *Freedom Road* by Howard Fast and *Out from this Place* by Joyce Hensen.

◗ Develop a historical narrative assessing the changes in the political and economic position of African Americans in the North in the post-Civil War era. *Did attitudes toward free blacks in the North change after the Civil War? To what extent were Jim Crow laws passed in the North? How did the social conditions of African Americans in the North compare with those in the South?*

◗ Explain why some freedmen (Exodusters) chose to migrate west. *What problems did they encounter in the West?*

◗ Drawing from historical evidence, construct sound arguments to support or refute the images of corruption reflected in the majority of political cartoons of the post-Civil War era. *Did political cartoonists accurately reflect the degree of corruption in the United States in the postwar era?*

Grades 9-12

◗ Analyze the successes and achievements of "Black Reconstruction." *To what extent were African American goals of education, economic development, and establishing and reaffirming community achieved? What examples illustrate the desire of African Americans to establish independence and gain control over their own lives and destinies?*

◗ Assess the impact of the uses of fraud and violence on the end of Reconstruction in 1877 as a means of testing a recent historian's assertion that: *"The end of Reconstruction would come not because propertyless blacks succumbed to economic coercion, but because a politically tenacious black community, abandoned by the nation, fell victim to violence and fraud."*

◗ Compare the various viewpoints on the nature of Recon-struction by analyzing different interpretations of the era. *How have historians viewed Radical Republicans, the former plantation owners, the freedmen, the carpetbaggers, and the scalawags over time? What factors may account for changes in interpretations?*

◗ Construct a sound argument, debate, or historical narrative on questions such as: *Was Reconstruction a half-way revolution?*

◗ Examine civil rights legislation passed during Reconstruction. *To what extent did Reconstruction lay the groundwork for the Civil Rights movement of the 1960s?*

◗ Analyze how economic expansion and development were affected by the Civil War and Reconstruction. *How did land grants, subsidies to railroads, and tariff and monetary policies affect U.S. growth and development? Was the government following a policy of laissez faire in economic development or actively engaging in aid?*

◗ Evaluate the extent to which gender roles and status were affected by the Civil War and Reconstruction. *Why did leaders like Elizabeth Cady Stanton, Susan B. Anthony, and others feel betrayed by Reconstruction? How did the National Women's Suffrage Association (NWSA) and the American Women's Suffrage Association (AWSA) differ?*

ERA 6

The Development of the Industrial United States (1870-1900)

From the era of Reconstruction to the end of the 19th century, the United States underwent an economic transformation that involved the maturing of the industrial economy, the rapid expansion of big business, the development of large-scale agriculture, and the rise of national labor unions and pronounced industrial conflict.

Students can begin to see a resemblance to possibilities and problems that our society faces today. The late 19th century marked a spectacular outburst of technological innovation, which fueled headlong economic growth and delivered material benefits to many Americans. Yet, the advances in productive and extractive enterprises that technology permitted also had ecological effects that Americans were just beginning to understand and confront. In the last third of the 19th century, the rise of the American corporation and the advent of big business brought about a concentration of the nation's productive capacities in many fewer hands. Mechanization brought farming into the realm of big business and turned the United States into the world's premier producer of food—a position it has never surrendered.

This period also witnessed unprecedented immigration and urbanization, both of which were indispensable to industrial expansion. American society, always polyglot, became even more diverse as immigrants thronged from southern and eastern Europe—and also from Asia, Mexico, and Central America. As newcomers created a new American mosaic, the old Protestant European Americans' sway over the diverse people of this nation began to loosen. Related to this continuing theme of immigration was the search for national unity amid growing cultural diversity. How a rising system of public education promoted the assimilation of newcomers is an important topic for students to study.

Students should appreciate the cross-currents and contradictions of this period. For example, what many at the time thought was progress was regarded by others as retrogressive. Paradoxes abound. First, agricultural modernization, while innovative and productive, disrupted family farms and led American farmers to organize protest movements as never before. Second, the dizzying rate of expansion was accomplished at the cost of the wars against the Plains Indians, which produced the "second great removal" of indigenous peoples from their ancient homelands and ushered in a new federal Indian policy that would last until the New Deal. Third, muscular, wealth-producing industrial development that raised the standard of living for millions of Americans also fueled the rise of national labor unionism and unprecedented clashes in industrial and mining sites between capital and labor. Fourth, after the Civil War, women reformers, while reaching for an unprecedented public presence, suffered an era of retrenchment on economic and political issues. Lastly, the wrenching economic dislocations of this period and the social problems that erupted in rural and urban settings captured the attention of reformers and politicians, giving rise to third-party movements and the beginning of the Progressive movement.

He mocks the people who proposes that the Government shall protect the rich and that they in turn will care for the laboring poor.

— GROVER CLEVELAND
ANNUAL MESSAGE TO CONGRESS, 1888

Essay

American Labor History*
By Leon Fink

Recent labor historians have expanded their research by examining the question of when and how working people have affected American society rather than passively looking at how society affected the labor movement. Analysis from a different angle has opened every era of American history to an incorporation of the role of working men and women, from colonial artisans to computer technicians. This has liberated labor history from its confines in pigeon-holes in selected eras of survey courses. Leon Fink argues for a multi-dimensional study, examining diverse social forces that have affected the ordinary workers without denying the effects of economics, politics, and other outside influences on the development of labor history. The article in its entirety examines labor history from the colonial period to the present; the excerpt that follows focuses on the Gilded Age and Progressive Era.

Leon Fink has written extensively on American labor history. His works include *In Search of the Working Class* and *Working Democracy: The Knights of Labor and American Politics.*

Historians over the past generation have rediscovered the American working class. In doing so, they have focused less on official labor organizations (although such studies have played their part) than on the larger processes of social and economic change as these affect workers. The definition of 'labor,' itself has expanded beyond wage work in factories and workshops to encompass the lives of slaves on plantations and women at home; the subject of study also includes new or relatively unorganized groups such as department store employees, nurses, and migrant farm laborers. While the work experience itself still receives central attention, some labor historians give at least equal consideration to the dimensions of cultural identity, politics and governmental policy, and the structure of the labor market.

Such departures have given a distinctive new feel to a field that long took a more modest and self-restricted view of its purpose and direction. Originally growing out of the dedicated scholarship of early twentieth century labor economists following John R. Commons, labor history traditionally concentrated on the impact of the economic marketplace on workers, skills, living standards, and organizing capacity. The trade union itself, the main subject of analysis, was regarded primarily as an economic institution; political activity, competing organizational models, and biographies of labor leaders received secondary emphasis.

The "new labor history," though encompassing many different thematic currents, has generally emphasized the ordinary worker as subject. Without denying the influence of markets, outside political events, and other forces, historians have attempted to reconstruct not only the behavior but the motivations and understandings of the common people.

...Branching out creatively toward social and cultural analysis, the new labor history has necessarily involved forays into immigration, Afro-American, and women's history. Industrial relations, urban geography, and popular culture have also become vital subjects. Even standard political topics such as the American Revolution, the Civil War, and political party development have been reshaped by this "history from the bottom up."

...Much that we think of as modern America was first consolidated during the late nineteenth century. The spread of the business corporation as the country's basic economic unit, the accompanying rise of large-scale factories, the growth of cities, and the urban culture of

---

*Reprinted from *The New American History,* edited by Eric Foner (Philadelphia, Pa.: Temple University Press, 1990), pp. 233-250. Reprinted by permission of the copyright owner.

consumption based on mass marketing were all products of what Mark Twain called the Gilded Age. We normally picture the period as one that celebrated the businessman as the mover and shaker of America's progress and established a dominant intellectual climate sanctioning unrestricted free enterprise. In this fiercely middle-class culture, according to the conventional historical wisdom, American working people were simply middle-class citizens without money and education. Possessed of the same desires as everyone else, they lived with Horatio Alger dreams of "moving on up" the economic ladder by individual effort. Both the stepladder of immigrant upward mobility and a labor movement geared to craft-based demands for "more!" offered evidence of the fundamental unity and stability of a business-dominated culture by the turn of the century.

Such a gloss on the late nineteenth century requires correction if we are to grasp the real play of social conflict and historical possibility at the time. The Gilded Age witnessed the last and most significant attempt by American workers to fashion an alternative to corporate capitalism from within traditional political and social values. During recent years labor historians have explored the workers' world during the late nineteenth and early twentieth centuries from a variety of angles. One of the most popular approaches has been the community study used to examine industrializing towns and immigrant communities in large cities such as Chicago, New York, and Philadelphia. A second focus has been on the study of the work process itself, with attention to specific occupational subcultures. A third emphasizes worker organizations and labor politics during the period. Together, these studies have reconstructed a lost world of working-class America.

Within the workers' world the work experience itself generated an ethic of mutuality foreign to the emphasis on individualism which is often assigned to the period. Amid changing technological and managerial constraints imposed from above, workers—first as autonomous craftsmen, then through union work rules, and finally through sympathy strikes—struggled to maintain or regain control over decisions on the shop floor. The craftsman's notion of the work "stint" (the self-imposed limit on worker output), a visceral resistance or defiant "manliness" toward unwarranted exactions from employers or supervisors, and a disciplined solidarity with fellow workers defined a workplace ethic enveloping not only skilled craftworkers but unskilled, immigrant factory workers as well. David Montgomery's study of "workers' control" has emphasized the strength of the early twentieth-century labor ethic; other studies have drawn attention to the divisions within the labor force occasioned by the heterogeneity of skill, gender, and ethnic background of American workers.

American workers' organizing efforts in the age of Carnegie, to be sure, drew on more than the daily fight for "control" at the workplace. A popular republicanism questioned the effects, indeed the very morality, of a corporate industrial order in which one class of citizens would have so much power over others. As a philosophical Ohio farmer put it, "In Europe labor is accustomed to oppression, and it's a hard part of God's destiny for them, to be borne patiently as long as they can get enough to hold body and soul together"; in America, however, "our people have been carefully educated to consider themselves the best on earth, and they will not patiently submit to privation such as this system is leading to. They not only feel that they are the best of the earth, but there is no power, no standing army, no organized iron rule to hold them down." The responsibility of democratic citizenship required workers to earn a "competence," enough income and time to sustain a healthy family, educate the children, and stay personally abreast of worldly affairs. In 1885 one labor agitator declared that lumbermen who toiled fourteen or fifteen hours a day were "not free men—they had no time for thought, no time for home."

Efforts to transcend "wage slavery," evident in much of the political and industrial activity of organized workers since the 1860s, peaked with the rise of the Knights of Labor in the mid-1880s. The Knights, numbering more than three-quarters of a million members by 1886 and aspiring to a universal crusade of the "producing classes" (excluding only "social parasites"—lawyers, bankers, and liquor salesmen), reflected the full range of social and political initiatives in Gilded Age laboring communities. Unlike the older view of the Knights, which relegated the organization to the dustbins of history as impractical and backward-looking, recent treatments have shown renewed respect for the Great Upheaval, labor's serious and rational challenge to the consolidation of corporate capitalism in the 1880s. Under the vast social umbrella of the Knights of Labor (skilled and unskilled, men and women, native and immigrant, white and black joined as equals), Leon Fink has argued, moral and political education produced cooperatives, land resettlement schemes, and Greenback-labor politics mixed uncertainly with trade union organization and the weapons of the strike and boycott. Reading rooms and family picnics as well as Labor Day parades and independent political tickets defined the socialization of individuals, families, and communities into the labor culture. Drawing on the traditions of fraternal lodges such as the Masons and Odd Fellows, the Knights began as a secret society, cloaking its activities in a rich veil of ritual and formal ceremony.

It was not only in formal organizations or overtly political activity, however, that the tensions of working-class versus middle-class values registered at the turn of the century. In popular leisure as well, historians have discovered a record of conflict, resistance, and, finally, adaptation by the immigrant working classes to outside pressures. Middle-nineteenth century recreation among the laboring classes generally centered on local neighborhoods; it was loosely self-organized; and because of both a traditional unruliness among working men and a self-styled brashness among young working women, it tended to affront middle-class Protestant standards of proper decorum. Neighborhood saloons, raucous celebrations of holidays such as the Fourth of July, untamed behavior in the public parks, and defiance of the quiet Sabbath all came in for critical scrutiny by middle-class reformers. Sunday closings, prohibition, museums, libraries, and supervised recreation were all prescribed from on high as ways to "civilize" the working-class immigrants. Just as certainly, such impositions were either politically resisted or, sometimes more effectively, simply ignored by their would-be beneficiaries.

But while the genteel leisure reformers generally failed to remake the behavior and values of American workers, another set of changes did have lasting effects on the popular culture. These involved the commercialization of leisure time, or the creation of what has come to be called mass, consumer culture. Higher incomes combined with a generally shrinking week had created, by the turn of the century, a mass audience for professional sports and entertainment industries. By 1910 the nickel theaters showing silent motion pictures (featuring talents usually drawn from the immigrant working class itself) could be labeled "the academy of the workingman and by the 1920s some 50 million, or half the U.S. population, could be counted in weekly attendance at the movies. Initially catering to working-class audiences with a tolerant indulgence of drinking and casual family comings and goings, the movie theaters began to take on more lavish, disciplined, middle-class standards only in the 1920s. In the end the new mass culture, argues Roy Rosenzweig, would be neither an autonomous creation of the common people nor a product created and packaged entirely apart from them. Drawing originally on popular and democratic impulses, leisure in America—like politics—would involve a continuous if often contested quest to harness the public impulse for private ends.

The examination of leisure and popular culture suggests the breadth of themes now invoked by the study of labor history. The transformation of work and the workers' community, the consequent struggle not only for material standards of living but for a voice in the direction of American society, and the changing meanings that working people themselves gave to their actions lend the study of labor history a broad territorial claim within the larger discipline. Indeed, much of the social and cultural history of the American people may be observed through these lenses.

Charitable distribution of bread, c1890s. Courtesy Library of Congress

Sample Student Activities

I. *How the rise of corporations, heavy industry, and mechanized farming transformed the American peoples.*

A. The connections among industrialization, the advent of the modern corporation, and material well-being.

Grades 5-6

▸ Construct a timeline listing the significant improvements in transportation and communication and the important inventions of the post Civil War era. *What contributed to the rapid economic growth of the United States? How did trade, shipping, railroads, large business and new farming practices change during the period? What were the effects of technological change on the environment? To what extent would life be different today without the benefit of technological change and the inventions of the latter part of the 19th century?*

▸ Research the lives of famous inventors such as Thomas Alva Edison (electric light), Alexander Graham Bell (telephone), and Granville T. Woods (automatic air brake), explaining how their inventions changed people's lives.

▸ Assemble evidence and write a newspaper story (ca. 1900) reflecting the major technological, transportation, and communication changes occurring since 1870 and explain how they changed the lives and standard of living of a majority of citizens.

▸ Write a biographical sketch of an American entrepreneur such as James Hill, John D. Rockefeller, Andrew Carnegie, J. Pierpont Morgan, or Leland Stanford.

Grades 7-8

▸ Draw evidence from popular literature, biographies and other historical sources to evaluate the influence of the Horatio Alger stories on the notion of the "American Dream." *How many of the great business leaders of the late 19th century fit the Horatio Alger model? What do the "rags to riches" stories tell about American values? To what extent is the "rags to riches" dream alive today? How does contemporary literature or television promote the dream of "rags to riches"?*

▸ Construct a historical narrative assessing the impact of modern technology, new inventions, advances in transportation and communication on society. *To what extent did advances in transportation and communication promote the development of urban areas? How did Americans move from steam power to electrical power? How did Edison's laboratory at Menlo Park stimulate industrial research?*

▸ Draw upon evidence from a variety of primary and secondary sources including letters, public addresses, and biographies to construct a character sketch of a prominent industrial leader. *What benefits did the individual's success bring to American society? How did these "captains of industry" build great fortunes? How did they use their wealth? What effects did the practices employed by these business leaders have on competition? What role did government take in promoting business? Were the prominent business leaders of the day "captains of industry" or "robber barons"?*

▸ Draw from historical sources and current events to compare prominent contemporary business leaders with the "industrial giants" of the late 19th century. *To what degree are the men and women in the forefront of American business today different from earlier entrepreneurs? What role has free competition played in the development of today's business leaders?*

Grades 9-12

▶ Using a variety of historical, literary, graphical, and visual sources, create a narrative explaining the changing nature of business enterprise in the late 19th century. *Which had a greater impact on economic expansion in the period 1870-1900, individual business leaders, such as Rockefeller and Carnegie, or market forces (e.g., supply and demand)? Did the judicial system help or hinder the economic transformation of the United States in the period?*

▶ Explain how industrialization increased the availability of consumer goods, raised the standard of living, and redistributed wealth.

▶ Utilize a variety of historical sources, including primary documents, to complete a case study of how a business leader gained dominance in a particular industry in the late 19th century. *To what extent did business leaders seek to maximize profits and limit competition? Did the business leader pursue horizontal or vertical integration? Why? To what extent did managerial organization, technological innovation, and individual decision making contribute to the success of the business?*

▶ Conduct a mock trial of John D. Rockefeller in which the defense and prosecution present evidence to refute or support a charge of price fixing and unfair competition.

▶ Write a response to the following passage from "Wealth" by Andrew Carnegie: "This, then, is held to be the duty of the man of wealth: To set an example of modest, unostentatious living, shunning display or extravagance; to provide moderately for the legitimate wants of those dependent upon him; and, after doing so, to consider all surplus revenues which come to him simply as trust funds, which he is called upon to administer, and strictly bound as a matter of duty to administer in the manner which, in his judgment, is best calculated to produce the most beneficial results for the community—the man of wealth thus becoming the mere trustee and agent for his poorer brethren, bringing to their service his superior wisdom, experience, and ability to administer, doing for them better than they would or could do for themselves." *What evidence would you use to support or refute Carnegie's statement regarding the responsibility of individuals of wealth?*

B. The rapid growth of cities and how urban life changed.

Grades 5-6

▶ Identify places and regions where industries and transportation expanded during the late 19th century and explain the geographic reasons for building factories, commercial centers, and transportation hubs in these places.

▶ Compare the size of major cities then and now, using census data and historical pictures. *Which cities had the best ports? What made some cities grow and others stay the same size or get smaller?*

▶ Describe living conditions in the growing cities in the late 19th century. Draw upon historical accounts, stories, and pictures, to compare opportunities and problems of 19th-century families in large cities to those who live in urban American today. *What drew different groups of people to the big cities in the late 19th century? What draws people to the cities today?*

▶ Construct a model or plan for a typical large urban center of the 1890s showing skyscrapers, transportation systems, and parks and recreation areas. *How did urban centers change since mid-century? What accounts for these changes?*

▶ Draw evidence from historical accounts, biographies, and political cartoons to provide examples of corruption in the period following the Civil War. Investigate the life of William Marcy Tweed. Explain what Tweed meant when he said: "I don't care so much what the papers write about me. My constituents can't read. But...they can see pictures." *How important were cartoonists in drawing attention to political corruption?*

Grades 7-8

▶ Construct a data sheet listing diverse and common factors of five selected large cities in different regions of the country (e.g., Boston, Philadelphia, Atlanta, Chicago, San Francisco). *How did physical geography influence the location of the selected cities? What influence did new methods of transportation and communication have on the growth and development of cities? To what extent did economic development such as industrialization and commerce contribute to the growth of these urban centers?*

▶ Draw from a demographic map, graphs, and statistical data to trace the internal migration from farm to city in the latter part of the nineteenth century. *What geographic factors contributed to the growth of cities? What accounted for the movement to the cities? How did urban living conditions differ from those in rural areas? Do the same factors attract people to large cities today? Do cities today have the same advantages as they did in the late 19th century?*

▶ Draw evidence from a variety of historical documents including eyewitness accounts, art, and period literature, to construct a pictorial essay explaining how industrialization and urbanization affected living conditions in late 19th-century cities.

▶ Construct an oral report which examines how urban political machines gained power and how they addressed the challenges of governing large cities. *Who were the most notorious political bosses of the era? What tactics did they use to govern cities? In what ways did machine politics help the urban poor? Why were immigrants willing to cooperate with political bosses?*

▶ Draw upon the works of political cartoonists and reform writers, such as Thomas Nast and Lincoln Steffens, to examine the criticism of machine politics.

▶ Use a map of a major 19th-century city to assess the elements of urban planning such as recreation, zoning patterns, and transportation. *How did the "city beautiful" movement transform the urban environment and change the character of American cities?*

Grades 9-12

▶ Select a city for study and, drawing upon a variety of sources, review its demographic, economic, and spatial expansion in the late nineteenth century. *What were the factors influencing the city's growth in the late 19th century? How did the city's population, work force, and residential patterns change in the period 1870-1900?*

▶ Draw upon such sources as Jacob Riis's *How the Other Half Lives* (1890), Stephen Crane's *Maggie: A Girl of the Streets* and *George's Mother*, pictures and diagrams of the "dumbbell tenement," and other visual and graphic material, to determine how city residents dealt with such problems as developing adequate water supplies, sewer systems, public health measures, public safety, public and private education, paving or roads, transportation, and housing in the late 19th century.

▶ Utilizing a variety of sources, including eyewitness accounts, construct a historical narrative or a case study examining the methods urban bosses used to win support of immigrants. *How effective were urban bosses in supporting the interests of immigrants and the urban poor? Were they demigods or demagogues? Explain. To what extent was Lord James Bryce's characterization of city government in the United States as a "conspicuous failure" in his* The American Commonwealth *(1888) a correct appraisal?*

▶ Construct a case study of political bosses such as George Washington Plunkitt and "Big Tim" Sullivan. *How did middle-class reforms and urban bosses view the role and responsibilities of city government? How democratic were the "goo-goos" (good government advocates)?*

▶ Evaluate the extent of corruption in state and national politics. *To what extent did crooked business deals, in securing contracts during the Civil War, encourage corruption in the government after the war? How was William Marcy Tweed able to come to power in New York? Why was the city called "Boss Tweed's New York"?*

▶ Examine the influence of Frederick Law Olmstead in establishing principles of urban planning nationwide. Evaluate the role of urban planners in transforming a major American cities. *How valid was the opinion of leading city planners, such as Frederick Law Olmstead and Richard Morris Hunt, that an improved urban environment would encourage good citizenship and social order?*

C. How agriculture, mining, and ranching were transformed.

Grades 5-6

▶ Draw from various resources including historical novels and physical maps, to examine how geography impacted the way people lived and worked in the West.

▶ Draw upon primary sources and literature including the Little House series by Laura Ingalls Wilder and *Prairie Songs* by Pam Conrad to explain the idea of the "frontier." *What kind of people were drawn to the West? Where did they come from and how well did they get along with one another? What was the role of women and children on farms, ranches, and in mining towns?*

▶ Compare life on the Great Plains with life in urban areas in the latter part of the 19th century. *What was the average work week like for farmers compared to urban workers in terms of hours worked, income, and leisure time and opportunities?*

Grades 7-8

▶ Draw upon topographical, climate, and land use maps, period literature, diaries and journals, and visual evidence of the late 19th-century frontier to explain the influence of geography and technology on farming, ranching, and mining in the West. *How did agricultural innovations such as those by Cyrus McCormick and John Deere improve agricultural production? How did the invention of barbed wire change ranching? How did the new technology change rural America?*

▶ Construct a simulated journal, classroom newspaper, or skit which reflects the different perspectives of ranchers, farmers, and miners in the west. Draw evidence from historical sources and novels such as *A Lantern in Her Hand* by Bess Streeter Aldrich, *Prairie Songs* by Pamela Conrad, *The Obstinate Land* by Harold Keith, and *Shane* by Jack Schaefer. *What were the issues behind the conflicts? What disputes developed over water rights and open ranges?*

▶ Debate the proposition, *Resolved: the West was won by barbed wire.*

▶ Draw evidence from letters, diaries, contemporary art, photography, and literary works, to construct a simulated journal or short story reflecting the daily life of women on the western frontier. *How did life experiences in the Great Plains and West differ from those in the East and Midwest? What impact did these experiences have on the expansion of woman's rights?*

▶ Examine cross-cultural encounters and explain the conflicts that arose among different racial and ethnic groups in western mining regions, farming communities, and urban areas. *To what extent were the old Spanish and Mexican land grants recognized by local and state governments and new settlers? What experiences did Asian immigrants encounter? What discriminatory practices existed? What conflicts developed between Native Americans and white settlers in mining regions and farming communities in the West? What were the experiences of African Americans in the West? What was the role of the Buffalo Soldiers in the West?*

Grades 9-12

▸ Contrast the romantic depiction of life in the West with the reality, and describe some of the hardships faced by settlers in the late 19th century. *What led to conflicts between cattle ranchers on the one hand and farmers and sheep herders on the other? How was ethnic conflict portrayed in the Murietta stories and the Cortina uprising? What was the role of vigilantes in the West?*

▸ Analyze the role of religion in stabilizing the new western communities.

▸ Review data from a variety of sources which reflect the extension of railroad lines, increased agricultural cultivation and productivity, and the effect of improved transportation facilities on commodity prices. *What was the average size of farms in the North, South, Great Plains, and West in 1870 and in 1900? What agricultural commodities were the principal source of farm income in these regions? How did the increased use of agricultural machinery affect productivity, indebtedness, farm ownership, and the average size of farms?*

▸ Research the importance of hydraulic engineering in the American West in the latter part of the 19th century. *How significant was hydraulic engineering in the "winning of the West"?*

▸ Draw from a variety of historical, literary, and statistical data, to analyze the racial, ethnic, and gender composition of farmers, miners, and ranchers in the West in the late 19th century. *How were gender and racial roles defined on the farming, mining, and ranching frontiers?*

▸ Utilize a variety of historical and graphic data, such as the social and political programs of the Patrons of Husbandry, Greenbackers, Northern, Southern, and Colored Farmers' Alliances to analyze the impact of the crop-lien system in the South, transportation and storage costs for farmers, and the price of farm staples such as wheat, corn, and cotton in the period 1870-1896. *What caused the decline in farm commodity prices? How did the government's monetary policy affect the price of farm commodities? What were the major grievances of the primary farm organizations in the West and South during the period? What major solutions did they offer?*

D. The effects of rapid industrialization on the environment and the emergence of the first conservation movement.

Grades 5-6

▸ Describe the efforts of late 19th-century reformers to control pollution, and compare their activities with current efforts.

▸ Examine photographs or art works which show the effects of mining and industrial development on health and scenic beauty. *What was the effect of strip mining on soil erosion?*

▸ Analyze the effect of men such as John Muir in promoting concern for the natural environment. *Why was the Sierra Club established? What were its goals?*

Grades 7-8

▸ Draw upon primary sources such as journals, letters, contemporary art, and photography to examine the environmental impact of industrialization and the depletion of natural resources. *What contrasts are presented in visual records of the period? What were the origins of the late 19th-century environmental movement? How successful were they? What role did local, state, and national government play in the attempt to preserve natural resources?*

▸ Draw from a variety of primary and secondary sources including period literature, to construct a well-reasoned argument, debate, or historical narrative on such questions as: *What measures could have been taken to provide for mining and industrial development and environmental protection? What are some current issues over the same question? What lessons regarding the conflict between economic expansion and environmental protection can be determined from the study of history?*

Grades 9-12

◆ Draw upon visual sources such as the paintings of the Hudson River School artists, Currier and Ives prints, the writings of John Muir, and Frederick Jackson Turner's celebration of the frontier to analyze how the emphasis on staple crop production, strip mining, lumbering, ranching, and the destructions of western buffalo herds led to environmental changes in the late 19th century. *Who were the leaders and primary supporters of the conservation movement in the late 19th century? What arguments did environmentalists and conservationists of the time employ? How did local, state, and national leaders respond to environmental and conservation concerns? How did ordinary people respond to environmental and conservation concerns?*

◆ Construct a historical narrative examining the impact of the rapid increase in population and industrial growth in urban areas in the late 19th century. Respond to H. L. Mencken's claim that Baltimore in the 1880s smelled "like a billion polecats" and the comment by Cleveland's mayor who, in 1881, called the Cuyahoga River "an open sewer through the center of the city." *Why did the "gridiron pattern" become the standard for urban growth in the late 19th century? What problems resulted? How did inefficient procedures for garbage collection and sewage disposal and treatment effect urban life? How did city leaders and residents cope with the major environmental problems facing cities?*

◆ Debate the issues raised by environmentalists in the latter part of the 19th century. *How did businessmen and farmers respond to these issues?*

> *II. Massive immigration after 1870 and how new social patterns, conflicts, and ideas of national unity developed amid growing cultural diversity.*

A. The sources and experiences of the new immigrants.

Grades 5-6

◆ Explain how immigration changed after 1870. Use maps and pictorial resources to show where people came from and where they settled. *Which immigrant groups came to your community in the late 19th century? Why did they leave their native land? What opportunities did they seek in America?*

◆ Describe the ways in which immigrants learned to live and work in a new country. Draw upon excerpts from first-hand accounts, stories, and poems which describe living and working conditions. *How did urban reformers like Jane Addams and Jacob Riis try to serve the needs of new immigrants? What role did public schools have in helping immigrants settle into their new communities?*

◆ Use old photographs, oral histories, and other sources to compile a history of the experiences of family members who immigrated to the United States.

◆ Use stories such as *Tales from the Gold Mountain* by Paul Yee and *Samurai of the Gold Hill* by Yoshiko Uchida to examine early Chinese and Japanese immigration to California.

◆ Examine the experiences of Jewish immigrants through children's stories such as *The Cat Who Escaped from Steerage* by Evelyn Wilde Meyerson.

Grades 7-8

◆ Compare and contrast immigration in the 1880s with that of the 1840s. *To what extent did the motives for immigration differ for the earlier and the later period? From what regions of the world did most immigrants come?*

▶ Draw evidence from a variety of historical sources to construct a chart showing different attitudes toward immigrants. *How did Americans react to the new immigration? Did the nativism of the 1840s differ from that of the 1880s? How did the languages and religious beliefs of the new immigrants affect the nativists? What factors contributed to changing attitudes toward immigrants? How did immigrants respond to hostility?*

▶ Draw upon evidence from biographies and other historical sources such as *The Life Stories of Undistinguished Americans*, edited by Hamilton Holt, to construct historical assessments of the contributions of immigrants in American society.

▶ Examine the efforts of individuals who worked to assist immigrants such as Jane Addams and Frances Xavier Cabrini. *How did they help immigrants? To what extent did individual assistance programs promote assimilation?*

▶ Interpret documentary evidence from diaries, letters, and political cartoons such as those of Thomas Nast to assess attitudes towards Catholic and Jewish immigrants.

Grades 9-12

▶ Draw upon such sources as copies of immigrants' letters written home and excerpts from ethnic newspapers to compare the experiences of the new immigrants in the period 1870-1900 with the message of Emma Lazarus's poem, "The New Colossus." *What were the expectations of the new immigrants? To what extent did they attain their goals? How did parochial and other religious schools serve the interests of the newer immigrants? Why were the last four lines of "The New Colossus" placed on the Statue of Liberty? How do they compare with the rest of the poem? Do the terms "melting pot" or "salad bowl" best describe the acculturation experience of the newer immigrants? Are both terms inadequate?*

▶ Research communal associations and institutions that immigrant groups organized. *How effective were these associations in preserving cultural and ethnic identity? In promoting economic opportunities?*

▶ Construct a narrative drawing upon historical evidence to examine the reasons for hostility to the "new" immigrants in the 1880s and 1890s using examples such as the antiforeign hysteria in the aftermath of the Haymarket Affair, attacks on Jewish merchants and residents in Louisiana and Mississippi (1880s and 1890s), anti-Italian sentiment in New Orleans (1891), and attacks on Polish and Hungarian strikers in Pennsylvania (1887).

▶ Develop a case study which examines the importance of public and parochial schools in integrating immigrants into the American mainstream. *What difficulties did the immigrants face in assimilating? How successful were schools in Americanization programs?*

B. "Scientific racism," race relations, and the struggle for equal rights.

Grades 5-6

▶ Draw upon evidence in historical studies, documentary photographs, political cartoons, and children's stories to explain how different people lived in America in the late 19th century. *How difficult was it to move up in American society? Did minority groups and immigrants establish and practice their own religions and customs?*

▶ Give examples of Jim Crow laws and explain how African Americans worked to end these restrictions.

▶ Compare and contrast a schedule of school activities in a 19th-century urban school and your own. *How does public education promote social mobility?*

Grades 7-8

- Define Social Darwinism and illustrate through specific historical examples the application of the philosophy.

- Use a chart or graph to illustrate social mobility in 19th-century American society. *What factors made it possible for people to move to a different social class? What hindered social mobility?*

- Draw from a variety of sources including letters, journals, popular literature, political cartoons, and Supreme Court cases, to construct a historical narrative examining racial and ethnic discrimination in the United States. *What forms of discrimination did Asian Americans and Hispanic Americans face in the West and Southwest? How did they respond to discriminatory practices? To what extent did legislation limit the rights of Asian and Hispanic Americans? What were Jim Crow laws? To what extent were discriminatory practices against African Americans different in the North and South? What were the issues involved in the* Plessy v. Ferguson *case? What impact did this decision have on race relations?*

- Construct a historical narrative examining the efforts of minority groups to attain equal rights in the latter part of the 19th century and appraise the leadership roles of individuals who were outspoken in opposition to discrimination and racial prejudice.

- Examine personal encounters with Jim Crow laws through literature using historical fiction such as *I Be Somebody* by Hadley Irwin.

Grades 9-12

- Assess the role of land grant colleges and public educational institutions in promoting social mobility.

- Drawing upon the arguments of advocates of Social Darwinism such as William Graham Sumner, John Fiske, and Andrew Carnegie, and opponents such as Lester Frank Ward, John Dewey, Richard T. Ely, and William James, analyze the impact of Social Darwinism on public policy in the late 19th century. *Did Social Darwinism justify the political, economic, and social dominance of one group over another?*

- Use examples of literacy tests and selections from the Mississippi Constitution 1890 and the South Carolina adoption of the Mississippi formula in 1896 to analyze the origin and purpose of the "Jim Crow" system. *How did poll taxes and residency requirements help to bolster the system? What were the goals and consequences of the Immigration Restriction League?*

- Utilizing selections from the anti-lynching appeals of Ida Wells Barnett, Booker T. Washington's "Atlanta Exposition Address," W. E. B. Du Bois's *The Souls of Black Folk*, and appeals of other African American leaders of the late 19th century, explain the various proposals advanced to combat political disenfranchisement, Jim Crow Laws, and the widespread lynching of the 1890s.

- Analyze the meaning of the *Yick Wo v. Hopkins* (1886) and *Plessy v. Ferguson* (1896) Supreme Court cases. *What do the decisions reveal about American society in the 1890s? What was the reasoning in the minority opinions? Were the implications of the decisions similar or different?*

- Use historical fiction such as *The Sport of Gods* by Paul Laurence Dunbar to explore the experiences of an African American family's migration from the South to New York City in the 1890s.

C. How new cultural movements at different social levels affected American life.

Grades 5-6

▸ Compare children's toys, games, and entertainment in the late 19th century with those of today. *Where did children go for entertainment in the late 19th century? How does it compare with entertainment opportunities available today? What inventions and media changes make our choices different from those of children in the late 19th century?*

▸ Use stories, narratives, and photographs to compare the expected behavior for children then with those in our time.

Grades 7-8

▸ Draw upon the art of the late 19th century to develop a historical narrative or construct a project that examines the ways in which leading artists such as Mary Cassatt and Winslow Homer portrayed life. *How does art reflect attitudes and values of society? How did the work of leading artists differ?*

▸ Compose a list of the different sports, entertainment, and recreational activities popular in the latter part of the 19th century and explain the reasons for their popularity. *What recreational activities were associated with the wealthy? Which were popular with the middle and working classes? What recreational activities are commonly shown in the art of the period? How did increased leisure time affect spectator sports and entertainment?*

▸ Examine the changes in lifestyles of the late 19th century. *How did department stores and chain stores illustrate the change in the role of the family from producers to consumers? How did public education reflect the changes taking place in the country? How were changes in childhood reflected in new games played and the differing expectations of children? How did women's clothing and dress styles (e.g., the "Gibson Girl") change in the late 19th century?*

Grades 9-12

▸ Evaluate the portrayal of regional life in the writings of social realist authors such as George Washington Cable, Willa Cather, Edward Eggleston, Hamlin Garland, Joel Chandler Harris, Bret Harte, William Dean Howells, Charles W. Chesnutt, Mary Noailles Murfree, O. E. Rölvaag, Mark Twain, Edith Wharton, and Constance Fenimore Woolson. *How did different authors portray life in the late 19th century? Why are most of the famous authors of the period referred to as social realist writers? What were the regional themes found in their works?*

▸ Compare the various forms of leisure activities available to different classes, such as organized and spectator sports, museums, theaters and symphonies, vaudeville, amusement parks, circuses, city parks, bicycling, croquet, and golf, tennis, polo, and horse racing.

▸ Draw upon evidence from a variety of sources including art and literature of the late 19th century to evaluate the effects of Victorianism on proper codes of conduct. *What do the architectural layouts and pictures of interior rooms tell about lifestyles, class differences, and gender roles during the Victorian era? How do the reform movements led by Frances Willard and Anthony Comstock reflect the enduring moral code of Victorianism?*

▸ Research voluntary organizations that worked to assist immigrants and assess the programs which they offered to promote national unity and American values during a period of massive immigration. Explain how public education promoted Americanization programs. *How successful were these programs in building national unity?*

> ### III. The rise of the American labor movement and how political issues reflected social and economic changes.

A. How the "second industrial revolution" changed the nature and conditions of work.

Grades 5-6

- List the changes in the way businesses operated after the Civil War and explain how workers lives were affected by these changes.

- Describe working conditions in urban factories. *What kind of working conditions did men, women, and children experience? How are workers protected from such conditions now?*

- Develop a skit or role-play activity which explores the reasons for child labor and its consequences.

Grades 7-8

- Draw upon a variety of primary and secondary sources to assess the connection between ethnic groups and occupational patterns in the late 19th century. *What factors were necessary to achieve skilled and high paying jobs? What were the highest paying jobs during this era? Do these occupations exist today? Do people today who hold these jobs have the same status in society as their late 19th-century counterparts?*

- Construct a historical narrative examining the changes in the size and shape of the work force and in working conditions in the manufacturing sector. *What affect did the rise of big business have on the number of manufacturing workers needed in American industry? Which jobs—both skilled and unskilled—were most affected by change during the period? What were working conditions like at the time? Wages? Benefits? Safety precautions? What place did women and children play in this work force? To what degree did their experiences differ from those of the men?*

- Examine typical working conditions interpreting documentary evidence from the period, including photographs, newspaper articles, and biographies. *What do the sources reveal about the nature and condition of work during the late 19th century? What comparisons or observations might be made to evaluate the differences between the past and the present day?*

Grades 9-12

- Examine how the rise of big business affected workers. *How did the running of factories by managers change the prior relationship of workers and owners? How did workers respond to the increasingly impersonal nature and strict timetables of factory work?*

- Assess the inroads women made in traditional male-dominated professions and occupations. *Why did early labor unions refuse to admit women? Why did the Knights of Labor admit women as members while other unions did not? How did the employment of African American women differ from immigrant and native-born white women?*

- Draw evidence from primary sources to examine the legal status of women in the late 19th century. *What were the issues raised by Myra Bradwell? What was the legal reasoning in Bradwell v. Illinois case (1873)? Why? To what extent did the Bradwell case typify the status of women in the professions throughout the latter part of the century?*

- Drawing on such sources as John Spargo's *The Bitter Cry of the Children* and a variety of other literary, historical, and visual sources, construct a narrative explaining the reasons for the increase in child labor, the type of work performed by children, the occupations in which they were employed, and the dangers they faced during the workday.

B. The rise of national labor unions and the role of state and federal governments in labor conflicts.

Grades 5-6

▸ Write a biographical profile of a labor leader such as William Sylvis, Terence Powderly, Mary Harris Jones, Isaac Myers, Eugene V. Debs, or Samuel Gompers. *How did this labor leader influence history? How effective was he or she in promoting the interests of workers?*

▸ Use historical fiction such as *Trouble at the Mines* by Doreen Rappaport to investigate the strikes in the coal mines and the organizing efforts of Mother Mary Jones.

▸ Explain why people organized to improve working conditions, hours, and wages. *Why did tension grow in factories and mines during the late 19th century? How do workers and owners solve their problems today?*

Grades 7-8

▸ Draw upon historical sources to examine the development of trade unions in the United States. *In what ways did trade unions differ from earlier reform unions? What circumstances prompted workers to attempt to band together? How did management from different regions and different industries respond to union organization?*

▸ Explain the rifts between workers and management in the Railroad Strike (1877), the Haymarket Affair (1886), the Homestead and Coeur d'Alene strikes (1892), and the Pullman Strike (1894). *What were the reasons underlying the workers decision to strike? What stance did management take in response to workers demands? How, why, and to what extent did government come to be involved in the crisis? What was the legacy of labor unrest in this period?*

▸ Investigate labor organizing and the experiences of immigrants in the labor movement by drawing upon historical novels such as *Breaker* by N.A. Perez and *The Tempering* by Gloria Skurzyuski.

▸ Conduct a mock trial of Eugene V. Debs in which the defense and prosecution present evidence to refute or support a charge of restraint of commerce in the 1894 Pullman strike.

Grades 9-12

▸ Compare the charters of the Knights of Labor and American Federation of Labor in terms of the types of workers organized; their view of immigrants; African Americans, Chinese, and women workers; and their position on strikes and reform agendas. *Why did most unions support a "lily white" policy in the late 19th century? How and why did the Knights of Labor differ? Why did the Knights of Labor display racial hostility to the Chinese in contrast to their policy toward African American and women workers? Why did the American Federation of Labor avoid involvement in broad-based reform and political movements?*

▸ Drawing evidence from the writings of Terence Powderly, Samuel Gompers, and Eugene V. Debs, and historical accounts of the Haymarket Affair (1886), the Homestead and Coeur d'Alene strikes (1892), and the Pullman strike (1894), analyze the extent of radicalism in the labor movement. *Why did Henry Clay Frick feel that he was defending American republicanism in the Homestead Affair? Why did the Amalgamated Association of Steel and Iron Workers believe their actions were in the true spirit of republicanism? Which point of view would you support?*

▸ Analyze the labor conflicts of 1894 and their impact on the development of American democracy. *Why was Coxey's Army formed and what was its impact? What did Thorstein Veblen mean when he argued that the men of Coxey's Army changed the phrase of Declaration of Independence from "life, liberty, and the pursuit of happiness" to "life, liberty, and the means of happiness"? Why did Attorney General Olney seek an injunction against the Pullman strikes? How did the Pullman strikers justify their actions? How did President Cleveland justify the use of the U.S. Army? Would you agree with the president's decision?*

C. How Americans grappled with the social, economic, and political issues.

Grades 5-6

▶ List the third parties that were formed in the post-Civil War period and explain why they were established.

▶ Examine Thomas Nast's political cartoons to explore the issues of importance in the period. Compare the Nast cartoons to present-day political cartoons. *What do the Nast cartoons tell about important political issues of the day? What symbols did Nast use to represent the Republican party? The Democratic party?*

▶ Research the lives of important individuals such as Grover Cleveland, Belva Lockwood, Samuel Gompers, Mary Elizabeth Lease, William Jennings Bryan, and George Washington Carver, and chart the significant events in their lives.

Grades 7-8

▶ Define socialism. *What were the goals of the Socialist party? How did socialism differ from capitalism? Who would be most likely to support the socialists?*

▶ Construct a historical argument in the form of balance sheets, debates, or narratives to examine the position of the major political parties on the paramount issues of the day. *How did the Democratic and Republican parties differ on issues relating to business regulation?*

▶ Draw upon evidence from biographies and other historical sources to assess the importance of individuals such as Samuel Tilden, Grover Cleveland, and Thomas Nast in promoting political reforms. *How did the Democratic and Republican parties respond to demands for political reform? Who were the Mugwumps and what were their goals? How did the Pendleton Act address political patronage?*

▶ Explain the goals of the Populist Party and identify the leading Populists of the period. *What did the founders of the Populist Party see as the major problems in America? What policies did they advocate in order to address the roots of their concerns? How effective were Mary Elizabeth Lease and William Jennings Bryan in arousing western farmers?*

Grades 9-12

▶ Draw from a variety of sources to construct a historical narrative that assesses the appeal of the Democratic, Republican, and Greenback Labor parties to socioeconomic groups and different sections of the country. *Why was voter turnout and party loyalty so high in the period 1870-1896? Why did a large majority of urban workers in the North support the Democratic party? Why did African American voters tend to support the Republican party? What was the role of third parties like the Greenback-Labor and Socialist parties in the last third of the 19th century? What impact did third parties have on the two major parties?*

▶ Draw upon historical and graphical data to evaluate whether or not the contraction of the money supply was the chief cause of the decline in farm prices and income in the period 1873-1896.

▶ Evaluate to what extent the Democratic and Republican parties deserved the label "Tweedledee and Tweedledum." *Who were the "Mugwumps" and why did they support Cleveland in the election of 1884? Was the tariff a major issue in the 1880s and 1890s? How did the Cleveland and Harrison administration deal with the tariff?*

▶ Using data such as the "Ocala Demands" and the writings of Tom Watson, analyze the reaction of western and southern farmers to the cycle of falling prices, scarce money, and debt. *What were the goals and achievements of the National Farmers Alliance and Industrial Union? What was its relationship to the National Colored Farmers' Alliance? To the Northwestern Alliance? Why did Jerry Simpson and Mary Elizabeth Lease become alliance leaders?*

▶ Use the Omaha Platform of 1892 as the focus of historical inquiry to uncover the problems that prompted the establishment of the Populist Party. *To what extent, if any, were provisions of the Omaha Platform incorporated into the platforms of the two major parties over the following generation? What influence did the Populists have on the later Progressive movement?*

▶ Construct a historical argument, debate, or narrative to present evidence on issues such as the following: *Farmers are to blame for their own inability to adjust to the changing industrial scene.*

▶ Assess the overall successes and failures of the Populist movement in meeting the needs of American society. *What were the issues raised by the Populists? To what extent did Populism differ in different sections of the country? What position did Populists take on immigration and woman suffrage? What leadership role did women play in the populist party? How did Populism contribute to the movement to disfranchise African Americans in the southern states?*

▶ Analyze William Jennings Bryan's "Cross of Gold" speech at the 1896 Democratic convention. *To what extent may it be argued that the "Cross of Gold" speech won Bryan the Democratic nomination but lost him the election?*

▶ Examine the election of 1896. *Why did Populists decide to endorse the Democratic nominee for President? What effect did that endorsement have on the future of the Populist party? Why were Populists and Democrats unable to gain substantial support from urban women in 1896? What were the principal arguments and strategies used by William McKinley and Mark Hanna to ensure a Republican victory? What were the major components of the "full dinner pail"? How did American farmers fare in the decade after 1896?*

> ### IV. Federal Indian policy and United States foreign policy after the Civil War.

A. **Various perspectives on federal Indian policy, westward expansion, and the resulting struggles.**

Grades 5-6

▶ Chart the movement of Native Americans to reservations in western states from the end of the Civil War to 1900. *Why did some Native Americans sign treaties to accept life on reservations? How did others resist?*

▶ Compare maps of Native American nations in the 1860s and at the end of the century. *What changes have occurred? How do you account for these changes?*

▶ Write a biographic profile of a Native American leader of the post-Civil War period. *What made him a leader? How well did he serve his people?*

Grades 7-8

▶ Draw from a variety of primary sources such as speeches, letters, and oral histories to construct a historical narrative explaining different attitudes toward Native Americans in the latter half of the 19th century. *To what extent had governmental policies towards Native Americans changed? What was the public's reaction to the Indian wars of the post-Civil War era? How did prevailing attitudes of easterners differ from westerners? What was the impact of Helen Hunt Jackson's* A Century of Dishonor *on public opinion?*

What attempts were made to assimilate Native Americans? What role did missionaries play in promoting the assimilation of Native Americans? What was the impact of the government's reservation policy? What was the intent of the Dawes Severalty Act of 1887? To what extent did it achieve its goals? How did Native Americans respond to the Dawes Act?

▶ Draw upon speeches and appeals by Indian leaders, military records, biographies, and other historical data to construct a historical narrative explaining the various strategies Native Americans societies employed in response to the increase in white settlement, mining activities, and railroad construction in the West. Assess the effectiveness of these survival strategies.

Grades 9-12

▶ Explain the Dawes Severalty Act of 1887 and assess its impact. *Why in the mid-1880s did support for dismantling the reservation system and assimilating Native Americans gain ascendancy? How did the effort to assimilate Native Americans affect Indian land holdings in the late 19th century? How did the admission of new western states affect relations between the United States and Native American societies?*

▶ Draw upon a variety of visual sources, including the paintings of such artists as George Catlin, Frederic Remington, and Charles M. Russell examine how Native American cultures were portrayed.

▶ Marshal historical evidence to construct a sound argument responding to the following statement: *"Over the long term, the completion of the transcontinental railroad and trunk lines and the willful and premeditated slaughter of the buffalo herds, did more to defeat the Plains Indians and their way of life, than all the military campaigns of the period 1870-1895."*

▶ Examine the life of a notable Native American leader such as Red Cloud, Chief Joseph, Crazy Horse, Black Elk, Geronimo, or Wovoka, and construct a character sketch evaluating his leadership, values, and determination to serve his people. *What were his leadership characteristics? What respect did he garner from his people? How did government officials portray Native American leaders? What was the reaction of the general public to Indian leaders? How were they represented in the eastern and western press?*

B. **The roots and development of American expansionism and the causes and outcomes of the Spanish-American War.**

Grades 5-6

▶ Locate on a world map areas which the United States annexed in the post-Civil War era and explain the primary reason or reasons for interest in each of these areas.

▶ Explain the conditions which led the United States to war with Spain in 1898. *Why was the U.S.S. Maine sent to Havana harbor? Should the United States have declared war because of the sinking of the Maine?*

▶ Develop biographical sketches of leading personalities of the Spanish-American War including Valeriano "Butcher" Weyler, William McKinley, Theodore Roosevelt, and Emilio Aguinaldo.

▶ Construct a biographical profile of Dr. Walter Reed explaining his work to improve conditions in Cuba after the Spanish-American War.

Grades 7-8

▶ Interpret documentary evidence from speeches, letters, and journals to construct historical arguments, debates, or narratives on reasons for U.S. expansionism in the late 19th century. *What were the geographic factors that motivated the United States to expand beyond the continental limits? What economic factors led the United States to pursue an expansionist policy in the late 19th century? To what extent was the theory of Social Darwinism used to justify expansion? What were the arguments advanced by individuals who opposed expansion?*

▶ Draw evidence from a variety of historical sources that provide different perspectives to debate the issue, *"Was the United States justified in going to war against Spain in 1898?"*

▶ Interpret documentary evidence from a variety of primary sources to construct a sound historical argument or debate on the necessity for a military occupation of Cuba after the Spanish American War. *How effective was the U.S. military government of Cuba in establishing schools, improving sanitation, addressing problems of disease, and rebuilding the economic infrastructure of the island? Did the U.S. occupation promote political and economic stability?*

▶ Use a variety of primary sources including cartoons, newspaper headlines, and editorials to explain the distortions and sensationalism of the press and its impact on public opinion.

▶ Construct a historical argument assessing the consequences of the annexation of the Philippines. *What were the basic arguments politicians used to justify annexation of the Philippines? What was the Filipino response to U.S. incursions? What were the human costs of the war compared with those of the Spanish-American War? What were the long-term consequences of U.S. annexation of the Philippines? How effective was the administration of Governor William Howard Taft? How did the Philippine Government Act (1902), the Jones Act (1916), and the Tydings McDuffie Act (1934) improve U.S.-Philippine relations?*

Grades 9-12

▶ Utilize such sources as Senator Albert Beveridge's "March of the Flag" speech, Alfred Thayer Mahan's *The Influence of Sea Power upon History,* and the program of the anti-imperialist league, to compare the positions and arguments of imperialists and anti-imperialists. *To what extent was "sea power" a factor in U.S. expansionism? What special interests did the United States have in acquiring Hawaii and Samoa?*

▶ Using selections from Josiah Strong's *Our Country,* analyze the Protestant missionary zeal for expansionism. *Why does Strong call it America's divine mission? To what extent did workingmen, business leaders, and farmers support expansion?*

▶ Analyze Rudyard Kipling's poem, "The White Man's Burden: The United States and the Philippine Islands" as to the reasons used to justify U.S. expansion. *Why did Theodore Roosevelt call the poem "rather bad poetry but good sense from the expansionist point of view"? What historical evidence supports or refutes Mark Twain's satirical remark about American expansionism, "Our usual flag, with the white stripes painted black and the stars and stripes replaced by a skull and crossbones"?*

▶ Assess the relative significance of the following factors as motives for the U.S. declaration of war with Spain in 1898: a) economic; b) geopolitical; c) humanitarian; and d) nationalistic, especially as reflected in public opinion.

▶ Evaluate changing U.S. attitudes toward Emilio Aguinaldo from Senator George Hoar's remark in 1898 that Aguinaldo was the "George Washington of the Philippines" to the issue of warrants for his arrest after the Treaty of Paris. *What was President McKinley's reasoning for taking control of the Philippines? Was the U.S. justified in annexing the Philippines? Why did Aguinaldo oppose U.S. annexation of the Philippines? What were his basic goals? How effective was Aguinaldo's leadership during the Filipino insurrection?*

▶ Examine the impact of the Supreme Court decisions in the Insular Cases. *What were the constitutional issues raised by the acquisition of new territories?*

ERA 7

The Emergence of Modern America (1890-1930)

The study of how modern America emerged begins with the Progressive Era. It deserves careful study because, among other things, it included the nation's most vibrant set of reform ideas and campaigns since the 1830s-40s. Progressives were a diverse lot with various agendas that were sometimes jostled uneasily, but all reformers focused on a set of corrosive problems arising from rapid industrialization, urbanization, waves of immigration, and business and political corruption. Students can be inspired by how fervently the Progressives applied themselves to the renewal of American democracy. They can also profit from understanding the distinctively female reform culture that contributed powerfully to the movement.

Two of the problems confronted by Progressives are still central today. First, the Progressives faced the dilemma of how to maintain the material benefits flowing from the industrial revolution while bringing the powerful forces creating those benefits under democratic control and enlarging economic opportunity. Second, Progressives faced the knotted issue of how to maintain democracy and national identity amid an increasingly diverse influx of immigrants and amid widespread political corruption and the concentration of political power. Of all the waves of reformism in American history, Progressivism is notable for its nearly all-encompassing agenda. As its name implies, it stood for progress, and that put it squarely in the American belief in the perfectible society.

Students cannot fully understand the Progressive movement without considering its limitations, particularly its antagonism to radical labor movements and indifference to the plight of African Americans and other minorities. As in so many aspects of American history, it behooves students to understand different perspectives. Progressivism brought fusion in some areas of reform, but it also created fissures. Among those was the ongoing, heated controversy about female equality, particularly in the area of economic protectionism.

All issues of American foreign policy in the 20th century have their origins in the emergence of the United States as a major world power in the Spanish-American War at the end of the 19th century and in the involvement of the United States in World War I. The American intervention in World War I cast the die for the United States as a world power for the remainder of the century. Students can learn much about the complexities of foreign policy today by studying the difficulties of maintaining neutrality in World War I while acquiring the role of an economic giant with global interests and while fervently wishing to export democracy around the world.

In the postwar period the prosperity of the 1920s and the domination of big business and Republican politics are important to study. The 1920s displayed dramatically the American urge to build, innovate, and explore—poignantly captured in Lindbergh's solo flight across the Atlantic in 1927, which excited more enthusiasm than any single event to that time. The cultural and social realms also contain lessons from history that have resonance today. First, students should study the women's struggle for equality, which had political, economic, and cultural dimensions. Second, students should understand how radical labor movements and radical ideologies provoked widespread fear and even hysteria. Third, they need to study the recurring racial tension that led to black nationalism, the Harlem Renaissance, and the first great northward migration of African Americans on the one hand and the resurgence of the Ku Klux Klan on the other hand. Fourth, they need to understand the powerful movement to Americanize a generation of immigrants and the momentous closing of the nation's gates through severe retrenchment of the open-door immigration policies. Lastly, they should examine the continuing tension among Protestants, Catholics, and Jews, most dramatically exemplified in the resurgence of Protestant fundamentalism.

Essay

A History of Technology: A Young and Vibrant Discipline*
by W. David Lewis

As W. David Lewis surveys the recent scholarly developments of the history of technology, he finds an impressive body of work that enhances our understanding of the role of technology in the American past. Numerous historians have demonstrated that technological developments have an impact on human lives that is more complex than is traditionally taught in K-12 classrooms. Teachers who take advantage of these studies will find a veritable goldmine of suggestive teaching practices that will emerge from studying technology as it developed in its broad economic, social, and historical context.

W. David Lewis, Hudson Professor of History and Engineering, Auburn University, has written extensively on the history of business and technology. He is the author of *The Airway to Everywhere: A History of American Aviation, 1937-1953* and *Delta: The History of an Airline* and edited *The Southern Mystique: The Impact of Technology on Human Values in a Changing Region.*

In 1958 a group of scholars led by Melvin Kranzberg established the Society for the History of Technology (SHOT). Late in 1959 the first issue of the Society's journal, *Technology and Culture*, appeared. Responding to the urgent need of an increasingly technological civilization to understand the evolution of its relationship with tools, machines, and other products of human inventiveness, SHOT and its members have produced a steadily growing body of historical literature documenting and interpreting this relationship in an increasingly sophisticated way.

Although SHOT is an international organization, its members are heavily concentrated in the United States. Accordingly, they have probed intensively, in a steady outpouring of books and articles, the role of technology in American development. The survey that follows is necessarily selective, but will convey some idea of the themes and approaches that have been most fruitful in this sustained effort, concentrating particularly on books and articles that have won prizes and awards. These include the Dexter Prize, awarded annually by SHOT to outstanding books and monographs, and the Abbott Payson Usher Prize, awarding to outstanding articles published in *Technology and Culture*.

As the title of their journal indicates, historians of technology have aimed to produce "contextual" studies that successfully integrate two perspectives: The "internalist," relating to the design and function of machines and other inventions, and the "externalist," relating to the political, economic, social, and intellectual milieu within which technology has developed. An outstanding work that effectively achieves this goal is Merritt Roe Smith's, *Harpers Ferry Armory and the New Technology: The Challenge of Change* (1977).

Demonstrating self-evident mastery of the "internal" dimensions of a series of highly intricate technological developments, Smith analyzed the way in which a highly mechanized approach to the manufacture of firearms was introduced into an extremely traditional craft-oriented setting at a federal armory located at Harper's Ferry, Virginia. In the process, he effectively challenged a common assumption that Americans in the period of the early republic were unfailingly receptive to technological innovation. Showing great sensitivity to agrarian traditions, regional folkways, local insularity, and the stake of skilled workers in a craft-dominated way of life, he showed how managers and employees at Harpers Ferry resisted pressures from the War Department in Washington to cooperate with such outsiders as John Hall, a New

---

*Reprinted from *Magazine of History*, Vol. 4, No. 2 (Spring 1989), pp. 10-15 with permission from the Organization of American Historians.

Englander who pioneered the manufacture of the first shoulder weapons successfully made with interchangeable parts. Conversely, Smith analyzed why Springfield, Massachusetts, provided a supportive cultural milieu for a much more successful armory whose workers readily embraced "change, specialization, and centralization of power."

In arguing that Hall, not Eli Whitney, was the true father of interchangeable parts manufacture, Smith built upon foundations laid earlier by such historians of technology as Robert Woodbury, who had won the Usher Prize for a seminal article, "The Legend of Eli Whitney and Interchangeable Parts," published in the Summer 1960 issue of *Technology and Culture*. Carefully examining how the new "armory practice" gradually spread from Springfield and Harpers Ferry to foundries and machine shops throughout the United States, Smith also showed how these methods laid the basis for later American achievements in mass production. His major contribution to a better understanding of the interplay between technology and other aspects of American culture led the Organization of American Historians to award Smith's book the Frederick Jackson Turner Prize in 1979.

Like Smith, a growing number of historians of technology, who wrote in the 1960s and 1970s, brought fresh insight to bear upon neglected or badly-understood aspects of the American past. One of their goals was to examine how the activities of engineers fit into the mainstream of American history. In *The Revolt of the Engineers: Social Responsibility and the American Engineering Profession* (1971), which won the Dexter Prize in the same year, Edwin T. Layton, Jr. traced the way in which the professionalization of engineering in the late nineteenth and early twentieth centuries was accompanied by a rising conviction among engineers that they could solve political, economic, and social problems through the application of scientific principles. Demonstrating that engineers, unlike many reformers in the Progressive Era, were animated by pro-big business and anti-labor ideologies, he ably documented their tendency to confuse scientific and moral laws, and searchingly analyzed the failure of such panaceas as scientific management to offer viable answers to complex public issues. In the process, he presented valuable case studies of such politically active engineers as Morris L. Cooke and Herbert Hoover.

Smith's analysis of the role played by the War Department in the genesis of "armory practice," and Layton's emphasis upon the intense commitment of most engineers to an implicitly conservative approach to public affairs, typified themes that would occupy the minds of historians of technology for years to come. In *Elmer Sperry: Engineer and Inventor* (1971), the first of his books to win the Dexter Prize, Thomas P. Hughes showed how a brilliant pioneer in cybernetics exemplified the transition from an age of individual inventive effort to one of institutionalized research and development, and yet managed to retain his own distinctive style. As Hughes indicated, Sperry's career typified a growing partnership on the part of engineers with business and government, and particularly with military constituencies. In his work in the development of the gyroscope and other servomechanisms, Sperry was obliged to think in an extremely structured and rational way about interactions that took place within highly complex technological systems.

Such themes would appear again and again in Hughes' later work. Studying the career of Thomas A. Edison, about which he wrote a short book and a probing chapter in Carroll Pursell's, *Technology in America: A History of Individuals and Ideas* (1981), he stressed the degree to which Edison was compelled to pursue such inventions as electric incandescent lighting in terms of complex variables interacting with one another as parts of an interdependent system that had to meet rigorous cost requirements in order to compete with gas lighting in the marketplace. Later, the same preoccupation with systems appeared on a much larger scale in, *Networks of Power: Electrification in Western Society, 1880-1930* (1983), for which Hughes won a second Dexter Prize and in which he searchingly analyzed key differences between large electrical distribution systems in the United States, Great Britain, and Germany.

More recently, in *American Genesis: A Century of Invention and Technological Enthusiasm* (1989), Hughes has traced the way in which Sperry, Thomas A. Edison, Alexander Graham Bell, and a number of other inventors and engineers contributed to the development of an American technological tradition, exemplifying faith in system-building efficiency, rationality, and centralized control that was not effectively challenged until the appearance of the counterculture in the 1960s. In so doing, he emphasized how the careers of his protagonists related to the origins and the development of the so-called "military-industrial complex" and how their outlook was manifested in such enormous ventures as the Manhattan Project, under which the first atomic bombs were made.

These studies are highly congruent with the work of yet another Dexter Prize winner, Bruce Sinclair, who examined developing tensions in a much earlier stage of American history between the institutionalization and systematization of technological creativity on the one hand and the democratic aspirations of American culture on the other in his book, *Philadelphia's Philosopher Mechanics: A History of the Franklin Institute, 1824-1865* (1974). Whereas the founders of the Franklin Institute dreamed of the educational benefits that it would confer upon upwardly-aspiring artisans and mechanics, the demands of a growing national economy forced the Institute to become involved in a variety of tasks, such as the testing of boilers and the development of standardized screw-threads. This demanded a high degree of professionalization, scientific expertise, and what Sinclair aptly called "the rational manipulation of power and materials in an industrial context."

Trends toward concentration and control were analyzed repeatedly by historians of technology as the discipline matured, following much the same pattern traced by business historian, Alfred D. Chandler in his much-admired study, *The Visible Hand* (1977). In *Images and Enterprise: Technology and the American Photographic Industry* (1975), still another Dexter Prize recipient, Reese Jenkins, probed the way in which photography evolved through a succession of stages from a highly individualistic industry characterized by small-scale firms into a highly concentrated one dominated by large companies that capitalized upon rationalized production techniques to command far-flung mass markets, both in America and abroad. George Eastman was the key figure whose entrepreneurial strategies exemplified this trend. As Jenkins pointed out in an essay later published in Pursell's *Technology in America*, Eastman ultimately saw that manufacturers of photographic equipment could not rely upon acquiring patents developed by individual inventors but, instead, had to institutionalize invention by creating large industrial research laboratories in which teams of scientists and engineers would bring about a dependable flow of innovations.

As they grappled with broad trends toward centralized control, and in the process, challenged facile notions about the relationship between technology and democracy, historians of technology also criticized standing assumptions about "Yankee ingenuity" and its supposedly peculiar congruence with American individualism. An early attack upon this legend, Norman B. Wilkinson's, "Brandywine Borrowings from European Technology," appearing in the Winter 1963 issue of *Technology and Culture* and subsequently winning the Usher Prize, demonstrated that many products of so-called early American inventiveness were actually imported from abroad. I myself noted similar trends in *Iron and Steel* in America (1976), pointing out how virtually every innovation that affected the production of ferrous metals in the United States was transplanted from Europe.

Historians of technology have explored the phenomenon of "technology transfer" in a variety of contexts. In *Early Stationary Steam Engines in America* (1969), Carroll Pursell analyzed in detail how the inventions of such great British engineers as Thomas Newcomen and James Watt were transplanted into a North American setting. In *Transatlantic Industrial Revolution: The Diffusion of Textile Technology between Britain and America, 1790-1830s* (1981), Dexter Prize winner David Jeremy showed how the emigration of skilled artisans from Great Britain to the United States contributed to the establishment of the American textile industry. Effectively using statistical data, Jeremy broke fresh ground not only by analyzing key differences between British and American working conditions, but also by comparing and contrasting textile manufacturing in such specific areas as New England and the Philadelphia region. Valuable perspectives on the way in which American technological practices gradually diverged from European prototypes also have been presented by Brook Hindle and Stephen Lubar's *Engines of Change: The American Industrial Revolution, 1790-1860* (1986), which is extensively illustrated with artifacts and drawings from the collections of the Smithsonian Institution.

Typically, as I indicated in my own study of iron and steel manufacturing, the distinctive American contribution to technological development lay not in an ability to originate revolutionary new concepts and ideas, but instead in the capacity of the United States, with its large domestic market and its strong commitment to mass consumption, to apply European innovations on a vast scale. To a great degree, this capacity also reflects a sheer zest for technological achievement that Hindle has stressed repeatedly, both in *Engines of Change* and in his pioneering work, *Technology in Early America* (1969).

The aircraft industry furnishes another good example. In *The Origins of the Turbojet Revolution* (1981), Dexter Prize recipient Edward W. Constant II traced in a masterly way how the jet engine was conceived and born in Europe in the minds and activities of such creative persons as Theodore von Karmann, Hans von Ohain, and Frank Whittle, who brilliantly foresaw that fundamental limitations in the performance of piston-driven aircraft engines would ultimately require power plants designed upon radically different principles. American manufacturers, who developed a succession of superb reciprocal engines underlying much of the revolution in commercial air transport that took place in the 1930s, failed to become involved in jet engine technology until they were forced to do so by the exigencies of World War II. Yet, as Roger E. Belstein has pointed out in his recent study, *Flight in America: From the Wrights to the Astronauts* (1986), aircraft manufacturers in the United States demonstrated a characteristic American flair for massive feats of production and ultimately won world dominance in the large-scale manufacture of jet transports in the postwar era. Today, they still cling to an increasingly precarious lead in this field despite the belated challenge posed by Europe's Airbus Industrie.

The American genius for quantity production naturally led historians of technology to follow Smith's *Harpers Ferry Armory*, in examining closely the origins and evolution of the methods that enabled American manufacturers to develop and exploit mass markets for harvesting equipment, sewing machines, watches, bicycles, automobiles, and other products. None have done so more successfully than David A. Hounshell, whose book, *From the American System to Mass Production 1800-1932: The Development of Manufacturing Technology in the United States* (1984), was subsequently awarded the Dexter Prize. Part of Hounshell's achievement lay in the effectiveness with which he challenged earlier facile assumptions about the development of mass production made by such popular writers as Roger Burlingame, who in such books as *Machines That Built America* (1953), had emphasized the roles purportedly played by such entrepreneurs as Cyrus McCormick and Isaac Singer in the use of interchangeable parts.

As Hounshell indicates, the firms founded by these men actually did not use interchangeable parts until their dominance had been securely established through other means, including "extensive use of advertising and other promotional techniques." On the other hand, Hounshell reinforced the image of Henry Ford as truly "radical" figure by emphasizing Ford's role as the first manufacturer to combine high-quantity production with the lowest possible unit prices by integrating preexisting techniques and using machines to replace labor rather than merely trying to make workers more efficient, as Frederick W. Taylor had previously done.

While acknowledging the impressive material results of the rationality, efficiency, and centralized control underlying the American technological achievement, historians of technology have more often than not been critical of the political, social, and emotional costs involved. In 1974, for example, SHOT selected mainstream historian Daniel Boorstin's, *The Americans: The Democratic Experience* (1973), as co-winner of the Dexter Prize for its mordant analysis of the way in which technological advance had taken place "at the cost of ephemeralizing and attenuating the quality of experience so that distinctions between the natural and the unnatural, the substantial and the evanescent, have been weakened and in many cases all but obliterated." Ten years later, the Society awarded the Dexter Prize to Ruth Schwartz Cowan for her trenchant book, *More Work for Mother: The Ironies of Household Technology from the Open Hearth to the Microwave* (1983), which argued that the development of various allegedly labor-saving devices, such as electric washing machines and vacuum cleaners, actually increased the workload of middle-class American housewives. Furthermore, according to Cowan, it was accompanied by the spread of advertising and other media pressures that made such women feel guilty if they did not efficiently discharge their functions as "household engineers."

The winner of the 1986 Dexter Prize, diplomatic historian Walter A. McDougall's *The Heavens and the Earth: A Political History of the Space Age* (1985), gave even greater cause for alarm in its analysis of the way in which the response of the United States to Soviet achievements in space technology contributed to the rise of a "technocratic state" which, like the Soviet Union itself, had "made the will to power over the forces of nature a categorical imperative subject to no political or philosophical constraints." In doing so, McDougall argued, Americans had placed at risk "the very values that make one's society worth defending in the first place."

Concern about the potentially dire consequences of technology put to improper use informed the writing of historians of technology as diverse as John Kasson, whose influential book, *Civilizing the Machine: Technology and Republican Values in America* (1976), began by emphasizing the desire of our founding fathers to achieve harmony between technology and republican virtue and ended with Mark Twain's nightmare vision of technology run amok in the chilling denouement of *A Connecticut Yankee in King Arthur's Court*. David Noble, whose books, *American by Design* (1979), and *Forces of Production* (1983), interpreted much of the American technological quest in terms of a conspiracy on the part of baleful capitalist forces and their allies to manage technological change so as to thwart the rightful interests of the working class, and Langdon Winner's *Autonomous Technology: Technics-out-of-Control as a Theme in Political Thought* (1977), enumerated the strategies by means of which entrenched special interests practiced what he called "system imperialism" to promote their ends.

If such books did not win anything approaching universal assent among practitioners of the discipline, they stimulated a great deal of thought. In his magisterial *The Continuous Wave: Technology and American Radio, 1900-1932* (1985), for example, two-time Dexter Prize recipient Hugh G. J. Aitken thoughtfully probed the applicability of Noble's and Winner's ideas to the way in which the development of such key inventions as the alternator, the oscillating arc, and the vacuum tube, as affected by the behavior of the business firms, military forces, and governmental units that attempted to control them, shaped the evolution of continuous wave radio technology.

In view of the way in which historians of technology had identified drives toward system-building, efficiency, centralization of power, and the achievement of control as being of key importance in the unfolding of American culture, it is not surprising that these were heavily stressed in a pioneering comprehensive scholarly overview, *Technology in America; A Brief History* (1989), by Alan I. Marcus and Howard P. Segal. Typical also of the historiographical trends mentioned here was a book-length manifesto edited by Merritt Roe Smith, *Military Enterprise and Technological Change: Perspectives on the American Experience* (1985), in which Smith and eight other historians of technology emphasized the degree to which American technological development had been shaped by military needs and purposes.

At SHOT's Silver Anniversary meeting in 1983, John M. Staudenmaier presented a critique of its accomplishments under the title, "What SHOT Hath Wrought and What SHOT Hath Not: Reflections on Twenty-five Years of the History of Technology." This critique was subsequently published in the October 1984 issue of *Technology and Culture*. In it, Staudenmaier, a Jesuit priest who had witnessed the dislocating impact of modern technology upon a South Dakota Indian reservation before studying for his doctorate under Thomas P. Hughes at the University of Pennsylvania, criticized the cumulative record represented by most of the articles that had been published to date in the Society's journal, charging that they overplayed technological "success stories," manifested too little interest in non-capitalist perspectives, and devoted inadequate attention to such groups as workers and women. These criticisms were elaborated in Staudenmaier's subsequent book-length study, *Technology's Storytellers: Reweaving the Human Fabric* (1985), which also explored a variety of themes and approaches that had been developed by historians of technology since the birth of the discipline.

Staudenmaier's indictment is to some degree justified, but the preceding analysis indicates that historians of technology have not been blind to aspects of American technological development that provoked the rise of the counter-culture of the 1960s and still arouse vigorous criticism today. Some practitioners of the discipline still adhere to a "progressive" view of technological change. In *How the West Grew Rich: The Economic Transformation of the Industrial World* (1986), for example, economist and veteran SHOT member Nathan Rosenberg joined lawyer L. E. Birdzell, Jr. in a ringing affirmation of the essentially beneficent function of technological progress in such countries as the United States. This is hardly a majority view, however, and drew a highly negative response from reviewer Gary Kulik in a subsequent issue of *Technology and Culture*.

Numerous indications exist that the central issues of our time involve our relationship with technological developments that have massive potential for good or ill. Historians of technology have firmly established a thriving discipline that has grown steadily in both a quantitative and a qualitative sense since its founding more than three decades ago. Having added greatly to a deeper understanding of American culture, it continues to yield a rich store of insight and information upon which teachers of American history can draw. Under the leadership of two successive presidents, Bruce Sinclair and Merritt Roe Smith, SHOT had adopted as a primary goal the enhancement of its impact upon American secondary education. The results of this development in future years should be highly significant both for young Americans and for the society they will inherit.

Sample Student Activities

I. *How Progressives and others addressed problems of industrial capitalism, urbanization, and political corruption.*

A. The origin of the Progressives and the coalitions they formed to deal with issues at the local and state levels.

Grades 5-6

▶ Use photographs of child labor, urban tenements, and slums, along with first-hand accounts and stories, to describe the conditions that led Progressives to propose far-reaching reforms. *How did migrants from rural areas and immigrants from other lands experience life in growing urban centers?*

▶ Generate a chart listing issues important to Progressives. Use newspapers and media reports to list and compare current social issues. *How do problems today compare to those tackled by the Progressives? How have social problems changed in our time?*

▶ Use census records, personal accounts, and pictorial sources to explain immigration to the United States. *Where did most immigrants settle? How did schools, religious groups, settlement houses, and philanthropists help immigrants cope with crowded urban living conditions?*

Grades 7-8

▶ Draw upon evidence from the work of muckrakers such as Upton Sinclair, Jacob Riis, Lincoln Steffens, Lewis Hine, and Ida Tarbell to reveal chronic problems of urban industrial society. *Why were individuals who attempted to instigate reforms called muckrakers? Who might be considered muckrakers in contemporary American society, and how do they go about bringing attention to their causes?*

▶ Chart Progressive social reforms of such areas as education, conservation, temperance, and the "Americanization" of immigrants. Identify the people who were instrumental in promoting these reforms, and evaluate the relative success of their efforts.

▶ Draw upon biographies to examine the contributions to Progressivism by such governors as Hiram Johnson (California), Robert La Follette (Wisconsin), and Charles Evans Hughes (New York).

Grades 9-12

▶ Draw upon such sources as the *Dictionary of American Biography*, a variety of literary sources, historical narratives, newspaper accounts, and political commentaries to analyze the personal background of Progressives, their critique of urban-industrial America, their goals and political strategies for effecting change, and their successes as well as failures. *How did the social background of Progressive reforms contribute to their critiques, goals, political strategies, and successes? What were the major structural changes they proposed for government at the local and state levels? What was the impact of the social gospel movement on the reform agenda? What were their proposals in education, conservation, the consumption of alcohol, and the assimilation of immigrants?*

◗ Read selections from *The Autobiography of Lincoln Steffens;* Ida Tarbell's *The History of Standard Oil,* Upton Sinclair's *The Jungle,* Henry Demarest Lloyd's *Wealth Against Commonwealth,* Jacob Riis's *How the Other Half Lives,* and articles from *McClure's Magazine* to evaluate the evidence and arguments offered by the social critics of urban-industrial society in the late 19th and early 20th centuries. *What were the Progressive proposals for the regulation of big business, the protection of consumers, and the improvement of working conditions? What were the targets of Progressive criticism? What were the primary arguments and evidence used in their brief against urban-industrial society?*

◗ Compare and contrast reforms pertaining to government and business at the local and state level of government to ascertain which changes had lasting impact. *What were the major reforms implemented at the local level? Which cities and mayors deserve recognition for outstanding leadership of the reform movement at the local level? What were the major reforms implemented at the state level during the Progressive Era? What states and governors deserve recognition for outstanding leadership of the reform movement at the state level?*

◗ Compare and contrast Progressive programs for reform in several states and explain their successes and failures in promoting meaning change. *How effective were direct lawmaking programs such as the initiative, referendum, and recall? Which states established regulatory commissions, provided for workmen's compensation, and initiated the direct primary?*

◗ Read selections from the writings of major leaders involved in social reform at the local level and analyze why some proposals were adopted throughout the nation and others failed. Select from such reformers as Jane Addams, John Dewey, Washington Gladden, Florence Kelley, and Walter Rauchenbusch.

◗ Develop a case study examining the work of Progressives in promoting different forms of city government; alternative tax structures; and public works programs. Write biographical profiles of Progressive leaders at the local level such as Hazen Pingree (Detroit), Edwin Curtis (Boston), Tom Johnson (Cleveland), Seth Low (New York), and Samuel "Golden Rule" Jones (Toledo). *How would Progressive journalist Lincoln Steffens appraise the selected individual's leadership in promoting good government and urban reform?*

B. Progressivism at the national level.

Grades 5-6

◗ Write biographic sketches of leading reformers during the Progressive era. *What reforms did they advocate? How successful were they?*

◗ Use biographies as references to compare Presidents Roosevelt, Taft, and Wilson and their ideas for reform. *How did each of these national leaders hope to solve human problems in urban centers and the work place. How well did they succeed in reaching their goals during their lifetimes?*

◗ Explain the 16th, 17th and 18th amendments. Using role-playing, an art project, or writing assignments, have students respond to such questions as: *How did these amendments reflect the ideas of the Progressives? Why, as senator from your state, would you have voted for or against each of these amendments? How would each of these amendments affect your life if you were one of the following people: (a) a store owner; (b) a homemaker; (c) a farmer; (d) a student or, (e) a mayor of a city?*

◗ Examine the movement for woman suffrage through historical fiction using stories such as *Never Jam Today* by Carol Bolton and *Does Anyone Care About Lou Emma Miller?* by Alberta Wilson Constant.

Grades 7-8

▶ List the major reforms initiated by the Roosevelt, Taft, and Wilson administrations and construct a historical argument evaluating the commitment of each to Progressive ideals.

▶ Utilize such visual sources as photographs, newsreel images, cartoons, and caricatures of Presidents Roosevelt, Taft, and Wilson to interpret how they were popularly portrayed as leaders of reform.

▶ Use maps and statistical data to investigate the results of the presidential election of 1912. *What factors contributed to Wilson's victory? In what way was the election of 1912 a high watermark for Progressivism?*

▶ Identify the Progressive amendments to the Constitution, trace the movements that culminated in each amendment, and analyze the issues during the debate over ratification. *Why was the Income Tax Amendment considered progressive? Why was there a movement for direct elections of senators? How did the alliance of the Anti-Saloon League and the Women's Christian Temperance Union produce the 18th Amendment? What arguments were presented for and against passage of the women suffrage amendment?*

Grades 9-12

▶ Draw upon a variety of historical narratives, biographical and newspaper accounts, personal letters, and memoirs to compare Presidents Roosevelt, Taft, and Wilson as leaders of the Progressive movement. *What was the substance of Progressive reforms during the presidency of Theodore Roosevelt? What were his major contributions to Progressivism? How did Taft's background and training influence his view of the presidency and his style of leadership? What kind of progressive qualifications did Wilson bring to the presidency?*

Was Theodore Roosevelt a "trust buster" in the progressive sense or was he resorting to political rhetoric? What was the progressive Republicans' case against Taft? Was it justifiable? How are the weaknesses and strengths of Progressivism illustrated in the Wilson administration? How did Wilson respond to the requests of African Americans, women, and labor?

▶ Analyze the Hetch Hetchy controversy by explaining the motives of the central participants and the impact of the controversy. *How did Gifford Pinchot defend his position? How did John Muir cast his opposing views? Which, in your opinion, presented the most compelling argument?*

▶ Assess the platforms of the Democratic, Republican, Progressive, and Socialist parties in the 1912 presidential elections; analyze their similarities and differences; and explain why the 1912 campaign was the high tide of Progressivism. *What were the political and issue-oriented factors affecting the rift within the Republican party after 1909? In what ways did the Square Deal, New Nationalism, and New Freedom differ? In what ways were they similar? What factors influenced the outcome of the election? To what extent was Wilson's reform program from 1913 to 1916 a simple updating of the Omaha Platform of 1892?*

▶ Analyze the methods that Carrie Chapman Catt used in her leadership of the National Woman's Suffrage Association to get the 19th Amendment passed and ratified. *Why did Wilson change his mind about the amendment? Which of Catt's tactics were most successful? Why?*

▶ Evaluate whether the Supreme Court aided or retarded Progressivism by analyzing key decisions and reasoning in such cases as: *United States* v. *E.C. Knight Company* (1895); *Northern Securities Company* v. *United States* (1904); *Lochner* v. *New York* (1905); *Muller* v. *Oregon* (1908); *Standard Oil of New Jersey* v. *United States* (1911); and *Hammer* v. *Dagenhart* (1918).

C. The limitations of Progressivism and the alternatives offered by various groups.

Grades 5-6

▶ Use stories, narratives, and biographies to identify issues that were important to African Americans, Native Americans, women, and organized workers. *How did the Progressives respond to the issues they raised?*

▶ Read biographical sketches of such persons as Ida Wells-Barnett, Booker T. Washington, and W. E. B. Du Bois, and create a collage illustrating what they sought to achieve during the Progressive period.

Grades 7-8

▶ Compare the goals and strategies for change advocated by Booker T. Washington and W. E. B. Du Bois. *How did African Americans use Progressive tactics to attempt change? How successful were they in securing the passage of legislation such as anti-lynching laws? What was the legacy of* Plessy v. Ferguson?

▶ Use primary documents such as speeches, posters, songs, and poems to explain the message of the Industrial Workers of the World (IWW). *Who were the leaders of the radical labor movement and what strategies did they advocate to achieve their goals? How did the IWW differ form the American Federation of Labor? How did the goals of the IWW differ from those of the Progressives?*

▶ Develop character sketches of individual women and examine the issues they raised during the Progressive era. *How did mainstream Progressives respond to women's issues? How did activists in the women's movement evaluate the Progressive's agenda for reform?*

Grades 9-12

▶ Construct a chart listing the goals of different labor movements in the United States including radical syndicalist unions. Contrast their goals with those of mainstream Progressives. *Which of the labor movements in the early twentieth century supported the Progressive agenda? How did the programs of radical labor organizations contrast with those of the Progressives? How did the political and social reform agendas of U.S. unions compare with the social democratic programs promulgated by unions in Western Europe?*

▶ Use selections from *The Souls of Black Folk* to show how W. E. B. Du Bois criticized Booker T. Washington. *Why did Du Bois believe that the substitute of "man training for materialism fostering intelligence and knowledge of the world" is progressive for African Americans? What was Du Bois's role in founding the NAACP? Why was it established? To what extent were the efforts of Washington and Du Bois complementary?*

▶ Use selections from Mary Church Terrell's *Autobiography* to explain her quest for social justice. *To what extent did the Progressives' emphasis on decentralization and localism work to the disadvantage of African Americans? What were the major contributions of Charlotte Hawkins Brown, Ida Wells-Barnett, and Mary Church Terrell?*

▶ Draw from a variety of historical sources including pictures and newspaper articles to explain how the International Ladies Garment Workers Union (ILGWU) and the "1909 uprising of the 20,000" exemplified an alternative to mainstream Progressivism.

▶ Analyze the debate among leading women on the suffrage movement. *How did Susan B. Anthony use the traditional ideas of domesticity to support her reasoning? How did Charlotte Perkins Gilman's reasoning differ? Who was threatened by Gilman's ideas and why? How did the activities of Margaret Sanger, Louise Bryant, and Emma Goldman add to Progressive fears about disorder? How did Alice Paul's Congressional Union and the NAWSA differ in their approach to suffrage?*

▶ Compare earlier white views of Native American assimilation at the time of the Dawes Act of 1887 with the changing perception in the first two decades of the 20th century. *How did the case of* Lone Wolf *v.* Hitchcock *(1903) and the Burke Act of 1906 affect Native Americans and the disposition of tribal lands? What was the impact of western politicians and their constituents on the decisions to decrease federal restriction on the sale and taxation of Indian allotments? What were the effects on ownership of tribal lands?*

▶ Evaluate the success of the Progressive movement. *How democratic was the Progressive movement? Did Progressives' views of the immigrant strengthen the position of urban bosses? What was the outcome of reforms such as the initiative and the direct primary? To what extent did voter registration laws affect the participation of voters? How did the disenfranchisement of African Americans in the South, which continued during the Progressive era, display the paradox of Progressive reform?*

II. *The changing role of the United States in world affairs through World War I.*

A. How the American role in the world changed in the early 20th century.

Grades 5-6

▶ Explain the Open Door policy. Locate China on a map and show areas that were dominated by European countries and Japan. *Why was the United States interested in having an "open door" in China? Why was trade with China important to the U.S.? What products did the U.S. want from China?*

▶ Construct a classroom newspaper examining the importance of an inter-oceanic canal. In addition to news stories, include editorials, letters to the editor, and political cartoons related to the construction of the Panama Canal.

▶ Construct a journal or classroom newspaper examining the importance of an inter-oceanic canal.

Grades 7-8

▶ Explain American diplomatic initiatives in East Asia. *To what extent did the "Open Door" policy differ from previous U.S. policy? How were goals of both the United States and Japan met by the Gentlemen's Agreement of 1907?*

▶ Define Roosevelt's Big Stick policy and explain how it was applied to Latin America. *Under what circumstances did Theodore Roosevelt believe that the United States had the right to intervene in the affairs of Latin American nations? How did the construction and control of the Panama Canal change the role of the United States in the region? How did contemporary political cartoonists depict Roosevelt's foreign policy?*

▶ Develop a historical argument assessing differences in the foreign policy approaches of Roosevelt, Taft, and Wilson. Conduct historical research to develop a case study of one such episode (e.g., Panama, Nicaragua, or Mexico). *What were the foreign policy goals of each administration? What was the reaction of Latin Americans to U. S. intervention in the Caribbean, Central America, and Mexico? What is the legacy of such policies in the present-day relationships between the United States and Latin America?*

Grades 9-12

▶ Use the Open Door Notes to explain the commercial basis of American foreign policy in East Asia. *To what extent were the Open Door Notes part of a quest for "informal empire" rather than open imperialism in East Asia? How did the Open Door Notes lay the basis for America's future protection of China's territorial integrity?*

154

◆ Use the texts of the Monroe Doctrine and the Roosevelt Corollary to determine to what extent there is a connection. *Is the Roosevelt Corollary a legitimate use of the Monroe Doctrine? To what extent did he Roosevelt Corollary undermine the sovereignty of Latin American nations?*

◆ Use cartoons and newspaper articles to explain the U.S. role in the Panama Revolution of 1903. *Was the construction of the Panama Canal in the U.S. national interest? Were Roosevelt's responses to the Panamanian Revolution justifiable? What were the long-range effects of his actions? Was Theodore Roosevelt abusing his powers as president to act on the canal without congressional approval?*

◆ Use primary sources illustrating the West Coast hostility to Japanese immigrants to explain the connection between the 1906 segregation of San Francisco schools and the Gentleman's Agreement. *What was the Japanese perspective on the segregation issue? How did the issue affect Japanese-U.S. relations? Why did Roosevelt feel it was necessary to send the Great White Fleet to Japan in 1908? How did it affect diplomatic relationships with Japan?*

◆ Draw from a variety of sources including Taft State Department documents to explain Dollar Diplomacy. *What reasons did Taft give for his administration's policy of Dollar Diplomacy in China and the Caribbean? To what extent was Dollar Diplomacy the implementation of the Roosevelt Corollary?*

◆ Use Wilson's "Mobile Declaration" to examine his views of appropriate U.S. diplomacy towards Latin America. *Did Wilson contradict his foreign policy goals when he sent General Pershing into Mexico and employed a large military force along the Mexican-U.S. border? What events prompted these actions? How did Wilson's policy in Mexico underscore the significance of Porfirio Díaz's lamentation: "Poor Mexico. So far from God, so close to the United States"?*

B. The causes of World War I and why the United States intervened.

Grades 5-6

◆ Describe the German and Allied use of new weapons. Using pictures, maps, and news accounts answer such questions as: *How did new weapons used in World War I, such as the "Big Bertha" cannon, poison gas, the airplane, and the tank, change warfare? How did the use of submarines and blockades push the United States toward a declaration of war?*

◆ Use a world map to locate the Allied and Central Powers and areas where the war was fought. *Why is this conflict called a "world war"?*

Grades 7-8

◆ Examine the system of alliances through which nations in Europe sought to protect their interests, and explain how nationalism and militarism contributed to the outbreak of war. *What measures might have been taken to avert the war? How did the war expand beyond European boundaries to become a world war? Why did the United States declare neutrality at the beginning of the war?*

◆ Examine the reasons why many Americans initially saw no reason to join in the war in Europe and construct a response to each of the following quotations: *The United States should "set an example for peace for the world"* (Secretary of State William Jennings Bryan), and *"Our whole duty for the present, at any rate, is summed up by the motto: 'America First: Let us think of America before we think of Europe'"* (President Woodrow Wilson).

◆ Analyze maps and photographs of battle scenes in order to explain the nature of the war in Europe. *How did the American public respond to the images of total war? What impact did Allied propaganda have on public opinion in the United States? How did ethnic American groups figure in the debate about the course of the war?*

▶ Debate the proposition, *"The United States should have maintained its neutrality during the course of World War I."* Prepare evidence considering such factors as British interference with U.S. shipping, the sinking of the *Lusitania*, Wilson's election pledge to keep the United States out of the war, unrestricted submarine warfare, and the Zimmermann Telegram.

▶ Assess the importance of aviation during World War I. Compare the effectiveness of the airplane as a war machine to that of the tank, long-range howitzer, and chemical weapons. *How effective was the airplane in determining the outcome of the war? How did chemical warfare, used by both sides during the war, influence military strategy? How effective were tanks in bringing an end to the stalemate on the Western Front?*

Grades 9-12

▶ Draw upon a variety of historical narratives, literary sources, newspaper accounts, and magazine descriptions to analyze the motivations of the leading world powers in August 1914. *Once hostilities began, what were the motivations of the various belligerents for fighting the war? To what extent were countries successful in mobilizing their people and resources for fighting the war? How successful were the propaganda campaigns the belligerents aimed at neutral nations? Prior to the entry of the United States, how successful were the military strategies pursued by belligerents?*

▶ Analyze Wilson's leadership during the period of neutrality. *Was Secretary of State William Jennings Bryan right in calling for a ban on loans and the sale of munitions to the belligerents? Was there any inconsistency between Wilson's warning American citizens to get out of Mexico and his refusal to warn them to stay out of the European war zone? How did Wilson respond to the Zimmermann Note? Do you agree with his response?*

▶ Draw upon biographies, historical narratives, newspaper accounts, and magazine descriptions to write an essay on Wilson's decision to call for a declaration of war. *During the presidential election of 1916, was Wilson forthright with the American people about our prospects as a participant? How did the Wilson administration respond to the propaganda campaigns conducted by Germany and Britain in the United States? How would you evaluate the response? Was Wilson following a policy of neutrality during the first three years of the war? Did Wilson's declaration of war focus primarily on U.S. national interest? Explain.*

▶ Investigate how technological developments employed in the "Great War" contributed to the brutality of modern war. Examine the visual impact of works by artists such as Henry Tombs and Harvey Dunn, and the imagery used by writers such as Wilfred Owen and Erich Maria Remarque, who portrayed the human tragedy of modern war.

C. The impact at home and abroad of United States involvement in World War I.

Grades 5-6

▶ Explain how the United States rapidly prepared for war in 1917 by examining memorabilia such as recruitment posters, war bond appeal flyers, pictures of women at work, and appeals urging African Americans to move north to fill jobs to support the war effort.

▶ Assess Wilson's call for a League of Nations to preserve peace. *How did the Congress, the press, and the people respond to this idea? Why did the United States not join the League of Nations?*

Grades 7-8

▶ Compare government actions to mobilize support and suppress opposition for the war effort. *What measures did the government utilize to win popular support for military conscription and the sales of liberty bonds? During wartime, should the government have the right to limit civil liberties?*

◆ Research the role of women in wartime industry using primary source materials such as journals, periodical literature, and photographs to write fictional diaries, letters, and narratives reflecting the impact of the war on women.

◆ Examine a map of World War I military engagements and indicate the campaigns in which the American Expeditionary Force participated. Investigate the importance of U.S. forces in the victory over the Central Powers. Analyze such things as photographs, poetry, literature, art, and music to appraise the impact of war on American troops.

◆ Research the causes of the Russian Revolution. *Why did the communist government withdraw from the World War I? To what extent did this change the course of the war?*

◆ Explain Wilson's goals in recommending the establishment of a League of Nations. *Why did domestic opposition to the League of Nations arise? What were the basic arguments against it?*

Grades 9-12

◆ Draw upon sources such as historical narratives, newspaper articles, and personal memoirs to analyze the reasons for passage of the Selective Service Act in May 1917, and explain what areas of the country most legislative opponents of the measure represented. *What reasons did opponents of the Selective Service Act offer against passage of the measure? To what extent did the Selective Service Act reflect the ideals and objectives of Progressivism?*

◆ Analyze President Wilson's declaration in 1917 that: *"It is not an army that we must shape and train for war, it is a nation."* Compare how U.S. mobilization in World War I differed from previous wars considering the role of the following in the mobilization effort: (a) War Industries Board; (b) Railroad Administration; (c) Food Administration; (d) Fuel Administration; (e) U.S. Shipping Board; and (f) Committee on Public Information (Creel Committee).

◆ Evaluate the reasons for the passage and enforcement of the Espionage and Sedition Acts. *On what grounds did Wilson support passage of such measures as the Espionage and Sedition Acts? To what extent did Justice Oliver Wendell Holmes's opinion in* Schenck v. U.S. *(1919) affect free speech? Do you agree with his reasoning? How did his opinion in* Abrams v. United States, *given eight months later, differ?*

◆ Explain the wartime contributions of labor. *How did the role of Samuel Gompers and the American Federation of Labor differ from that of "Big Bill" Haywood and Eugene Debs in terms of support for the war? How did the Wilson administration attempt to ensure labor support for the war effort?*

◆ Draw upon newspaper reports, editorials, advertisements, cartoons, historical narratives, and literary sources such as Richard Wright's *Native Son* to explain the "Great Migration" of African Americans to northern cities. *What opportunities were open to African Americans in northern urban centers? How difficult was it for African Americans from the rural south to adapt to life in urban areas? What did African American migrants contribute to the culture of northern cities? What were the major causes and consequences of racial tensions and conflict in the North (e.g., East St. Louis, Illinois, 1917) and South (e.g., Houston, 1917) during the war?*

◆ Examine point six of the Fourteen Points, which dealt specifically with Russia. *Did Wilson's subsequent actions in regard to Russia violate the principles set forth in his Fourteen Points? What was the nature and purpose of the U. S. Siberian expedition? What were the consequences of Allied military intervention in Russia?*

◆ Draw upon the Fourteen Points and supplementary declarations negotiated by U.S. and Allied leaders to evaluate the efficacy of the Treaty of Versailles. *Were the terms that Germany agreed to in the armistice realized in the Versailles Peace Treaty? How did the Allied secret treaties, negotiated during the war, complicate Wilson's task at Paris in 1919? What major conflicts over self-determination arose at Paris and embittered the settlement?*

◆ Construct a sound argument or debate such questions as: *Did Wilson miscalculate early popular support for the League of Nations and therefore refuse to compromise with his opponents? Was Henry Cabot Lodge really an "irreconcilable" disguising himself as a "revisionist" in order to defeat "Wilson's treaty"? How did Wilson's medical problems and subsequent incapacitation affect the Treaty and League ratification struggle in 1919-1920?*

III. *How the United States changed from the end of World War I to the eve of the Depression.*

A. Social tensions and their consequences in the postwar era.

Grades 5-6

◆ Using census charts, compare rates of immigration before and after the passage of immigration laws in the 1920s. *Why did nativists feel that immigration had to be restricted in the early 1920s? Who did they think should live in this country? Why did Congress pass laws which limited immigration? Did these laws further restrict the immigration of Asian peoples?*

◆ Assess the spread of the Ku Klux Klan's influence in different sections of the country in the 1920s. *Which groups were targets of Klan hostility?*

◆ Draw historical evidence from narratives, stories, diaries, and photographs to describe how women's lives changed after World War I. *How did women contribute to improvement in schools, hospitals, settlement houses, and social agencies? How did the spread of electrification and growing use of household appliances improve family life?*

◆ Use historical fiction such as *Shadrach's Crossing* by Avi to examine smuggling during Prohibition.

Grades 7-8

◆ Debate the proposition: *In order to defend American society from the threat of Communists it may become necessary to restrict civil liberties.*

◆ Construct a sound historical argument, or conduct a Socratic seminar on the topic: "Immigration restrictions of the 1920s contradicted the spirit of the Statue of Liberty." *How did the quota impact particular groups of immigrants? How did the restriction of European immigration affect Mexican immigration?*

◆ Read historical accounts of the revival of the Ku Klux Klan and analyze photographs of the "New Klan" such as the march in Washington, D.C. and violence against African Americans and immigrants. *What accounts for the development of large Klan organizations in northern states?*

◆ Construct a historical narrative comparing attitudes toward women with changing values and new ideas regarding such things as employment opportunities, appearance standards, leisure activities, and political participation.

Grades 9-12

◆ Analyze the major causes of the Red Scare and explain the role of Attorney General A. Mitchell Palmer in the deportation of suspected subversives. Draw historical evidence from speeches, political cartoons, news reports, editorials, and journal articles to analyze how words and images were used to stir fears of Bolshevism and foreigners. *To what extent was Bolshevism a threat to the United States? How effective was propaganda in winning public support for the Palmer Raids?*

◗ Draw evidence from the Sacco and Vanzetti trial proceedings and commentary by journalists to analyze the issues raised by the celebrated case. Examine recent historical interpretations of the case. *Do current historical studies verify or refute earlier interpretations? Did Sacco and Vanzetti get a fair trial?*

◗ Use statistical charts and the immigration laws of 1917, 1921, and 1924 to explain the changes in the ethnic composition of immigrants and the fears it represented. *What factors contributed to the passage of restrictive immigration laws in the twenties? How was "American" being defined?*

◗ Draw historical evidence from biographies, newspapers, and works of authors reflecting different attitudes on race, such as Madison Grant, Thomas Dixon, James Weldon Johnson, W. E. B. Du Bois, and Claude McKay, to construct a historical narrative assessing the impact and consequences of racism in the postwar era. *What were the underlying causes of the northern race riots of the postwar era? What were the origins and goals of the Garvey movement? How successful was Marcus Garvey?*

◗ Gather evidence from a variety of sources to explore the growth of the Ku Klux Klan in the 1920s. *How did it differ from the earlier Klan? To what extent was immigration related to the revival of the Klan? What was the role of women in the organization?*

◗ Use selections from the Scopes trial or excerpts from *Inherit the Wind*, to explain how the views of William Jennings Bryan differed from those of Clarence Darrow. *To what extent did Bryan's arguments relate to fundamentalist thinking? What techniques did Clarence Darrow use to counter Bryan's arguments? To what extent did Darrow represent modernist thought?*

◗ Trace the history of the temperance movement from the early nineteenth century and explain the factors which led to the establishment of prohibition in 1920. *Which groups supported the 18th Amendment? Why did reformers consider prohibition a "noble experiment"? To what extent did the dry crusade reflect urban-rural tension? What factors led to the ratification of the twenty-first amendment in 1933?*

◗ Use pictures, journal articles, and the writings of H. L. Mencken and Charlotte Perkins Gilman to explain how the image of the "flapper" symbolized the "New Woman." *Why were clothes called "The Great Liberator of the Decade"? How did the media image of women conform to reality? How did the images and goals of the "New Woman" affect middle-class behavior and family relationships? What fears did the "New Woman" image arouse?*

B. How a modern capitalist economy emerged in the 1920s.

Grades 5-6

◗ Assess the changes in your community and urban/suburban settings by examining historical pictures, visiting museum displays, and interviewing people who lived in the 1920s. *How did earlier improvements in steel construction and elevators allow for great change in cities in the 1920s? Why did people prize home ownership? Why did so many people leave the cities for the suburbs? What made travel to work easier for people in cities and suburbs?*

◗ Investigate how inventions and technology changed American society in the early 1900s. *How significant were the 1903 Wright Brothers experiments in powered flight? What was the importance of Robert Hutchings Goddard's experiments in rocket propulsion of 1926? How did the Wright Brothers and Goddard's experiments in aerotechnology lead to significant advances in future generations?*

◗ Research how advances in science and technology reduced the cost of products and helped raise the standard of living. Investigate scientists such as William Davis Coolidge and Irving Langmuir who improved the efficiency and lowered the cost of electric lights.

Grades 7-8

▶ List new inventions and technological advances which affected the lives of Americans in the 1920s, and describe how management techniques changed the methods of production. *Why was Henry Ford the symbol of the new industrial order in the twenties? In what respects was automobile manufacturing the characteristic industry of 1920s America? How did the automobile change American life in the 1920s?*

▶ Analyze the impact of advertising on the desire for new products. Compare advertising media from the 1920s with contemporary media, using the Sears Roebuck Catalogue or automobile, cigarette, and appliance advertisements from newspapers and magazines.

▶ Develop a case study of a major city of the late nineteenth century and explain how new technology transformed the modern city. *How did new and more advanced transportation systems affect American cities? What factors contributed to the development of skyscrapers? How did the development of suburbs change the composition of American cities in the late nineteenth century?*

Grades 9-12

▶ Examine such companies as General Electric, the Endicott-Johnson Shoe Company, or International Business Machines (IBM) to explain how new inventions, technological advances, and improvements in scientific management revolutionized productivity and the nature of work in the twenties. *How did the expanded "rule of reason" decision in the 1920 U.S. Steel case favor the growth and development of modern corporations? How did Frederick W. Taylor's evaluation of shop organization, task analysis, industrial engineering, and worker motivation contribute to increased efficiency and productivity in the 1920s?*

▶ Explain how the "new paternalism" of the modern corporation, as illustrated in the rise of "welfare capitalism" and the rapid growth of personnel departments seeking to create a cooperative, highly motivated, and productive work force, contributed to the improvements in industrial efficiency and production in the postwar period.

▶ Construct a historical narrative explaining how new forms of advertising, installment buying, and sales techniques contributed toward the creation of a new consumer culture in the twenties. *How was a deodorant advertising slogan, "Make your arm pits, charm pits," reflective of new methods of advertising? How did national advertising and sales campaigns impact the American economy?*

▶ Analyze the reasons for development of skyscrapers and their impact on the concept of community and individualism. *What were Frank Lloyd Wright's contributions to urban architecture?*

▶ Investigate the work of Luther Burbank and explain how his work in hybridization with plants promoted agricultural productivity.

▶ Explain the factors which made the United States a major agrarian producer.

C. How new cultural movements reflected and changed American society.

Grades 5-6

▶ Construct projects such as wall charts, murals, short stories, poems, skits, or songs to compare media and recreation available in the 1920s. Compare the print media, radio, and movies produced in the 1920s to information sources available today. *What did families do at home to get information and entertain themselves? Where did they go outside their homes for recreation? Which inventions and technologies have changed the ways in which we get information and entertainment since the 1920s?*

◗ Investigate the work of an individual who contributed to the Harlem Renaissance to define the movement. Draw from the music, art, and literature of major figures in the Harlem Renaissance such as Langston Hughes, James Weldon Johnson, Zora Neale Hurston, Bessie Smith, Duke Ellington, and Archibald Motley. *What issues and ideas did they portray in their work?*

◗ Draw evidence from a variety of sources, such as maps, historical narratives, and photographs, to examine the growth of professional sports facilities, fair grounds, amusement parks, and recreational areas in your region. *When were these places developed in your community, county, or state? How did people reach these places? How did these recreational areas change the local environment?*

◗ Draw evidence from photographs, movies, or family albums to examine the changes that contribute to the reason why people call this era the "Roaring Twenties." *How did clothing and fashion change in the 1920s? What was the dance rage of the period? What would it have been like to live in the 1920s?*

Grades 7-8

◗ Define mass culture and describe examples of the means by which cultural norms and fads are disseminated today. Compare these findings with the society of the 1920s. *How were such things as fashion and hair styles, slogans or phrases, and popular dances introduced into mainstream society? How have movies, radio, and print media influenced change in American culture?*

◗ Examine how literature and art in the 1920s questioned traditional values and culture. *What did the writers of the "Lost Generation" think about American society? Who were the prominent writers and what were the themes of their works? To what extent did the Harlem Renaissance capture the diversity of African American culture? Who were the leading writers and artists of the Harlem Renaissance? What was the impact of their works?*

◗ Investigate how Americans used the luxury of increased leisure time. Answer such questions as: *What accounted for the increase of leisure time in the 1920s? How did the automobile promote the use of national parks? Why have the 1920s been called the "Golden Age of Bat, Club, Glove, and Ball"? Who were the popular sports figures of the era?*

◗ Describe the origin of the Blues and explain how it reflected the Jazz experience of African Americans. *Why did the Blues and Jazz become a part of the national culture? What messages did the music contain?*

Grades 9-12

◗ Assemble evidence regarding the national impact of radio, high circulation print media, and movies, and construct a valid historical argument on such questions as: *To what extent was a national popular culture created by syndicated presses or national press associations? In the 1920s, was the radio a more powerful form of media for the shaping of a national popular culture than television is today? How constructive were the movies in shaping national popular culture?*

◗ Describe how World War I contributed to a general spirit of disillusionment in the 1920s by analyzing evidence from a variety of historical, visual, and literary sources including the distinctive American art and literature which emerged in the post-war period. *How did cultural changes, industrialization, and the disillusionment following War I influence writers of the "Lost Generation" such as F. Scott Fitzgerald, Ernest Hemingway, John Dos Passos, Edith Wharton, and Theodore Dreiser?*

◗ Draw from literature, poetry, art, and music of the Harlem Renaissance to analyze how literature and the arts reflected the experiences of African Americans in the 1920s and 1930s. *How did the poetry of Langston Hughes illustrate the themes of the Harlem Renaissance? To what extent did authors such as Claude McKay, Zora Neale Hurston, and Countee Cullen employ similar themes in their works?*

▶ Construct a historical narrative or visual display which explains how the work of such artists as Georgia O'Keefe, Robert Henri, William Glackens, George Luks, Everett Shinn, John Sloan, George Bellows, and Edward Hopper reflected the urban landscape of the early 20th century. *In what respects was the Armory Show of 1913 revolutionary? Why did its display of modern art shock so many people? How did the themes of cynicism and disillusionment influence the work of artists in the postwar period?*

▶ Drawing upon a variety of historical narratives, literary sources, newspaper accounts, and magazine descriptions, analyze how the increased leisure time achieved in the 1920s promoted the growth of professional sports, amusement parks, and national parks. *How did the desire for the emerging leisure time comport with the Protestant work ethic dominant in the 19th century?*

▶ Examine how authors used fiction to explore issues in society drawing from literary works of the 1920s such as F. Scott Fitzgerald's *The Great Gatsby* and William Faulkner's *The Sound and the Fury.*

▶ Construct biographical profiles of artists such as George Balanchine, Arturo Toscanini, Bertolt Brecht, Thomas Mann, Igor Stravinsky, and Salvador Dali who fled repressive communist and fascist regimes in Europe in the 1920s and 1930s to practice their arts in America. Assess their influence on American culture, film, architecture, literature, and music. *What were the reasons for the increase in the numbers of expatriates who flocked to the United States?*

▶ Examine the reasons for and effects of the extension of secondary education in the Progressive era. *What were the results of a dramatic increase in enrollment in public high schools? What segments of American society were among those that now attended high school for the first time?*

D. Politics and international affairs in the 1920s.

Grades 5-6

▶ Construct a timeline of the woman suffrage movement from the Seneca Falls Convention of 1848 to the ratification of the 19th Amendment. *Why did women want to be able to vote? How did the 19th Amendment change political life in America? How have voting rules changed since the ratification of the 19th Amendment?*

▶ Examine efforts to outlaw war in the 1920s by investigating the Kellogg-Briand Pact of 1928 (Pact of Paris). *What countries played a major role in promoting the agreement to outlaw war? What nations signed the agreement? Why did Secretary of State Frank Kellogg receive the Nobel Peace Prize in 1929? What other Americans have received the Peace Prize? Why were they awarded the prize?*

Grades 7-8

▶ Investigate the changes in Progressivism during the Harding and Coolidge administrations. *Were the 1920s an extension of the Progressive era or a retreat from Progressive ideals? How would a Progressive respond to Coolidge's statement: "The man who builds a factory builds a temple. The man who works there, worships there"?*

▶ Examine the impact of woman suffrage on American society in the decade following the passage of the 19th Amendment. *Did the right to vote guarantee equality for women? Why did women such as Alice Paul call for the passage of an Equal Rights Amendment as a means to end gender discrimination?*

◗ Locate on a world map United States territories and spheres of influence in the 1920s and investigate the foreign policy of Republican administrations. *What was the role of the U.S. in disarmament conferences? Was the United States willing to enter into associations or make treaties with major European powers? Did U.S. policy in Latin America differ from that of previous administrations? To what extent did Presidents Harding, Coolidge, and Hoover carry out the Big Stick policy of Theodore Roosevelt?*

Grades 9-12

◗ Gather evidence from a variety of historical sources to assess the Harding and Coolidge administrations and analyze the effects of World War I on the vitality of Progressivism. *Did the "return to normalcy" reflect a rejection of Wilsonianism and Progressivism? How did Harding's support of federal anti-lynching legislation, rights for African Americans, and his record in civil liberties contrast with his predecessor? What was the impact of the Coolidge-Mellon economic program? To what degree was it a break with the economic policies of Progressives?*

◗ Examine the effect of woman suffrage on women and society in the 1920s. *Why was Alice Paul's sponsorship of the Equal Rights Amendment so little supported by women in the 1920s? What issues concerning protective labor for women and children arose in the 1920s? How unified were women on these issues?*

◗ Describe Republican efforts to ensure a peaceful and stable world order in the 1920s and evaluate their success. *Were there discernible differences in U.S. foreign policy toward Asia, Europe, and Latin America in the 1920s? How effective were the agreements reached at the Washington Naval Conference of 1921-22 in protecting the long-term interests and security of the United States? In what respects were Republican foreign policies in the 1920s different from Progressive policies? How did the Clark Memorandum (1928) and the Hoover administration reorient U. S. foreign policy toward Latin America?*

Teacher Gloria Sesso with students, Half Hollow Hill High School East, New York

ERA 8

The Great Depression and World War II (1929-1945)

Participants of this era are still alive, and their common memories of cataclysmic events—from the Crash of 1929 through World War II—are common points of reference today. Our closeness to this era should help students see how today's problems and choices are connected to the past. Knowledge of history is the precondition of political intelligence, setting the stage for current questions about government's role and rule, foreign policy, the continuing search for core values, and the ongoing imperative to extend the founding principles to all Americans.

The Great Depression and the New Deal deserve careful attention for four reasons. First, Americans in the 1930s endured—and conquered—the greatest economic crisis in American history. Second, the depression wrought deep changes in people's attitudes toward government's responsibilities. Third, organized labor acquired new rights. Fourth, the New Deal set in place legislation that reshaped modern American capitalism.

In its effects on the lives of Americans, the Great Depression was one of the great shaping experiences of American history, ranking with the American Revolution, the Civil War, and the second industrial revolution. More than Progressivism, the Great Depression brought about changes in the regulatory power of the federal government. It also enlarged government's role in superimposing relief measures on the capitalist system, bringing the United States into a mild form of welfare state capitalism, such as had appeared earlier in industrial European nations. This era provides students with ample opportunities to test their analytic skills as they assay Franklin Roosevelt's leadership, the many alternative formulas for ending the Great Depression, and the ways in which the New Deal affected women, racial minorities, children, and other groups.

World War II also commands careful attention. Although it was not the bloodiest in American history, the war solidified the nation's role as a global power and ushered in social changes that established reform agendas that would preoccupy public discourse in the United States for the remainder of the 20th century. The role of the United States in World War II was epochal for its defense of democracy in the face of totalitarian aggression. More than ever before, Americans fought abroad, not only winning the war but bringing a new cosmopolitanism home with them. As before, the war was an engine of social and cultural change. In this war Americans of diverse backgrounds lived and fought together, fostering American identity and building notions of a common future. Similarly, on the homefront public education and the mass media promoted nationalism and the blending of cultural backgrounds. Yet students should learn about the denial of the civil liberties of interned Japanese Americans and the irony of racial minorities fighting for democratic principles overseas that they were still denied at home as well as in military service itself.

Students will need to assess carefully the course of the war, the collapse of the Grand Alliance, and its unsettling effects on the postwar period. Also, they should evaluate the social effects of war on the homefront, such as internal migration to war production centers, the massive influx of women into previously male job roles, and the attempts of African Americans and others to obtain desegregation of the armed forces and end discriminatory hiring.

Essay

Comparative Biography as Political History: Huey Long and Father Coughlin*
by Alan Brinkley

A curricular mainstay of many history classrooms is the ubiquitous "presidential project," or some similar type of research report. In the following piece, Alan Brinkley illustrates how the product of traditional biographical studies can extend well beyond superficial hagiography to reveal important lessons about social, political, and/or economic history. The comparative approach he advocates is one that could be used to good effect in most any history class, with students working individually or in groups to discover and evaluate the roles and contributions of particular people in the broader context of the times in which they lived.

Alan Brinkley is Professor of American History at Columbia University, where he teaches the history of American politics and society in the late nineteenth and twentieth centuries. Professor Brinkley is the author of *Voices of Protest: Huey Long, Father Coughlin, and the Great Depression,* which was awarded the 1983 American Book Award for History.

Is the task of the biographer synonymous with the task of the historian? The answer, of course, depends on our definition of historical inquiry. If we assume that the study of history involves simply the reconstruction of the past, the illumination of human experience in all its variety and nuance, then the study of any individual is a contribution to historical understanding. But there is another, broader conception of the historian's task: the belief that the purpose of scholarship is not simply to reveal the past, but to explain it; to make connections and identify transformations; to look at the individual pieces of history in terms of how they fit into a larger pattern. By that definition, the connection between biography and history becomes less clear, and all historians engaged in biographical inquiry must grapple with an important question: how does the study of individual lives illuminate the larger history of a society or an era?

There is no additional question facing those historians whose excursions into the field of biography take them into the lives of more than one person: what can they study of several lives, juxtaposed against one another, teach us that an ordinary biography, or another mode of analysis, can not? My own work in the field of what some have called "comparative biography" has forced me to confront both these questions and has led me to answers that have discomfited some traditional biographers but that suggest, I believe, several avenues for enhancing the connection between the study of individuals and the illumination of the larger patterns of the past.

In the case of the two popular dissident leaders of the 1930s—Huey Long and Father Charles Coughlin—the comparative perspective helps us less in understanding the two men themselves than in understanding the larger culture of dissent that they both came to represent and to lead. Viewed in isolation, Long and Coughlin have often seemed little more than quirky aberrations, who must be explained in terms of their own inner natures, their vaulting ambition, and the susceptibility of the marginal people to whom they appealed. Viewed together, however, they illuminate a series of deeper and more universal impulses, impulses not new to the 1930s and not unique even then to Long and Coughlin, impulses whose survival—and debilitation—suggest a great deal about the larger contours of American society. The comparative approach, in short, helps in this case to put biography to the service of social and political history.

As individuals, Long and Coughlin could, on the surface at least, hardly have had less in common. Long was a product of the American South, born and raised in the hill country of

*Reprinted with permission from *The History Teacher,* Vol. 18, No. 1 (November 1984), pp. 9-16.

northern Louisiana, imbued with that region's Baptist pieties and populist political inclinations. Coughlin was of Irish Catholic descent, born and raised in Hamilton, Ontario, immersed in the life of the Church almost literally from the moment of his birth. Long was a lawyer and politician, who from a very young age pursued elective office with an unrelenting fury and who, having obtained office, brooked no opposition to the consolidation of his power. Coughlin was a Catholic priest, presumably removed from politics by his vocation, subject always to the will of his Bishop and the rules of his Church. Long openly and deliberately spurned the conventions of "respectable society" and tried instead to pose as a renegade, as the embodiment of popular will, struggling and attempting to replace a hostile and unrepentant establishment. Coughlin craved respectability, cultivated the mighty with an almost pathetic sycophancy, wished for nothing more than acceptance by and influence within the circles of established power, and turned against them only when it became clear that acceptance by them would forever elude him.

Yet for all their differences in background, station, personality, Long and Coughlin pursued public careers that were strikingly similar in their foundations and their trajectory. Both began to become involved in national politics and to develop national followings in the first year of the Great Depression; both first supported and then broke with Franklin Roosevelt and the New Deal (Long earlier, but no more bitterly, than Coughlin); both placed themselves at the head of imposing national political movements (Long as the leader of the Share Our Wealth Society, Coughlin of the National Union for Social Justice); both extended their influence through skillful use of the radio (Long irregularly, in national political broadcasts of increasing frequency, Coughlin weekly, through his enormously popular political sermons every Sunday afternoon); both reached the peak of their popularity in mid-1935.

But the public impact of Long and Coughlin was not simply similar. To an increasing degree by the mid-1930s, it was of a piece. As both men increased the range of their influence and the size of their followings, their movements began to overlap, in some cases to merge. Their admirers, and many of their opponents as well, began to view the two leaders as allies fighting in a common cause. Long and Coughlin themselves, although they were barely acquainted and although they viewed one another with great suspicion and some contempt, came to recognize how closely their movements were becoming connected, how important it was to each of them not to antagonize or alienate the admirers of the other.

The first question, then, is why did two men so strikingly different seem so appealing to many of the same people? Why did they seem to mainstream politicians of the 1930s—Franklin Roosevelt among them—to represent a similar, even a common danger?

One answer, of course, is that Long and Coughlin were not really as different from one another as they appeared. Both were intensely ambitious and highly self-centered men, as most successful politicians are. Both were accomplished speakers, effective radio personalities. Both were skilled at raising money (both openly and illicitly), and in spending it effectively on their own political advancement. Both had an intense personal magnetism that, however difficult to define, was an essential element in their popular appeal. But the real connection between Long and Coughlin lay less in their personal similarities, than in their social and ideological relationship to American society.

Long and Coughlin were, first, both products of cultures that were somehow marginal to the larger society of which they were a part. Long emerged from a region of Louisiana that had for decades felt itself on the periphery of the state economy and at odds with the state political oligarchy; his original constituents were men and women who had, for generations, considered themselves powerless and voiceless. Coughlin emerged from the Catholic working class and built his initial following primarily among second and third generation Irish and German laborers (usually skilled or semi-skilled workers) and small entrepreneurs in the industrial cities of the northeast and the midwest. His followers, like Long's, looked with suspicion and unease at the national corporate culture that was coming to dominate their society and their own lives. Long and Coughlin were, in short, outsiders, speaking for outsiders, in a society increasingly dominated by an educated middle class closely allied to the national corporate institutions of industrial America.

Long and Coughlin were, second, both imbued with the ideological currents of populism, broadly defined. Long's ties to the populists were both obvious and direct. Winn Parish in Louisiana, Long's birthplace and home, had been the center of populist sentiment in the states in the 1890s; it had been a bastion of agrarian socialism in the early twentieth century; and it had remained politically contrary every since. Long's own family was not particularly radical, although his father maintained at least a veneer of populist sympathies. But Huey's own political instincts were clearly honed on what he recognized as the prevailing sentiments of his community. In his first major legal case, he represented a poor widow in a suit against the local bank; one of his first political associations was with a socialist state senator from Winn who opposed American involvement in World War I as a Wall Street conspiracy.

Coughlin's connections with populism are less immediately apparent, but were no less powerful. His early education with the Basilian order in Canada brought him into close contact with the new social activism of European Catholics in the early twentieth century, the revival of interest in St. Thomas Aquinas, and the concerns about industrial growth that helped produce Catholic populist uprisings in Austria and Germany both before and after World War I. Coughlin's bishop and mentor in Detroit, Michael Gallagher, had spent a portion of his youth in Austria immersed in the anti-socialist, vaguely populist activism of the Catholic clergy there. Coughlin may have had no direct connection with the agrarian populism of the late nineteenth century America; but his ideological roots owed much to the related populist sentiments that were emerging in other societies at roughly the same time.

But the force that drew the Long and Coughlin movements together most effectively in the end was less the similar backgrounds of the leaders themselves than the similar messages that they presented to their supporters. And it is here, I think, that the comparative approach is most clearly valuable.

On the surface, these messages appeared strikingly different, at least in emphasis. Long came to national attention by promoting a grandiose scheme for the redistribution of wealth— through confiscatory taxes to scale down large fortunes, and through guaranteeing decent incomes to all citizens (a guarantee to be financed out of the surplus wealth that the new taxes would bring in to the government). Coughlin, for his part, based his national appeal on a series of proposals for inflating the currency and overhauling the banking system. Both men, it is true, expressed at least cautious approval of the proposals of the other; neither believed that the other's ideas were incompatible with his own. But a significant difference always existed between their concrete economic proposals.

But there was more to the appeal of Long and Coughlin than the specifics of their programs. For both men were expressing a deeper anxiety—a complex, often muddled anxiety, but one that can be described in relatively simple terms. Long and Coughlin were, in essence, raising similar challenges to the form of the modern, industrial state—not a genuinely radical or genuinely philosophical challenge; not a challenge to industrialism or capitalism per se; but a challenge to the structure the economy was assuming in the twentieth century, a structure shaped increasingly by the rise of large, centralized national bureaucracies. Both directly and indirectly, they were denouncing the process by which power and wealth were flowing away from individuals and toward remote, inaccessible institutions, toward obscure forces that were controlling people's lives while remaining outside the people's control.

They were, in short, appealing to one of the fundamental anxieties of any modern, industrial society: the fear of lost autonomy, of powerlessness; the terrifying sense—all the more terrifying in a time of economic distress—of losing control, of discovering that one's fate is in the hands of forces one cannot affect or even know. Virtually all members of modern society suffer such anxieties in some form, to some degree; Long and Coughlin, however, were appealing to those afflicted with such fears with special intensity.

Long identified the source of the problem as the bloated power of a few wealthy plutocrats; and he saw the solution in the destruction of their power and the redistribution of their wealth. Coughlin denounced the national and international banking and financial system; and to him the solution lay in the destruction of its power and its control over the currency. The difference is not insignificant; but the connection is, I believe, clear. Both were expressing an essentially populist vision of a small-scale, localistic economy; both were seeking explanations for the disappearance of that economy and prescriptions for its regeneration.

But there were two other important connections between the ideologies of Long and Coughlin, which illustrate not only the extent, but the limits, of their willingness to challenge the dominant trends of their society. Both Long and Coughlin were, first, calling on government to play a major role in the reconstruction of the economy; but the role they were prescribing for government was, they insisted, to be a largely passive and restricted one. The Share Our Wealth Plan would, Long insisted, require the creation of no menacing, intrusive federal bureaucracy; it would create, instead, a system of simple, clean, self-regulating tax codes. Coughlin's plans for banking and currency reform, similarly, envisioned no major expansion of federal power; the government would simply supervise the creation of new, more localistic financial institutions and then allow them freely to do their work of regeneration.

Concentrated power in the hands of the states, both men implied, was to be feared just as much as concentrated power in the hands of plutocrats, or banks, or corporations. And the importance of this concern was particularly clear in the contrast between the claims Long and Coughlin made for their own proposals and the charges they leveled against the New Deal.

Their attack on Franklin Roosevelt had a dual thrust. First, they charged, the New Deal was not doing enough. It was not acting sufficiently forcefully to break up great fortunes, redistribute wealth, reform the banks and the currency, and decentralize power. It was timid and weak, controlled by the very bankers and plutocrats whom Roosevelt had once promised to attack. But, second, and of at least equal significance, they attacked the New Deal for doing too much: for creating a menacing, tyrannical bureaucracy of overbearing intrusiveness, for expanding the role of the state in national life to the point that government was becoming a menacing, meddling force—threatening to freedom in precisely the same way that concentrated private power was threatening.

But what Long and Coughlin shared in addition to this strictly limited view of government power was an inability to translate that view into a coherent, realistic program of reform. What was missing in both their messages was a genuine belief in possibilities. There was, instead, an unspoken but very real sense of resignation, which became evident on those few occasions when they tried to spell out in detail how their programs would work.

Long, for example, offered a detailed picture of his Share Our Wealth Plan in a book published shortly after his death and entitled *My First Days in the White House*. In it, he described the enactment of his plan through the creation of a Federal Share Our Wealth Corporation. This new government-owned institution would hold all the wealth confiscated under the Long plan; and it would then issue stock in itself to the public at large, through which universal prosperity would be assured. The obvious unworkability of this scheme is less striking, I think, than its grandiose dimensions. The restoration of power to communities and individuals was to be accomplished by the creation of a huge government corporation, an agent of centralized power greater and more influential than any institution hitherto imagined.

Coughlin, for his part, only rarely spoke in specific terms of his vision of a new financial system. But when he did, he too seemed unable to envision any structure that was not dominated by powerful federal institutions. He called for a new national reserve board, to be staffed by elected representatives from around the nation, but to be granted almost dictatorial power over the behavior of banks and the size and composition of the currency. The menacing institutions of Wall Street would be transformed into benign arms of the federal government—institutions less menacing, perhaps, but no less centralized, no more localistic.

What Long and Coughlin reveal to us, in their confused and contradictory ideological wanderings, and in their ability to arouse intense popular support, is the power that the long tradition of localism, decentralization retained in American life in the 1930s; how the forces that had sustained republicanism and populism throughout the nineteenth century had survived and, in some respects, flourished in the twentieth. But they reveal to us as well how much more difficult it was for those forces to offer a credible basis for reform in a modern, industrialized America; how debilitated the localistic vision had become in the face of the realities of the centralized social organization of the twentieth century world. The dream of decentralization had not yet, in the 1930s, turned into the purely rhetorical stance that it would become in the postwar era; but the contradictions and ambiguities in the Long and Coughlin movements suggest that it was already well on its way—doomed by its growing irrelevance in a modern, increasingly consolidated nation in which basic choices had long since been made.

The comparative study of Huey Long and Father Coughlin, therefore, offers no particular advantage in the effort to understand the personalities, the inner lives, the motives, the dreams and frustrations of Long and Coughlin themselves. But it helps us to understand something far more important. We see here two very different men, from different backgrounds, representing (at first, at least) different constituencies offering closely related ideological messages and evoking highly similar, and ultimately identical popular responses. We see in them, in their successes and their failures, evidence of the endurance and the universality of several powerful social impulses with deep roots in American history; and we see in them, too, evidence of the fate those impulses had encountered, and would encounter, in the world of the twentieth century.

Sample Student Activities

I.   The causes of the Great Depression and how it affected American society.

A.   The causes of the crash of 1929 and the Great Depression.

Grades 5-6

▸ Contrast pictures of life in the "roaring twenties" with those showing depression conditions of the 1930s. Draw evidence from graphs and charts, documentary photographs, and oral history interviews to explain the changes in American life after the stock market crash of 1929.

▸ List the factors that contributed to the causes of the Great Depression.

▸ Through a role-playing activity, skit, or reader's theater, examine the effects of the depression on farmers, city workers, and military veterans. *Why were farm products destroyed while people were hungry in the towns and cities? Why were workers unable to find jobs? How did mechanization displace workers? What did World War I veterans do to demand bonuses and jobs?*

Grades 7-8

▸ Construct a chart illustrating the effects of the economic decisions of the Coolidge administration on large businesses, urban labor, and agriculture. *To what extent did the Coolidge economic program promote economic growth? What were the arguments used by those who supported and those who opposed the policy? According to Coolidge, what role was government to play in the system? To what extent did economic policies of the 1920s benefit owners or large businesses, laborers, and farmers?*

▸ Explain the factors that contribute to the fluctuation of the stock market and construct a historical narrative to examine the causes and consequences of the market crash of 1929.

▸ Explain the factors which contributed to the Great Depression. Draw upon evidence from a variety of primary and secondary sources, including data from graphs and charts, to assess the central political and economic causes of the Great Depression. *How did the distribution of income and wealth affect the U.S. economy in the 1920s? To what extent did the agricultural problems of the post-World War I era contribute to the depression?*

▸ Evaluate the effectiveness of programs instituted by the Soil Conservation Service, Bureau of Reclamation, Army Corps of Engineers, Civilian Conservation Corps, or the Tennessee Valley Authority to address issues of conservation during the New Deal. *How did the photography of Dorothea Lange and films of Pare Lorentz, produced for the Farm Security Administration, help to marshal public awareness of environmental issues?*

▸ Chart the measures the Hoover administration took to stem the tide of the Great Depression and construct a historical argument, debate, or narrative evaluating the effectiveness of these measures. *What programs did the Hoover administration initiate to meet the crisis? To what extent did President Hoover's philosophy of "rugged individualism" influence his recommendations for measures to stop the depression? What factors contributed to the continuing economic crisis? What impact did the closing of banks have on the economy? How did the worldwide depression impact the United States economy?*

Grades 9-12

▶ Draw upon the historical, literary, and graphic evidence to answer such questions as: *Did the application of "laissez-faire" economic policies ensure prosperity and growth? What factors contributed to the increasing consolidation of business in the 1920s? What major scientific and technological changes contributed to the increased productivity of business in the 1920s? Did Sinclair Lewis's character Babbitt reflect the business creed of the 1920s? How and why did the depression tarnish the popular image of American businessmen? Why did union membership decline so significantly in the 1920s? What major changes affected the lives and prosperity of workers in the 1920s? How did American tariff policy and international economic developments affect the Great Depression?*

▶ Research measures President Herbert Hoover took to stem the tide of the Great Depression. Consider different historical interpretations of and evaluate debates among historians regarding the effectiveness of the Hoover administration in dealing with the crisis. Analyze arguments used to evaluate Hoover's response to the depression and assess the validity of opposing viewpoints.

B. How American life changed during the 1930s.

Grades 5-6

▶ Draw evidence from diaries, journals, oral histories, literature, documentary films, and photographs to develop a skit or role play activity which examines life in the Midwest during the depression and the experiences of farmers who migrated to California in search of work.

▶ Use Children's literature such as *Nelda* by Pat Edwards and *Elderberry Thicket* by Joan Zeier to illustrate the effects of the depression on families.

▶ Explore the effects of the Great Depression on the local community using library and local historical society resources and interviews with family members and long-time community residents. Compare photographs of homes and businesses then and now. *What happened to local families, businesses, farms, and banks during the depression? Did people in the local community lose their homes and farms? How did this compare to what was happening in the rest of the country at that time? Where did people turn for help in their community?*

▶ Describe how the drought of 1932 changed farming conditions in the Midwest. Draw upon documentary photographs, literature, and personal accounts to demonstrate how farm owners, tenant farmers, and sharecroppers were affected. Develop skits or stories depicting their problems.

▶ Draw upon evidence from diaries, journals, oral histories, documentary films, and photographs to develop picture boards, role-play activities, or stories examining the lives of diverse groups during the depression. *How did farm families fare when they moved westward to California? Where did unemployed city workers turn for help? How did people manage when homes were foreclosed?*

▶ Examine folk songs, pictures, and public art to learn about problems during the depression. Develop a classroom musical program or art show comparing issues faced during the depression with problems in our communities now. *How did aid for families during the depression compare with efforts to help the homeless today?*

Grades 7-8

▶ Use historical fiction such as *I Remember Valentine* by Liz Hamilton, *No Promises in the Wind* by Irene Hunt, *Lackawanna* by Chester Aaron, and *Tracks* by Clayton Bess to explore the impact of the depression on young adults.

▶ Draw upon documentary photographs, ballads, demographic data, and unemployment trends to evaluate the effects of the Great Depression on the American people. *What was the response of Dust Bowl farmers to the crisis? What was the nature of their migration—where did they go and how did they get there? How did factory workers and other urban dwellers respond to rising unemployment, and bank failures? What programs were developed by local officials to aid the affected?*

▶ Gather evidence from oral histories, letters, journals, and documentary photographs to examine the effects of the depression on American families and gender roles. *What pressures did unemployment place on families? What effect did the depression have on women who were employed outside the home? What employment opportunities were open to women during the depression?*

▶ Chart the effects of the Great Depression in various regions of the country and construct a historical argument, debate, or narrative comparing the experiences of diverse groups in different regions. *How were African Americans in the South and industrial centers of the North affected by the depression? How were Mexican Americans in the West and Southwest affected? How were their experiences similar or different from those of white farmers in the Midwest and industrial workers in the Northeast?*

▶ Investigate the plight of African Americans and white sharecroppers during the depressing drawing evidence from *Roll of Thunder Hear My Cry* by Mildred Taylor. Draw upon Taylor's sequel, *Let the Circle Be Unbroken* to examine a family's determination to combat prejudice.

Grades 9-12

▶ Draw upon such historical, literary, and visual sources as Carey McWilliams's *Ill Fares the Land*, John Steinbeck's *The Grapes of Wrath*, James Agee and Walker Evans's *You Have Seen Their Faces*, Pare Lorentz's documentaries for the Farm Security Administration—*The River* and *The Plow That Broke the Plains*—and the photographs of Dorothea Lange and others to analyze the reasons for and effects of the Dust Bowl on farmers and their families in the Great Plains.

▶ Draw upon the historical evidence to answer such questions as: *How do you account for the poverty amidst plenty during the depression? What was the purpose and success of the Southern Tenant Farmers' Organization? Did farmers have legitimate complaints concerning exploitation by a variety of middlemen as the chief source of their problems, or did their economic hardship result primarily from overproduction and the vagaries of a market economy?*

▶ Draw on a variety of personal reminiscences and periodicals of the period to write a historical account of the impact of the Great Depression on local, state, and charitable resources in the period 1930-1938.

▶ Draw upon a variety of historical, literary, and visual sources to explain the impact of the Great Depression on the lives of workers and their families. *What effect did the Great Depression have on traditional gender roles? Why did the number of working women increase in the 1930s? Did women take jobs from men? What effect did the Great Depression have on marriages, divorces, and the number of children born in the 1930s? How did the Great Depression affect the lives of children and teenagers? What effect did prolonged unemployment have on male heads of families and how did the Great Depression affect traditional authority relationships within the family?*

▶ Explain how racism affected the conditions and position of African Americans in the 1930s.

▶ Draw on a variety of sources, including oral histories, to examine the experiences of Mexican-Americans during the depression. *What was the policy of state and local governments in dealing with Mexican and Mexican-American migrant workers? To what extent did Mexican-Americans seek repatriation to Mexico? To what extent were they forced into leaving the United States?*

▶ Draw on the tradition of documentary expression in the 1930s by such practitioners as Erskine Caldwell, Dorothea Lange, Arthur Rotherstein, Ben Shahn, Roy Stryker, James Agee, Walker Evans, John Grierson, Pare Lorentz, and Dwight Macdonald to explain how their work reflected American conditions in the 1930s. *How did the Works Progress Administration promote art in the period 1935-41?*

▶ Assess the impact of mass media on the American culture in the 1930s. *What factors contributed to the nationalization of culture? What kinds of movies and radio shows were most popular and why? How did popular culture divide along class lines? How did popular sports and athletic heroes reflect the ideals and interests of people? How did regionalist artists such as Thomas Hart Benton and Grant Wood portray American life?*

II. *How the New Deal addressed the Great Depression, transformed American federalism, and initiated the welfare state.*

A. The New Deal and the presidency of Franklin D. Roosevelt.

Grades 5-6

▶ Draw upon library resources to compare the leadership styles that Herbert Hoover and Franklin D. Roosevelt brought to the presidency. *How did the public respond to both presidents? Was public reaction to these two presidents fair?*

▶ Construct a pictorial biography of the life of Franklin Roosevelt.

▶ Explain what is meant by the "New Deal." *How did the New Deal attempt to provide for relief from the Great Depression?*

▶ Gather evidence from interviews, community libraries, and historical societies to investigate ways in which New Deal legislation touched the lives of local families and people in your state or region. *How did people in your community participate in New Deal programs?*

▶ Research how women in your local community tried to improved life for children and families. *What roles did they play in organizing day-care centers, medical clinics, and food pantries?*

▶ Draw upon biographies to determine how women like Eleanor Roosevelt, Frances Perkins, and Mary McLeod Bethune contributed to New Deal programs.

Grades 7-8

▶ Compare Herbert Hoover and Franklin Roosevelt with regard to their personal and political responses to the Great Depression. *To what degree were the personal backgrounds of these leaders alike? To what extent were they different? How might one account for the different mind-set with which each leader responded to the Great Depression? How have recent historians evaluated the two presidential administrations?*

▶ Interrogate historical data from a variety of sources to explain the link between Progressivism and the early New Deal.

▶ Chart the relief, recovery, and reform measures associated with the "first" and "second" New Deal and construct a historical argument, debate, or narrative evaluating the relative success of each program. *What were the social, economic, and political ramifications of these two New Deal plans? How might one account for the different responses to the continuing depression?*

▶ Draw upon historical accounts and personal narratives to assess how the Tennessee Valley Authority extended the benefits of electro-technology in the rural South. *How did other New Deal programs disseminate knowledge and advances in science and technology? What were the practical benefits of these programs?*

▶ Evaluate Eleanor Roosevelt's role in promoting change in American society during the New Deal. *What specific efforts did the First Lady make in response to the crisis? How successful was she in fulfilling her agenda?*

Grades 9-12

▶ Evaluate journalist Walter Lipmann's characterization of Franklin Roosevelt during the 1932 campaign as: *"[He] is no crusader. He is no tribune of the people. He is no enemy of entrenched privileges. He is a pleasant man who, without any important qualifications for office, would very much like to be President." How accurate was Lipmann's characterization in 1932? How would you evaluate these remarks at the close of the Hundred Days? Today?*

▶ Assemble the evidence to answer such questions as: *How did philosophical and political approaches of Hoover and Roosevelt in dealing with the depression differ? To what extent did Hoover pave the way for Roosevelt and the New Deal? Which groups benefited most from the early New Deal? In what ways did the New Deal complete the work of the Populists and Progressives or venture into new fields?*

▶ Examine the economic theories of John Maynard Keynes and evaluate the influence of Keynesian economics on major legislation of the first and second New Deal. *To what extent did Roosevelt and his "Brain Trust" adopt Keynesian economics? In what ways was this a departure from previous economic policy? To what extent did Keynesian economics lead to economic recovery in the 1930s?*

▶ Draw evidence from New Deal legislation to assess how specific agencies such as National Industrial Recovery Administration, Social Security Administration, and Civilian Conservation Corp positively or negatively affected minorities and women. *Were specific New Deal programs designed to benefit minorities and women? Did New Deal legislation treat all people in the same way?*

▶ Drawing upon the historical evidence, evaluate FDR's commitment to advancing the civil and political rights of African Americans. *How aggressive was the Roosevelt administration in advancing civil rights? Why did African American voters increasingly change their political allegiance from the Republican to the Democratic party after 1934? How did increased African American support for the Democrats affect Democratic policies? How did southern Democrats respond to the New Deal and efforts to improve the life and conditions of African Americans?*

▶ Drawing on a variety of historical sources, assess how African Americans planted the seeds of a civil rights revolution during the 1930s. *How did Charles Houston and his law students at Howard University lay the groundwork for the legal assault on segregation in the 1930s? To what extent did African American leaders like Mary McLeod Bethune, Robert Weaver, William Hastie, Booker T. McGraw, and Robert J. Vann influence the New Deal?*

▶ Investigate the Indian Reorganization Act of 1934 and explain how it affected Native Americans. *What role did John Collier play in securing a "new deal" for Native Americans?*

B. The impact of the New Deal on workers and the labor movement.

Grades 5-6

▶ Use lyrics of songs such as "Brother, Can You Spare a Dime?," "Union Maid," and "Which Side Are You On?" to examine the effects of the depression and New Deal on the American labor movement. *What do the songs tell you about the condition of working men and women in the United States in the 1930s?*

▶ Assemble a collection of photographs showing American workers during the New Deal. Place yourself in the pictures and write a diary entry describing how your life had changed or remained the same since the early 1930s.

Grades 7-8

▶ Interrogate historical data from a variety of sources including personal narratives, newspapers and periodicals, historical photographs, and documentary films to determine the impact of the first and second phases of the New Deal on the labor movement. *How valuable was Section 7a of the NIRA in promoting unionism? How successful were New Deal measures in reducing the number and frequency of strikes? How militant were these unions? To what extent did the New Deal support unions over management?*

▶ Explain how labor unions organized African Americans, Mexican Americans, and women. *Which unions had as a major goal to secure equitable conditions and pay for minorities? How effective were unions in organizing minorities and women?*

▶ Write a character sketch of one labor leader or advocate for labor during the New Deal. Describe the stated objectives of the individual and how he or she responded to the crises of layoffs, anti-union tactics, and unemployment. Select from individuals such as: John L. Lewis, Frances Perkins, A. Philip Randolph, Upton Sinclair, and Robert Wagner.

▶ Drawing data from art and photographs depicting the depression era labor movements and lyrics of labor songs, examine the emotional appeal to support unions.

▶ Analyze how the WPA projects affected local areas. Survey the local community for buildings, bridges, murals or other public works projects sponsored by New Deal agencies. *How did the Federal Theatre Project drama companies influence small town America? How did artists working for the Federal Arts Project transform post offices, schools, and other public buildings?*

Grades 9-12

▶ Drawing upon a variety of historical sources, explain the factors contributing to the success of CIO leadership in organizing the rubber, auto, and steel workers in the period 1937-1941. *Why did the American Federation of Labor prove reluctant to organize workers in the mass production industries? What role did the Communist party organizers play in organizing workers in the 1930s? To what extent did Roosevelt and the New Deal advance the interests of working class Americans? What workers benefited most from the New Deal? How did the general public respond to the "sit-down strikes" of 1937-38 and what effect did public perception have on support for the New Deal? What workers were least affected by unions? How did the New Deal affect nonunion workers?*

▶ Draw upon methods of historical research including oral history to formulate questions in assessing labor's commitment to organizing African Americans, Mexican Americans, and women workers during the 1930s. *To what degree did the American Federation of Labor (AFL) encourage women and minorities to join unions? What role did A. Philip Randolph play in promoting unionization of African American workers? How did the Congress of Industrial Organizations (CIO) differ from the AFL in promoting interracial industrial unions? How committed were unions in organizing migrant farm workers? What unions did Mexican American workers establish to protect their interests? What impact did the Great Depression have on women in the work place? What was the impact on women workers of the AFL's program to restore "family life"?*

▶ Construct a historical investigation assessing the causes, strategies, and leadership of major strikes during the New Deal. Evaluate strikers' success in attaining their stated goals. Select from the rash of strikes in 1936 and 1937, including the celebrated General Motors sit-down strike.

▶ Explain the effects of New Deal agricultural programs on farm laborers by examining the Agricultural Adjustment Administration (AAA) and the Southern Tenant Farmers' Union (STFU). *Why was the STFU outraged by the implementation of the AAA? What methods did they use to change the system? To what extent did white and African American tenant farmers in the South work together in the STFU?*

C. Opposition to the New Deal, the alternative programs of its detractors, and the legacy of the New Deal.

Grades 5-6

▶ Construct an illustrated project such as a poster board, bulletin board display, or pictorial quilt to show the effects of the New Deal on the lives of people.

▶ Construct a balance sheet listing major New Deal programs which are still in effect today. Explain how these New Deal programs affect our life today.

▶ Examine political cartoons which show support for or opposition to Franklin Roosevelt and the New Deal. Explain the cartoons. Draw your own cartoon expressing your views of Franklin Roosevelt.

Grades 7-8

▶ Draw upon evidence from a variety of primary and secondary sources including speeches and political cartoons to explain the controversy over Roosevelt's "court packing" proposal. *What constitutional arguments did the Supreme Court use to strike down New Deal legislation? What was Roosevelt's plan in response to the decisions of the Supreme Court? How successful was he in carrying out his plan? How did the public respond to Roosevelt's plan?*

▶ Examine film documentaries and speeches of Dr. Francis Townsend and Senator Huey Long to explore the ideas of the Townsend Plan and the "Share the Wealth" program. *To whom did they appeal? Why did they attract public attention? What threats did they present to the New Deal?*

▶ Use a "meeting of the minds" activity or a Socratic seminar to explore different perspectives of the New Deal such as that of Progressives Robert and Philip LaFollette, California gubernatorial candidate Upton Sinclair, radio priest Charles Coughlin, Union Party candidate Gerald L. K. Smith, and former president Herbert Hoover.

▶ Construct a sound historical argument, debate, or narrative evaluating the significance and legacy of the New Deal and the extent to which the New Deal influenced the public's belief in the responsibility of government to deliver public services.

Grades 9-12

▶ Examine the Supreme Court's reasoning in such cases as *Schechter* v. *United States* (1935), *United States* v. *Butler* (1936), *West Coast Hotel Company* v. *Parish* (1937), and *National Labor Relations Board* v. *Jones and Laughlin* (1937). Investigate Roosevelt's response to the rulings and debate such questions as: *Was Roosevelt's "court packing" scheme constitutional? Would its acceptance have destroyed the constitutional system of checks and balances? Were the rulings by the Supreme Court the death knell of the New Deal?*

◆ Construct a sound argument, debate, or historical narrative examining the opposition to the New Deal from the perspective of the conservative Liberty League, the radical Communist party, or the protest movement of Huey Long, Charles Coughlin, and Francis Townsend. *How did the proposals of the "Share the Wealth" movement differ from those of the Communist party? How did they differ from the Liberty League's agenda? What was the effect of such programs on the New Deal? Was the criticism of Roosevelt and the New Deal justified? To what extent did the opposition of these groups solidify popular support for the New Deal?*

◆ Examine the proposals of Upton Sinclair's EPIC campaign in California. *What groups opposed it? Why did it fail? What were the reasons for the growth of the American Communist party during the 1930s? To whom did the party have the greatest appeal?*

◆ Utilizing a variety of historical and statistical sources, analyze the class basis for support and opposition to the New Deal in the Northeast, South, Midwest, and Far West. *What social classes most supported the New Deal? Who did the New Deal help the most? Would American voters in the 1930s have supported more radical changes?*

◆ Assess ways in which the New Deal changed the relationship between state and federal government.

◆ Evaluate Roosevelt from different perspectives. *How do current historians evaluate Roosevelt's domestic programs?*

◆ Debate the proposition: *The New Deal failed to provide a solution to the Great Depression.*

III. The causes and course of World War II, the character of the war at home and abroad, and its reshaping of the U.S. role in world affairs.

A. International background of World War II.

Grades 5-6

◆ Define isolationism. Use physical maps to explain the geographic features which influenced isolationist policies after World War I.

◆ Use political and physical maps to examine the international conflicts before World War II. Locate countries that were affected by prewar events such as Manchuria, Ethiopia, Spain, Czechoslovakia, and Poland. Identify on a map those countries that formed the Allied and Axis powers at the beginning of World War II.

◆ Locate Pearl Harbor and explain why it was an important U.S. naval base. Describe the events that brought the United States into World War II in 1941.

Grades 7-8

◆ Research Fascist and Communist philosophies of government. *How did these philosophies differ from those of a democratic system?*

◆ Construct a chart showing the political and economic factors that contributed to the rise of dictatorships in Europe.

◆ Construct a historical narrative that explains the Roosevelt administration's response to international conflicts. *What were American interests in Europe and Asia? To what extent did the Neutrality Acts limit Roosevelt's options in dealing with international aggression? Why did public opinion oppose U. S. intervention in Africa, Asia, and Europe in the 1930s?*

⬧ Construct a timeline from 1900 to 1941 listing the events which caused tensions between the United States and Japan. Draw from a variety of sources such as newspaper stories and editorials, treaties, international agreements, propaganda graphics, and documentary photographs to explain the reasons for rising tensions.

Grades 9-12

⬧ Construct a sound historical argument or debate examining statements such as: *"The failure to enforce the Treaty of Versailles led to World War II;"* or *"the lack of support for the League of Nations encouraged aggressive policies by dictatorial regimes."*

⬧ Draw on examples of Roosevelt's foreign policy toward Latin America and explain the reasons for the Good Neighbor Policy. Compare Roosevelt's policy to earlier U.S. policies toward Latin America.

⬧ Explain the events which led to the outbreak of war in Europe. *What was the role of Fascist dictatorships? The role of the Soviet Union? How did the U.S. respond?*

⬧ Use speeches, laws, and actions to decide whether the U.S. was already at war in the Atlantic when the Japanese attacked Pearl Harbor. *To what extent did Roosevelt's foreign policy evade U.S. neutrality laws? Was the arming of American merchant ships an offensive or defensive act? What actions led Roosevelt to justify "cash and carry" and "lend lease" policies? What were the consequences of each action?*

⬧ Use diplomatic correspondence, legislative actions, and political speeches to analyze U.S.-Japanese relations prior to December 7, 1941. *Why did Japan set up the East Asian Co-Prosperity Sphere? How did the United States respond? Were the differences between the United States and Japan in the 1930s negotiable or irreconcilable? How did Japan justify its attack on Pearl Harbor? Why did Roosevelt call it a "day that will live in infamy"?*

B. World War II and how the Allies prevailed.

Grades 5-6

⬧ Locate the major theaters of war in North Africa, Europe, and the Pacific on a world map.

⬧ Investigate the impact of the Holocaust by examining the personal stories of individuals. Draw evidence from books such as *Alan and Naomi* by Myron Levoy.

⬧ Construct a picture board, sketchbook, or report showing the contributions of men and women during the war.

⬧ Examine the photography of U.S. Marines raising the flag atop Mount Suribachi on Iwo Jima. *What stories are captured in this photograph?*

⬧ Draw evidence from diaries, interviews, and documentary films and photographs to explain the human tragedy of the war on civilians.

Grades 7-8

⬧ Trace the war through the participation of young adults by using books such as *The Last Mission* by Harry Mazer.

⬧ Draw upon historical data and evidence from maps of Axis and Allied movements in Europe, Africa, and Asia to explain military strategy during World War II. *Why did Germany and the USSR sign a nonaggression pact in 1939? What military strategy did Germany use in its conquest of France in 1940? What was the importance of the "Battle for Britain"? What was the Japanese strategy in East Asia and the Pacific? What was Roosevelt's logic in fighting an aggressive war against the Axis powers in Europe and a defensive war in Asia? Why did the Allies launch an invasion of North Africa in 1942, Sicily in 1943, and Normandy in 1944?*

- Explain what was meant by the "final solution" and draw from primary sources such as eye-witness accounts, oral history, testimony of Nazi officials, and documentary photographs and films to examine the human costs of Nazi genocide. *How did Roosevelt respond when he learned of the Nazi death camps?*

- List the major turning-points during World War II in Africa, Europe, and Asia and explain there impact on the outcome of the war. *Who were the most prominent U.S. military leaders in the war? How did their leadership help determine victory?*

- Draw upon visual data including documentary photographs, newsreels, and graphs to construct a chart appraising the human costs of World War II.

- Construct historical narratives, oral reports, diagrams, or displays which explain the structure of the United Nations and compare its goals and objectives with those of the League of Nations. *How did the United Nations differ from the League of Nations? To what extent has the United Nations achieved its stated goals?*

- Draw evidence from oral histories, letters, diaries, and documentary films to examine how military experiences brought people from all walks of life and religions and ethnic backgrounds together in a common cause. *How did the war promote a cohesiveness in American society? To what extent did racial segregation of military units affect morale? To what extent did the military experiences during the war help to promote a civil rights movement in the post-war years?*

Grades 9-12

- Compare Norman Rockwell's illustration of Roosevelt's Four Freedoms speech in January 1941 with the ideas presented in the speech. *What images of America do they both convey? Is Rockwell's portrayal accurate? To what extent was Roosevelt's speech idealistic? Rockwell's paintings?*

- Investigate the strategic and logistical factors involved with planning Operation Overlord. *How did the Allied military leadership decide on the timing and location of the D-Day invasion? What accounts for its military success?*

- Examine the naval strategy of "Island Hopping" in the Pacific theater. *What logistical and political factors led to its development? What were its goals? How effective was it in bringing an end to the war?*

- Interview World War II veterans and research oral histories such as Studs Terkel's *The Good War* to examine the experiences of American servicemen as combatants.

- Examine the decisions made at the major war-time conferences. *How did the allied military situation impact the decision to seek unconditional surrender, open a second front, and create a United Nations? What was the Roosevelt vision for the postwar world? What were the Soviet Union's objectives?*

- Construct a historical argument or debate to examine Allied response to the Holocaust. *What was U.S. immigration policy toward Jewish refugees from Europe? When did the Allies discover the scope of Nazi persecution of European Jewry, as well as the persecution of Jehovah's Witnesses, Gypsies, homosexuals, and other groups? What was the Allied response? What were alternative courses of action the Allies may have taken?*

- Draw evidence reflecting different perspectives to analyze within its historical context the decision to use the atomic bomb on Japan. Construct a sound argument, debate, or position paper on Truman's decision considering various factors such as: the Allied military position in the Pacific in 1945; estimated military and civilian casualties in a prolonged war; long-term consequences as understood in 1945; Japanese surrender overtures; and, the probability of Soviet entry into the war.

C. The effects of World War II at home.

Grades 5-6

▶ Draw upon historical records, photographs, and stories such as *A Time Too Swift* by Margaret Poynter to examine the war effort at home. Interview people who remember wartime experiences and create albums, stories, or plays to show ways in which people's lives were affected by the war. *How were men and women mobilized to take part in the war effort? How did shortages and rationing affect people's lives?*

▶ Locate the places where large numbers of Japanese Americans were living on the West Coast and the centers to which they were removed during the war. Construct an album of photographs and sketches which trace a Japanese American family from their home on the West Coast through their internment in a relocation center. Use personal stories such as *The Bracelet* by Yoshiko Uchida to examine childhood experiences in internment camps. Write journal entries, poems, or draw illustrations to express the feelings of the forced movement of Japanese Americans.

▶ Create a timeline or wall chart showing major developments in aviation, weaponry, communication, and medicine during the war years. Explain how these inventions and discoveries changed our lives.

▶ Draw evidence from books, movies, and cartoons that show how entertainment changed during the war years.

Grades 7-8

▶ Analyze visual images of women workers, such as "Rosie the Riveter" and poster art, to examine how women were portrayed during the war. *Were these complimentary images?*

▶ Explain the factors that led to the internment of Japanese Americans. Use oral histories and novels such as *Farewell to Manzanar* by Jeanne and James Houston, *Nisei Daughter* by Monica Itoi Sone, and *Journey to Topaz* by Yoshiko Uchida, and *Citizen 13660* by Mine Okubo, to compile case studies of the experiences of Japanese Americans during the war. *How did Japanese Americans cope with their internment? How was family life affected by the camps? How did the contributions of the Nisei Battalion contrast with the treatment of Japanese Americans at home?*

▶ Plot on a U.S. map the great migrations during World War II, locating the cities to which most migrated. Analyze the tensions that resulted from the rapid increase in population. *What drew people to these cities? How did local governments respond to demographic changes. What were the factors behind the Detroit race riot of 1943? The Los Angeles "Zoot-suit" riot of 1943?*

▶ Examine the effects of rapid technological change during the war years. *What new employment opportunities were available? How was the wartime technology transferred to a peacetime economy? How did military research in synthetic fabrics, plastics, television, and aviation change American society in the post-war years?*

▶ Draw upon evidence from a variety of primary and secondary sources to examine the role of Hollywood movies, radio programs, and musical recordings on American culture during the war years.

Grades 9-12

▶ Interrogate historical data from a variety of sources including industry and military draft records, economic and employment statistics, and historical narratives to explain United States mobilization during World War II. *How did the industrial sector adapt to meet the necessities of war production? What types of jobs—both within and outside the factories—developed as a result of domestic mobilization? What role did women play in the workforce? To what extent were their experiences similar to or different from those of women during World War I?*

◗ Analyze how African Americans, Mexican Americans, and Native Americans contributed to the war effort. *How did they respond to the contradiction between the discrimination within American society and the goals that they were fighting for as soldiers?*

◗ Assemble historical evidence to explore such questions such as: *On what grounds did government officials justify the internment of Japanese-Americans? Was this an example of racism? What were the Supreme Court's decisions in* United States *v.* Hirabayashi *(1943);* United States *v.* Korematsu *(1944);* United States *v.* Ex parte Endo *(1944)? What constitutional issues were involved in the cases? Was the restriction of civil liberties during wartime justified? Why did Congress issue a public apology and vote to compensate surviving Japanese American internees in 1988?*

◗ Use periodicals and local newspapers to research the public's expectations at the conclusion of the war. *To what extent did the American public expect a "return to normalcy"? Did public opinion support a continued U.S. role in world affairs or a return to isolationism? What was the prevailing attitude toward the Soviet Union at war's end? How did Americans view their global responsibilities at the end of the war?*

◗ Research the significant changes in science, medicine, and technology after World War II. *How did technological and scientific innovations during the war impact American society? What were the civilian applications of military research in fibers, sonar, nuclear physics, aviation, and rocketry?*

New Yorkers Celebrate VE Day, 1945. Courtesy Library of Congress

ERA 9

Postwar United States (1945 to early 1970s)

Although the study of the era following World War II can easily be dominated by a preoccupation with the Cold War, our understanding of present-day American society will be deficient without grappling with the remarkable changes in American society and culture in the 1950s and 1960s. It should be remembered that the closeness of the period makes it one of continuing reinterpretation, reminding us that historical judgements should be seen as provisional, never cut in stone.

Students will need to understand how the postwar economic boom, mightily affected by the transforming hand of science, produced epic changes in American education, consumer culture, suburbanization, the return to domesticity for many women, the character of corporate life, and sexual and cultural mores—both of which involved startling changes in dress, speech, music, film and television, family structure, uses of leisure time, and more.

All of this can take on deeper meaning when connected to politics. Politically, the era was marked by the reinvigoration of New Deal liberalism and its gradual exhaustion in the 1970s. In the period of liberal activism, leaders sought to expand the role of the state to extend civil liberties and promote economic opportunity. The advent of the civil rights and women's movements thus became part of the third great reform impulse in American history. Conservative reaction stressed restrictions on the growth of the state, emphasized free enterprise, and promoted individual rather than group rights.

The Cold War set the framework for global politics for 45 years after the end of World War II. The Cold War so strongly influenced our domestic politics, the conduct of foreign affairs, and the role of the government in the economy after 1945 that it is obligatory for students to examine its origins and the forces behind its continuation into the late 20th century. They should understand how American and European antipathy to Leninist-Stalinism predated 1945 that it was obligatory for students to examine its origins and the forces behind its continuation into the late 20th century. They should understand how American and European antipathy to Leninist-Stalinism predated 1945, seeded by the gradual awareness of the messianic nature of Soviet communism during the interwar years, Stalin's collectivization of agriculture, and the great purges of the 1930s. Students should also consider the Soviet Union's goals following World War II. Its catastrophic losses in the war and fear of rapid German recovery were factors in Soviet demands for a sphere of influence on its western borders, achieved through the establishment of governments under Soviet military and political control. Students should also know how the America policy of containment was successfully conducted in Europe: the Truman Doctrine, the Marshall Plan, the Berlin airlift, NATO, and the maintenance of U.S. military forces in Europe under what was called the nuclear "balance of terror."

They should also recognize that the U.S. government's anti-Communist strategy of containment in Asia confronted very different circumstances and would involve the United States in the bloody, costly wars of Korea and Vietnam. The Vietnam War is especially noteworthy. It demonstrated the power of American public opinion in reversing foreign policy, it tested the democratic system to its limits, it left scars on American society that have not yet been erased, and it made many Americans deeply skeptical about future military or even peacekeeping interventions.

Essay

The Personal Dimension in Doing Oral History*
by Roger D. Long

An important objective for any history teacher is for students in the course to appreciate the historian's craft and to reach an understanding about how the people who study the past seek out clues and interrogate a variety of evidence in order to construct arguments and reach conclusions about what occurred and why. Roger Long tells how a traditional term paper assignment reaps powerful benefits when students are asked to do the work of historians; that is, to conduct interviews and consult primary sources in order to uncover the lessons of history. Oral history assignments can be powerful for students of all ages, as demonstrated by a San Diego sixth grader who wrote: "There are two sides to every story. Maybe three. The book's. The TV's. And my grandfather's."

Roger D. Long is Associate Professor of History at Eastern Michigan University. He has taught in England, Pakistan, Japan, and Italy. He is author of a forthcoming study of Liquat Ali Khan, the first prime minister of Pakistan, as well as the editor of a volume of essays on British Empire history.

Using oral history in the classroom in nothing new and the special care which needs to be exercised when using this kind of approach is generally acknowledged, but it can be a very effective means of stimulating students and of introducing them in a practical way to the dilemmas and excitement which writing history can offer.

...In thinking about this I decided that instead of the usual term paper "on any aspect of twentieth century history which interests you" I would require a paper based on an oral history project. Furthermore, the contributor of the oral history would have to be someone they knew or someone their family knew. I had thought about this idea for some time but the decision became final when a student, who normally volunteered nothing in class, and for whom getting a response to the readings was like pulling teeth, came to me after class one day with copies of some documents which were his late great-grandfather's. They were in German and concerned his great-grandfather's service in the Austrian army at the beginning of this century, and he wanted to know what there was to know about them and how and where he could find out more. We spent some time discussing the documents, how he could find out about his great-grandfather's immigration into the United States, and some issues dealing with research. For the first time in the course the student looked like he was coming alive! Whether an oral history project of a personal nature could stimulate all the students in the class in the same way would be put to the test.

The result has been very encouraging and the experiment continues. Some of the students knew immediately what they were going to write about—their father's experiences in the Vietnam War—but others had to think about the subject and worry over it before they could decide on a topic. Those students who quickly came to a decision and became emotionally involved in the project produced the best reports and seemed to have got the most out of it. The papers, interestingly enough, covered the same sorts of topics that you typically find in this kind of class but the focus was, of course, different; it was history from the bottom up. There were no biographies of FDR or Hitler or other studies of the rich and famous although one student, in tracing the history of her family, found a connection with the founder of Yale University.

Looking at the papers I received in more-or-less chronological order, the first paper dealt with chemical warfare in World War I and how the student's grandfather—the grandfather he never

---

*Reprinted with permission from *The History Teacher*, Vol. 24, No. 3 (May 1991), pp. 307-311.

knew—was poisoned and disabled for life. The second paper spoke about the Depression and its effects on the family as remembered by the student's grandmother. This was an interesting narrative where the student compared what her grandmother remembered with what the secondary sources revealed: it was clear that the student's grandmother's experience was typical of many during the 1930s. The next four papers were concerned with World War II with the third also covering the Korea War as the interviewee became a career military man first in the navy and then the air force. Some interesting insights were revealed in the interview process, the kinds of things you do not find in the standard textbooks. In the Korean War, for instance, the Turkish troops fighting in Korea as part of the United Nations forces were proud, fierce fighters. In response to the U.S. Army's Second Division motto of "Second to None" they called themselves "None." They were also renowned for bringing back the heads—only the heads—of those they suspected of being North Korean spies! One paper dealt with a people who welcomed the arrival of the German invaders—the Lithuanians. This story was a remarkable one of a family being divided when the Russians reinvaded Lithuania in 1944; the interviewee did not see her mother again for twenty-three years. Her story was full of hardships and of chance such as visiting Dresden and deciding not to stay there just three weeks before it was destroyed by fire bombs.

Another subject dealt with was the one you might expect to be covered quite widely—the Vietnam War. Many of the students' fathers served in the war or were in the military at the time of the war and four of them wrote their papers on that subject. There were others who might also have written about the war but their father or their family's friend whom they had asked to be part of the project refused to talk about it with the result that all but one of the students had to change topics. Even for that one student who persevered, it was difficult to get anything out of his father as the experience was still so painful. A helicopter pilot in 1961 when the U.S. was fighting a secret war in Vietnam, the man told his son that the casualty rate of fighting behind enemy lines at that time was about seventy-five percent, and as a result he had lost nearly all of his friends. The effect was that while his mother had many friends, he had none and could make none because he was always afraid of losing them. Others were in the military at the time, had not fought in Vietnam, had not volunteered to fight in Vietnam when asked if they wanted to do so, or had served in the Army Reserves, and their stories showed many sides of the picture and brought up the ambiguity of the whole situation. All of those interviewed said that involvement in the war was wrong but if they had to do their time again they would always follow orders, no matter where it led them. Whether they fought in Southeast Asia or not, and even when the interviewees said they opposed the war, they all expressed their patriotism saying they had served their country even in the Reserves. The lesson which was brought home to the students in a very vivid way was that the war could be viewed from many different sides, that historical issues are not clear-cut, least of all to those living and remembering the events, and that the historian has to see all sides of the picture before taking a position. It was an interesting exercise for the students as they identified with the person they interviewed and gave his point of view in class.

The remaining nine papers were on various social and artistic topics such as fashion, movies, television, the beat poets and the civil rights movement. One of the papers concerning civil rights dealt with a riot in Detroit in an area that the students were familiar with; others discussed companies the students had grown up hearing about. As a result, history became something very real and concrete rather than remote and far removed.

The exercise did several things for the students and pointed out some of the problems in doing oral history. The first thing it did was to teach the students things about topics which they were interested in but which they had never had the chance or the motivation to delve into before—the Vietnam War, for example. It also made them more conscious about the world around them, even that the places of their everyday life had been, at various times, at the center of events of historical significance. The riots of 1968 in Detroit occurred in streets which were familiar to some of the students. It also taught them about the people they knew and how war could change their lives. For example, the person a student thought was "weird" because he always wore a cap and dark glasses was found in interviews to do so because his eyes had been affected by injuries sustained in Vietnam. One student felt sorry for a Vietnam veteran who could never have children and believed this was because of his connection with the Agent Orange program. Another was deeply impressed by the fact that a woman did not see her husband for two years during World War II. These personal narratives which caused the students to feel the anguish that the interviewee felt had more impact on these students than I think most history books would have.

The students also learned a great deal about primary source materials and the problems of doing oral histories. One student who did a history of her family interviewed her grandmother, who talked knowledgeably about a variety of people and their descendants. The student asked how she knew all this and the grandmother replied that it was "in the book." "What book?" asked the student. The reply was the book which was a history of the family. Where was the book? It was supposedly somewhere in the house and they made a cursory search for the book but the grandmother was legally blind and could not remember where it was and the student was not in a position to turn the house upside down to search for it. This reliance on the memory of an elderly informant was also one of the issues raised by another student who complained that there was just not enough information to work with. This was a good lesson on how a historian will sometimes have to build up a thesis from a limited amount of material and how historical controversies can arise because of theories based on just a single source or a few pieces of evidence. Another issue which arose was the difficulty of getting information from informants. The interviewee was generally a very busy person and it was difficult to arrange for the initial interview let alone the follow-up discussions. Remembering could also be painful, as in the case of a Vietnam veteran who reluctantly discussed his experiences for the first time with his son.

These experiences of the students in conducting oral histories with people they either knew personally or came to know made history come alive. It heightened their sense of the past and helped to make the subject a living one. In discussing the class with the students a common wish as that the course should begin with 1945 rather than 1900 and give more time to the 1970s and 1980s—a period with which the students could identify. While not concurring with this I think the sentiment reveals the effectiveness of making the term assignment one which the students could become personally involved with and which could bring the subject alive to students who only enrolled in a history class because it was a requirement for graduation. The experiment of requiring an oral history assignment was, I believe, successful. It challenged the students and encouraged them to grapple with many of the issues which are exciting to historians: a student's comment said it all and reflected the opinion of the class—"different, interesting, personal."

Sample Student Activities

I. The economic boom and social transformation of postwar America.

A. The extent and impact of economic changes in the postwar period.

Grades 5-6

▸ Develop journals, albums, videos, or presentations answering questions concerning local life in the postwar decades. *What economic opportunities did members of the armed forces find when they came home after World War II? How did people find housing and work after the war? How did the landscape of America change after the war? How did transportation change?*

▸ Give examples of service sector jobs and explain why more service jobs were available after World War II.

▸ Construct a collage to show the difference in standards of living of the urban poor and suburban middle class.

Grades 7-8

▸ Interrogate historical data from a variety of sources to evaluate the economic and political ramifications of demobilization after World War II. *What were the effects of demobilization and reconversion on American industry? How was the working life of women and minorities altered in the aftermath of the war? What was the economic effect of suburbanization and the return of women home from the factories?*

▸ Assess the economic impact of opportunities in the service sector and develop questions to guide historical research in appraising the expansion of service jobs in government and the private sector. *What factors contributed to the development of new government jobs? How did the expansion of hospitality and recreation industries offer service sector jobs?*

▸ Construct a sound argument, debate, or historical narrative examining the effects of postwar industrial development on the environment.

Grades 9-12

▸ Drawing upon a variety of memoirs, newspapers, and periodicals, examine the contrary proposals advanced for promoting postwar prosperity. *Why did so many economic advisors fear a postwar depression?*

▸ Construct a historical narrative explaining how increased defense spending and the unique position of the U.S. economy in the postwar era vis-à-vis European and Asian economies, led to unprecedented economic growth. *What opportunities were open to corporate employees? How did the growth of large corporations affect the lives of their employees? To what extent were women and minorities represented in the corporate structure?*

▸ Draw evidence from works such as Michael Harrington's *The Other America* and James Baldwin's *Notes of a Native Son* to examine the extent of poverty in the midst of affluence in postwar America. *Who were the "invisible poor"? What were the social and political factors that made the poor "invisible"? What groups made up the urban poor? To what extent did new technology contribute to poverty in Appalachia? How did geography contribute to poverty in areas like Appalachia?*

▶ Use oral histories to develop a case study of an American family during the post-war period and examine the extent to which life has changed since the Great Depression. *What were the dreams and aspirations of the family during the depression years? What aspects of the unprecedented affluence represented a dream fulfilled?*

▶ Assess the impact of the Cold War on the American economy. *How did increased military spending affect post-war employment? What resources were allocated for defense and how did the reallocation affect the American consumer? What was the domestic economic significance of the allocation of funds for the Marshall Plan and military defense against Communist encroachments in Europe, the Middle East, and Asia? How significantly did foreign aid impact the American economy?*

B. How social changes of the postwar period affected various Americans.

Grades 5-6

▶ Create a scrapbook, play, or song showing how family life changed in local communities in the decades following World War II. Drawing upon stories, pictures, and media clips, contrast local experiences with those in other regions. *What happened when Americans moved from cities to suburban areas? Did most women work outside the home? How did movies, television, and advertisements influence ideas about family life? What did the "ideal family" look like in the media then? What do families look like in the media and advertisements now?*

▶ Use magazine advertisements, lyrics from popular songs, and documentary films to examine how American popular culture changed after the war. *What were the dress styles of the day? What were the most popular forms of entertainment?*

Grades 7-8

▶ Use a variety of historical sources including oral histories, magazine advertisements, and catalogues to examine social changes in the postwar era. *What factors contributed to changing attitudes and values? What was the impact of the GI Bill? To what extent did the GI Bill improve the standard of living? What were the social effects of the return of women home from the factories in the postwar period? How did suburbanization promote social change?*

▶ Draw evidence from oral histories, documentary photographs, films, music, and dress to construct a historical narrative, audiovisual presentation, or classroom newspaper illustrating the influence of popular culture in the postwar periods.

▶ Draw evidence from television, movies, photographs, and lyrics of popular songs to assess the homogenizing tendencies of popular culture and mass media in the 1950s. *How did clothing and hair styles portrayed in situation comedies such as* Father Knows Best, Leave it to Beaver, *and* I Love Lucy *or* Dick Clark's American Bandstand *set a pattern for accepted dress for adults, teenagers, and children? To what degree were the Hollywood portrayals of Americans and their lives representative of the people of the United States?*

▶ Contrast popular attitudes towards women in the work force during World War II with those of the post-war era. *To what extent did these attitudes shape the popular image of family life?*

Grades 9-12

▶ Research the social and economic effects of the GI Bill. *What impact did the GI Bill have on higher education? What opportunities did it open? What effect did it have on new home construction? How did it foster a trend towards mass production? What impact did it have on the development of small businesses?*

▶ Draw evidence from documentary films, editorials, and periodical literature to evaluate how Soviet successes in space impacted the American educational system. *Why did the federal government appropriate increasing funds for educational programs? What was the effect of public spending on educational institutions? What new opportunities were opened to individuals?*

▶ Use advertisements, newspaper commentaries, and statistics to explain the meaning of the term "crabgrass frontier." *Why was the "house and the yard" considered an ideal? To what extent was the ideal real?* Explain the symbols involved in the term "Levittown." *What did people look for in suburbia? What did they find? What changes in social and economic patterns were brought about by the Interstate Highway System? What was the impact of suburbia? on the central cities?*

▶ Using pictures from women's magazines, the plots of TV programs, and selections from Betty Friedan's *The Feminine Mystique*, explain the impact of the Cold War on the lives and roles of women. *What was the impact of the "Baby Doll" look, the movies of Doris Day and Debbie Reynolds, the TV shows* Leave It To Beaver *and* I Love Lucy, *and McCall's definition of "togetherness" on women? What was the "Problem That Has No Name" that Betty Friedan was talking about?*

▶ Construct a historical narrative examining the development of ecumenicalism and the growing vitality of religious fundamentalism in postwar society. *To what extent did the ecumenism movement lead to a decline in overt anti-Catholic and anti-Semitic feelings? How did the reforms of the Second Vatican Council transform the social and political ideas of the Catholic Church?*

C. How postwar science augmented the nation's economic strength, transformed daily life, and influenced the world economy.

Grades 5-6

▶ Interview parents to prepare a list of new inventions and technology which affected their lives. Construct a chart illustrating new inventions which are affecting your lives today.

▶ Research the development of the U.S. space program and explain how it has served the public. *How important are communications and weather satellites? How has the space program affected medical research? How has the space program improved our knowledge of the universe?*

▶ Construct biographical profiles of prominent persons involved in medical research in the post-war period including such persons as Charles Drew, Jonas Salk, Albert Sabin, and Michael DeBakey. *How has research in medical science changed our lives?*

Grades 7-8

▶ Investigate how World War II provided a stimulus to scientific research and technical innovations which advanced health care and improved our standard of living.

▶ Research the "Green Revolution." *What agricultural techniques contributed to the growth in agricultural productivity? What new varieties of crops appeared? What were the benefits of these changes? How have scientists and governmental officials responded to unintended consequences of the "Green Revolution"?*

▶ Analyze the development of communications technology in the post World War II era. *How did the advent of television, magnetic recordings, and communications satellites change daily life?*

♦ Trace the development of computer technology from World War II to the present. *How did Steve Jobs and Steve Wozniak revolutionize the personal computer industry? How has the widespread use of computers affected the daily life at home and at work? To what extent has computer technology facilitated scientific research in other fields?*

Grades 9-12

♦ Examine the "high tech" revolutions which defined the base of the nation's economic strength and revolutionized medical science and opened the way for the information revolution.

♦ Construct a historical narrative that explains the increased life expectancy of 20th-century Americans. *What medical, agricultural, and scientific factors contributed to this progress?*

♦ Examine the role of the federal government in promoting research. *What was the effect of federal spending? To what extent did the National Science Foundation and the Department of Defense promote research in aviation, space, electronics, and scientific instruments? What new technologies emerged?*

♦ Examine the changes that have transformed the ability of medical practitioners to diagnose illness. *What technologies are most effective in the treatment of diseases such as cancer, heart disease, and diabetes?*

♦ Respond to *Life* magazine publisher Henry Luce's 1941 declaration that the world had entered into "The American Century" where the United States was "the intellectual, scientific and artistic capital of the world." *What evidence can be given to support Luce's declaration? Why have increasing numbers of foreign students sought advanced degrees from American universities since the end of World War II? In what fields has American science dominated? What factors account for innovations in scientific research in the U.S.?*

II. How the Cold War and conflicts in Korea and Vietnam influenced domestic and international politics.

A. International origins and domestic consequences of the Cold War.

Grades 5-6

♦ Compare maps of Europe and Asia before and after World War II. *What land areas changed hands? What countries were divided at the end of the war? What role did the United States play in maintaining peace?*

♦ Identify East and West Germany on a map and read accounts of the Berlin Airlift. *What did the Soviet Union try to achieve by blockading Berlin? What was the goal of the western governments in delivering supplies by air?*

♦ Locate and define the area in Europe that fell behind the "iron curtain." *What did Winston Churchill mean when he used the "iron curtain" metaphor?*

Grades 7-8

♦ Examine the political events in Central and Eastern Europe at the conclusion of World War II. *How did Poland, Czechoslovakia, and Hungary fall under the domination of the Soviet Union? In what ways did the people of these countries resist communism? How did U.S. foreign policy respond?*

♦ Explain what was meant by the terms "containment" and "massive retaliation." *What were the circumstances that led to President Harry Truman's development of containment as a strategy for U.S. foreign policy? What events led President Dwight Eisenhower to expand the policy? What were the international confrontations that fueled the Cold War? What influence did atomic weapons have in sustaining the Cold War?*

♦ Describe the circumstances that led to the Marshall Plan and assess its accomplishments. *Why was the program offered to eastern as well as western Europe? How effective was the Marshall Plan in rebuilding Western Europe?*

♦ Investigate the reasons for the division of the Korean peninsula at the close of World War II and examine the events which led to the outbreak of the war. *What was the primary goal of the United States in the Korean War? What role did the United Nations play in the conflict? How did the United States respond to China's entry into the conflict? Why did Truman call for a "limited war"? What conflict developed between the president and General Douglas MacArthur? What were the terms of the armistice?*

♦ Investigate U.S. responses to the spread of communism abroad. *Did the Korean War and conflicts in Europe and the Middle East stimulate "red-baiting" in the United States?*

♦ Draw evidence from weekly periodicals and documentary films to examine the popular uprisings in East Germany (1953), Poland (1956), and Hungary (1956). *How did repression of popular uprisings in eastern Europe heighten the Cold War? How did these uprisings affect U.S. foreign policy? What steps were taken to strengthen the North Atlantic Treaty Organization?*

♦ Research U.S.-China policy from the end of World War II to the Communist revolution of 1949. *How did the communist take-over of China affect U.S. foreign policy?*

♦ Construct a graphic illustration, chart, or timeline indicating the relations between the United States and the Soviet Union from confrontation to détente during the Truman through Nixon administrations.

Grades 9-12

♦ Examine the decisions of the Big Three at Yalta and Potsdam and explain how these decisions contributed to the start of the Cold War.

♦ Draw upon a variety of contemporary accounts, including newspapers and periodicals, government documents, and personal memoirs, to analyze the historical origins of the Cold War and evaluate the mutual suspicions and divisions fragmenting the Grand Alliance at the end of World War II. *Was the Cold War avoidable? If not, how could it have been avoided? How did U.S. support for "self-determination" conflict with the USSR's desire for security in eastern Europe at the end of the war? To what extent did the U.S. and Soviet Union pursue "atomic Diplomacy" in the postwar period?*

♦ Examine the factors which contributed to the successes of the Chinese Communist revolution. Debate the proposition: The Truman administration was responsible for the "fall of China." *How did the "loss of China" escalate the tensions of the Cold War both at home and abroad? How did Communist control of mainland China alter U.S. policy in Asia? How did it contribute to the start of the Korean War?*

♦ Examine the causes and consequences of the Korean War and evaluate the strategy in achieving a military victory. *Why did Truman seek assistance from the United Nations? To what extent did U.S. goals change during the War? What military factors accounted for the stalemate? What was the impact of the Korean War on U.S. domestic politics and foreign affairs?*

B. United States foreign policy in Africa, Asia, the Middle East, and Latin America.

Grades 5-6

♦ Work with maps to show the development of nation states in Africa, Asia, and the Middle East after World War II. Draw from biographies and stories to explain the establishment of independent nations. *Why did African countries change their names from those used by European colonizers? What countries in Asia became independent nations after World War II?*

♦ Locate the modern state of Israel on a map and explain how it became an independent country after World War II.

♦ Investigate ways in which the United States sought to encourage Eastern Europeans to resist communist domination through such programs as Radio Free Europe. Develop a script for a Radio Free Europe broadcast in the mid-1950s. *What news reports and stories would you feature to help people resist communism?*

Grades 7-8

♦ Explain the Truman and Eisenhower doctrines in the context of the international tensions which prompted each.

♦ Draw evidence from a variety of sources including public speeches, memoirs, biographies, editorials, and documentary films to construct a sound argument, debate, or historical narrative appraising the Kennedy administration's Cuban policy. *Should President Kennedy have carried out the Eisenhower administration's plan to overthrow Fidel Castro? Should Kennedy have committed the U.S. military in the Bay of Pigs affair? How did the Cuban missile crisis differ from the Bay of Pigs? How was the Cuban missile crisis resolved?*

♦ Trace changes in U.S. foreign policy toward the Soviet Union during the Kennedy and Johnson administrations and explain reasons for these changes. *How did U.S. policy toward the Soviet Union change during the Kennedy and Johnson years? What was the significance of the Nuclear Test Ban Treaty of 1963? How did escalation of the war in Vietnam influence U.S.-Soviet relations?*

Grades 9-12

♦ Evaluate the United States's response to "wars of national liberation" in Africa and Asia in the 1960s. *What were the guiding principles that governed U.S. foreign policy regarding independence movements in Africa and Asia? To what extent did the Cold War determine U.S. response?*

♦ Compare the Kennedy administration's Latin America policy to that of the Eisenhower administration.

♦ Analyze NSC-68 [National Security Council Paper #68], explain how it reoriented U.S. foreign policy in 1950, and evaluate its long-range effects on domestic policies and institutions. *How did the Korean War affect the basic premises of NSC-68? What was the fundamental disagreement between President Truman and General MacArthur during the Korean War? Which individual supported the better strategy? Why? How did the Eisenhower administration's emphasis on massive retaliation and the negotiation of alliances seek to modify the containment policy?*

♦ Examine documents relating to the Bay of Pigs and the Cuban missile crisis, including the recently declassified documents to assess the wisdom of Kennedy's response to the crisis. *How would you account for the idealism of Kennedy's Alliance for Progress with the overt and covert interventionism of his Cuban policy? How did Kennedy's Cuban policy threaten the goals of the Alliance for Progress? What was "Operation Mongoose" and what were some of its major consequences? To what extent did President Lyndon Johnson follow Kennedy's policy in Latin America? How did Latin American countries and the Organization of American States respond to the Kennedy-Johnson policies in the Americas? What were the "lessons" of the Cuban missile crisis? Did it contribute toward détente or accelerate the arms race?*

♦ Draw upon such documents as George F. Kennan's "Mr. X" article, "The Sources of Soviet Conduct," in *Foreign Affairs* (1947), and Walter Lippman's *The Cold War* (1947), to analyze the major arguments supporting and opposing the "containment" policy. *How and why did the Truman administration implement the containment policy in Europe? How successful were these policies?*

▶ Research the popular uprisings against Soviet domination in Eastern Europe during the 1950s and assess the role of the Western alliance in dealing with the abortive revolts. *Should the Western Allies have intervened? What role did the Eisenhower administration take during the Hungarian Revolution of 1956? What courses of action were open to the U.S.? What were the risks involved in each scenario?*

▶ Assess the role of presidential administrations from Truman to Nixon in pursuing a policy of mutual cooperation between the U.S. and U.S.S.R. *How effective was the Nuclear Test Ban Treaty (1963) and the Strategic Arms Limitation Agreement (1972) in building better relations? What factors contributed to changes in U.S. policy toward the U.S.S.R.?*

▶ Explain U.S. policy regarding the British mandate over Palestine and the establishment of the state of Israel. *Why did the U.S. State Department oppose recognition of the new state of Israel in 1948 and why was the U.S. the first country to extend recognition? What role did the U.S. take during the Suez War of 1956? To what extent did U.S. policy toward Israel change in subsequent wars in the Middle East? What factors account for a change in U.S. Middle Eastern policy?*

C. Foreign and domestic consequences of U. S. involvement in Vietnam.

Grades 5-6

▶ Draw upon a variety of primary sources including letters, diaries, songs, documentary films, and photographs to explain the personal impact of the war on Vietnamese civilians and U.S. and Vietnamese combatants in Southeast Asia.

▶ Use children's literature such as *Charlie Pippin* by Candy Dawson Boyd to examine a young adult's perspective on the Vietnam war.

▶ Locate Southeast Asia on a Pacific Rim map and trace the migration of peoples from the area after the Vietnam War. *Why did so many people become refugees? Where did these refugees settle?*

Grades 7-8

▶ Research evolution of U.S. policy in Vietnam from the end of World War II to the Paris Peace accords. Construct a timeline illustrating both the escalation and "Vietnamization" of the war. *Why did President Eisenhower send military advisers to Vietnam? What was the "domino theory"? How did it later influence U.S. policy in Vietnam? How did the Kennedy and Johnson administrations increase U.S. involvement? To what extend did Nixon's Vietnam policy differ from those of his predecessors?*

▶ Construct a sound argument, debate, or narrative which marshals historical evidence on such questions as: *Was it necessary to escalate U.S. involvement in Vietnam to stop the spread of communism in Southeast Asia?*

▶ Interrogate historical data from a variety of sources to evaluate the impact of the Vietnam War on American society. *What factors contributed to the advent of opposition to American involvement in Vietnam? What were the moral and ethical issues involved in the protest movement?*

▶ Develop an oral history project interviewing civilians who supported and opposed the war and Vietnam veterans in order to examine to what extent the war divided American society. *How divisive was the Vietnam War? What opinion did men and women who served in Vietnam have towards the war? How did they feel about domestic opposition to the war? To what extent do these divisions still exist today?*

▶ Explain President Richard Nixon's Vietnamization policy and construct a historical argument assessing its effectiveness in bringing an end to the conflict.

♦ Draw evidence from speeches, contemporary literature, documentary films, and photographs to measure the impact of saturation bombing on North Vietnam and the effect of the invasion of Cambodia on the antiwar movement in the United States. *What factors led to the growth of student radicalism? What was the impact of violence at Kent State and Jackson State on public opinion? To what extent did television coverage of the war advance the antiwar movement?*

♦ Examine the controversy over the Vietnam War using novels such as *And One for All* by Theresa Nelson and *After the Dancing Days* by Margaret Rostkowski.

Grades 9-12

♦ Assemble the evidence and develop a sound historical argument on such questions as: *How did the "fall of China" syndrome affect the response of Democratic presidents to events in Vietnam? How did the overthrow of Diem in 1963 contribute to political instability in South Vietnam? What were the long-term consequences for the U.S.? What was the significance of the Tonkin Resolution? What was the gravity of the Tet offensive? Did President Johnson's withdrawal speech of March 31, 1968, result in a significant change in U.S. policy?*

♦ Drawing on contemporary newspapers and periodicals and available secondary sources, analyze the diverse groups and major arguments advanced against the war. *What groups protested the war? How did the bombing of North Vietnam and the invasion of Cambodia impact the anti-war movement? What were the arguments advanced by groups which supported U.S. policy? To what extent did television coverage advanced the anti-war movement?*

♦ Analyze why the war contributed to a generational conflict and concomitant lack of respect for traditional authority figures. *How did the development of the "counterculture" impact American music, art, and literature?*

♦ Use historical sources, including statistical information, to assess the validity of the class basis of combat service in Vietnam.

♦ Drawing on the historical evidence, assess the success and impact of Vietnamization and evaluate President Nixon's expansion of the war and bombing in Southeast Asia. *What were the terms of the Paris Peace Accords? What is the legacy and lessons of the Vietnam War?*

♦ Debate the proposition that national security during the Vietnam War necessitated restriction of individual civil liberties and the press. *To what extent did public dissent hinder the American war effort? Does the public's right to know take precedence over national security? What were the paramount constitutional issues raised during the Vietnam War? How were they settled?*

III. Domestic policies after World War II.

A. Political debates of the post-World War II era.

Grades 5-6

♦ Draw evidence from historical research to develop stories, skits, and readers' theater activities on the civil rights movement during the Truman administration. *What rights did African Americans gain during the Truman presidency? Who were the leaders in the movement for equal rights during the Truman administration?*

▶ Write a biographical sketch of an important person in the 1950s to explain how individuals make a difference in American life during this period and explain how he or she is regarded today. Include nationally recognized leaders such as Harry Truman, Dwight Eisenhower, Eleanor Roosevelt, Thurgood Marshall, or people in your state or local community who were important leaders during the 1950s.

Grades 7-8

▶ Chart the measures of the Truman Administration in the area of civil rights and construct a historical argument, debate, or narrative evaluating the effectiveness of his efforts. *What steps did President Truman take in the area of race relations? How successful was he in achieving his goals? What were the issues raised in the presidential election? How did the split in the Democratic party affect the outcome of the election?*

▶ Analyze the success of Truman's Fair Deal program for securing fair employment practices and desegregation. *What impact did his efforts at desegregation have on the Democratic party? What were the goals of the States Rights ("Dixiecrat") and Progressive Democratic parties?*

▶ Explain how the spread of Communism abroad and domestic subversive activities such as the Fall of China, the Communist invasion of Korea, and the Alger Hiss and Rosenberg cases contributed to the rise of McCarthyism. *What factors contributed to McCarthy's loss of support?*

▶ Research the 1952 presidential campaign. *What were the issues? What was the basis of President Eisenhower's popularity? What did Eisenhower mean when he referred to his beliefs as "dynamic conservatism" and "modern Republicanism"?*

Grades 9-12

▶ Use charts, laws, and speeches to determine how the Fair Deal compared to the New Deal. *In which ways did the Fair Deal's goals and achievements build on Roosevelt's New Deal? In which ways did the goals and achievements go beyond those of the New Deal?*

▶ Analyze Truman's message vetoing the Taft-Hartley Bill for what it says about America's commitment to organized labor. *Why did Truman veto the bill?*

▶ Analyze writings of Eleanor Roosevelt, the publications of the NAACP, and the special presidential committee report, *To Secure These Rights*, in order to explain the civil rights program of the Truman administration. *Why did southern Democrats object to the civil rights proposals of the Truman administration? How did the Cold War influence the struggle for civil rights? Why was Truman able to win the 1948 election, even though newspapers projected his loss?*

▶ Examine the domestic sources of popular anti-communism. *How did the public respond to investigations of the House Committee on Un-American Activities and the celebrated espionage cases such as those of Amerasia, Hiss, Hollywood Ten, and the Rosenbergs?*

▶ Explain the emergence of McCarthyism and its impact on civil liberties. *What was the impact of the McCarran Internal Security Act and the Dennis v. United States case (1951)? How did the Army-McCarthy hearings of 1954 affect McCarthyism?*

▶ Compare the "red scare" in the post-World War I period with the "second red scare" that emerged after World War II in terms of causes and consequences. *Did the activities of American communists in the 1920s and 1950s justify the restrictions of civil liberties? How did Truman's support of the Federal Employee Loyalty Program contribute to the growing "red scare" in the postwar period? What was the basis for McCarthy's attack on Eisenhower? How did Eisenhower respond?*

◗ Drawing on the 1952 election campaign, analyze Republican opposition to the New Deal and the Fair Deal. *What image did Eisenhower project in the campaign? To what degree were Eisenhower's domestic and foreign policy priorities and objectives similar to and different from his predecessors? How have recent historians and political scientists re-evaluated the Eisenhower legacy?*

◗ Analyze Eisenhower's Farewell Address of January 17, 1961. *What was his warning regarding the military-industrial complex? What were the goals Eisenhower set for the nation in this farewell address?*

◗ Examine the Eisenhower administration and evaluate the credibility of changing historical interpretations. *What accounts for different evaluations of the Eisenhower administration over the past 40 years? How has new evidence changed views of Eisenhower's political leadership?*

B. The "New Frontier" and "Great Society."

Grades 5-6

◗ Construct a chart or mural on the Kennedy and Johnson administrations. Drawing upon biographies, stories, and pictorial sources, chart major issues in each administration. List steps taken to try to meet problems. Made a collage or bulletin board contrasting those issues with current problems.

◗ Use pictures and quotations to explain how Jacqueline Kennedy developed the images of Camelot to depict her husband's presidency.

Grades 7-8

◗ Compile a list of the major issues in the 1960 presidential campaign and assess Kennedy's stance on each. *What were the central domestic issues that divided candidates John Kennedy and Richard Nixon? To what extent was religion an issue in the campaign? How did candidate Kennedy respond to issues relating to Cold War foreign policy?*

◗ Select several political cartoons on different issues in the 1960 campaign and explain the issue and the visual impact of the cartoon.

◗ Construct arguments in the form of balance sheets, debates, or narratives to marshal historical evidence to assess the impact of New Frontier and Great Society domestic programs. *How did the New Frontier differ from the Great Society? What impact did the Kennedy assassination have on the passage of reform legislation during the Johnson administration? How did Johnson's leadership style differ from that of Kennedy? What factors contributed to greater popular support for Great Society legislation? What New Frontier and Great Society legislation has had a lasting impact on American society?*

◗ Assess the environmental legislation during the Johnson administration and compare it to the measures enacted by the Theodore Roosevelt administration at the beginning of the century. *How do the two environmental movements compare? What factors promoted environmental legislation of the 1960s? To what extent did environmental protection legislation alter American federalism? What was the response of the business community, labor organizations, and farm associations to the environmental protection legislation of the 1960s?*

Grades 9-12

◗ Use video selections of the TV debates, campaign speeches of Richard Nixon and John Kennedy, and newspaper and periodical articles covering the campaign to analyze the "New Politics" introduced in the election of 1960. *How did the television debates shape the outcome of the election? How did charisma and image play a role in the campaign? Did they overshadow the issues? Why did Kennedy win the election? Was the election a mandate for liberalism?*

▶ Analyze Kennedy's inaugural address for what it says about citizenship, rights, and responsibilities. *Did the inaugural address intensify the Cold War or was it a response to it? Was it a momentary, pragmatic political speech or one that embodies a long-lasting American passage?*

▶ Use Kennedy's acceptance speech at the 1960 nominating convention and historical accounts of the Kennedy administration to define and explain the meaning and impact of the "New Frontier." *Was there a "New Frontier" in domestic legislation?*

▶ Explain Lyndon Johnson's statement: "They say Jack Kennedy's got style, but I'm the one who's got the bills passed." *How did the Kennedy assassination affect the implementation of the Great Society? Was Johnson trying to implement Kennedy's program or break experimental ground? Explain.*

▶ List Great Society legislation and programs and explain their goals. *What impact did the Great Society have? How did Great Society proposals compare with the New Deal? Were the Great Society programs a success or a failure? How did Great Society legislation affect American federalism?*

▶ Examine excerpts of Senator Barry Goldwater's *Conscience of a Conservative* to assess his critique of modern liberalism. *How did his views on the role of the federal government compare with Johnson's?*

IV. The struggle for racial and gender equality and for the extension of civil liberties.

A. The "Second Reconstruction" and its advancement of civil rights.

Grades 5-6

▶ Define terms such as "freedom ride," "civil disobedience," and "nonviolent resistance" and explain how they were important in the civil rights movement

▶ Present a dramatic reading of Martin Luther King, Jr.'s "I Have a Dream" speech and construct a collage, mural, or bulletin board display using excerpts from his speech to explain pictures of events in the civil rights movement.

▶ Construct a skit, role playing activity, or readers theater to explain issues brought before the U.S. Supreme Court in the *Brown v. Board of Education* case in 1954.

▶ Explain the lyrics of civil rights songs such as "We Shall Overcome," "Blowin' In the Wind," "If I Had a Hammer," and "O Freedom."

▶ Use children's trade books such as *Freedom's Children: Young Civil Rights Activists Tell their Own Stories* by Ellen Levine and *The March on Washington* by James Haskins to examine the goals and accomplishments of individuals and groups in the civil rights movement.

▶ Develop profiles of Asian Americans who have become congressional leaders in contemporary American society such as Daniel Inouye, Hiram Fong, Patsy Mink, and Spark Matsunaga.

▶ Drawing on biographies, stories, poetry, music, and pictorial resources, trace the achievements of Asian Americans, Mexican Americans, and Native Americans in the civil rights movement.

▶ Interview local people and investigate historical resources in the community to learn about issues important to cultural groups in the region.

♦ Construct biographic profiles of two major leaders in the struggle for equal rights and compare their goals, accomplishments, and failures. *Who were the major leaders in the struggle for equal rights? How did these men and women advance their ideas? What methods did they use to achieve their goals? Did their efforts make a difference in the way we think about equality and civil rights and the way we live now?*

Grades 7-8

♦ Construct a historical argument, debate, or narrative assessing the origins of the modern civil rights movement.

♦ Construct a time line illustrating important milestones in the civil rights movement between 1954 and 1965 and critically evaluate the effects of white resistance in the South. *What developments prompted African Americans as well as other American citizens to challenge entrenched economic, political, and social power? What direction did these resistance measures take? To what extent did leaders in the civil rights movement agree on the means to reach their goals? How did the work of Martin Luther King, Jr., and Malcolm X differ? What is the legacy of each in contemporary society, and how does each fare in the nation's historical memory?*

♦ Draw evidence from a variety of sources including court cases, laws enacted by Congress, and executive orders to assess the effects of constitutional steps taken in the judicial, legislative, and executive branches of the government as part of the civil rights movement. *What actions were taken to resist federal civil rights policy?*

♦ Draw evidence from President Eisenhower's address to the nation to explain the president's reasons for dispatching federal troops to Little Rock in 1957.

♦ Draw upon a variety of historical evidence including literature, poetry, art, and music to investigate the efforts of various organizations and individuals to improve the status of minority groups in contemporary American society.

♦ Examine personal accounts of migrant farmworkers using children's tradebooks such as *Voices from the Fields: Children of Migrant Farmworkers Tell Their Stories* by S. Beth Atkin.

♦ Use stories such as *Jimmy Yellow Hawk* by Virginia Driving Hawk Sneve, *And Now Miguel* by Joseph Krumhold, and *Sea Glass and Child of the Owl* by Laurence Yep to investigate personal narratives of young Native Americans, Hispanics, and Asians in searching for their own identity in American society.

♦ Construct a historical narrative assessing the means by which individuals and groups worked to improve civil and equal rights. *Who were the leaders in the struggle for civil and equal rights? What methods were used to achieve their goals? How did the struggle differ among groups? To what extent was civil disobedience used to attain their goals?*

Grades 9-12

♦ After reading the decisions in *Plessy* v. *Ferguson* (1896) and *Brown* v. *Board of Education* (1954), analyze the social and constitutional issues involved. *Are separate schools inherently unequal? How does the historical context explain the reversal of* Plessy v. Ferguson? *Why is the Brown decision called "sociological jurisprudence"? Was Eisenhower justified in sending troops to Little Rock, Arkansas?*

♦ Use "Letter From a Birmingham Jail," "I Have a Dream," and other writings of Martin Luther King, Jr., to analyze his leadership of the civil rights movement. *How did Malcolm X feel about the March on Washington in 1963 and the philosophy of nonviolence? In what ways were King and Malcolm X similar and different in their goals and ideas? How did the Freedom Riders affect the civil rights movement? Why did the civil rights movement undergo a change from an emphasis on "Black Rights" to "Black Power" after passage of the Voting Rights Act in 1965?*

◖ Examine the role of women such as Ella Baker, Fannie Lou Hamer, Viola Liuzzo, Rosa Parks, Jo Ann Robinson, in the civil rights movement and explain their influence in shaping and affecting the struggle for civil rights. *What was the significance of the change?*

◖ Analyze the connection between legislative acts, Supreme Court decisions, and the civil rights movement. *How did the Supreme Court's decision in* Heart of Atlanta *v.* United States *(1964) use the commerce clause of the Constitution to expand the scope of the Civil Rights Act? What was the impact of the decision? To what extent did the civil rights movement alter American federalism?*

◖ Explain the issues that led to the development of civil rights movements among Asian Americans and investigate the efforts of organizations such as the Japanese-American Citizens League and Pan Asian Association in efforts to marshal community action and redress grievances. *How did young Asian Americans influence older members of their communities to become more involved in the political process? How did political activism encourage the expansion of social service agencies, health clinics, and bilingual education programs in Asian communities?*

◖ Interrogate historical data, contemporary poetry, literature and political biographies of César Chávez, "Corky" Gonzalez, and Delores Huerta to analyze the issues and goals of the Farm Labor movement, and La Raza Unida. *How does César Chávez describe the life of the migrant workers? How is this connected to Hispanic American rights? How do poems like Inez Hernandez's "Para Teresa" describe the emotions of Mexican Americans? How does it compare to the writings of Martin Luther King, Jr. and Malcolm X?*

◖ Use newspaper and magazine reports of the seizure of Alcatraz (1969) and Second Wounded Knee (1973), and books such as Vine Deloria's *Custer Died for Your Sins* to explain the reasons for the Native American Civil Rights movement. *How has "Red Power" been defined? Why did the American Indian Movement (AIM) seize Alcatraz Island in San Francisco Bay? How did the occupation end? What were the issues that led to Second Wounded Knee? Did AIM achieve its goals? Why or why not?*

B. The women's movement for civil rights and equal opportunities.

Grades 5-6

◖ Explain why the National Organization for Women was established. *What are the issues women raised in the postwar period? Were these issues resolved or are they still present today?*

◖ Draw evidence from documentary photographs, films, and newspaper and magazine advertisements to explain attitudes regarding women in the postwar period. Contrast the image of women today with that of the 1950s and 1960s.

Grades 7-8

◖ Use a timeline to trace the evolution of the movement for women's rights in the 20th century and construct a historical narrative examining the accomplishments and setbacks in the development of the modern feminist movement. *To what extent were the gains women made in the work force during World War II continue in the postwar period? What factors contributed to the development of the modern feminist movement? What factors led to the development of the National Organization for Women (NOW)? How did individuals such as Eleanor Roosevelt and Betty Friedan spur the development of the modern women's movement? To what extent has the modern feminist movement reshaped American society?*

◖ Draw upon evidence from different perspectives to construct a historical argument, debate, or personal narrative explaining the conflicts originating from within and without the women's movement in the 1970s.

▶ Construct a sound argument, debate, or historical narrative presenting historical evidence on such questions as: *Was the Equal Rights Amendment (ERA) a necessary step in securing and maintaining women's rights? What were the arguments presented by Phyllis Schlafly and other opponents of ERA? What is the appropriate role of government in promoting equal employment opportunities for women? Are women's affirmative action programs necessary?*

Grades 9-12

▶ Use articles from *Ms.* magazine or selections from such books as *Sisterhood is Powerful,* edited by Robin Morgan, or *The Rebirth of Feminism* by Judith Hole and Ellen Levine and examine how feminism addressed women's problems and the solutions offered. Explain how Jacqueline Kennedy epitomized the transition from the fifties to the sixties woman. *How were minority women affected by feminism?*

▶ Using Supreme Court decisions, Title VII of the Civil Rights Act of 1974, Title IX of the Educational Amendment Act of 1972, and the Equal Credit Opportunity Act of 1974, explain the impact of modern feminism. *What does the slogan "the personal is political" mean? What factors contributed to the failure of three-fourths of the states to ratify the ERA? Was the ERA necessary? How are the civil rights movement and the women's rights movement connected?*

▶ Draw upon evidence reflecting different perspectives to examine the controversies over the Supreme Court decision in *Roe* v. *Wade.* Examine the legal and moral issues raised by the "Right to Life" and "Free Choice" movements. *How has the Supreme Court modified the* Roe v. Wade *decision through such court cases as* Webster *v.* Reproductive Health Services *(1989),* Rust *v.* Sullivan *(1990), and* Planned Parenthood *v.* Casey *(1992)? What are the constitutional issues raised by* Roe v. Wade?

C. The Warren Court's role in addressing civil liberties and equal rights.

Grades 5-6

▶ Construct role-playing activity, skit, or classroom newspaper explaining the importance of the separation of church and state and freedom of religion in contemporary American society.

▶ Interview local people to investigate issues regarding religious freedom which are important to the community or region.

▶ Write a biographical sketch of Chief Justice Earl Warren and explain why some regard him as a great leader and others oppose the positions he took while serving on the Supreme Court.

Grades 7-8

▶ Define "due process of law" and examine the Warren Court's stand on the extension of due process rights for the accused. *What landmark Supreme Court cases extended due process rights? What were the controversies raised by these cases?*

▶ Examine the Warren court's decisions in *Engle* v. *Vitale. Why did the decision provoke widespread opposition?*

▶ Investigate the major decisions of the Warren Court that aroused public opposition. *What were President Eisenhower's views of Earl Warren and his decision to appoint him as Chief Justice? Why did Southern congressional leaders accuse the Court of an abuse of judicial power in 1956? What was the basis for the movement to impeach Chief Justice Earl Warren?*

Grades 9-12

♦ Use selections from transcripts of several major court cases, speeches, and political cartoons to analyze the extension of due process rights by the Warren court. *What is the reasoning used to justify the decision in* Gideon v. Wainright? Miranda v. Arizona? *Does the Sixth Amendment's "right to an attorney" mean that a citizen should be provided with one if he/she can't afford it? Is there such a thing as tainted evidence? Is the following statement a justifiable criticism of the Warren court's decisions: "The prisoner goes free because the constable has blundered"? Do you agree or disagree with the statement: "It is better that nine guilty men go free if one innocent man is saved"? Did the* Miranda v. Arizona *and* Escobedo v. Illinois *decisions undermine the ability of the police to apprehend criminals?*

♦ Examine the Warren court's reasoning in the *Reynolds* v. *Sims* and *Baker* v. *Carr* cases, and explain their effect on representation. *What is the "one man, one vote" principle?*

♦ Examine the Warren court's interpretation of the First Amendment guarantee of freedom of religion. *What were the landmark Supreme Court cases regarding freedom of religion? Why did the court rule that nondenominational prayers were a violation of the First Amendment? When, if ever, do you think that prayers should be allowed in public schools? Is a moment of silence a violation of the First Amendment? Why or why not? Were the decisions of the Warren court consistent with the concept of separation of church and state?*

♦ Examine biographical sketches of members of the Warren Court. *How did the background of justices differ? How effective has the Supreme Court been in protecting rights of the minority? To what extent did the majority of the court abandon judicial restraint and advocate judicial activism?*

♦ Trace the historic roots of arguments over judicial activism and judicial restraint since the passage of the 14th Amendment. *How did the Hughes Court of the 1930s use judicial power to invalidate acts of Congress? How has Justice Stone's famous "Footnote 4" (Carolene Products Dictum) been used to place stricter standards for the review of laws that are prejudicial against "discrete and insular minorities"? How did the judicial activism of the Warren Court compare to that of the Hughes Court?*

♦ Use Article III of the Constitution and The Federalist Papers to examine the role and function of the Supreme Court. Debate the proposition: *The Warren Court violated the Constitutional doctrine of separation of powers by "legislating from the bench."*

Women's Equality Day,
Washington D.C., 1977.
Courtesy Library of Congress

ERA 10

Contemporary United States (1968 to the present)

Examining the history of our own time presents special difficulties. The historian ordinarily has the benefit of hindsight but never less so than in examining the last few decades. Furthermore, the closer we approach the present the less likely it is that historians will be able to transcend their own biases. Historians can never attain complete objectivity, but they tend to fall shortest of the goal when they deal with current or very recent events. For example, writers and teachers of history who voted for a particular candidate will likely view his or her actions in office more sympathetically than a historian who voted the other way.

There can be little doubt, however, that in global politics the role of the United States has led to seismic changes that every student, as a person approaching voting age, should understand. The detente with the People's Republic of China under Nixon's presidency represents the beginning of a new era, though the outcome is still far from determined. More epochal perhaps is the collapse of the Soviet Union, the overthrow of communist governments in Eastern Europe, and the consequent end of the Cold War and the nuclear arms race. Students can understand little about American attempts to adjust to a post-bipolar world without comprehending these momentous events.

In politics, students ought to explore how the political balance has tilted away from liberalism since 1968. They should also study the ability of the political and constitutional system to check and balance itself against potential abuses as exemplified in the Watergate and Iran-Contra affairs. They can hone their ability to think about the American political system by exploring and evaluating debates over government's role in the economy, environmental protection, social welfare, international trade policies, and more.

No course in American history should reach a conclusion without considering some of the major social and cultural changes of the most recent decades. Among them, several may claim precedence: first, the reopening of the nation's gates to immigrants that for the first time come primarily from Asia and Central America; second, renewed reform movements that promote environmental, feminist, and civil rights agendas that lost steam in the 1970s; third, the resurgence of religious evangelicalism; fourth, the massive alteration in the character of work through technological innovation and corporate reorganization; and lastly, the continuing struggle for *e pluribus unum* amid contentious debates over national vs. group identity, group rights vs. individual rights, and the overarching goal of making social and political practice conform to the nation's founding principles.

Essay

Refugees in History and in the History Classroom*
by Paula Gillett

Teachers of American history face the particularly daunting task of helping students understand the pervasive ambiguity explicit in our history which has among its most prominent signposts the establishment of liberty, democratic processes, and freedom of opportunity on one hand the scourge of racism, discrimination, and inequality on the other. In her discussion of the plight of refugees over the past half-century, Paula Gillett suggests that ambivalence in our communities and in our schools toward recent immigrants—both documented and undocumented—represents a powerful teaching opportunity in history classrooms, and that the unhealthy mixture of compassion and wariness that pertains may have its antidote in thoughtful, informed, history curriculum.

Paula Gillett is Associate Professor of Humanities and coordinator of liberal studies at San Jose State University. She also directs New Faces of Liberty, publisher of a series of essays that explain the cultures of the major groups of newcomers and offer insight into the student's adjustment to American schools.

The United States has been the world's most generous country of resettlement for people fleeing oppression. Since 1945, our country has accepted two million people who have left their homelands because of political, racial, or religious persecution, a number over and above those who have been part of the far greater immigration stream. The United States has also borne the largest financial share of the costs of international programs to assist refugees.

The admission of refugees is regulated by legislation enacted in 1980 in the aftermath of the acceptance of several hundred thousand refugees from Communist takeovers in the countries formerly known as Indochina. Operationally, the Refugee Act of 1980 was an effort to replace piecemeal legislation and discretionary executive action with a clearly articulated policy, a sequence of procedures, and the expectation of a "normal flow" of fifty thousand annual admissions (an estimate that has regularly been exceeded). Philosophically, the Refugee Act represented an effort to remove refugee admissions from the service of Cold War goals: refugee status was to be awarded for humanitarian reasons, whether or not the source of persecution was a Communist government. In practice, the operational goal has been met with far greater success than the humanitarian one. Refugee admissions have continued to reflect the aims of foreign policy and to manifest a strongly anti-communist bias.

According to the Refugee Act, the actual number of refugee visas is decided upon each year by the President in consultation with Congress. Areas of the world are allocated specific proportions of refugee admissions; within these designated areas, the law gives preference to persons deemed to be of "special humanitarian concern" to the United States. Only a small proportion of those among the world's fifteen million refugees who long to make a fresh start in the United States can be accepted by this country. As for regular immigration channels, the world's three major immigration countries—the United States, Canada, and Australia—have strict criteria for selecting limited numbers of would-be migrants. Refugees without sponsors, close family, or special skills can seldom qualify.

Even though the United States prides itself on a tradition of offering hope and refuge to the oppressed—the opening lines of Emma Lazarus' poem may well be the most familiar poetic lines to Americans of all ages—opinion polls taken during the past half-century have consistently revealed a strongly negative current towards immigrants and refugees. These ambivalent

---

*Reprinted from *Magazine of History*, Vol. 4, No. 4 (Spring 1990), pp. 14-18, with permission from the Organization of American Historians.

attitudes—compassion and humanitarian concern on the one hand and wariness, especially concerning refugees and their agenda of human needs, on the other—are mirrored in countless resettlement communities and in public schools in many parts of the nation.

President Reagan provided a revealing example of this ambivalence. In July of 1980, Reagan accepted the nomination as the Republican Party's presidential candidate with this prayer:

Can we doubt that only a Divine Providence placed this land, this island of freedom here as a refuge for all those people who yearn to breathe free? Jews and Christians enduring this persecution behind the Iron Curtain; the boat people of Southeast Asia, Cuba, and of Haiti; the victims of drought and famine in Africa; the freedom fighters in Afghanistan.

A year later, President Reagan issued an executive order directing the United States Coast Guard to interdict boats bringing Haitians toward the shores of Florida and to return all but those who could demonstrate a clear case for political asylum to the country from which they had sought so desperately to escape. Lacking a knowledge of English, weakened by deprivation, and often terrified of the uniformed officers who questioned them, hardly any of these "boat people" succeeded in having their claims for asylum considered inside the United States since 1981; only six Haitians out of the 21,406 interdicted have been brought to this country in order to pursue these claims.

This forced repatriation of asylum seekers has not escaped the notice of Thailand, whose government has received international criticism for allowing Indochinese arriving by sea to be pushed back from its own shores. More recently, Michael Hanson, the Coordinator for Refugees in Hong Kong, cited U.S. precedent to justify a policy aimed at the "repatriation" of the overwhelming majority of refugees who have arrived there from Vietnam. The United States, said Hanson, picks people up off the coast of Haiti, "screen[s] them on board the boat, den[ies] them refugee status, and then push[es] them off. Now why are the Vietnamese different?"

The dilemma of deciding who are genuine political refugees and who are "economic migrants" easily becomes overwhelming in the presence of large and continuous flows of people into countries of first asylum. But the practice of repatriating asylum seekers without giving due consideration to their claims to refugee status violates the international norm of *nonrefoulement*, a principle established by the United Nations protocol of 1967 and signed in the following year by the United States. According to this principle, nation-states, although not obliged to offer asylum—even to refugees who can thoroughly document their life-threatening situations—*are* prohibited from returned asylum seekers to countries where their lives are likely to be in jeopardy.

In an age that has passed through the stage of "compassion fatigue" to enter a new era recently characterized as one of "compassion exhaustion," the best answers to the refugee dilemma depend upon international cooperation. These must include the continued development and legitimization of widely accepted norms designed to dissuade governments from pursuing policies of mass expulsion and from bringing about situations that lead to refugee flight. When this kind of pressure is unsuccessful, international cooperation is needed in order to protect persecuted and stateless people. Such cooperation, now in place under the auspices of the United Nations High Commissioner for Refugees and other agencies, might have saved hundreds of thousands from Nazi terror. But a critical level of support in public opinion is necessary to ensure continued international cooperation. David Wyman's book, *The Abandonment of the Jews: America and the Holocaust* (1984), shows the tragic consequences of a lack of public support for refugee assistance. After the pace of measures against German Jews was sharply accelerated in 1938, opinion polls showed that between seventy-one and eighty-five percent of the American public were against a proposal to increase immigration quotas. In 1939, sixty-six percent opposed a plan to allow 10,000 refugee children to enter outside quota limits. Only 21,000 refugees were accepted into the United States during the three and a half years of war against Germany.

In the late twentieth century, California is the favored destination for about a third of all the nation's newcomers, an estimate which includes immigrants and refugees both of legal and undocumented status. While the great majority of legally recognized refugees in this state are Southeast Asian (almost eighty percent), undocumented seekers of refuge from the political turmoil and violence in Central America may well be equally numerous. The "push" factors from that region have been brutally powerful, but our country has offered refugee status to few of those seeking to escape them. (In 1989, three regions accounted for almost ninety percent of refugee admissions: the Soviet Union, Southeast Asia, and Eastern Europe. The Refugee Act of 1980 anticipated the granting of 5,000 asylum requests per year; yet in 1989 alone, over 100,000 asylum applications were filed with the Immigration and Naturalization Service (INS). The great majority of these were filed by Central Americans. And while the average rate of INS approval for asylum applicants of all nationalities was eighteen percent, it was under three percent for Salvadorans and Guatemalans.

The experience of Oscar, a young Salvadoran in San Francisco, is representative of that of many refugee students. Oscar grew up in the care of his paternal grandmother in a town from which his father, unable to earn a decent living, had migrated to the United States. He attended the local public school, but the intensified civil war made it a dangerous place for boys once they reached the age of ten or eleven: both soldiers and leftist guerrillas regularly "conscripted" young male students from the school and its immediate vicinity. Although her circumstances were barely above subsistence level, Oscar's grandmother managed to pay a woman whom she met at church each Sunday to tutor her grandson now that his formal education was in abeyance. Other clandestine students in the town studied under similar arrangements.

By 1985, when Oscar was thirteen, his father had saved enough money to arrange for his son to join him in California. Oscar has worked hard to learn English and is grateful for the help he received from the teachers at his American high school. Fortunately for him and for thousands of young people brought to this country by circumstances far beyond their control, an important Supreme Court decision in 1982 (*Plyler* v. *Doe*) made it illegal for public school districts to discriminate against students on the basis of illegal status in this country, Oscar and his father hope to return one day to a peaceful El Salvador. Public opinion in the United States, which has been greatly troubled by the problem of illegal immigration, seldom distinguishes between Central Americans seeking refuge from violence and political persecution and other undocumented immigrants. But the distinction is an important one for us (and for our students) to understand. For many years, our government's activities in Central America have contributed to the tragic suffering so widespread in that area and our refugee policy has foreclosed the possibility of legal refuge for most applicants from that region.

In addition to the anguish and fears caused by undocumented status (only those who entered the United States prior to January 1, 1982—and remained in "continuous residence"—were eligible to apply for amnesty under the Immigration Reform Act of 1986), Central American refugees face the hostility engendered by racial and linguistic prejudice. Legally-recognized refugees, too, encounter serious problems; for example, members of host communities are often resentful of the resettlement assistance that refugees receive during their first year in this country. By far the greatest number of California's legal refugees are Southeast Asian: Vietnamese, Cambodians, Lao, and Hmong. California is now the home of forty percent of the Indochinese who have settled in this country. Often, they have encountered the same prejudice that closed the door to Asian immigration for so many years.

Leon Gordenker, in his recent book, *Refugees in International Politics* (1987), points out that the response of host communities to newly settled refugees in countries of first asylum is typically characterized by expressions of jealousy. He has found this to be the case even in places where refugees receive only minimal assistance. Refugee populations often include energetic, highly motivated people whose willingness to work hard can intensify local resentment. "The creation of an unwelcoming atmosphere bodes little good, either for the refugees or the surrounding community," Gordenker writes. Resentment seems to be a frequently encountered response both when refugees succeed, either in academic life or as entrepreneurs, or when the difficulties of vocational and linguistic adaptation lead refugees into patterns of welfare dependency. Where members of the host community have themselves suffered from discrimination and economic disadvantage, it is easy to understand a negative response to newcomers. However, resentment towards immigrants and refugees seems to be just as strong a factor in middle-class communities.

A recent visit with teachers in a prosperous California community located in the heart of the Silicon Valley demonstrated the potency of the resentment often evoked by immigrants and refugees. The occasion was staff development conference on the effects of immigration and demographic change on the public schools. The largest minority in this school were Vietnamese refugees, and their numbers were growing rapidly with secondary and tertiary migrations. Before the conference, the principal had commented that although a significant number of newcomer students were experiencing personal and academic problems, most were doing extremely well and a remarkable number were honors students. He added that ethnic relations in his school were harmonious.

The presentation to the teachers began with a historical overview on immigration which included information on the racial quotas established during the 1920s which remained in effect until 1965. Teachers of southern and eastern European background were shocked to learn that their own families had been so long, and so officially, relegated to inferior status when compared to the favored groups from northern and western Europe. The teachers were completely unfamiliar with this aspect of American history and knew nothing about pre-1965 restrictions on Asian immigration. When the discussion turned to the responses of communities and schools to demographic change (and after a few teachers had alluded to the notable academic success of some of the newcomer students in this school and district), it became immediately clear that a raw nerve had been touched. The tenor of the discussion immediately changed. "It's the fault of the grading system that 'they' do too well in math," said one young teacher. "We should change the grading structure so that won't happen." An older man stood up, clearly agitated. "I'm so angry about this," he said. "I have to say this. We worked hard to build this country up, and now they're taking it all."

This incident is of course an anecdote rather than a representative research finding. Most teachers are concerned about the welfare of all their students and many work hard to combat hostility towards newcomers as well as the prejudices and stereotypes that all groups hold as part of their image of others. But on the basis of other school visits, information from educators and from immigrant and refugee students, and on the basis of some acquaintance with the literature on intergroup relations in the schools, it is amply clear that the attitudes expressed at this meeting are widespread in communities of refugee settlement.

While the history curriculum is not the immediate instrument for dealing with these attitudes, neither is it wholly irrelevant to such efforts. Some kinds of historical understanding, both among teachers and students, can support the goal of building community in multiethnic and polyglot classrooms. For example, greater attention to the theme of migration in many times and places would provide American-born young people with an important perspective on the experience of immigrant and refugee classmates and on their own family histories. Some understanding of the legal framework of immigration (and refugee admissions) in this country, both pre- and post-1965, will help students understand a central aspect of our national experience and prepare them to participate as citizens in issues that are not likely to become less divisive during their lifetimes. For future public school teachers, a stronger background in world history will enable them to enrich their own teaching by drawing upon the cosmopolitan makeup of their classes as a resource for group learning. Education in American political theory and practice is of course an essential part of the social studies curriculum that prepares students for citizenship. By sharing their experiences of the violations of rights typically taken for granted, refugees who have risked so much to escape oppression can contribute a great deal to the civic education of American-born youth even as they learn about the political traditions of their new country.

Additional implications for the history curriculum are suggested by the presence in our schools of such large numbers of the foreign-born, whose families represent a great diversity of backgrounds as well as varying degrees of continuing contacts with their homelands. Their very presence points to the inadequacy of teaching history exclusively within the confines of individual nation-states. In some way, the history curriculum, certainly at the secondary level, should be informed by an awareness of what Aristide Zolberg has termed a "fundamental paradox of our historical situation," that is, the understanding that while our era has seen the global spread of the nation-state as the basic form of political organization, it is also the period when it has become clear "that the destiny of the inhabitants of these nation-states is shaped to a large, and perhaps even determinative extent, by social forces originating beyond the political communities of which they are members(14)."

Stanley Hoffmann concludes his book, *Duties beyond Borders* (1981), by singling out three groups within open societies which hold a special responsibility for moving the world toward a more humane order: intellectuals, the media, and the educational system. Intellectuals, according to Hoffman, must work to fight prejudice and chauvinism and must protest against injustice and violence; the media should move away from entertainment and glib explanations of issues and events and dedicate themselves to exploring current affairs and contemporary problems in far greater depth and complexity. The educational system, writes Hoffmann, should become more cosmopolitan; it should give far more emphasis to the teaching of foreign languages and to "the interconnection of ethical and other issues."

The international response to refugees is one such issue. Teaching about it requires us to raise and grapple with important ethical questions, not the least of which is the need to balance responsibilities to our own citizens with the moral imperative to contribute to the protection and humane treatment of the oppressed in other parts of the world. Teaching about international mechanisms of cooperation which, whatever their shortcomings or inequities, have eased the plight of millions of refugees, can in itself be an important component of citizenship education, showing students the possibility of humane and efficacious action in a world whose devastating wars form a central portion of the history curriculum.

Sample Student Activities

I. *Recent developments in foreign and domestic policies.*

A. Domestic politics from Nixon to Carter.

Grades 5-6

▸ Write a biographical sketch of Richard Nixon and highlight his accomplishments as president.

▸ Examine political cartoons dealing with issues surrounding the Watergate Affair. Explain the cartoons and evaluate how they portrayed Nixon and his administration. Describe the role of prominent people affiliated with the Watergate scandal.

▸ Analyze charts, documentary photographs and films that illustrated how inflation, high unemployment, and escalating energy prices affected Americans during the Ford and Carter administrations. Interview family members to find out how they felt about changes during these years. Use interview data and graphs to show how much it cost to buy essentials such as bread, milk, gasoline, and clothes then and now. *How have prices of basic foods and services changed from the 1970s to our time? What did inflation mean to families in the 1970s?*

▸ Locate the OPEC countries and describe how they controlled oil prices in the 1970s. *What led to the rise in gasoline prices in the 1970s? Why did people have to wait in long lines to buy gasoline for their cars? How did Americans try to limit reliance on foreign oil supplies?*

Grades 7-8

▸ Define what was meant by the term "silent majority" and explain the factors that caused so many Americans to support President Nixon and his "law and order" stance.

▸ Chart the legislative measures debated in the years 1968-74 that dealt with family assistance and employment opportunities. *What was unique about Nixon's advocacy of these social programs? Why was the administration unsuccessful in attaining congressional approval?*

▸ Draw evidence from public records, special interest groups, newspapers, and magazines to evaluate the Nixon administration record on the environment. *What new programs were established? How did special interest groups react to environmental legislation? To what extent did the Nixon administration sponsor environmental programs?*

▸ Draw upon evidence from a variety of primary and secondary sources including documentary films, books, diaries, audio tapes, news magazines, and newspapers to reconstruct the events of Watergate. *Who was involved in the attempt to cover-up the Watergate Affair? How did the attempt to cover up the crime take shape, and what was the role of the media in exposing Watergate? How did Congress react to Watergate?*

▸ Conduct a mock Judiciary Committee hearing examining impeachment charges.

▸ Debate President Gerald Ford's decision to pardon Richard Nixon.

▸ Explain President Jimmy Carter's program for dealing with the energy crisis and evaluate the effectiveness of his leadership. *To what extent did Carter's "outsider" status affect his dealings with Congress?*

Grades 9-12

▶ Explain how President Richard Nixon and Attorney General John Mitchell sought to strengthen respect for law and reestablish order in the aftermath of the riots and violence that had occurred during the Johnson years. *Did the Nixon-Mitchell emphasis on public law and order conflict with their use of illegal wiretaps and surveillance, the "enemies list," and the "dirty tricks" campaign?*

▶ After investigating the formation of a new political coalition of southern whites, residents of the rapidly growing western Sunbelt, white working-class ethnics in the North, and conservative white suburbanites, construct a sound argument, debate, or historical narrative on such questions as: *Did the civil rights and antiwar movements splinter the old "Roosevelt coalition"? Did the racial and gender characteristics of voters lead them to support one or the other of the major parties? Why or why not? To what extent did Nixon as president create a new political coalition?*

▶ Define the "New Federalism" and explain why Nixon supported it. *What was the significance of the administration's program? What welfare, health, safety, and environmental programs were instituted under Nixon? How did these programs correlate with the administration's New Federalism? What was the role of "revenue sharing" in the New Federalism? What prompted the president to impound congressional appropriated funds? How was the issue settled?*

▶ Explain the reasons for congressional imposition of wage and price controls and the devaluation of the dollar. Evaluate their success in dealing with the inflationary spiral. *How did the Nixon administration's sale of wheat to the Soviet Union in 1972 affect the subsequent inflationary spiral? What other factors contributed to inflation? Was Nixon responsible for the inflation affecting the nation during his years in office?*

▶ Drawing on the evidence of the Watergate break-in and involvement of the Nixon administration in the subsequent cover-up, analyze the evidence accumulated by the special prosecutor, the Ervin Committee, and the House Judiciary Committee. *What were some of the illegal actions of officials of the Nixon White House? What role did the media play in exposing the illegal actions engaged in by Nixon administration officials? On what grounds did Nixon refuse to turn over subpoenaed tapes of private conversations in the Oval Office to the special prosecutor and congressional investigating committees? What were the grounds for impeachment of the president advanced by the House Judiciary Committee in July 1974? Why did Nixon decide to resign? What major figures in the Nixon administration were convicted of illegal actions in the Watergate affair?*

▶ Draw evidence from unemployment statistics and economic appraisals of the Ford and Carter administrations to address such questions as: *What factors contributed to the high inflation rates in the 1970s? What factors contributed to the high unemployment of the period? How did Presidents Ford and Carter attempt to deal with the problem of "stagflation"? What political factors underlined their approaches? Were their programs successful? Why or why not?*

▶ Examine how Presidents Ford and Carter, in the aftermath of Watergate, attempted to address the problems associated with the "Imperial Presidency." *To what extent did Ford and Carter restore credibility to the presidency?*

B. Domestic politics in contemporary society.

Grades 5-6

▶ Draw evidence from documentary films, newspaper and magazine accounts, and interviews with family members to examine the reasons for President Ronald Reagan's popularity.

▶ Construct a balance sheet listing in one column the major domestic problems facing Presidents Ronald Reagan and George Bush and in the second how their administrations sought to deal with these issues.

Grades 7-8

▶ Draw evidence from Reagan's first inaugural address to determine the goals of his administration and compare these to his accomplishments. *What were the central issues presented in the address? What did the new administration propose regarding the role of government? What is meant by the "Reagan Revolution"?*

▶ Construct a historical narrative, debate, or project, such as a classroom newspaper, mock congressional hearing, or speeches in support of or opposition to Reagan's environmental program. *What were the economic issues involved in the debate over the environment? To whom did the administration's program appeal? What was the basis of Sierra Club opposition to the program?*

▶ Construct a balance sheet listing the domestic issues facing President Bush and the programs his administration presented to deal with them. *How effective was the administration in dealing with the economic recession? How effective was the Republican administration in dealing with the Democratic congress?*

▶ Construct a timeline listing legislation that has promoted or restricted the growth of organized labor in the post-World War II era. Define terms such as "open shop," "closed shop," "featherbedding," and "right to work" laws. *What political and economic factors explain the decline in union membership and influence?*

Grades 9-12

▶ Analyze Reagan's assessment of the Soviet Union as the "evil empire" and explain how it shaped U.S. defense policy. *Did his views of the Soviet Union change?*

▶ Use selections from memoirs, monographs, newspaper articles, and the testimony of Oliver North to analyze the Iran-Contra affair. *How did the relations with the civil war in Nicaragua contribute to the affair? To what extent did the Boland Amendment restrict executive foreign policy initiatives? Was the amendment constitutional? Was the president's staff acting above the law? How does the Iran-Contra affair compare to the Watergate crisis?*

▶ Examine the economic theories of conservative economists such as Milton Friedman and explain how they are a departure from previous economic policies. *To what extent did the Reagan administration implement conservative economic policy?*

▶ Explain the impact of Reagan's tax policies on the national economy. *What were the elements of "supply-side" economics? How did the increased spending on defense affect the outcome of Reagan's economic program? How did deregulation fit in the overall economic plan? How was the federal deficit affected by the economic program?*

▶ Draw evidence from statistical data, unemployment figures, union contracts, current periodicals, and public opinion polls to examine the status and perception of labor in the postindustrial economy. *What factors contributed to the rapid decline in manufacturing jobs? How has the public attitude toward labor unions changed in the latter half of the 20th century? What accounts for this change?*

▶ Explain how economic recession and the deficit influenced the 1992 election. *What was the impact of the deficit on the Clinton administration's priorities and programs? What were the immediate and long-term consequences of the budget stalemate of 1995-96?*

C. Major foreign policy initiatives.

Grades 5-6

▶ Identify crisis areas around the world and list some of the major peace initiatives made during recent presidential administrations. Locate places where recent presidents tried to influence world events. *How successful has the U.S. been in efforts to resolve conflicts?*

▶ Compare maps of Europe in 1985 with current maps to show changes after the fall of the Soviet Union and communist states in eastern Europe.

▶ Locate on a world map places in the Middle East, Central America, the Caribbean, Africa, and Asia where U.S. advisers and military forces have been involved since the end of the Vietnam War. Post current news stories describing the role of the United States in these places today.

Grades 7-8

▶ Interrogate historical data from a variety of sources including contemporary newspaper accounts, weekly news magazines, television journalism, and biographies to evaluate the Nixon administration's policies toward the Soviet Union. *What were Nixon's objectives? To what extent was he successful in achieving his goals in arms control?*

▶ Construct a historical narrative comparing the view of the American public and government toward China in today's world to that at the beginning of the Nixon presidency. *Why was Nixon's trip to China a historic occasion? What effect did the venture have on U.S. relations with the People's Republic of China? How did the public respond to the China initiative? What are the outstanding issues between the United States and the People's Republic of China today? How are they similar or different from those of the Nixon era?*

▶ Explain the factors that prompted President Nixon to send his secretary of state on numerous trips to the Middle East. *Why did Secretary of State Henry Kissinger devote considerable time and effort traveling throughout the Middle East? What challenges did he undertake on behalf of the United States? How successful was he in resolving the Arab-Israeli conflict?*

▶ Chart the measures that led President Carter to assume a leadership role in the Camp David accords, and construct a historical narrative evaluating the importance of that peace initiative for the Middle East. *How successful was Carter's personal diplomacy in negotiating the Camp David Accords? How did it compare with other Carter foreign policy initiatives such as the Panama Canal Treaty, and Salt II?*

▶ Explain the factors that led to the Iranian hostage crisis and evaluate the effects of public opinion about the crisis on Carter's reelection efforts.

▶ Construct a speech, editorial, poster board, or collage analyzing one aspect of President Reagan's foreign policy. Illustrate different domestic and foreign reactions to the initiative. *What impact did the Strategic Defense Initiative (S.D.I. or "Star Wars") have on the Soviets? What was the basis of domestic opposition to the S.D.I.? To what extent did the Grenada affair signal a new era in American foreign policy? Did the air strikes on Libya represent a change from previous U.S. policy or was it a continuation of prior policy?*

▶ Construct an argument, debate, or historical narrative on the proposition: *Reagan's defense and military initiatives led to the collapse of communism.*

▶ Explain the foreign policy goals of the Bush administration and evaluate its effectiveness. *What was the Bush administration's response to the end of the Cold War? How effective was the administration's policy in Panama? Eastern Europe? The Persian Gulf? How did the end of the Cold War influence President Bill Clinton's foreign policy actions? How did human rights issues impact U.S. policy toward the People's Republic of China?*

Grades 9-12

▶ Compare Nixon's foreign policy with that of his Democratic predecessors in the Cold War era. *Why did Nixon, who began his career as an anti-communist crusader, devote his energies as president to negotiate an easing of tensions and conflict with communist states?*

▶ Explain Nixon's policy of "linkage" and provide examples of its implementation. *How did Nixon use the "China card" and detente with the Soviet Union to further his foreign policy objectives? How did the Nixon Doctrine redefine the role of the United States in the world? What factors influenced Nixon to issue the doctrine?*

▶ Drawing evidence from congressional debates, speeches, newspaper, and magazine articles, maps of the Middle East and monographs, analyze U.S. goals and objectives in the Middle East. Evaluate the success of Secretary of State Henry Kissinger's "shuttle diplomacy" in stabilizing tensions in the Middle East following the Yom Kippur War in 1973 and resolving the oil crisis in the aftermath of the OPEC boycott. Evaluate the significance of the Camp David Accords.

▶ Evaluate the success of Operation Desert Storm. Drawing on a variety of historical sources analyze the pros and cons of U.S. intervention in the Persian Gulf during the Reagan and Bush administrations. *What were the factors that lead to Operation Desert Storm? Was Desert Storm justified?*

▶ Analyze the U.S. role in furthering the Arab-Israeli peace talks. *What are the obstacles to peace in the Middle East? How effective has recent U.S. foreign policy been in securing peace in the Middle East?*

▶ Evaluate the changing U.S. policy toward South Africa in the 1970s and 1980s. *What was the U.S. role in furthering democracy in South Africa? Was corporate divestment in South Africa a proper response to apartheid? What were the economic and social ramifications of economic sanctions on the black majority in South Africa?*

▶ Analyze the reasons for the collapse of communism in eastern Europe and the Soviet Union. *To what extent did American foreign policy influence the collapse of communism?*

▶ Analyze the meaning of human rights and explain how it has been used in American foreign policy. *What measures has the United States government taken to insure support for the United Nations Declaration of Human Rights? How did the Helsinki Accords of 1975 promote human rights? How have recent presidential administrations promoted human rights as an aspect of foreign policy?*

II. Economic, social, and cultural developments in contemporary United States.

A. Economic patterns since 1968.

Grades 5-6

▶ Create a scrapbook of the new technologies. Identify and explain the impact of computers, satellites, robotics, telecommunications, and microchips on how people do their jobs.

▶ Drawing on graphical data and newspaper employment advertisements, examine the kinds of jobs available and the education and skills required.

▶ Prepare a list of consumer goods available in your home and the countries they came from. Using a large map of the world create a display of the worldwide network of international trade and explain how international trade affects your local community.

Grades 7-8

▶ Drawing on examples from everyday life, analyze the ways in which computers and accessories, such as modems and CD-ROM drives, increase worker productivity and efficiency.

▶ Using areas such as "Silicon Valley," the "Sunbelt," or the "Rustbelt," explain how the new technologies and increased global competition affect the contemporary U.S. economy. *What is the impact of the new technologies on educational requirements, job training and job creation, the nature of work, and standards of living?*

⁍ Define "post-industrial economy" and explain its impact on the changing nature of work and job creation. *What are the social benefits and costs of the new technologies? What impact do the new technologies have on wealth distribution, gender, race, and class relationships? What effect do the new technologies have on regional, urban, rural, and suburban developments?*

Grades 9-12

⁍ Use recent census data to examine the changing demographies of the American work force with regard to factors such as age, education, income, and ethnic background.

⁍ Examine the influence of the new technologies on education and learning? *What is the relationship between earning and learning?*

⁍ Analyze the advantages and disadvantages of increased global trade and competition on the U.S. economy. *What economic groups and regions benefit from the NAFTA Treaty? What economic groups and regions are hurt by the treaty? Is free trade beneficial or harmful to American workers, businessmen, farmers, and consumers?*

⁍ Research how the modern American corporation has employed new technology to remain competitive in the world market. *How has American business adapted to changes in the last decades of the 20th century? To what extent have federal and state governments helped or hindered the new entrepreneurs?*

⁍ Investigate the growth of business ventures such as MCI, Turner Broadcasting, and Apple Computers. *How did the new entrepreneurs of the last quarter of the 20th century raise needed venture capital funds? What problems have developed in financial schemes associated with junk bonds"? How do current business leaders compare with the "industrial giants" of the Gilded Age?*

B. New immigration and demographic shifts.

Grades 5-6

⁍ Compare current immigration and migration patterns to earlier times by preparing a class chart showing where ancestors lived before moving to their present residence.

⁍ On a classroom map locate areas of the U.S. where immigrants have settled in large numbers. Explain the reasons that sparked increased immigration to the U.S. in recent times. *From which areas of the world have most immigrants come in recent times?*

Grades 7-8

⁍ Investigate life stories of recent immigrants to explain the reasons for their decisions to emigrate and the challenges they faced in moving to a new land. *What problems do immigrants face in their new home? What organizations help immigrants? How have immigrants relied on their families, friends, or religious communities to help make life easier in their new homeland?*

⁍ Construct a historical narrative comparing past immigration history with the reality of present immigration. *What are the push/pull factors that have caused people to move to the United States in the past? How do they compare to the reasons that impel immigrants today? To what extent is the reception afforded immigrants today similar to that of the past? To what extent is it different?*

⁍ Construct a chart to show how the immigration acts of 1965, 1986, and 1991 changed immigration patterns.

▶ Draw upon evidence from demographic maps, census reports, and periodicals to chart the internal migration from the Northeast to the South and Southwest. *What prompted the migration? Why did industries relocate in the "Sunbelt"? What have been the effects of the reduction in military spending and the recession of the 1990s on growth in the Sunbelt?*

▶ Identify and explain the expression "greying of America." *What are the political, economic, and social implications of the "greying of America"? What are the new issues raised by the elderly? How did the legislative raising of mandatory retirement from 65 to 70 in 1978 impact younger workers?*

Grades 9-12

▶ Explain the demographic changes resulting from the Immigration Act of 1965. *What areas of the world have provided the most immigrants to the United States since passage of the act? What major factors have promoted immigration to the U.S. from these areas of the world? What effects have the new immigration had on economic opportunity, education, and government services?*

▶ Construct a historical investigation of the factors that led to the Immigration Reform and Control Act of 1986 and examine arguments for and against the legislation and its application. Draw evidence from INS studies, congressional reports, and public opinion polls. *How does the increase in immigration in the 1980s compare to that of the early 1900s in terms of the country of origin and size? How did immigration change after the passage of the 1965 and 1991 immigration acts? How did the 1985 and 1986 acts seek to control undocumented immigrants? Does the act offer fair and balanced treatment? To what extent has the act impacted social services and health care?*

▶ Examine the social, political, and economic arguments in the current debate over immigration.

▶ Debate the following question: *Is American society best described as a "melting pot" or "salad bowl"?*

▶ Compare the size and composition of the traditional American family of the 1950s to that of the 1980s. *What changes have taken place in the American family? What are the ramifications of these changes? What are the pressures placed on single parents?*

▶ Draw on data depicting demographic and residential mobility since 1970 and analyze the factors contributing to the population shift from the "Rustbelt" to the "Sunbelt." Explain how this has affected representation in Congress. *How have the major political parties adjusted to such demographic changes?*

C. Changing religious diversity and its impact on American institutions and values.

Grades 5-6

▶ Use the local community to prepare a survey of the different religious groups represented. *What role has immigration played in the growth of religious diversity?*

▶ Identify and describe important issues relating to religious beliefs in contemporary American society. *What solutions have religious groups proposed to solve these important issues?*

▶ Interview family members and friends to investigate the importance of religious beliefs on choices made in the family such as the selection of television programs, movies, and the purchasing of goods and services.

Grades 7-8

▸ Develop a timeline indicating the prominent issues regarding the guarantee of no establishment of religion and the free exercise clauses of the First Amendment. Construct a sound historical argument or debate on questions such as: *What is the Constitutional issue involved over school prayer?* Explore the pros and cons of local government promoting public signs of religions in seasonal displays. Analyze Supreme Court action in cases dealing with free exercise of religion.

▸ Research the growth of religious evangelism in the post-World War II era. *To what extent has the growth of evangelism been a reaction to secularism in American society? What has been the appeal of television evangelists? What social issues are at the forefront of evangelical crusades? To what extent have the major political parties responded to issues raised by evangelical Christian organizations?*

▸ Conduct a local survey on the significance of religious groups in the local community. *What are the concerns of local religious groups? What differences are evident in their approaches to social issues?*

Grades 9-12

▸ Draw on statistical sources such as census data to analyze the changing immigration patterns from the 1970s to the present. Compare how religion and family have eased the transition of past and present immigrants to the U.S.

▸ Examine how major religious institutions have addressed controversial issues such as: capital punishment, abortion, school prayer, women in the clergy, and gay rights.

▸ Analyze the causes and significance of the religious evangelical movement and its effect on American political and religious culture in the 1980s. *What is religious fundamentalism? How has it been a part of American history? How is the religious fundamentalism today similar or different from that of earlier periods in American history? How does television contribute to the growth of religious evangelism?*

▸ Analyze how Supreme Court decisions since 1968 have affected the meaning and practice of religious freedom. Contrast the position of the Democratic and Republican parties on issues arising from the religious clauses of the First Amendment.

▸ Examine how religious organizations have influenced U.S. policies toward the Middle East, Latin America, South Africa, and Eastern Europe. *In what ways have major religious organizations promoted human rights as a standard for U.S. foreign policy? What influence have religious institutions had on resolving international and regional conflicts?*

D. Contemporary American culture.

Grades 5-6

▸ Survey your classmates to discover who their heroes are and examine why they chose such individuals. *How did television and movies influence their selections?*

▸ Using examples from the local community, examine how ethnic art, music, food, and clothing have been incorporated into the mainstream culture and society.

▸ Research the lives of Americans who have become popular heroes in recent history. *What lessons can be learned from their determination and perseverance?*

▸ Interview members of the community to determine the popularity of professional sports. *What changes have occurred in sports participation and viewing habits in recent American history. What role has television played in these changes?*

Grades 7-8

▶ Examine the influence of popular music including MTV (Music Television) on contemporary culture. *What is the role of image in the success of popular music figures? To what extent does popular music shape and reflect social values?*

▶ Examine the role of television in defining ethnic groups in American society. *Are television shows accurate in their portrayal of individuals and family life? What effect do television situation comedies and documentaries such as "The Autobiography of Miss Jane Pittman" have on shaping public opinions of ethnic groups in contemporary American society?*

▶ List major figures in contemporary American music, sports, and the arts, and describe how their popularity has become universal. *How have popular forms of entertainment such as Hollywood movies and professional sports become more international? How has American culture grown in popularity throughout the world?*

▶ Examine the influence of Hollywood movies on contemporary American culture drawing from popular thrillers such as "Star Wars" and "Indiana Jones," and social commentaries like "Driving Miss Daisy" and "On Golden Pond." *How do movies such as "Dances with Wolves," "The Color Purple," and "Glory" portray minorities and women?*

Grades 9-12

▶ Construct a position paper or debate the appropriateness of censorship of music and art. *How does the Constitution balance free speech rights with community standards of propriety? To what extent does unrestricted expression undermine traditional values?*

▶ Examine advertisements in newspapers, periodicals, billboards, and television commercials to determine how issues in contemporary society are reflected in popular culture. *How do the lyrics of popular songs reflect current issues?*

▶ Drawing on the works of artists such as Willem de Kooning, Roy Lichtenstein, and Jasper Johns to explain how abstract expressionism is an art form illustrating changing societal concerns.

▶ Analyze the reflection of values in such popular TV shows as *The Bill Cosby Show, Murphy Brown, Roseanne, Married With Children,* and *The Simpsons,* and compare to those expressed in programs popular in the 1950s and 1960s like *Ozzie and Harriett, The Honeymooners, Father Knows Best, My Three Sons,* and *All in the Family. Which of the contemporary TV situation comedies is more reflective of the values portrayed on television in the earlier period? Do television programs reflect contemporary values or do they promote a value system?*

▶ Assess the influence of "high culture" in contemporary American society by examining the popularity of art museums, philharmonic orchestras, and Shakespeare festivals. *How have operatic superstars such as Luciano Pavorotti, Placido Domingo, and José Carreras established a place in American popular culture?*

▶ Investigate how architects such as Paolo Soleri have drawn upon the earlier work of Buckminster Fuller in merging architecture and ecology to develop utopian city schemes. *What has been the impact of Soleri's Arizona desert city Arcosanti? How practical are schemes such as Arcosanti?*

E. How a democratic polity debates social issues and mediates between individual or group rights and the common good.

Grades 5-6

▶ Create a collage using the preamble to the U.S. Constitution to show issues involving justice and the common welfare. *Which groups continue to seek rights and opportunities to solve their problems? How successful have they been?*

▶ Draw evidence from biographies, newspapers and magazine articles, and diaries of women in the arts, science, sports, and professional worlds to compare opportunities for women now and in the past. *What accounts for changes since World War II? To what extent have women's roles remained unchanged?*

▶ Draw evidence from biographies to create a booklet using illustrations and short quotations to reflect how ethnic groups have retained cultural heritage.

Grades 7-8

▶ Use letters, speeches, documentary photographs, stories, and diaries to show how interest groups have tried to achieve their goals of equality and justice. *How have Americans worked to change laws about such things as child labor, unsafe working conditions, and limited suffrage?*

▶ List the issues that are important to the women's movement and examine different methods in achieving their goals. Draw upon evidence from personal interviews, speeches, newspapers and magazines to appraise the successes of the women's movement in modern America. *What are the most important gains of the women's movement since the late 1960s? To what extent is the women's movement responsible for an increase of women in local, state, and federal offices? What are the unresolved issues? What are the issues dividing the women's movement?*

▶ Survey local community efforts to adapt facilities for the physically disabled. *When did the local community begin addressing the needs of the physically challenged? Were local efforts begun before federal government requirements were established? Do additional steps need to be taken?*

▶ Analyze how racial and ethnic stereotyping has affected social relations among African Americans, Asian Americans, Hispanic Americans, and Native Americans. *How have Americans challenged these perceptions?*

▶ Construct a historical narrative explaining how affirmative action policies were initiated and assess their goals. *What are the basic arguments given in support of and opposition to affirmative action?*

Grades 9-12

▶ Explain the *Roe* v. *Wade* case (1973) and evaluate its impact on the women's rights movement. *What are the arguments for and against abortion?*

▶ Analyze the diversity of the women's rights movement. *How do race and class affect the women's rights movement.*

▶ Assemble the evidence and explain the extent to which the modern feminist movement has been both a success and a failure.

▶ Draw evidence from oral histories, films, museum exhibits, literature, and the fine arts to evaluate the contributions of diverse peoples and cultures to American society.

▶ Draw evidence from public debates and court cases such as *Regents of the University of California* v. *Bakke* (1978) to analyze issues and explain the arguments for and against affirmative action. *What was the court's decision regarding quotas?* Evaluate the argument that the economic and social costs of affirmative action outweigh its benefits. *How has affirmative action affected the economic and social standing of women and minorities? How has affirmative action affected groups that do not directly benefit from it? Does affirmative action promote "reverse discrimination"?*

◗ Research newspaper articles that present the controversy surrounding equal rights for gay Americans. Examine local, state, and federal statutes that protect gay Americans from discrimination. *What are the constitutional arguments for extending civil rights laws? What is the constitutional basis for opposition? What evidence is presented by both sides on the issue?*

◗ Draw on a variety of historical and statistical data to analyze the demographic, educational, occupational, and residential characteristics of African Americans, Asian Americans, Hispanic Americans, and Native Americans. *How have changing economic conditions and the decline in entry-level manufacturing jobs, affected such groups? How have such organizations as the American Indian Movement, Pan Asian Congress, La Raza Unida, and the United Farm Workers sought to improve the lives of their constituents? What are the criticisms raised in opposition to these organizations and their goals?*

Former President Jimmy Carter greeting Samuel Gompers High School Students, San Diego, CA, 1980. Photograph by Patricia Sumi.

Student Mural, Theodore Roosevelt Junior High School, San Diego, CA

PART III

Teaching Resources

Introduction to Resources

While traditional printed sources are still invaluable, the revolution in information-processing technologies provides a new wealth of possibility for studying the past. Today's teachers and students have a wide array of sophisticated resources and materials available for the improved study of history. The rapid advances in telecommunications and satellite technologies enable learners to engage in a variety of "distance learning experiences," including interactive field trips to historical sites and the use of modems and communications software to tap into distant data banks and sources. Making use of current technology, students have the opportunity to interview policy makers, conduct oral history projects, and explore different perspectives through the links to individuals and students from throughout the world.

The evolution of CD-ROM and laserdisc technologies also provide access to an abundance of diverse printed, audio, and visual data. In addition, publishers increasingly incorporate such multimedia resources into their textbook packages. Finally, an extensive variety of public history resources and materials are available to enhance the study of history. Museums, art galleries, and folk art exhibits provide information and resources for studying history while local historical societies offer another avenue for exploring the impact of world events on local communities.

The following list is meant to be suggestive rather than inclusive and needs to be updated periodically.

Symbols

Media resources

CD-ROM

Text-based resources

Primary resources

Art

General Resources

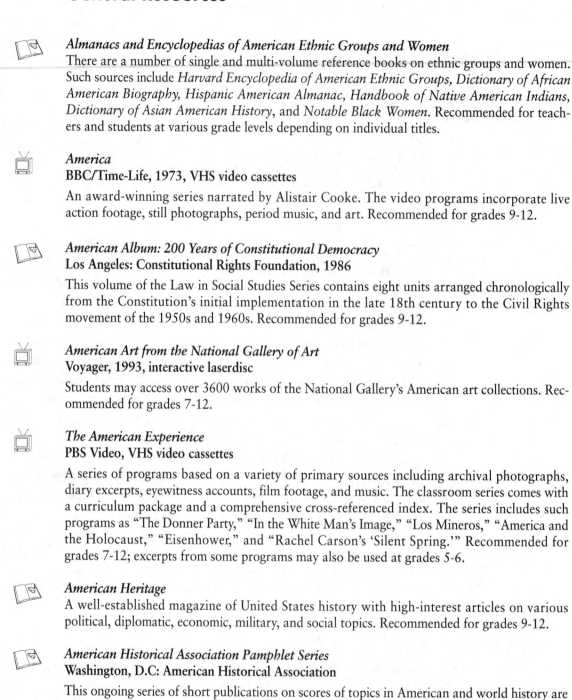

Almanacs and Encyclopedias of American Ethnic Groups and Women
There are a number of single and multi-volume reference books on ethnic groups and women. Such sources include *Harvard Encyclopedia of American Ethnic Groups*, *Dictionary of African American Biography*, *Hispanic American Almanac*, *Handbook of Native American Indians*, *Dictionary of Asian American History*, and *Notable Black Women*. Recommended for teachers and students at various grade levels depending on individual titles.

America
BBC/Time-Life, 1973, VHS video cassettes

An award-winning series narrated by Alistair Cooke. The video programs incorporate live action footage, still photographs, period music, and art. Recommended for grades 9-12.

American Album: 200 Years of Constitutional Democracy
Los Angeles: Constitutional Rights Foundation, 1986

This volume of the Law in Social Studies Series contains eight units arranged chronologically from the Constitution's initial implementation in the late 18th century to the Civil Rights movement of the 1950s and 1960s. Recommended for grades 9-12.

American Art from the National Gallery of Art
Voyager, 1993, interactive laserdisc

Students may access over 3600 works of the National Gallery's American art collections. Recommended for grades 7-12.

The American Experience
PBS Video, VHS video cassettes

A series of programs based on a variety of primary sources including archival photographs, diary excerpts, eyewitness accounts, film footage, and music. The classroom series comes with a curriculum package and a comprehensive cross-referenced index. The series includes such programs as "The Donner Party," "In the White Man's Image," "Los Mineros," "America and the Holocaust," "Eisenhower," and "Rachel Carson's 'Silent Spring.'" Recommended for grades 7-12; excerpts from some programs may also be used at grades 5-6.

American Heritage
A well-established magazine of United States history with high-interest articles on various political, diplomatic, economic, military, and social topics. Recommended for grades 9-12.

American Historical Association Pamphlet Series
Washington, D.C: American Historical Association

This ongoing series of short publications on scores of topics in American and world history are designed to help secondary teachers stay abreast of current historiography, changing interpretations, and significant writings in special fields. Recommended for teachers.

American History Through Narration and Song
WEM, not dated, audio cassettes, notes

Audio-cassettes boxed in five sets: "Colonial and Revolutionary Songs," "Moving West," "Civil War Songs," "Cowboy Songs," and "Working and Union Songs." Each set includes historical narration and notes on the songs. The cassettes vary in length from 1.5 to 3 hours. Recommended for grades 5-12.

The American Indian: A Multimedia Encyclopedia
Facts On File, 1993, CD-ROM for IBM

The program uses documents, photographs, drawings, images, maps, and sounds to explore the history of American Indians. Students may access biographies of over 700 leading figures along with a collection of legends and folktales. Recommended for grades 5-12.

The American Indians
Time-Life Books

A comprehensive series of illustrated books chronicling the history and culture of Native Americans. Books in the series include: *Keepers of the Totem, The Buffalo Hunters, The Way of the Warrior, Tribes of the Southern Woodlands,* and *War for the Plains.* Recommended for grades 7-12.

American Literature
Center for Learning, 1990

A two-volume resource of activities which examine U.S. history and culture through literature. Volume 1, "Beginnings through the Civil War," covers 15 authors from Bradstreet through Whitman. Volume 2, "Civil War to the Present," includes 13 authors from Twain to Updike. Recommended for grades 9-12.

The Annals of America
Chicago: Encyclopedia Britannica, Inc., 1976

A 21-volume collection of primary source material from the European discovery to last decade of the 20th century. An invaluable library resource for secondary schools. Recommended for grades 9-12; however, selected readings may be used with grades 7-8.

An Annotated Bibliography of Historical Fiction for the Social Studies, Grades 5 through 12
by Fran Silverblank
Dubuque, Iowa: Kendall/Hunt Publishing Co., 1992

A bibliography of historical fiction with grade level recommendations. Brief annotations of hundreds of children's trade books in United States and world history. Recommended for teachers.

The Archives of American History: A Moving-Image Retrospective of the 20th Century
Multimedia, 1993, CD-ROM for Macintosh

Film and video archives from 1896 to the present. Materials include the Spanish-American War, the Nuremberg trials, Nixon's visit to China, and the Challenger disaster. Recommended for grades 7-12.

Art Resources
Art museums often feature special exhibits focusing on individual artists or themes in United States history. Although educational field trips may be impractical in some cases, special exhibit catalogues such as the Corcoran Gallery's *Facing History: The Black Image in American Art 1710-1940* and the Smithsonian's National Museum of American Art *Homecoming: The Art and Life of William H. Johnson* are exceptional classroom resources. In addition illustrated theme books such as *Propaganda, The Art of Persuasion: World War II* demonstrate the power of visual images through art, architecture, motion pictures, poster art, cartoons, and caricatures. Museum catalogues and art books may be used at different grade levels depending on student maturity.

Atlas of U.S. Presidents
Applied Optical Media, 1992, CD-ROM for MPC compatibles

The program includes biographies of the presidents, speeches, political appraisals, and traditions and symbols of the executive office. Recommended for grades 7-12.

Band Music in American Life: A Social History: 1850-1990
Golden Owl Publishing Company

A Jackdaws portfolio of historical documents and audio documents on cassette. The portfolio explores the great band movement from the end of the Civil War. The audio cassette presents 15 representative selections from Gospel to Sousa marches. The program was developed in conjunction with the Smithsonian Institution. Recommended for grades 7-12.

Caricatures and Cartoons

There are a wide variety of books and portfolios of political cartoons which enrich the study of history. Among those available are portfolios such as "History Through Political Cartoons," and numerous books including *Rebellion and Reconciliation: Satirical Prints on the Revolution at Williamsburg, Draw! Political Cartoons From Left to Right, A Cartoon History of American Foreign Policy, 1776-1976, The Image of America in Caricature and Cartoon*, and the series *Best Editorial Cartoons of the Year*. Recommended for grades 7-12.

CD Sourcebook of American History
Infobases, 1992, CD-ROM for IBM

A collection of primary sources, selections from the works of eminent historians, and visuals. The program consists of thousands of entries including Madison's notes on the Philadelphia Constitutional Convention, *The Federalist Papers*, Alexis de Tocqueville's *Democracy in America*, presidential inaugural addresses, the journal of Meriwether Lewis, and the Emancipation Proclamation. Recommended for grades 7-12.

A Century of Political Cartoons, by Allan Nevins and F. Weitenkampf
New York: Charles Scribner Sons, 1944, republished by Octagon Books

A well-selected collection of 19th-century political cartoons. The text includes an introductory essay analyzing American cartoon development and commentaries on the selected cartoons. Recommended for grades 7-12.

Civilization

A bi-monthly magazine of The Library of Congress which features articles on topics in history, literature, and the arts. Recommended for teachers and students, grades 9-12.

Civitas: A Framework for Civic Education edited by Charles F. Bahmueller
Calabasas, CA: Center for Civic Education, 1991

Civitas is a comprehensive framework for civic education. The work provides objectives, key understandings, and historical background information for curriculum developers and classroom teachers. Recommended as a teacher resource.

Classroom Plays and Simulations

Numerous short classroom plays and simulation activities enhance the study of history. A number of companies have produced excellent interactive activities in U.S. history. Among the many plays and activities which should be reviewed for classroom use include "American History through Plays," "Southwest: A Simulation of the Spanish/Mexican Influence Upon American History," and "Great American Confrontations." Grade level recommendations vary.

Cobblestone, The History Magazine for Young People
A magazine for students, grades 5-8, which focuses on a different in-depth theme or topic in U. S. history each month. "The Cobblestone American History CD-ROM: 1980-1994" is a full-text database with a menu-driven search strategy which makes for easy retrieval of articles which appeared in issues between 1980 and 1994. Articles and lists of references can be either printed or exported to disk. A printed index is included with the CD-ROM. Recommended for grades 5-8.

Dictionary of American History, edited by James Truslow Adams *(Revised Edition)*
New York: Charles Scribner's Sons, 1976

A multi-volumed dictionary of American history recommended for teachers and students, grades 9-12. A companion work, *Album of American History* (1961) is an illustrated six-volume dictionary edited by Adams. *Album of American History*, recommended for grades 5-8, focuses on all aspects of American life including arts and crafts, housing, costume, and weaponry.

Documentary Photographs
A number of companies produce documentary photographs and posters which may be used as an integral part of instruction. Among the many documentary visuals are: "Child Labor," "America Revisited," and "The Living Constitution Poster Series." Recommended for various grade levels depending on the scope of each publication.

Documents of American History, 10th edition, edited by Henry Steele Commager and Milton Cantor
Englewood Cliffs: Prentice Hall, 1988

A two-volume collection of primary sources arranged in chronological order from privileges granted to Columbus by Ferdinand and Isabella to the Report of the Congressional Committees investigating Iran-Contra. An invaluable source book. Recommended for grades 9-12.

Encyclopedia of American Biography, edited by John A. Garraty
New York: Harper and Row, 1974

A one-volume encyclopedia of notable Americans. Recommended for grades 9-12.

Encyclopedia of American History, edited by Richard Morris. *6th edition*
New York: Harper and Row, 1982

A one-volume reference encyclopedia. Recommended for teachers and students, grades 9-12.

Encyclopedia of the American Left, edited by Mari Jo Buhle, Paul Buhle, and Dan Georgakas
Urbana: University of Illinois Press, 1992

A one-volume reference encyclopedia on radicals and radicalism in American society. Recommended as a reference for teachers and students, grades 9-12.

Eyes: Images from the Art Institute of Chicago
Voyager Co., interactive laserdisc, Macintosh

Over 200 works from the Chicago Institute with music, poetry, sound effects, and narration about each work. The program provides an introduction to the world of art for younger students. Recommended for grades K-6.

Facing History: The Black Image in American Art 1710-1940 by Guy C. McElroy
San Francisco: Bedford Arts, 1990

This comprehensive study of African Americans by American artists documents and interprets the changing visual representation of black Americans from the colonial period to the mid-twentieth century. Recommended for grades 7-12; however the illustrations may be used at all grade levels.

"Geography and History: Partners in Understanding the American Experience"
Magazine of History, **Vol. 7, No. 3 (Spring 1993)**

Articles in this special National History Day edition offer practical suggestions for including geographical perspectives in history courses. Recommended for teachers and students, grades 7-12.

GTV: A Geographic Perspective on American History
National Geographic Society, interactive laserdisc, Apple and IBM

Approximately 40 short programs which define the broad concepts of U.S. history from the pre-Columbian era to the present. Recommended for grades 5-8.

Harvard Guide to American History, edited by Frank Freidel
Cambridge, MA: Belknap Press, 1974

A two-volume reference guide to monographs and journal articles on all aspects of U.S. history. Recommended for teachers and as a student reference for grades 9-12.

"History of Sport"
Magazine of History, **Vol. 7, No. 1 (Summer 1992)**

Articles in this issue cover topics as different as "The Labor-Leisure Relationship in Stuart England and its American Colonies" to "The Negro Leagues." Teaching lessons include "Bellows, Boxing, and Progressivism," "American Women in Sport," and "Baseball and American Cultural Values." Recommended for teachers and students, grades 7-12.

Landmark Documents in American History
CD-ROM. Facts on File, 1995

A compendium of over 1,000 primary source documents on CD-ROM including short introductions which explain the significance of each document, brief biographies, period photographs, and illustrations. Documents include famous speeches, party platforms, legislation, treaties, Supreme Court decisions, and literary excerpts.

Legacies: An Audio cassette on the History of Women and The Family in America
Annenberg, CPB Project

Diary excerpts, songs, and stories about women in different periods of U.S. history. The program includes "New England Farm Families" and "Black Families in Freedom." Recommended for grades 7-12.

The Library of America

An on-going series supported by the National Endowment for the Humanities and the Ford Foundation. The series includes speeches, debates, letters, and memoirs of important historical figures and the selected writings of American literary luminaries. The series includes *The Debate on the Constitution, Autobiographies of Frederick Douglass, Abraham Lincoln: Speeches and Writings,* and *Writings of W. E. B. Du Bois.*

Living With Our Deepest Differences: Religious Liberty in a Pluralistic Society
First Liberty Institute

Curricular notebooks for upper elementary, junior and senior high school which focus on the place of religious liberty in society. Lessons are designed to provide teachers with maximum flexibility so that they may be used either together as a unit or infused into the study of United States history.

MacGregor, Molly Murphy. Women and the Constitution
National Women's History Project, 1988

This unit presents women's relationship to the Constitution since its inception. It provides narrative sections, documents, biographies, assignments, and discussion questions. A brief overview of women and the Supreme Court precedes examples of Court decisions that have defined women's legal and political rights. Recommended for grades 10-12.

Mac TimeLiner
Tom Snyder Productions, Inc., 1990

This timeline maker sorts the entered events into chronological order and arranges them proportionally. Recommended for grades 4-8.

Milestone Documents in The National Archives
National Archives, 1995

This revision of *The Written Word Endures* features 22 of the most important government records from the Declaration of Independence to the Marshall Plan. Recommended for grades 7-12.

Native Americans: An Illustrated History, edited by David Thomas, et al.
Atlanta: Turner Publishing, Inc., 1993

A one-volume, richly illustrated history of Native Americans. Recommended for grades 9-12; however, the illustrations may be used effectively with grades 5-8.

Nearby History: Exploring the Past Around You by David Kyvig and Myron A. Marty
Nashville: American Association for State and Local History, 1983

This reference book explains how to find and use visual sources, artifactual records, interviews, and published and unpublished records in exploring family and community history. Kyvig and Myron are editors of the "Nearby History Series," a set of books on the study of local history. Recommended for teachers.

On Doing Local History: Reflections on What Local Historians Do, Why, and What it Means by Carol Kammen
Nashville: American Association for State and Local History, 1986

A guide for exploring local history. The text examines the special factors which confront historians in local history projects. The book also investigates how local history is practiced around the world. Recommended for teachers.

Ordinary Americans: U.S. History Through the Eyes of Everyday People,
edited by Linda R. Mink
Washington, DC: Close Up Publishing, 1994

A collection of nearly 200 first person accounts of American history from the people not traditionally found in U.S. history textbooks. Recommended for grades 7-12.

Past Imperfect: History According to the Movies, edited by Ted Mico, John Miller-Monzon, and David Rubel
New York: Henry Holt and Company, 1995

A useful guide to the selection of films. This examination of the historical accuracy of 60 Hollywood movies, including "Gone With the Wind," "The Birth of a Nation," "Matewan," "Tora, Tora, Tora," and "JFK," is a useful reference for teachers who use movies in their instruction.

"Peacemaking in American History"
Magazine of History, Vol. 8, No. 3 (Spring 1994)

The articles and lessons in this issue cover different eras in American history from Quakers in colonial America to conscientious objection to the Vietnam War. Recommended for teachers and students, grades 7-12.

Peoples of the American West by Mary Hurlbut Cordier and Maria A. Perez-Stable
Scarecrow Press, 1989

An annotated bibliography of over 100 children's literature books that deal with the settlement of the American West. A good resource for elementary and middle school libraries. Recommended for teachers.

The Presidents: It All Started With George
National Geographic/IBM, 1991, CD-ROM for IBM

Students use timelines, texts and audios of famous speeches, personal views of the presidents, and photo essays to investigate the presidency at their own pace. The program includes color photographs and video clips of major events surrounding the presidents. Recommended for grades 4-8.

Prologue

A quarterly magazine published by the National Archives which lists resources and special programs for the National Archives and the regional archives. Recommended for grades 9-12.

Readers Companion to American History, edited by Eric Foner and John Garraty
Boston: Houghton Mifflin, 1991

An encyclopedic reference book recommended for grades 7-12 as a resource for teachers and students.

Religion in American History, What to Teach and How, by Charles Haynes
Alexandria, VA: Association for Supervision and Curriculum, 1990

A series of lessons based on religious issues in United States history. The lessons are based on primary source materials and provide reproducible facsimiles of documents. Recommended for grades 9-12 but may be adapted for grades 7-8.

"Science and Technology in History"
Magazine of History, Vol. 4, No. 2 (Spring 1989)

This issue deals largely with science and technology, and includes an article "Does the History of Science and Technology have a Future?" as well as several lessons on subject on different eras in American history. Recommended for teachers and students, grades 7-12.

"Smithsonian's America"
Creative Multimedia, 1994

CD-ROM. A treasury of American history and culture with over 700 artifacts, photographs, documents, posters, and video segments drawn from the Smithsonian. Students explore American ideals, politics, family life, entertainment, achievements in science, the West, and other aspects of our collective experience. Recommended for grades 4-8.

Social Education

Published periodically by the National Council for the Social Studies with articles of interest to educators. The magazine regularly features annotations of children's trade books, reviews of newly developed computer programs, and lessons using primary source documents. Recommended for teachers.

Social Studies and the Young Learner

A quarterly magazine of the National Council for the Social Studies which includes articles of interest for K-6 teachers. Issues provide critiques of children's trade books. Recommended for teachers.

Teaching With Documents: Using Primary Sources From the National Archives
Washington, D.C.: National Archives, 1989

A collection of over 50 short lessons using facsimiles of a variety of documents, maps, photographs, drawings, and cartoons. This is a compilation of lessons published since 1977 in *Social Education* along with practical suggestions for using documents in classroom settings. The documents are appropriate for upper elementary through high school. Worksheets in analyzing written documents, data retrieval, and cartoon analysis are extremely helpful in introducing students to work with documents. Recommended for grades 7-12, although some lessons can be easily adapted for grades 5-6.

Telling America's Story: Teaching American History Through Children's Literature
Produced by Tom McGowan and Meredith McGowan

A resource book which incorporates popular children's literature into the study of U.S. history from the colonial era to the 20th century. Selections include a story summary, lesson plans, and critical thinking activities. Recommended for grades 5-8.

United States History: Eyes on the Economy, by Mark Schug et al.
New York: National Council on Economic Education, 1993

A two-volume guide using economic concepts to supplement the study of U.S. history. Units such as "The Road to Revolution," "Boom and Bust in the Early 1800s," "The Emergence of Big Business," and "Economic Growth after World War II" include various lessons exploring economic issues in American history. Recommended for grades 7-12.

United States History: Origins to World War II
Schlessinger Video Productions, 1996

This 20-volume video series examines American history from pre-Columbian civilization through World War II. Thoroughly researched and meticulously crafted, the series draws from an extensive collection of archival imagery, artifacts, historical re-enactments, and interviews with prominent historians. Recommended for grades 5-12.

War and Conflict: Selected Images from the National Archives, 1765-1970,
edited by Jonathan Heller

A catalog of 1500 black-and-white images including copies of prints, paintings, and posters as well as photographs relating to American wartime history from the national Archives collection. Nearly 40 percent of the images depict scenes from World War II.

We the People: The Citizen and the Constitution
Calabasas: Center for Civic Education, 1995

A course of study, complete with teaching suggestions, student readings, and daily lesson plans, which explores the foundations of American democracy and the American political system. Recommended for grades 9-12. Two other editions are designed for grades 5-6 and 7-8.

The West
PBS, 1996

A vivid study of the American West using archival photographs, music, diary entries, and commentaries by prominent historians and writers. PBS Video offers a teaching edition which includes curriculum material. Recommended for grades 7-12.

With Liberty and Justice for All: The Story of the Bill of Rights
Calabasas, CA: Center for Civic Education, 1991

A unit of study designed to give students a better understanding of the background, creation, and application of the Bill of Rights. A teacher's guide states objectives and offers practical lesson strategies. Recommended for grades 9-12.

The World's Great Speeches, edited by Lewis Copeland and Lawrence Lamm
New York: Dover Publications, 1973

A collection of 278 speeches from United States and world history. Speeches include Jonathan Edwards's "Sinners in the Hands of an Angry God," Tecumseh's speech to Governor Harrison in 1810, Susan B. Anthony on woman's suffrage, Fiorello LaGuardia on American labor, Bernard Baruch on the control of atomic weapons, and Eleanor Roosevelt on the United Nations. Recommended for grades 9-12.

Era Specific Resources

ERA 1

Cahokia and the Hinterlands, edited by Thomas E. Emerson and R. Barry Lewis
Urbana, IL: University of Illinois Press, 1991

This collection of essays gives a detailed study of the last cycle of moundbuilding. Recommended for teachers.

"The Columbian Encounter"
Los Angeles: National Center for History in the Schools, 1991

Drawing on a wide variety of sources, this unit allows students to explore the Columbian Encounter from the perspective of Europeans, Native Americans, and Africans. The unit traces the background of the encounters, including motives for exploration and analyzes relations among the races as well as animal and plant exchanges. Recommended for grades 5-8.

"Columbian Quincentenary"
Magazine of History, **Vol. 5, No. 4 (Spring 1991)**

This issue contains a special section on the Columbian Quincentenary. A number of short articles written by historians address a variety of issues from historiography to the voyages in historical perspective. "A Year Long Voyage of Investigation," "An Examination of the 1893 World's Columbian Exposition," and "Before Oglethorpe: Hispanic and Indian Cultures in the Southeast United States" are the three lesson plans included in this issue of the journal. Recommended for teachers and students, grades 7-12.

Estevanico and the Seven Cities of Gold
All Media Productions, 1993, VHS, video cassette

The story of Estevan, a Moroccan, who accompanied Cabeza de Vaca in the journey across the Southwest following the failed Narvaez expedition and Coronado in the search for the "Seven Cities of Gold." Recommended for grades 5-8.

"The Great Convergence: The Pueblo and Spaniards Meet"
Los Angeles: National Center for History in the Schools, 1996

Drawing on a wide variety of primary and visual sources that represent differing perspectives, students explore the great convergence of native Americans and Spaniards in the American Southwest. The unit introduces students to the indigenous Anasazi, the Spanish colonists, and the ensuing conflict of cultures culminating with the Pueblo Revolt of 1680. Recommended for grades 9-12.

Seeds of Change: A Quincentennial Commemoration, edited by Herman J. Viola and Carolyn Margolis
Washington, DC: Smithsonian Institution Press, 1991

An examination of the Colombian encounter prepared for a special exhibit at the National Museum of Natural History. Recommended for grades 7-12.

ERA 2

"Bacon's Rebellion"
Los Angeles: National Center for History in the Schools, 1992

By examining primary source documents, students explore Virginian society between 1640 1676 and study the causes of Bacon's Rebellion of 1676. This unit examines the conseque of colonial thirst for land and gives insights into why the Southern colonies shifted from v indentured labor to black slave labor. Recommended for grades 5-8.

"Early Jamestown"
Los Angeles: National Center for History in the Schools, 1991

This unit explores the founding and early development of Jamestown and the rel between the colonists and the indigenous peoples. Recommended for grades 5-8.

"Peoples in the Past"
Old Sturbridge Village Museum

A series of resource packets with accompanying teaching notes and a guide to doc variety of topics dealing with 18th-century daily life in New England. Recon grades 5-8.

"A Society Knit as One: The Puritans, Algonkians, and Roger Williams"
Los Angeles: National Center for History in the Schools, 1992

Relying on primary sources, students explore the Puritans' attempt to create a utopian community in New England. The lessons in the unit examine the importance of religious beliefs and how they affected daily life, the interaction between the Narragansetts and Puritans, and government in the Puritan colony. Recommended for grades 5-8.

Three Sovereigns for Sarah
PBS, 1985

An engaging and thought-provoking dramatization of the Salem witchcraft trials starring Vanessa Redgrave. Recommended for grades 9-12.

"William Penn's Peaceable Kingdom"
Los Angeles: National Center for History in the Schools, 1991

Through this unit, students explore the founding of Pennsylvania by examining a wide variety of documents, including Penn's letter to the Delaware Chiefs, land deeds, theological writings, laws, and paintings. Recommended for grades 5-8.

"Women in Colonial and Revolutionary America, 1607-1790" by Bonnie Eisenberg
National Women's History Project, 1989

A teaching unit designed as supplemental reading on women during the colonial era. The unit provides an important perspective on the early history of our nation. Biographies of ten women who lived between 1630 and 1800 are included. Recommended for grades 5-8.

ERA 3

"The Bill of Rights: Evolution of Personal Liberties"
Boca Raton, FL: SIRS, Inc.

This teaching kit includes a variety of documents from the National Archives and a teacher's guide. Recommended for grades 7-12.

The Black Presence in the Era of the American Revolution by Sidney Kaplan and Emma Nogrady Kaplan.
Amherst, MA: University of Massachusetts Press, 1989

A chronicle of the military, political, economic, and cultural experiences of Blacks during the American Revolution. This is a revised and expanded edition of the authors' catalog that accompanied a 1973 exhibition at the National Portrait Gallery. Recommended for grades 7-12.

"Congress Debates Slavery, 1790-1800"
Los Angeles: National Center for History in the Schools, 1991

Students analyze biographical information of congressmen and evaluate the positions taken during the debates over slavery during the First Congress. Arguments on the constitutionality of congressional action to purchase the freedom of all slaves is considered. Recommended for grades 9-12.

"The Constitution: Evolution of a Government"
Boca Raton, FL: SIRS, Inc.

This teaching kit includes a variety of documents from the National Archives and a teacher's guide. Students actively engage facsimiles of primary source documents in studying the formation of the American political system. Recommended for grades 7-12.

"Constitution of the United States"
Magazine of History, Vol. 3, No. 1 (Winter 1988)

This issue of the *Magazine of History* contains a special section on the Constitution. "An Angle of Vision: Black Women and the United States Constitution, 1787-1987" by Darlene Clark Hine and "How Five (Partly True) Myths Can Help Teachers Teach About the Constitution" by David Nichols are among the articles and lesson plans included in this issue. Recommended for teachers and students, grades 7-12.

"Documents from the Continental Congress and Constitutional Convention, 1774-1789"
The National Digital Library Program, Library of Congress Multimedia Historical Collections

These 274 broadsides chronicle the founding of our nation from resistance to the British through drafting and ratification of the Constitution. The collection includes the Articles of Confederation, journals of Congress, resolutions, proclamations, and treaties. Access on the World Wide WEB through the Library of Congress Multimedia Historical Collections, http://www.loc.gov. Recommended for grades 5-12.

"Equal Justice Under Law" Series
Metropolitan Pittsburgh Public Broadcasting, VHS, 3 video cassettes

A dramatization of three landmark Supreme Court cases, *Marbury* v. *Madison, McCulloch* v. *Maryland*, and *Gibbons* v. *Ogden*. Each video program examines the historical and legal significance of the court case. Recommended for grades 7-12.

"The Evolution of the Bill of Rights"
Los Angeles: National Center for History in the Schools, 1992

Students explore the story history of the Bill of Rights from the original Virginia Declaration of Rights in 1776 to the states' ratification of the first 10 amendments in 1791. This teaching unit concludes with several cases involving the application of principles embraced by the Bill of Rights. Recommended for grades 9-12.

The Federalist Papers, edited by Jacob E. Cooke
Middletown, CT: Wesleyan University Press, 1961

This is considered by historians to be the most complete and accurate edition of *The Federalist Papers*. Recommended for grades 9-12.

Federalists and Antifederalists: The Debate Over Ratification of the Constitution
edited by John P. Kaminski and Richard Leffler.
Madison, WI: Madison House, 1989

A collection of the writings of leading Federalists and Anti-Federalists. The documents presented in the work are organized around key ideas in the ratification debate. Recommended for grades 9-12.

James Madison and The Federalist Papers by John J. Patrick
Bloomington, IN: ERIC Clearing House, 1990

An in-depth study of the Federalist and Anti-Federalist positions during the ratification debate over the Constitution. The lessons are based on primary source documents. Recommended for grades 9-12.

Lessons on the Northwest Ordinance of 1787 by John Patrick
ERIC Clearing House, 1987

This is a set of nine lessons written for the bicentennial of the Northwest Ordinance. The lessons use primary source documents and discuss such issues as civil liberties and governance of new states. Recommended for grades 9-12.

"Life in Revolutionary America"
Magazine of History, Vol. 8, No. 4 (Summer 1994)

This issue of the magazine includes several articles and four lesson plans applicable to the era. "Federalists and Anti-Federalists: Is a Bill of Rights Essential to a Free Society?" by Joseph Gotchy is one of the teaching activities printed in this issue.

Mary Silliman's War
Heritage Film and Citadel Film, 1993

This powerful dramatization brings together an array of issues central to one woman and her family during the American Revolution. The film is based on a biography of Mary Silliman, *The Way of Duty,* by Joy Day Buel and Richard Buel, Jr. Recommended for grades 9-12.

"The Revolutionary War: Gallery of Images"
CD-ROM. National Archives, 1994

140 historical images depicting various scenes, battles, and figures in the era of the American Revolution. Patrick Henry delivering the "Give me liberty or give me death" oratory, Molly Pitcher at the Battle of Monmouth, and Washington's farewell to his officers are a few of the images that can be incorporated in classroom presentations or student projects. The images, from the holdings of the National Archives are in the public domain and are royalty-free. Recommended for grades 5-12.

We the People
Calabasas, CA: Center for Civic Education, 1993

A series of teaching units divided into books for elementary, middle, and senior high school students. The units are intended to give students an understanding of the background, creation, and subsequent history of the Constitution and Bill of Rights.

"Women of the American Revolution"
Los Angeles: National Center for History in the Schools, 1991

From a variety of contemporary accounts, students discover that the struggle for American independence drew upon extensive support of and participation by women. The unit explores the varied roles of women in the Revolutionary movement. Recommended for grades 5-8.

ERA 4

"African-American Pamphlets from The Daniel A. P. Murray Pamphlet Collection, 1820-1920"
The National Digital Library Program, Library of Congress Multimedia Historical Collections

This collection of 351 pamphlets presents a panoramic and eclectic review of African American history and culure spanning one hundred years. Notable people represented in the collection include Frederick Douglass, Booker T. Washington, and Ida B. Wells-Barnett among others. Access on the World Wide WEB through the Library of Congress Multimedia Historical Collections, http://www.loc.gov Recommended for grades 5-12.

"The American China Trade," Jackdaws Teaching Kit
Amawalk, NY: Golden Owl Publishing

A Jackdaw collection of six essays and 12 historical documents on the early China trade between 1784 and 1850. Recommended for grades 7-12.

"Duel of Eagles: Conflicts in the Southwest"
Los Angeles: National Center for History in the Schools, 1996

This unit traces events from the opening of Spanish Texas to colonization in the early nineteenth century through the Treaty of Guadalupe Hidalgo in 1848. Lesson strategies and documents provide students with the opportunity to study in-depth the Texas War for Independence, the removal of the Cherokee from Texas, and the causes of the Mexican-American War of 1846. Recommended for grades 7-12.

"The Immigrant's Experience, 1840-1890, Volume 1," *Teaching With Primary Sources Series*
Peterborough, NH: Cobblestone Publishing, 1996

A collection of facsimile documents, photographs, ship diagrams, cartoons, and newspaper articles from the Library of Congress and National Archives on immigration through Castle Garden, Ellis Island, and Angel Island. Recommended for grades 5-8.

The Oregon Trail
MECC, 1993, CD-ROM for Macintosh

A simulation of mid-19th century westward expansion. Animated color graphic, music, and digitized speech. Recommended for grades 5-8.

"The Shakers: Hands to Work, Hearts to God"
Ken Burns' America Series (VHS, 58 minutes)

An examination of the Shakers from their origins in the antebellum period with a devoted following of some 6,000 to the present where a handful still expose Shaker ideals. Recommended for grades 7-12.

"Slavery in the Nineteenth Century"
Los Angeles: National Center for History in the Schools, 1991

Through a variety of documents, including letters by abolitionists, slave codes, parish records, and folktales, student explore the effects of slavery throughout society in the first half of the nineteenth century. This unit includes lessons on African American culture, slaves' resistance, abolition, women's rights, and an annotated bibliography. Recommended for grades 5-8.

ERA 5

"Abraham Lincoln and Slavery"
National Center for History in the Schools Teaching Unit. Los Angeles: Regents, University of California, 1994

This unit uses primary source documents to examine Abraham Lincoln's attitudes and actions regarding slavery, its abolition, and the use of African American troops during the Civil War. Recommended for grades 8-12.

"The Civil War"
PBS, 1990, laserdiscs (CLV) or VHS video cassettes

The award-winning series directed by Ken Burns using archival photographs, music, diary entries, and commentaries by leading historians. Teachers would benefit from reading Ken Burns's *The Civil War: Historians Respond*, edited by Robert Brent Toplin (New York: Oxford University Press, 1996) to gain a better understanding of the debates over the interpretations presented in the popular video series. Recommended for grades 7-12.

"The Civil War"
Magazine of History, Vol. 8, No. 1 (Fall 1993)

A collection of essays and lesson plans devoted to various topics dealing with the Civil War. Two of the teaching activities deal with prison camps, one on Point Lookout, a Union camp, and the other with Andersonville, a Confederate camp. The documents presented in each of these lessons offer a excellent opportunity for students to compare and contrast prison camps operated by both sides in the conflict. Recommended for teacher and students, grades 7-12.

"The Civil War: A Newspaper Perspective"
CD-ROM, Malvern, PA: Accessible Archives, Inc.

This database contains the full text of articles from the *New York Herald*, the *Charleston Mercury*, and the *Richmond Enquirer* published between November, 1860 and April, 1865. Recommended for grades 7-12.

"The Civil War: Soldiers and Civilians"
Boca Raton, FL: SIRS, Inc.

The unit is make up of five topics that relate to military and civilian life. Each topic uses reproductions of documents from the National Archives in conjunctions with classroom exercises based on the documents. The kit includes battlefield maps and Mathew Brady photographs. Students study the effects of the war on the development of technology and the war's impact on civil rights. Recommended for grades 7-12.

"The Divided Union: The Story of the American Civil War, 1861-1865"
Laserdiscs (CLV) or VHS video cassette

Reenactments of key Civil War battles, archival photographs, paintings, excerpts from diaries and letters, and analyses by historians. The index and guide provides quick access by bar codes or chapter stops. Recommended for grades 7-12.

"Lincoln"
PBS Video, VHS video cassettes

A four-part series on Abraham Lincoln and the Civil War drawn largely from Lincoln's writings and letters and diaries of his contemporaries. An educational resource package including a teacher's guide, a class set of a student magazine, and a cross-referenced index accompany the series. Recommended for grades 7-12.

Lincoln Live
Griessman & Associates, Inc., 1993

An audio cassette in which Gene Griessman portrays Abraham Lincoln. The cassette includes the Gettysburg Address, period songs, and humor, Recommended for grades 5-8.

Lincoln's Decisions: Simulation
Educational Activities, not dated, Apple 5.25" disk, IBM 5.25" disk, IBM 3.5" disk

A computer simulation which focuses on important events and turning points in Lincoln's life. Recommended for grades 7-8.

"Long Shadows: The Legacy of the American Civil War"
James Agee Film Project, Johnson City, TN

"Long Shadows" explores the ways in which the Civil War can still be felt in American society: from politics to economics, from civil rights to foreign policy, from individual to collective memory. Recommended for grades 9-12.

National Archives
World Wide Web

Civil War materials from the National Archives including photographs and records of the 54th Massachusetts Infantry Regiment, whose story was the basis for the film "Glory," may be electronically retrieved through http://www.nara.gov. Recommended for grades 5-12.

"The Port Royal Experiment: Forty Acres and a Mule"
Los Angeles: National Center for History in the Schools, 1991

Students read about the military emancipation of slaves in South Carolina during the Civil War and learn of promises of land ownership. Documents in this unit give different points of view including that of President Lincoln, the abolitionists, and the former plantation owners. Recommended for grades 7-12.

"The Reconstruction Era"
Magazine of History, Vol. 9, No. 1 (Winter 1989)

A special issue devoted to assisting teachers find new ideas about Reconstruction and to suggest interesting ways in which these ideas can be taught. Teaching materials are provided on several topics including Reconstruction through role play and comparing Emancipation in the United States to that of Imperial Russia. Recommended for teachers and students, grades 7-12.

"Selected Civil War Photographs from the Library of Congress, 1861-1865"
The National Digital Library Program, Library of Congress Multimedia Historical Collections

Over 1,100 photographs which feature Civil War encampments, battlefields, and portraits as captured by Mathew Brady and his staff of photographers. Access on the World Wide WEB through the Library of Congress Multimedia Historical Collections, http://www.loc.gov. Recommended for grades 5-12.

ERA 6

"Agriculture and Rural Life"
Magazine of History, Vol. 5, No. 3 (Winter 1991)

This issue is devoted to a study of American rural life. "The Farm in American History" by James Shideler and "The Tenancy System: The Forgotten Farmer" by George Chilcoat are among the articles and lesson plans included in this issue. Recommended for teachers and students, grades 7-12.

"The American Dream and the Gospel of Wealth in Nineteenth-Century American Society"
Los Angeles: National Center for History in the Schools, 1991

Through this unit students examine the writings of P. T. Barnum, Thorstein Veblen, Andrew Carnegie, and Nathaniel West to learn about both positive and negative interpretations of the "gospel of wealth." Recommended for grades 9-12.

"Child Labor: The Shame of the Nation"
Amawalk, NY: Golden Owl Publishing, 1996

This Jackdaw photo collection consists of 12 poster-size, black-and-white photographs by photojournalist Lewis W. Hine, a historical essay, timeline, and reproducible activities. Recommended for grades 7-12.

"Coxey's Army" Jackdaws Teaching Kit
Amawalk, NY: Golden Owl Publishing

This Jackdaw recreated the factors which prompted Coxey's march on Washington and its aftermath. It included five essays and 12 historical documents. Recommended for grades 7-12.

"Environmental History"
Magazine of History, Vol. 10, No. 3 (Spring 1996)

This issue on the environment includes a lesson plan based on the movie "A Sea of Grass" and Willa Cather's novel, *O Pioneers!* Recommended for teachers and students, grades 7-12.

"The Ghost Dance: The Indian Removal After the Civil War"
Los Angeles: National Center for History in the Schools, 1991

Students read account by government agents and Indians describing conditions in the west after the Civil War. The documents set the stage for understanding the religious revitalization movement of the 1870s, its suppression by the U.S. government, and the massacre at Wounded Knee in 1890. Recommended for grades 9-12.

"If Your Name Was Changed at Ellis Island"
CD-ROM, Scholastic, 1994

Based on Ellen Levine's book by the same name, this CD-ROM enriches the text with photographs, video, maps, and supplemental readings. Students may venture beyond Ellis Island and investigate Asian immigrants at Angel Island and involuntary migration of African slaves. Recommended for grades 3-6.

"Immigration"
Magazine of History, Vol. 4, No. 4 (Spring 1990)

A special section devoted to immigration history includes articles on historiography, refugees, and immigrant women in the early twentieth century. One of the teaching lessons focuses on using poetry to teach about immigration. Recommended for teachers and students, grades 7-12.

"The Immigrant's Experience, 1890-1925, Volume 2," Teaching With Primary Sources Series
Peterborough, NH: Cobblestone Publishing, 1996

A collection of print and photographic documents from the Library of Congress and National Archives on immigration principally from Europe and Latin America. The dedication of the Statute of Liberty, Jacob Riis photographs of immigrants at work, and documents relating to the quota system are included in this teaching kit. Recommended for grades 5-8.

"Keeping them Apart: Plessy *v.* Ferguson *and the Black Experience in Post-Reconstruction America"*
Los Angeles: National Center for History in the Schools, 1991

Students study the effects of Reconstruction-era legislation on race relations in the later 19th century. In addition to the *Plessy* v. *Ferguson* decision, students connect to contemporary events in the civil rights movement. Recommended for grades 9-12.

"Photographs from the Detroit Publishing Company, 1880-1920"
The National Digital Library Program, Library of Congress Multimedia Historical Collections

These 25,000 commercial photographs of turn-of-the-century America served as the basis for picture postcards of the time. Prominent subjects include buildings and views in towns and cities, colleges and universities, battleships and yachts, resorts, natural landmarks, and industry. Access on the World Wide WEB through the Library of Congress Multimedia Historical Collections, http://www.loc.gov. Recommended for grades 5-12.

"Early Motion Pictures, 1897-1916"
The National Digital Library Program, Library of Congress Multimedia Historical Collections

This collection makes available 99 motion pictures which represent the earliest period of film production. Three featured groups of films include sensational footage of San Francisco before and after the earthquake and fire of 1906, the growing metropolis of New York City, and events surrounding the assassination of President William McKinley. Access on the World Wide WEB through the Library of Congress Multimedia Historical Collections, http://www.loc.gov. Recommended for grades 5-12.

ERA 7

Blues In America: A Social History
Golden Owl Publishing Company

A Jackdaws portfolio of essays, historical documents, and 13 audio documents on cassette. The portfolio traces the Blues from the Mississippi Delta to the industrial cities of the North and West. The program was developed in conjunction with the Smithsonian Institution. Recommended for grades 7-12.

"The Constitution in Crisis: The Red Scare of 1919-1920"
Los Angeles: National Center for History in the Schools, 1991

This unit uses passages from the Espionage and Sedition Acts, and excerpts from Supreme Court decisions in the Schenck, Abrams, and Gitlow cases. In addition, students read what prominent political, civic, and religious leaders said regarding the threat of communism in the 1920s and the need to protect the right to free speech and expression. Recommended for grades 9-12.

"The Harlem Renaissance"
Los Angeles: National Center for History in the Schools, 1996

Through a variety of documents, art work, poems and music, students study the evolution of the Harlem Renaissance in the 1920s and its role in defining African American cultural identity in the rapidly changing world of the early twentieth century. Recommended for grades 9-12.

"In the Aftermath of War: Cultural Clashes of the Twenties"
Los Angeles: National Center for History in the Schools, 1991

Through a variety of primary sources, including literary excerpts, advertisements, and trial transcripts, students learn about the fundamental changes in the 1920s that transformed the United States. Tensions between urban and rural populations, and between native-born and immigrant Americans, are explored through lessons on prohibition, the Sacco and Vanzetti trial, and the Scopes trial. Recommended for grades 9-12.

Jazz: A Multimedia History
Compton's NewMedia, 1993, CD-ROM for IBM compatibles and Macintosh

This history of jazz from its origins to the 1990s includes swing, bebop, fusion and the avant-garde. The program incorporates audio clips, historic photographs, and profiles of leading musicians including Louis Armstrong to Miles Davis. Recommended for grades 7-12.

"The Nation's Forum Sound Recordings, 1918-1920"
The National Digital Library Program, Library of Congress Multimedia Historical Collections

This collection contains 59 sound recordings of speeches by American leaders. The speeches focus on issues and events surrounding World War I and the presidential election of 1920. Access on the World Wide WEB through the Library of Congress Multimedia Historical Collections, http://www.loc.gov. Recommended for grades 5-12.

"The National American Woman Suffrage Association Collection, 1848-1920"
The National Digital Library Program, Library of Congress Multimedia Historical Collections

This collection consists of books, pamphlets, memorials, scrapbooks, and proceedings from the meetings of women's organizations which document the struggle for suffrage. Access on the World Wide WEB through the Library of Congress Multimedia Historical Collections, http://www.loc.gov. Recommended for grades 5-12.

"The 1920's"
Boca Raton, FL: SIRS, Inc.

This teaching kit includes a variety of documents from the National Archives and a teacher's guide. The collection includes facsimile documents, photographs, and cartoons of the era. Recommended for grades 7-12.

"The Progressive Era"
Magazine of History, Vol. 1, No. 3/4 (Winter/Spring 1986)

This special section on the Progressive Era contains several articles and lesson plans on the Progressive Era. The classroom lessons highlighted in this issue focus on conscription during World War I, the Progressive Era through popular culture, and the Federation of Women's Clubs. Recommended for teachers and students, grades 7-12.

"The Progressive Years, 1898-1917"
Boca Raton, FL: SIRS, Inc.

This teaching kit includes a variety of documents from the National Archives and a teacher's guide. The collection include facsimiles of printed documents in the National Archives as well as photographs of the era. Recommended for grades 7-12.

Who Built America? From the Centennial Celebration of 1876 to the Great War of 1914
Voyager, 1993, CD-ROM for Macintosh

Archival films, audio, still images, and a multitude of documents extend two chapters of the two-volume textbook written by the American Social History Project. Recommended for grades 9-12.

"Women in the Progressive Movement"
Los Angeles: National Center for History in the Schools, 1991

This unit provides students with the opportunity to examine women's efforts to reform American society between 1890 and 1920. Students explore an array of Progressive reform movements including the women's club movement, efforts to increase women's educational and occupational opportunities, women's involvement in the labor movement, the promotion of birth control, and the struggle for women's suffrage. Recommended for grades 9-12.

"World War I: The Home Front"
Boca Raton, FL: SIRS, Inc.

This teaching kit, designed to supplement a study of World War I, focuses on five topics that relate to life on the home front, each represented by reproductions of documents in the National Archives. Recommended for grades 7-12.

"World War I: The Home Front, Perspectives"
Procter and Gamble Educational Services, 1987

This unit discusses some of the home front activities specifically those of the business community. Students analyze primary source documents to support hypotheses about the role of business during wartime. Recommended for grades 9-12.

ERA 8

"The American Documents Series"
VHS video cassettes

Newsreel and motion picture footage, still photographs, and radio recordings document the culture and social history of the 1920s, immigration, woman suffrage, the Great Depression, and presidential inaugurals. Recommended for grades 9-12.

The Censored War: American Visual Experience During World War Two
by George H. Roeder, Jr.
New Haven, CN: Yale University Press, 1993

A powerful book that explains how public opinion was manipulated by wartime images that citizens were allowed to see and by those that were suppressed. The text is enhanced by dynamic visual essays composed of photographs from censored files which have not been previously published. Recommended for grades 9-12.

"The CIO and the Labor Movement," **Jackdaws Teaching Kit**
Amawalk, NY: Golden Owl Publishing.

This Jackdaw kit traces the existence of the CIO, from its formation in 1935, when eight unions split from the American Federation of Labor, to the merger of those two organizations twenty years later. The complete portfolio includes five essays, 12 historical documents, a study guide, and reproducible masters. Recommended for grades 7-12.

"Color Photographs from the Farm Security Administration and the Office of War Information, 1938-1944"
The National Digital Library Program, Library of Congress Multimedia Historical Collections

This is a collection of 1,616 digitized prints, photographs, and films along with interpretative text on small town America and the scenes of the World War II mobilization effort. Access on the World Wide WEB through the Library of Congress Multimedia Historical Collections, http://www.loc.gov. Recommended for grades 5-12.

"Gordon Hirabayashi v. The United States"
Produced by John de Graaf with the Constitution Project, 1992, VHS, video cassette

The story of Gordon Hirabayashi who refused to be interned in 1942, defying Executive Order 9066. The video chronicles Hirabayashi's 42-year struggle to overturn his conviction. Recommended for grades 9-12.

"Huey Long," Ken Burns' America Series
(VHS, 88 minutes)

The film, employing the techniques used in The Civil War series, probes Huey Long's career as governor, senator, and potential rival to Franklin Roosevelt. Recommended for grades 7-12.

"The Depression Hits Home," Jackdaw Photo Collection
Amawalk, NY: Golden Owl Publishing, 1996

This collection of poster size black-and-white photographs examines the human side and far-reaching effects of the Great Depression. Recommended for grades 7-12.

Documents from the National Archives: Internment of Japanese Americans
Dubuque, IA: Kendall/Hunt Publishing Co., nd.

A teaching unit based on 14 documents from the National Archives including war department pamphlets, political cartoons, photographs, letters, and Executive Order 9066. Recommended for grades 7-12.

Documents from the National Archives: Women in Industry World War II
Dubuque, IA: Kendall/Hunt Publishing Co., nd.

A teaching unit based on 14 documents from the National Archives. Students work with letters, photographs, cartoons, executive orders, and information leaflets to discern the role of women in the war industries and attitudes toward their employment. Recommended for grades 7-12.

"The Great Depression and The New Deal"
Boca Raton, FL: SIRS, Inc.

This teaching kit includes ten suggested classroom exercises, a teacher's guide and a variety of facsimiles of documents from the National Archives.

"Live from the Past: The New Deal"
New York Times Media, 1995

Each of the three modules in this series examines a different aspect of the Roosevelt administration. Each module contains reproducible archival sheets of key *New York Times* articles and editorials, a poster, educator's guide, and video which explore Roosevelt's first term, the Supreme Court's reaction to New Deal legislation, and the court-packing controversy of 1937. Recommended for grades 9-12.

"Live from the Past: World War II"
New York Times Media, 1994

This set of three independent teaching modules examines the beginning of the war in Europe, D-Day, and the end of the war in 1945. Each of the three modules contains reproducible archival sheets of key *New York Times* articles and editorials, a poster, educator's guide, and video. Recommended for grades 9-12.

Norman Rockwell's Four Freedoms: Images that Inspire a Nation, compiled by
Stuart Murray and James McCabe
Stockbridge. MA: Berkshire House and The Norman Rockwell Museum, 1993

A collection of Norman Rockwell's art reflecting the basic freedoms enjoyed by Americans. The art works selected for this book follow the theme expressed by Franklin Roosevelt's Four Freedoms address and the United Nation's Universal Declaration of Human Rights. Each of Rockwell's illustrations of the Four Freedoms is accompanied by an essay. Recommended for grades 7-12.

Propaganda, The Art of Persuasion: World War II, by Anthony Rhodes
Secaucus, NJ: The Wellfleet Press and Chelsea House, 1987

A visual compendium of all forms of propaganda used by the Allies and Axis powers during the war, including stills from John Huston, Noël Coward, and Leni Riefenstahl films, photographs of Tokyo Rose and Fritz Kuhn, comic books, magazine covers, paintings, stamps, postcards, sheet music, and other forms of the art of persuasion. Recommended for grades 7-12.

"Thomas Hart Benton"
Ken Burns' America Series (VHS, 86 minutes)

A profile of the artist who idealized small town life in the 1930s. Recommended for grades 7-12.

"World War II: The Home Front"
Boca Raton, FL: SIRS, Inc.

This teaching kit includes a variety of documents from the National Archives and a teacher's guide. The collection includes facsimile documents, artifacts, and photographs. Recommended for grades 7-12.

ERA 9

ABC Interactive Program
ABC, 1989-1991, interactive laserdisc (CAV) or Macintosh

These interactive laserdisc programs are part of the ABC Instant Replay of History series. The programs include interviews, speeches, and news footage. With Macintosh HyperCard programs students may print documents and use video clips to compile individual or group reports. The series includes programs such as "Martin Luther King, Jr.," "Communism and the Cold War," and "In the Holy Land." Recommended for grades 7-12.

"America's Civil Rights Movement"
Teaching Tolerance Kit, Montgomery, AL: Southern Poverty Law Center, 1992

The activity kit includes a 38-minute videotape, a student text, and a teacher's guide. The text entitled *Free at Last: A History of the Civil Rights Movement and Those Who Died in the Struggle,* profiles 40 people who died in the civil rights movement. Recommended for grades 7-12.

The Cuban Missile Crisis: A Resource Unit
John F. Kennedy Library and Museum

A collection of declassified primary source documents on the Cuban missile crisis which students use to reconstruct the negotiations from the U.S. and Soviet perspectives. Recommended for grades 7-12.

Escalation: Decision Making in the Vietnam War, 1964-1968
Kevin O'Reilly, 1990, Apple 5.25" disks, IBM 5.25" or 3.5" disks

A computer simulation on Johnson and the Vietnam War. Students work in small groups with different disks at separate terminals. The program includes reproducible handouts, maps, and other student information. Recommended for grades 9-12.

Eyes on the Prize, Parts I and II
PBS Video, 1987, laserdiscs (CLV) or VHS video cassettes

A highly acclaimed chronicle of the civil rights struggle between 1954 and 1985. The programs are based on eyewitness accounts and dramatic news footage. Recommended for grades 7-12.

The Fabulous 60s
VHS video cassettes

A kaleidoscopic view of the political, social, and cultural climate of the 1960s. Peter Jennings narrates the documentary which includes the Bay of Pigs, civil rights marches, Watts and Detroit riots, and Woodstock. Recommended for grades 7-12.

"Harvest of Shame"
CBS (VHS, 60 minutes)

Media journalist Edward R. Murrow narrates this 1960 documentary on the harsh living conditions of America's migrant workers. Recommended for grades 7-12.

"Hometown: A Local Area Study
Active Learning Systems, Apple, IBM

A computer program which guides students in collecting, storing, and analyzing demographic data about their local community. Recommended for grades 4-8.

"Live from the Past: The Civil Rights Movement"
New York Times Media, 1994

Recommended for grades 9-12. Four teaching modules trace the civil rights movement from Booker T. Washington's Atlanta Exposition speech to the March on Washington in 1963. Each module contains reproducible archival sheets of key *New York Times* articles and editorials, a poster, educator's guide, and video. Recommended for grades 9-12.

"Live from the Past: The Cold War"
New York Times Media. 1995

Four teaching modules, containing reproducible archival sheets of key *New York Times* articles and editorials, teacher's guides, videos, and posters, examine Truman's containment policy, the Korean War, the Cuban crises of 1961 and 1962, and Nixon's search for Détente, 1971-1972. Recommended for grades 9-12.

"Live from the Past: The Vietnam War"
New York Times Media, 1995

Four teaching modules, each containing reproducible archival sheets of key *New York Times* articles and editorials, a poster, educator's guide, and video, which trace key events in the Vietnam War. Recommended for grades 9-12.

May It Please the Court: The Most Significant Oral Arguments Made Before the Supreme Court Since 1955
New Press, 1992

The audio tapes present edited oral arguments before the Supreme Court for 12 landmark cases including *Miranda* v. *Arizona*, *Gideon* v. *Wainwright*, and *Roe* v. *Wade*. The tapes are accompanied by a hard cover book with transcripts of the tapes. Recommended for grades 9-12.

"The Origins of the Cold War"
Los Angeles: National Center for History in the Schools, 1991

Students analyze the cultural, political, historical, military and economic factors contributing to the Cold War, as well as its effects. Recommended for grades 9-12.

"Peace and Prosperity: 1953-1961"
Boca Raton, FL: SIRS, Inc.

This teaching kit includes a variety of documents from the National Archives and a teacher's guide. The collection includes a variety of documents which help students comprehend the changes in American society and the economic prosperity of the era. Recommended for grades 7-12.

"Rethinking the Cold War"
The Magazine of History, Vol. 8, No. 2 (Winter 1994)

In addition to several articles on the topic, this issue gives a detailed lesson plan on the Cuban Missile Crisis including declassified CIA maps, secret memorandum, intelligence data, and a timetable of Soviet military build-up in Cuba. Recommended for teachers and students, grades 7-12.

"The Shadow of Hate"
Montgomery, AL: Southern Poverty Law Center, 1995

This "teaching tolerance kit" includes a 40-minute documentary video and student text, Us and Them, and a teacher's guide. The program chronicles the history of hatred and intolerance in America from religious intolerance during the colonial era to the present. Recommended for grades 7-12.

"Stride Toward Freedom: The Aftermath of Brown *v.* Board of Education *of Topeka"*
Los Angeles: National Center for History in the Schools, 1991

This collection of lessons is a valuable resource for teachers. Students read Chief Justice Earl Warren's opinion on the Brown case, the reaction to the ruling by the North Carolina legislature, as well as letters regarding the decision. Recommended for grades 9-12.

Talking History
Produced by Spencer Nakasako, 1984, VHS, video cassette

Oral histories of Japanese, Chinese, Korean, Filipino, and Laotian women immigrants. Recommended for grades 9-12.

"The Truman Years"
Boca Raton, FL: SIRS, Inc.

This teaching kit includes a variety of documents from the National Archives and a teacher's guide. The collection includes facsimile documents, political cartoons, and photographs. Recommended for grades 7-12.

ERA 10

Documents from the National Archives: Watergate
Dubuque, IA: Kendall/Hunt Publishing Co., nd.

A teaching unit based on nine documents from the National Archives. The teaching unit contains a document analysis worksheet and a "Cast of Characters" which is a helpful list of persons involved in the break-in, cover-up, and investigation of the Watergate affair. Documents include the House Judiciary Committee's report on Impeachment, excerpted transcripts of the Oval Office tape of June 23, 1972, *Washington Post* article about Watergate, and President Ford's draft remarks on granting a presidential pardon.

History of the 1980s
ABC Video, VHS video cassettes

Documentary films of the major political, social, and cultural events in the 1980s. Recommended for grades 7-12.

"Live from the Past: The Rise and Fall of the Soviet Union"
New York Times Media, 1995

Each of the four teaching modules in this kit include 18 to 24 reproducible archival sheets of key *New York Times* articles and editorials, a poster, educator's guide, and video. The modules trace the rise and fall of communism in Russia and Eastern Europe from 1917 to 1991. Recommended for grades 9-12.

"The 1993 Time Magazine Compact Almanac"
Compact Publishing, 1993, CD-ROM for IBM, MPC compatibles, and Macintosh

A full text reference of every issue of *Time* for 1989 through the January 4, 1993 issue with CNN videos of major stories. The disk also includes a *"Time* Capsules" section with some articles dating to the first issue of the magazine in 1923, a "Compact Almanac," maps, and the CIA World Factbook with State Department notes. Recommended for grades 9-12.

"Thomas"
Library of Congress, World Wide WEB.

Search Thomas for legislative information, access services of the Law Library of Congress, or locate government information. Thomas includes full text of the Congressional Record, full text of legislation, bill summary and status and the Constitution of the U.S. Access http://thomas.loc.gov. Recommended for grades 9-12.

Notes

Notes

Notes

Notes

Notes

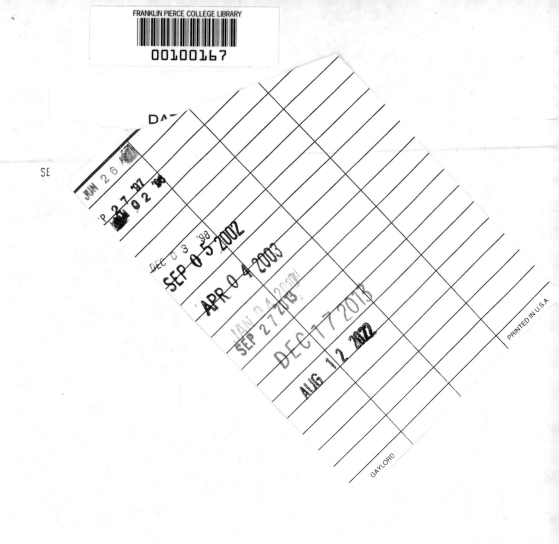